FEMINIST VISIONS OF DEVELOPMENT

Gender, Analysis and Policy

Edited by

Cecile Jackson and Ruth Pearson

London and New York

First published 1998
by Routledge
11 New Fetter Lane, London EC4P 4EE

Simultaneously published in the USA and Canada
by Routledge
29 West 35th Street, New York, NY 10001

Reprinted 2000

Routledge is an imprint of the Taylor & Francis Group

Typeset in Baskerville by M Rules
Printed and bound in Great Britain by
MPG Books Ltd, Bodmin

British Library Cataloguing in Publication Data
A catalogue record for this book is available from the British Library

Library of Congress Cataloguing in Publication Data
Feminist visions of development : gender analysis and policy / edited by
Ruth Pearson and Cecile Jackson.
p.   cm. – (Routledge studies in development economics)
Includes bibliographic references and index.
ISBN 0-415-14234-2 – ISBN 0-415-15790-0 (pbk.)
1. Women in development.   2. Sex role–Developing countries.
3. Feminism–Developing countries.   I. Pearson, Ruth.   II. Jackson,
Cecile, 1952- .   III. Series
HQ1240.F464   1998   97-45904
305.42—dc21   CIP

ISBN 0 415 14234 2 (hbk)
ISBN 0 415 15790 0 (pbk)

FEMINIST VISIONS OF DEVELOPMENT

In the wake of the 4th World Conference on Women this volume brings together leading gender and development scholars who interrogate the last twenty years of work in this area.

Feminist Visions of Development throws fresh light on key issues including:

- gender and the environment
- education
- population
- reproductive rights
- industrialisation
- macroeconomic policy
- poverty

Inspired by recent feminist theoretical work it re-examines previous structural analysis and opens the way for further research in the field.

Cecile Jackson and **Ruth Pearson** lecture at the School of Development Studies at the University of East Anglia.

CONTENTS

v

CONTENTS

CONTRIBUTORS

Sally Baden is a socio-economist working on gender issues, with specialist interests in economic reform, markets and poverty. For the past six years, she has been manager of the BRIDGE project (Briefings in Development and Gender) at the Institute of Development Studies, University of Sussex, where she is also involved in teaching on the MA in Gender and Development.

Diane Elson is Professor of Development Studies at the University of Manchester. She has been active in the women's movement since the late sixties. She has acted as adviser to numerous development agencies, both governmental and non-governmental, including Commonwealth Secretariat, United Nations Development Programme, UNIFEM, Department for International Development, Oxfam and Women Working Worldwide. Her publications include *Women's Employment and Multinationals in Europe* (ed. with Ruth Pearson), Macmillan, London, 1989; *Male Bias in the Development Process*, Manchester University Press, Manchester, 1991 and 1995; and 'Gender Awareness in Modelling Structural Adjustment,' *World Development*, Vol 23, No 11, 1995.

Anne Marie Goetz is a Fellow of the Institute of Development Studies, University of Sussex. She is a political scientist and her research focuses on the politics of gender in development institutions. She has studied the politics of implementing GAD policy at the grassroots level, in rural credit programmes in Bangladesh, and at the state level through 'national women's machineries' in a range of developing countries. She has also researched the politics of implementing poverty-reduction policies in Africa. She is currently researching gender issues in grassroots anti-corruption movements in India.

Cathy Green has a background in natural resources and gender and development. While at the Institute of Development Studies, Sussex she worked on the BRIDGE Project (Briefings in Development and Gender) and with Susan Joekes and Melissa Leach on a USAID consultancy entitled 'Integrating Gender into Environmental Research and Policy'. She is currently a social development consultant and projects manager with Options Consultancy Services, the UK Department for International Development's Resource Centre in Reproductive Health.

Barbara Harriss-White is a Reader in Development Studies at Oxford University. A field economist, she has three decades of intermittent field experience of markets for grain and state regulative policy in South Asia and West Africa. Her interest in gender arose from direct experience, field research and a spell in the Department of Human Nutrition at the London School of Hygiene and Tropical Medicine. She has published in the areas of rural development and social welfare.

Cecile Jackson is a lecturer at the School of Development Studies, University of East Anglia, UK.

Patricia Jeffery is at the Department of Sociology and Centre for South Asian Studies, University of Edinburgh, UK.

Roger Jeffery is at the Department of Sociology and Centre for South Asian Studies, University of Edinburgh, UK.

Susan Joekes has been for many years a Fellow of the Institute of Development Studies and also on the staff of the International Center for Research on Women in Washington DC. Her work is on gender analysis in relation to (a) international trade and labour markets and (b) natural resource management and environmental change. On the first subject she has published *Women in the World Economy*, OUP, New York, 1987, and, with Ann Weston, *Women and the New Trade Agenda*, UNIFEM, 1994. On Environment she is the author of 'Environment, Gender and Livelihoods in the Third World' (forthcoming), with case studies of gender relation and community level adaptation to environmental change in Kenya, Malaysia, Morocco and Pakistan.

Naila Kabeer (Fellow, Institute of Development Studies) is a socio-economist with research interests in gender, poverty, population and household economics and she has worked in India, Bangladesh and Vietnam She has been extensively involved in gender training and gender advisory work with NGOs, government donor agencies and researchers from a variety of different countries, with a particular focus on the institutional dynamics of social inequality. She is the author of Reversed Realities: Gender Hierarchies in Development Thought, Verso, 1994. Her next book, 'The power to choose: structure, agency and Bangladeshi women workers in London and Dhaka' is due out at the end of 1998.

Deniz Kandiyoti is Senior Lecturer in the Department of Development Studies at the School of Oriental and African Studies. She is the author of Women in Rural Production Systems (Unesco, 1985), the editor of Women, Islam and the State (Macmillan, 1991) and Gendering the Middle East (I.B. Tauris, 1996).

Jocelyn Kynch is at the Centre for Development Studies, University of Wales, Swansea.

Melissa Leach is a Social Anthropologist and Fellow of the Institute of Development Studies at the University of Sussex.

Maxine Molyneux, a Senior Lecturer at the Institute of Latin American Studies, University of London, has written exclusively in the fields of feminist theory and development studies. She was a member of the Subordination of Women Group, and a founder member of *Feminist Review*. Her most recent work has been on gender and post-authoritarian transitions, and includes the publication *State, Gender and Institutional Change in Cuba's 'Special Period': The Federación de Mujeres Cubanás* (ILAS Research Paper Series, London 1996). She is currently co-editing a collection with Elizabeth Dore, *Historical Perspectives on Gender and the State in Latin America*, to be published by Duke University Press.

Ruth Pearson is a lecturer at the School of Development Studies, University of East Anglia, UK.

Ines Smyth is a sociologist who has worked on women and industrialization in Indonesia. Her recent work has focused on gender analysis and reproductive rights and she is the author of numerous journal articles and book chapters on these issues. She has taught gender, development and population at the Institute of Social Studies, the Hague, and the Development Studies Institute at LSE. She is currently a senior manager at the Gender and Learning team at OXFAM UK/I.

INTRODUCTION:
INTERROGATING DEVELOPMENT

Feminism, gender and policy

Ruth Pearson and Cecile Jackson

Shortly before the 4th UN Conference on Women in Beijing, a group of academics and feminists concerned with gender and development gathered at the University of East Anglia to discuss where we were, and where we might be heading, in a field now at least 25 years old.[1] The essays in this book are a selection of what was presented there. What emerged was a diversity of work, all of which examined 'development' in its many meanings,[2] from which we have collected a group of papers which are not about projects and donors, but address broad and long-standing concerns emerging from particular discourses with roots in 1970s socialist feminism.

Much has changed since the early 1970s. Now it may be strange to many (potential) readers that this book is not about NGOs (non-government organisations) and development projects – or even donor led efforts to empower women, in spite of the pervasive fashionability of such endeavours. The essays here are concerned with an *interrogation of development* from the perspective of gender analysis. Given that we understand by 'development' both development policy and social and economic change, the chapters take up issues of macro-policy design and implementation as well as theoretical debates and analytical frameworks.

Twenty-five years on this volume marks a coming of age of gender analysis of development. The objectives of feminist analysis, as set out in the introduction to Young *et al.* (1980), are still relevant:

> Our aim was to develop better analytical and conceptual tools for the development of a theory of social relations which would encompass not only the so-called economic relations of society but what have also been called the relations of everyday life.
>
> (p. viii)

At the macro level, new concerns reflecting new interests such as the environment, markets, disasters, macro-economic policy and civil society have been added to

1

long-standing focuses on education, industrialisation, agrarian change and population policy. At the same time, the extension of development practice has taken on the concerns of gender analysis so that 'Women in Development' has come to describe a field bounded by concerns of targeting women for development cooperation and/or integrating women within the general activities of such practices.

Feminist analysis versus women and development

Even at the outset of interest in gender analysis of development, there were already different approaches to policy analysis and development. The positive approach of the international development agencies of the 1970s was largely aimed at integrating women into development, particularly influenced by Boserup's pathbreaking book published in 1970 which articulated a concern that women had been left out of development – defined in terms of the programmes for development following post-war reconstruction. Women in Development then became the policy response to the concern that the fruits of development were not trickling down to women; the response was therefore that women should be factored into such programmes.

However, a critique was already developing amongst feminist academics in development. First, there was a critique of the notion that 'development' itself was unproblematic, the problem was to integrate women into policy and practice, parallel to the liberal feminist view that extending education and employment opportunities to women in Western states would eliminate gender discrimination and oppression (Bandarage, 1984). In the UK, the Subordination of Women collective, affectionately known as SOW, financed by the Institute of Development Studies at the University of Sussex, provided the basis for much of the theoretical and analytical work reflected in the international conference on 'The Continuing Subordination of Women' held in 1978 (*IDS Bulletin*, 1979). The work carried out for this conference was significant in various ways. First, it distanced itself from the reduction of gender issues in development to the practice of Development agencies. Second, it problematised social relations within 'developing countries', seeing the relevance of gender as a lens through which to understand the dynamics of social and economic change in societies in transition, adopting a comparative approach in contrast to much 'women's studies' scholarship in Britain at that time. Many of the presentations at that conference were included in the conference volume, *Of Marriage and the Market* (Young et al., 1980). A major feature of the analysis of that time was a truly interdisciplinary approach, which rejected the artificial differences between disciplines such as anthropology, sociology or economics, as well as genuine collective discussion and scholarship. A number of the original authors of that text have contributed to the present volume.

Although not engaging in the subsequent debates in feminist theory about feminist methodology or standpoints the SOW perspective explicitly took a feminist position as a starting point for the examination of some of the positivist models of development intervention – export oriented production, agricultural technological change, etc. An explicit rejection of

> the growing literature concerned with 'women and development' [which was] predominantly descriptive, was equivocal in its identification and analysis of women's subordination, and tended to isolate women as a separate and often homogeneous category.
>
> (Pearson *et al.*, 1984: x)

This work also rejected an essentialist and universal notion of the category of women, again prefiguring subsequent work which has emphasised difference and deconstructed universal categories:

> our point of departure was that the relations between men and women are social and therefore not immutable and fixed. The form that gender relations take in any historical situation is specific to that situation and has to be constructed inductively; it cannot be read off from other social relations nor from the gender relations of other societies.
>
> (ibid.: x)

Central to this analysis was also the critical deconstruction of key social institutions which were the building blocks of traditional social theory. Critical feminist attention was brought to bear on the household, the notion of the economy, the separation of the economic and the social and the division between production and reproduction, structures which were central to contemporary Marxist analysis as well as neoclassical theory. The development of the domestic labour debate (Molyneux, 1979) helped pave the way for the creative fusion between feminist and socialist analysis (Hartmann, 1979), and the subsequent irreverent deconstruction of theory of intra-household relations and budgeting, from both sides of the political spectrum (Folbre, 1986).

All these theses have a resonance in subsequent debates in gender analysis of development and are taken up in this volume. By the 1980s the manifest failure of the central role of the state and international agencies had deflated the confidence of the 1970s that international agencies and conferences could determine the way in which development policy was to be evolved and delivered. Conventional Keynesian based sectoral intervention strategies of such agencies delivered through increasingly problematic state governments had floundered in the instability generated by the oil crisis of the 1970s and 1980s. The subsequent rising indebtedness of many Third World states in all continents stimulated a change in development strategy: the international agencies reversed their previous policies. Instead of using governments as the agents of international development cooperation and assistance the international agencies changed their framework.

The continuing inability of Third World governments to generate sufficient resources to repay international obligations, let alone in many cases to ensure a continuing upward rise in living standards, was the catalyst for a review of the old orthodoxy of development assistance. In line with the conservative monetarism which was the feature of most Western governments in that period, a new orthodoxy of development assistance was born. Third World states had to reform their economies in order to be able to meet international obligations in the long run, a process known as structural adjustment. To assist them the main international financial agencies, the World Bank and the IMF, offered transitional stabilisation and adjustment loans on condition that policy reforms were met. These now familiar reforms included a range of supply side and demand cutting measures designed to reduce balance of payments and domestic government deficits. Implicit and often explicit was a change in the role of the government as a development agency. In order to meet the new objectives the role of the state, including government expenditure and services as well as redistributory functions such as subsidies, was to be curtailed. Many activities previously carried out by the government, including a range of para-statals and transport and communications services, were privatised.

One consequence of this was that social services, those most connected with reproduction, were both cut back in expenditure terms and reorganised. Instead of the state being the sole or principal agent of organisation and provision of such services, regardless of whether they were externally or domestically financed, private 'not-for-profit' non-governmental organisations were charged with many of these functions.

For the increasingly vociferous movement which was calling for the 'integration of women into development' (WID) there was a certain amount of serendipity in this turn of events. Given that the earlier WID movement had been premised on a notion that women were excluded from development and that there was a growing feminist analysis of the patriarchal nature of the state and the ways in which it ignored the interests of women, this new scenario opened spaces for organisations of women and for the creation of women's NGOs, and was able to insist that women were targeted as beneficiaries of the new organisations in order to give them access to international development funding.

Much of the literature on gender and development since the 1980s has continued to be concerned with this area of activity. The attack on the state coincided with a rise in interest in the efficacy of organisations within civil society to respond more effectively to the 'real' needs of people at the 'grassroots', a position which oddly fitted in with the trenchant complaints of Third World feminists that current development policies furthered the needs of imperialist states and their allies, rather than the aspirations of poor women themselves (Sen and Grown, 1988).

The earlier critiques have not gone unheard. There has been a significant analysis of the need to reform the 'Women in Development' (WID) approach to development cooperation and many have chronicled the shift from WID to Gender Analysis in Development (GAD) (Rathgeber, 1990), arguing for approaches informed by a gender analyses of social relations (Kabeer, 1994), and even aspiring to the ultimate 'empowerment of women' (Moser, 1989, 1993).

4

These changes are not just cosmetic. In principle the enthusiasm for gender rather than women in development approaches signals not just a change in language or a depoliticising of the field,[3] but reflects the fact that at all levels of the development 'business' there is an acceptance that it is not women *per se* who are to be problematised, but gender relations in which women are subordinated which must be problematised, and that this analysis not only justifies the concentration of resources on women's development activities and access to resources, but also points to the centrality of gender analysis in the development of effective policies at all levels (Elson, 1995). This implies, and has delivered, the extension of analysis from issues which were clearly concerned with women's reproductive roles (health, family planning, education), through economic roles (employment, income generation, household budgeting) to generic issues of macro-economic planning, structural adjustment and debt, environmental degradation and conservation and civil and political organisation – which are clearly of general rather than sectoral relevance.

This book takes on this analytical approach in the context of development policy and practice in the 1990s, which has become infused with gender.[4] Gender has become not only a desirable attribute but a development goal of agencies and policy-makers.

Where this leaves us in the late 1990s is facing a series of paradoxes and uncertainties which, however, we see as an opportunity for, rather than a failure of, gender analysis. Issues of representation, of positionality and of practice transform old questions of integration, interests, struggles for resources and well-being, but do not replace them. Here a number of authors explicitly reflect on their own earlier work (see the chapters by Pearson, Molyneux and Kandiyoti), for gender analysis itself has produced an orthodoxy, which we and others continue to critique.

Commonalities and difference

In the 1970s, at the birth of 'gender', the concern was to theorise a social identity not given by 'sex', free from biological determinism and the arbitrary naturalisation of the gender order. Feminists needed to deny that biology was destiny and anthropologists provided the necessary scholarship on the enormous range of different gender identities which formed around biological females and males in other cultures. That the sex:gender distinction might lead logically to the argument of social constructionism biting back at the foundational feminist concept of 'woman', denying its existence, was hardly anticipated (Sayers, 1982). Crudely, biology could not be the basis of feminism, yet it framed what women appeared to have in common, whilst the cultural specificity of gender differences was equally problematic since it suggested the absence of commonalities. The questions of how to define commonalities and what to do about difference have become potentially disabling.

In policy discourses the sex:gender shift was accompanied by the similar move from Women in Development to Gender and Development discussed on pp.4–5, which stressed difference and the relational quality of gender. The charge that WID ethnocentrically universalised a particular white Western middle-class vision (Mohanty, 1988; Ong, 1988) was not perhaps entirely undeserved, but the extension of this critique to GAD (e.g. Hirschman, 1995) may be something of a distortion, since GAD had its roots in a feminist anthropology which was centrally concerned with cross-cultural and intra-cultural difference, and in socialist feminism where class:gender interactions were widely debated both within Britain and in other countries of the South (e.g. Robertson and Berger, 1986; Rubin, 1975).

These tensions are not easily resolved and neither should they be. The chapter by Sally Baden and Anne Marie Goetz engages with the contestations over the term 'gender', emerging from a number of opposing directions, and in both theory and practice. The institutionalisation of gender has been experienced as depoliticising by women's organisations, and in the analyses of feminist critics who see bureaucratised gender concepts stripped of political content deployed towards other development ends. The terms 'sex' and 'gender' continue to embody the problematic essentialism of a universalised feminism on the one hand, and a politically empty social constructionism which dissolves any notion of commonality in the acid bath of difference, on the other. Ways out of this impasse are indicated in notions of a politics of coalition and a recognition that biological sex can be experienced by actually existing women as meaningful even if it is always and everywhere socially constructed. Overcoming the congealed opposition of essentialism and social constructionism is an important priority for gender and development, and for feminism more widely.

Historical change and gender relations

Since the 1970s historical analysis of transformations in gender relations has been central in dispelling the essentialism of early formulations of concepts such as women, men and patriarchy, in analysing the unintended consequences of social change, and in deconstructing the continuities and discontinuities of gender relations in particular contexts. An example of the value of such analyses is in Jocelyn Kynch's chapter, which documents both the important differences within the category 'women', especially age based, for patterns of famine survival and the gender roles of men in generating patterns of both famine vulnerability and survival. She shows, using a modified entitlements framework, the ways in which famines have been ratchets of change in gender relations in which public policy initially operated to introduce gender relations of greater equality. However, local ideologies of seclusion, the 'customary' dependence of women, and their lower wages, combined with official desire for cost-effectiveness, through family rather than individual famine relief, to reassert the weakness of young women's fallback positions and bargaining power in households. Kynch argues that famine relief operations may have increased the rigidity of gender divisions of labour and by limiting coping strategies increased the mortality risks to women in their reproductive years. The paradox of immediate individual rational coping strategies and choices giving rise to unintended consequences which are negative in the longer term for women collectively is illustrated in Kynch's study.

Gender interests and emancipatory projects

Development policy has itself of course changed over the decades, from the 1970s when states were still seen as the key actors, whilst, curiously, dependency theory held sway in academic and activist circles, to the 1980s when the critique of the failure of states as development implementors was matched with a rise in non-governmental organisations and the discourse of participation became the new orthodoxy. Postmodernist interest in positionality and problems of representation chimed in towards a renewed legitimacy and necessity for Southern 'women's voices' to be engaged with; and Spivak wrote in 1985 of our need 'to learn to speak to (rather than listen to or speak for) the historically muted subject of the non-elite ("subaltern") woman'(1985: 120). The importance of the experiences and self-perceptions of the women affected by development can barely be dismissed in the light of the trenchant critique of the objectification in, as Spivak so memorably put it, 'white men saving brown women from brown men', and in development discourses the perceptions of 'beneficiaries' have come to be recognised as centrally important. Nevertheless, those who claim to be, or to speak for, 'women of the South' must also take care not to (mis)represent the diverse positions of different women, nor to collapse the complex multiple social identities of women into a simplistic notion of gender identity.[5]

These debates have contributed to the tension in the ways in which women's gender interests are conceived and investigated, between the ideas of false consciousness and a superior 'we know best' attitude of Western feminisms on the one hand and an uncritical acceptance of the epistemologically privileged voices of 'women', with their essentialist connotations on the other. Maxine Molyneux reflects, in her chapter on women's collective action and interest representation, how problematic and contested ideas of women's interests remain, and she asks: 'from where does the authority to define women's goals, priorities and actions, come?' (see p.70). She points out that the women's movement contains many kinds of organisation, that there is no necessary connection between organisational form and political goals and that women's *gender* interests are both ambiguous and coexist with other interests formed through their other social identities. In the 1990s gender analysis goes beyond an acceptance that women's gender interests cannot be given from their biological or structural positioning which was signalled in the SOW debates of the 1970s, for it is also necessary to refer to women's own understandings and perceptions. However, it is clear that a purely subjective account of women's gender interests cannot suffice because subjective constructions do not stand outside of prevailing gender ideologies. This particular ongoing tension in gender analysis has been central to debates over the nature of households, of well-being of members within them and of the gendered

7

processes of resource and work allocation, consumption, and the connections between gender relations within domestic groups and those at a societal level.

Domestic groups: cooperation, conflict and struggle

The past 25 years have seen intense debate on the nature of households and the relations between men and women, as well as women and women and men and men, within them. In Chapter 4 Naila Kabeer reviews the progression of neo-classical economists' concepts of households from the unified structures of New Household Economics to more recent concepts of non-unified households where the power differentials between genders and the differentials in well-being outcomes are recognised, but where the 'limits of economism' (Hart, 1995) are revealed, for example, in the attempts to explain excess female mortality in India. One of the changes of the past few decades is that disaggregation by gender within economics has become professionally interesting, but at the same time formal modelling seems to have increased its hold on the discipline and the complexities of power within gender relations continue to elude such approaches. For gender analysts the most influential of economists working on household models has been Amartya Sen (1990) precisely because of his recognition of the tensions between the objective and subjective gender interests of women, and his efforts to analyse the significance of perceptions of value to bargaining processes, forms of cooperation and well-being outcomes. In this regard he followed in a line of feminist scholarship which has problematised the notion of 'false consciousness' in work such as that of Deniz Kandiyoti on the 'patriarchal bargain' (1988).

In Chapter 6 Kandiyoti looks again at questions of power and agency within different social and historical contexts, and in so doing she picks up a theme, alluded to also by Kabeer, that frameworks which have evolved to explain class struggle and consciousness have serious limitations when extended to gender struggles and consciousness. For behind ideas of intra-household bargaining are assumptions about personhood and subjectivity which deserve scrutiny. Are women's perceptions of their gender interests mystified by dominant ideologies, as Sen argues, or are women aware of this mystification but externally constrained from struggling for their interests as Scott (1985) suggests? Furthermore, how do we conceptualise 'gendered identities and subjectivities in a manner that avoids both essentialism and the unproblematic assumption of the self-determining individual'? (p.138 of the present volume). Recovering a female subject risks essentialism; refusing a female subject risks erasing gender difference. If gender identity always coexists with other identities then it cannot be assumed to propel resistance, and nor do mobilised women necessarily express gender interests; where women's power is dramatically fractured by age and life cycle, the connections between gender as relations of power and actually existing women become potentially rather tenuous. If gender, however, is conceptually disconnected from actually sexed bodies then the political consequences for feminism as a movement, and for GAD's concern for social transformation in a world of 'target groups', are paralysing. From this perspective the constant slippage from gender to women, in spite of the widely approved case for GAD as an advance on WID, appears less a regrettable habit and more a 'tactical essentialism', in Kandiyoti's phrase.

Feminisms and green fundamentalism

Other essentialisms have emerged particularly strongly in recent years in the work of ecofeminist theorists, and any account of changes in developmentalism since the 1970s would give a prominent place to the rise of environmentalist discourses which couple women and nature. The chapter here by Cathy Green, Susan Joekes and Melissa Leach critiques this linkage and reviews a range of sectoral issues with an alternative social relations perspective. They argue that environment and development policy has consistently, across a number of sectors, taken a WID-oriented position which identifies women as subsistence providers, as an untapped labour resource and an homogeneous social category, and which deals neither with the relational meanings of gender or the possible disbenefits to women of participation in environmental projects and activities; they name this Women, Environment, Development (WED). Ecofeminist discourses have become increasingly popular in the West in recent decades, are echoed in WED, and have offered their own essentialist logic (Jackson, 1994) for targeting environmental initiatives at women, whilst Green, Joekes and Leach suggest the value of alternative approaches based on social and political relations. Arguing for a social relations approach to environment and development issues is, however, not always compatible with the drift of radical environmentalism in which it is *natural* relations, of humanity within nature, which define the critical political and analytical interface. The significance of anti-speciesism for feminism and GAD is still unfolding, but it is perhaps ironic to consider the relative weight of the land rights of women (Agarwal, 1994) and endangered species, reflected in the global movement for nature and biosphere reserves. One could argue that it is the very separation of women from the context of economic, social and political reproduction rather than their insertion into a notion of a sustainable future that differentiates a socially grounded feminist analysis from a free floating 'naturalistic' perspective which equates women's realities with natural futures.

Gendered economies: relations of production and reproduction

If women's subordination is to be understood in the context not just of the dynamics of gender relations but of the dynamics of accumulation, globalisation and polarisation in their totality, gender analysis must also engage with the dominant development discourses of our time. Unfortunately much of the gender and development literature of recent years has been *reactive* with respect to macro-policies, particularly in the economic arena. The extensive debates about the impact of structural adjustment on women (Commonwealth Secretariat, 1989; Afshar and

9

Dennis, 1992; Sparr, 1994) have been concerned to engage with generalised positions which argue that the reduction of social expenditure on health and education, as well as the reduction of protective subsidies for the consumption and services of the poor, make women 'vulnerable' in a situation of structural economic change. Diane Elson (1995) has argued that the economic models underpinning adjustment policies are based on gendered assumptions concerning the (lack of) rigidities between men's work and women's work between and with the productive and reproductive sectors of the economy. By deconstructing the elements of such policies she has also pointed to a paradox that many gender and development experts are unhappy to accept – namely that markets are not necessarily against women's interests and that the outcome of economic reforms in terms of their effect on women, on the sexual division of labour and entitlements to the outcome of production will depend on the political as well as the technical strength of the gender analysis applied to their construction.

A more pessimistic view pervades Barbara Harriss-White's chapter, which compares the engagement of women in South Asia and West Africa. She concludes for both cases, 'male' and 'female' marketing systems respectively, that marketplaces and staple food institutions are highly gendered complexes of social institutions (see p.190) in which male domination is reproduced. The dynamics of gender relations as well as the 'bearers of gender' within both social institutions and economic models clearly do change in complex ways over time. Whilst Harriss-White and Elson speculate on the policy directions which might offer some feminist leverage, both claim that the gendering of markets reduces efficiency.

In fact, Diane Elson's chapter takes on the challenge of 'transforming practice' and moving towards 'the use of macro-economic policy as an instrument for empowering rather than burdening women, see p.153. She argues that for feminist analysis to have any real effect on the construction of macro-policy we must stop talking only to ourselves and initiate an engagement with those on the 'inside' of the policy process – within Ministries of Finance, Central Banks and international institutions such as the World Bank and the IMF. An important element of such engagement is to make transparent to women themselves what the issues are which underpin the technical analysis taking place, given that the objective of gender analysis is not just to understand the gendering of policy, but to transform it in a gender-equitable manner. She contributes to this task by presenting an accessible account of the main economic growth models currently underpinning economic policy formation. She argues that such models are themselves 'bearers of gender', and argues that measures to restructure gender relations, particularly at the interface of production and reproduction, can be a powerful force for producing policies which both support human development and balance demands for different kinds of activities – i.e. which contribute both to equity and also to efficiency in economic terms. Such a position might appear to contradict much of the received wisdom about women and economic reform of recent years but it opens up to scrutiny the ways in which gender analysis can play a role in generating policies for sustainable development at the most basic level.

Another of the received wisdoms in the gender and development literature is that wage employment for women will dissolve gender asymmetries. Ruth Pearson goes back to her earlier work (co-authored with Diane Elson, 1981) which established an analytical framework based on questioning, rather than assuming the outcome of the incorporation of women into the new industrial labour force of the global economy. She argues that much analysis of women in the labour force veers between an Engels-derived framework which assumes that incorporation into waged labour is the basis of dissolving gender discrimination (Pearson, 1994) and a critique of this position which refutes an alternative (though invented) position that exploitation as wage labour is inevitably negative for Third World women. By discussing a range of research findings on women factory workers she shows that modernisation and Marxist theory share the same simplistic assumptions; neither problematises the relationship but assumes a direct causal connection between women's wage earnings and notions of liberation or empowerment, a point also stressed by Harriss-White. Given that much of the employment in question is classified as semi-skilled and organised in a way which is aimed at precluding the development of either workers' consciousness or women's consciousness, it is not surprising that many have come to an alternative position of dismissing such work as being inimical to women's interests. The conflation of employment with empowerment (or the assumption of their inverse relationship) is analogous to the conflation of women and poverty and is in just as much need of a nuanced analysis which applies a gender critique to theories of exploitation and internationalisation.

One of the other ways in which gender has become conventionally 'mainstreamed' into development policies in the 1990s is via the recognition that women are concentrated in the poorest sections of all population because of divisions of labour between paid and unpaid work, the gendering of opportunities and rewards in paid employment and the ongoing responsibility for household and generational reproduction which women carry, very often in the absence of contributing men (see Chant, 1997). This has resulted in a conflation of concerns about poverty alleviation with gender-focused policies which has infused all levels of policy analysis. Jackson's chapter challenges this conflation of women and poverty and the way in which development agencies have merged different objectives – poverty alleviation and integrating gender into development programmes and policies. She insists on a deconstruction of these objectives, arguing that the feminisation of poverty is not just about the concentration of women amongst those deemed to be living under a (internationally variable) poverty line; what gender analysis offers is an understanding of how the experience and implications of poverty are different for men and women who face different sets of constraints and responsibilities; that poverty refers to more than the level of household income and includes the context in which household survival takes place – the public space, access to services and opportunities for change – and that gender concerns are both mediated by poverty and transcend the poverty debate.

Recent debates at the Cairo conference on Population and Development in 1994 as well as the 1995 world conference on women underline the centrality of

11

women's connections with reproduction and the many political battles over population control, women's rights to control their own fertility, access to services, and state policy. Ines Smyth draws out the history of family planning policies and points to the ways in which the new 'reproductive rights' discourse is both an advance for feminist concerns in the field and also represents a cooption of feminists to an agenda set by others in which the adoption of the notion of reproductive health and rights is as much a political renaming as a radical change in policy and practice.

Sheila and Roger Jeffery confront another shibboleth of women and development policy – the notion that education is the key means of changing women's status and behaviour in a way which is positive for all agents involved. They set about dismantling the assumption that education is a 'silver bullet' policy instrument which can reduce women's fertility, and therefore population growth, as well as being the key to changing households' income-generating aspirations and activities. Instead they raise questions about the implications of schooling for girls for achieving greater social equity and autonomy for women. In some situations education can lead to greater autonomy and choices; but as research in South India indicates, it can also lead to less autonomy as education becomes part of the commoditisation of women for the marriage market. Moreover the macro-environment, particularly the reduction of social investment under structural adjustment programmes, has decimated education for poorer individuals in many countries, making female-targeted programmes a mirage. They also raise the controversial possibility that women, given reproductive choice, might opt for more rather than fewer children.

Feminism as deconstruction

The interrogation of development policy and analysis constitutes a deconstruction of many of the assumptions and concepts which are commonplace in such literatures. This reflects a trend in feminist theory in a wide range of disciplines not necessarily related to the study of development and change, which has over the last three decades maintained a continuous assault on the limits and limitations of gender neutral social sciences. As Gatens (1992: 121) explains:

> feminist theorists do not go to Marxism or liberalism hoping for 'the answer' or 'the solution' to 'the woman question' but . . . will approach dominant theories, and their implicit biases, as themselves part of the problem. For this reason it seems appropriate to name these contemporary feminist approaches to dominant socio-political theories 'deconstructive' . . . deconstructive feminism is concerned to investigate the elemental make-up of [these theories] . . . for example much political theory treats the family as a natural rather than a social phenomenon. A deconstructive approach highlights what is at stake in opposing the family, understood as natural, to the public sphere, understood as social.

As Nanneke Redclift reminded us at the end of the conference which inspired this volume, feminist research on development policy and practices presents feminism with a series of paradoxes, uncertainties and contradictions. Rather than try and resolve or dissolve them we should embrace them as a genuine reflection of the tension between the essentially *modernist* project of development, and the subversive *deconstructing* tendencies of feminist analysis. Feminism in general may reject grand narratives and policies and approaches founded on essentialist and universalist notions of women's experiences and priorities; at the same time, as this volume indicates, it cannot fall back on a 'different places, different voices' position which evades the challenge of theorising gender and development. As we noted at the beginning of this chapter, our positionality as academics in a post-colonial state requires that we continuously question the received wisdom concerning women's interests and gender analysis in development. Moreover, in the context of what many have recognised as the institutionalisation of 'gender in development', to maintain an independent questioning feminism is paramount. As many of the chapters in this volume bear testament, the gendering of development is in many instances vulnerable to a reinterpretation as focusing on women, often as instruments of other development cooperation objectives, or as hiding behind an expressed concern for women's interests the pursuit of strategies which have never taken gender relations of women's conflicting and multiple interests as their starting point.

This means chewing over what had seemed to be easy-to-digest positions – on giving women credit, on supporting reproductive choice, on creating employment or educational opportunities for women, on maintaining communities in the face of natural disasters, on writing in women's non-productive work into macro-economic policy formulation. Such positions may well appear progressive and uncontroversial in the circles in which gendering development has become part of the new vocabulary of participatory and concerned development policy and practice. But we should be suspicious of policy objectives or prescriptions made in an exhortatory mode, which declaim what should be done to or by women in developing countries. The analysis presented here is evidence that such approaches are insufficient to meet the complexity and contradictions of women's gender interests in the context of myriad multiple identities and realities. The chapters here are intended to deconstruct these gender and development positions, as much as the gender-blind policies and institutions in which they are embedded, and lay bare the intricate network of contradictory social relations which they claim to analyse and represent. Whilst many volumes may claim to present a feminist analysis of women in developing countries, the aim here is to interrogate the connections between gender and development, to provide an analytical syntax which we hope will provoke future debate, illuminate the implicit theoretical positions and contradictions of much contemporary policy as well as bear witness to the maturing of a field.

Notes

1 The conference was also attended by a number of NGO staff and activists; even so, the majority of those present were white and middle class.
2 For many the term 'Development' means the policies and practices of development agencies – be they national governments, international bodies, multilateral or bilateral aid agencies or local and international NGOs. However, 'development' also refers to social and economic change over time as well as the development of human capital. Most of the chapters in this book take this latter, wider view of development.
3 There are indeed still some feminists and activists from both sides of the North/South divide who reject the notion of 'gender' on the grounds that it decentres women as political subjects and reduces to a technical strategy what is at base a political struggle.
4 This has taken over from the observation by Phillips and Taylor (1980) that labour markets were 'saturated by sex'.
5 Ann Whitehead's contribution to the conference also took up some of these themes. She reviewed the agenda of feminist research in the areas of the rural economy and agrarian change from a contemporary feminist perspective, arguing for the importance of listening to the ways in which women in sub-Saharan Africa, for example, decided on their own list of priorities, rather than deducing issues from a pre-given political economy framework.

References

Afshar, H. and Dennis, C. (1992) *Women, and Adjustment Policies in the Third World.* Macmillan.

Agarwal, B. (1994) *A Field of One's Own: Gender and Land Rights in South Asia.* Cambridge: Cambridge University Press.

Bandarage, A. (1984) 'Women in Development: Liberalism, Marxism and Marxist Feminism', *Development and Change* Vol. 15, pp.495–515.

Boserup, E. (1970) *Women's Role in Economic Development.* London: George Allen and Unwin.

Chant, S. (1997) *Women-Headed Households: Diversity and Dynamics in the Developing World.* Basingstoke: Macmillan Press.

Commonwealth Secretariat (1989) *Engendering Adjustment for the 1990s: Report of a Commonwealth Expert Group on Women and Structural Adjustment.* London: Commonwealth Secretariat.

Elson, D. (1995) 'Male Bias in Macroeconomics: The Case of Structural Adjustment' in D. Elson (ed.) *Male Bias in the Development Process* 2nd Edition. Manchester: Manchester University Press, pp.164–190.

Elson, D. and Pearson, R. (1981) 'Nimble Fingers make Cheap Workers', *Feminist Review* No. 7, pp.87–107.

Folbre, N. (1986) 'Hearts and Spades: Paradigms of Household Economics', *World Development* Vol. 14, No. 2, pp.5–40.

Gatens, M. (1992) 'Powers, Bodies and Difference' in M. Barrett and A. Phillips (eds) *Destabilising Theory: Contemporary Feminist Debates.* London: Routledge, pp.120–137.

Hart, G. (1995) 'Gender and Household Dynamics: Recent Theories and Their Implications' in M. Quibnia (ed.) *Critical Issues in Asian Development: Theories, Experiences, Policies.* Hong Kong: Oxford University Press, pp.39–74.

Hartmann, H. (1981) 'The Unhappy Marriage of Marxism and Feminism: Towards a

More Progressive Union' in L. Sargeant (ed.) *Women and Revolution: A Discussion of the Unhappy Marriage of Marxism and Feminism.* London: Pluto Press, pp.1–41.

Hirschman, M. (1995) 'Women in Development: A Critique' in M. Marchand and J. Parpart (eds) *Feminism/Postmodernism/Development.* London: Routledge, pp.42–45.

IDS Bulletin (1979) 'The Continuing Subordination of Women' Vol. 10, No. 3.

Jackson, C. (1994) 'Gender Analysis and Environmentalisms' in T. Benton and Redclift (eds) *Social Theory and the Environment.* London: Routledge, pp.113–149.

Kabeer, N. (1994) *Reversed Realities: Gender Hierarchies in Development Thought.* London: Verso.

Kandiyoti, D. (1988) 'Bargaining with Patriarchy', *Gender and Society* Vol. 2, No. 3, pp.274–290.

Mohanty, C. T. (1988) 'Under Western Eyes: Gender Scholarship and Colonial Discourses', *Feminist Review* No. 30, pp.61–88.

Molyneux, M. (1979) 'Beyond the Domestic Labour Debate', *New Left Review*, No. 116, pp.3–27.

Moser, C. O. N. (1989) 'Gender Planning in the Third World: Meeting Practical and Strategic Gender Needs', *World Development* Vol. 17, No. 11, pp.1799–1825.

Moser, C. O. N. (1993) *Gender Planning and Development: Theory, Practice and Development.* London: Routledge.

Ong, A. (1988) 'Colonialism and Modernity: Feminist Re-representations of Women in Non-western Societies', *Inscriptions* 3/4, pp.79–93.

Pearson, R. (1994) 'Gender Relations, Capitalism and Third World Industrialization' in L. Sklair (ed.) *Capitalism and Development.* London: Routledge, pp.339–58.

Pearson, R., Whitehead, A. and Young, K. (1984) 'Introduction: The Continuing Subordination of Women in the Development Process', in K. Young, C. Wolkowitz and R. McCullagh (eds) *Of Marriage and the Market: Women's Subordination Internationally and its Lessons.* London: Routledge and Kegan Paul, pp.ix–xix.

Phillips, A. and Taylor, B. (1980) 'Sex and Skill: Notes Towards a Feminist Economics', *Feminist Review* No. 6, pp.79–88.

Rathgeber, E. (1990) 'WID, WAD, GAD: Trends in Research and Practice', *Journal of Developing Areas* July, pp.489–582.

Robertson, C. and Berger, I. (eds) (1986) *Women and Class in Africa.* New York: African Publishing Company.

Rubin, G. (1975) 'The Traffic in Women: Notes on the "Political Economy" of Sex', in R. Reiter (ed.) *Toward an Anthropology of Women.* New York: New York Monthly Review Press, pp.157–210.

Sayers, J. (1982) *Biological Politics.* London, Tavistock.

Scott, J. (1995) *Weapons of the Weak: Everyday Forms of Peasant Resistance.* New Haven: Yale University Press.

Sen, A. K. (1990) 'Gender and Cooperative Conflicts' in I. Tinker (ed.) *Persistent Inequalities.* Oxford: Oxford University Press.

Sen, G. and Grown, C. for DAWN (Development Alternatives with Women for a New Era) (1988) *Development Crises and Alternative Visions: Third World Women's Perspectives.* London: Earthscan Publications.

Sparr, P. (ed.) (1994) *Mortgaging Women's Lives: Feminist Critiques of Structural Adjustment.* London: Zed Press.

Spivak, G. (1985) 'Can the Subaltern Speak? Speculations on Widow Sacrifice', *Wedge* Vol. 7/8, pp.120–130.

Young, K., Wolkowitz, C. and McCullagh, R. (1980) 'Introduction' in *Of Marriage and the*

Market: Women's Subordination in International Perspective. CSE Books, pp.vii–xi. (Subsequently republished by Routledge in 1984 and 1989.)

Young, K., Wolkowitz, C. and McCullagh, R. (1980) *Of Marriage and the Market: Women's Subordination Internationally and its Lessons.* London: Routledge and Kegan Paul.

Part I

INTERESTS, IDENTITIES AND STRATEGIES

1

WHO NEEDS [SEX] WHEN YOU CAN HAVE [GENDER]?

Conflicting discourses on gender at Beijing

Sally Baden and Anne Marie Goetz

Introduction

For academics working in the gender and development (GAD) field, the concept of 'gender' is everyday currency. In the UK, at least, social relations of gender analysis, with its roots in socialist feminism, is a major foundation for GAD thinking (Young *et al.*, 1981; Razavi and Miller, 1995a: 27–32). Understanding the concept of 'gender' in the context of social relations analysis remains a touchstone of gender and development research, teaching and training in many institutions in the UK and elsewhere. However, outside of academia, within policy and activist arenas, the utility and relevance of 'gender' has been highly contested. Indeed, in some policy applications, 'gender' has come to lose its feminist political content. This chapter explores conflicting discourses on the relevance and meaning of gender in policy and activist contexts. We draw on debates over 'gender' aired at the NGO (non-government organisation) Forum of the United Nations (UN) Fourth World Conference on Women, in Huairou, China, in September 1995.[1] This conference provided an extraordinary opportunity to investigate a vast range of contemporary policy and activist discourses, given the very broad spectrum of interest groups represented there.

The first section of this chapter is inspired by the challenge to GAD from grassroots development workers and women activists in the South. This challenge is linked to the current debate over the institutionalisation of gender in development policy and practice, and relates to the perceived depoliticisation of the concept of gender. The second part explores a completely different critique of 'gender' from conservative groups, who attacked 'gender' during the Beijing process on the grounds that it is an over-radical and unrepresentative approach to thinking about social relations. We consider the ways the conservative critique illuminates contradictions and lacunae in feminist theorising about gender. Underlying both sections are questions about what happens to feminist concepts in activist and policy arenas and about our own role in this process, as gender and development researchers.

The mainstreaming agenda

The Beijing Conference reflected the extent to which gender issues have entered the 'mainstream', at least at the level of rhetoric. The entire range of bilateral and multilateral development agencies and institutions vied to display their gender-sensitivity with a range of policy documents and promotional literature as well as presence at workshops and on panels at both official and NGO events. For example, the World Bank launched its analytical framework *Toward Gender Equality: The Role of Public Policy*; while the United Nations Development Programme (UNDP) proferred the 1995 *Human Development Report* focusing on gender.

In the 1990s, 'mainstreaming' has become a dominant theme in gender and development policy circles. Mainstreaming evolved from the earlier call for the 'integration' of women in development, dating back to the 1970s. It arose following the Nairobi UN Women's Conference in 1985, in part reflecting the perceived failure of national women's machineries, many set up in the 1970s and early 1980s, to achieve significant results or influence over government policy. Mainstreaming signifies a push towards systematic procedures and mechanisms within organisations – particularly government and public institutions – for explicitly taking account of gender issues at all stages of policy-making and programme design and implementation. It also represents a call for the diffusion of responsibility for gender issues beyond small and underfunded women's units to the range of sectoral and technical departments within institutions (Razavi and Miller, 1995b).

Mainstreaming has been heavily promoted within international development circles by gender policy advocates in a relatively small group of bilateral agencies, sometimes leading to accusations of a donor driven agenda. It has also been argued that the mainstreaming agenda focuses on process and means rather than ends, leading to a preoccupation with the minutiae of procedures at all levels, rather than clarity or direction about goals (Razavi and Miller, 1995b). Feminist (or radical and Marxist) critiques of bureaucracies and their potential for promoting women's interests – or indeed those of any other disempowered social group – are not new although they have only relatively recently filtered into the GAD field (Staudt, 1990; Razavi and Miller, 1995b; Goetz, 1995). Echoing these critiques, disquiet about the mainstreaming agenda and the way in which the GAD discourse is evolving was in evidence at the NGO Forum in Huairou, from both the Left and the Right.

The Platform for Action of the official conference in Beijing had comprehensively adopted the language of gender and, specifically, of gender mainstreaming. In the final chapter on Institutional Arrangements, a commitment was made to 'promote an active and visible policy of mainstreaming a gender perspective . . . in the monitoring and evaluation of all policies and programmes' (United Nations, 1995a: 134). The preoccupation with institutionalisation was also evident in the number of workshops at the Forum (and panels at the official conference in Beijing) which focused on the issue from a variety of perspectives.

One of these, early on in the Forum, was entitled 'Feminism: From Movement to Establishment' convened by the Applied Socio-economic Research (ASR) organisation of Pakistan. Nighat Khan, Director of ASR and a panellist at this workshop, argued that gender analysis had become a technocratic discourse, in spite of its roots in socialist feminism, dominated by researchers, policy-makers and consultants, which no longer addressed issues of power central to women's subordination. She identified factors underlying this shift as the professionalisation and 'NGOisation' of the women's movement and the consequent lack of accountability of 'gender experts' to a grassroots constituency. A more radical perspective on the Beijing process and associated discourse on gender came from the Revolutionary Women of the Philippines, whose pamphlet *The Gender Trap: An Imperialist Scheme for Coopting the World's Women*, attacked gender mainstreaming as a scheme to buy off once committed activists (Makibaka, 1995: 5).

Nighat Khan asserted that the focus on gender, rather than women, had become counter-productive in that it had allowed the discussion to shift from a focus on women, to women and men and, finally, back to men. This latter point was echoed by others at the NGO Forum. Eudine Barriteau, presenting on a panel for Development Alternatives with Women in a New Era (DAWN), described how in Jamaica the shift in discourse from women to gender had resulted, in policy circles, in a focus away from women, to 'men at risk', reflecting concern about men's failure in education and in securing employment, while women perform much better educationally and many support families alone.

This view is also reflected in other accounts. A Bangladeshi development worker is quoted by Kabeer as saying: 'Do you think we are ready for gender in development in Bangladesh when we have not yet addressed the problems of women in development?' It transpired that 'the new vocabulary of gender was being used in her organisation to deny the very existence of women specific disadvantage and hence the need for specific measures which might address this disadvantage' (1994: xii). According to Razavi and Miller, in their recent review of conceptual shifts in the women and development discourse:

> Although the gender discourse has filtered through to policy-making institutions, in the process actors have re-interpreted the concept of gender to suit their institutional needs. In some instances, 'gender' has been used to side-step a focus on 'women' and on the radical policy implications of overcoming their disprivilege.
>
> (1995a: 41)

Mainstreaming in research: from subordination to disaggregation

The contradictions generated by mainstreaming resonate closer to home. As gender has become a more mainstream and therefore more respectable and fundable field of research, new players are entering the field, who bear no allegiance to feminist research and may not even have any familiarity with its basic texts, concepts and methodologies. Economists, statisticians and econometricians (many, though not all of them, men), responding to the growth in demand from major development bureaucracies for research and analysis to inform their new 'gender-aware' policy directions, have taken up research into gender issues. This recent body of research has tended to look at gender as an interesting statistical variable although certainly not a defining or universally relevant one (e.g. Appleton *et al.*, 1990; Haddad, 1991). Elson (1995) refers to this as 'the gender-disaggregation approach'. Drawing heavily on the neoclassical economic paradigm, it tends to a static and reductionist definition of gender as (woman/man) – stripping away consideration of the relational aspects of gender, of power and ideology and of how patterns of subordination are reproduced. To the extent that such approaches do consider the factors underlying gender disadvantage or inequality, they tend to look to information problems (e.g. women's tendency to follow female role models), or to 'culture' (defined as outside the purview of mainstream economics) as explanatory factors (see Lockwood, 1992 on Collier, for example). While such research may be of great interest and can provide invaluable insights and empirical evidence, it can under-specify the power relations maintaining gender inequalities, and in the process, de-links the investigation of gender issues from a feminist transformatory project.

Bureaucratic requirements for information tend to strip away the political content of information on women's interests and reduce it to a set of needs or gaps, amenable to administrative decisions about the allocation of resources. This distillation of information about women's experiences is unable to accommodate or validate issues of gender and power. Women are separated out as the central problem and isolated from the context of social and gender relations. Furthermore, bureaucracies tend to privilege certain kinds of information perceived as relevant to dominant development paradigms and attribute significance to information in proportion to the perceived social and political status of the informer. Thus, the information provided by Western feminists has tended to get a better hearing than the perspectives of Southern women (Goetz, 1994). It now appears that the quantitative expertise of male economists on gender is gaining increasing weight as the discourse becomes more technocratic, with the danger that in-depth, qualitative, feminist research may be devalued.

The Beijing Conference itself saw the production of several compendia of gender-disaggregated data, including a new edition of *The World's Women* produced by the UN Statistical Office (UN, 1995b) and the UNDP's *Human Development Report* (UNDP, 1995). This latter featured two new indices – the Gender Disparity Index (GDI) and the Gender Empowerment Measure (GEM). The GEM is an interesting departure in that it attempts to establish a universal index by which 'empowerment' (a highly culturally loaded concept) can be measured and compared between countries, based on a composite of measures of income, participation in professional and managerial jobs and formal political participation.[2] It is especially ironic that the rhetoric of grassroots, collective, bottom-up development ('empowerment') is invoked to name a top-down and universalising statistic.

This is not to say that quantitative data or analysis of gender issues is not valuable. One key victory at Beijing was the successful campaign for the Platform of Action to include a commitment to the valuation of women's unpaid labour in satellite national accounts, making concrete a long-standing feminist rallying cry. In this case, an organised feminist campaign was able to exploit the increasing sophisitication of gender-disaggregated statistics and of statistical method in general.

Advocacy and accuracy: lies, damned lies and gender statistics

As feminist researchers we felt it important in the build-up to Beijing to forge alliances with activists and campaigners within NGOs and women's organisations, who are attempting to change the policies of public institutions. This proved challenging, in a number of ways. Specifically, it highlighted our distance from the language used in the lobbying process, in both its conceptual underpinnings and style: our proclivity for academic rigour, complexity and critique seemed at times to be in direct opposition to the demands of consensus building, political utility, and direct campaigning messages.

A couple of examples illustrate the point. We are all familiar with the claim that 'Women [account] for two-thirds of all working hours, receive only one-tenth of the world income and own less than one percent of world property' (UN, 1980, cited in Duley and Edwards, 1986: 48). It has recently come to light that the figure was made up by someone working in the UN because it seemed to her to represent the scale of gender-based inequality at the time.[3] It has since been taken up and repeated endlessly, to the point of becoming a cliché, as a justification for attention to gender inequality in access to resources. The point is that, while highly effective as an advocacy slogan (still in circulation 15 years on!), the claim had no basis and thus had the potential to backfire and discredit feminist research. In the context of 'mainstreaming', such slogans may have little credibility.[4]

Nevertheless, similarly dubious statistical claims continue to be made by activists and gender advocates in order to justify attention to women. DAWN's position paper for the Beijing Conference asserts that 'Women world-wide produce half of the world's food, constitute 70 per cent of the world's 1.3 billion absolute poor and own only 1 per cent of the world's land' (DAWN, 1995: 6). Throughout the conference, the 'feminisation of poverty' featured prominently as a topic of discussion and as a justification for channelling resources to poor women. The Platform of Action features a chapter on the 'persistent and increasing burden of poverty on women' which specifically refers to the 'feminisation of poverty', and identifies female-headed households as a particularly vulnerable group in this context (UN, 1995a: 21).

At the conference, we distributed a briefing paper on gender and poverty reduction strategies, which, drawing on recent work in the GAD field (Jackson,

1996; see also Chapter 2 by Jackson in this volume) questioned the growing ortho-doxy on the feminisation of poverty and, specifically, the claim that rising female headship is responsible for this.[5] But other critics of the 'feminisation of poverty' at Beijing tended to be those on the religious right who viewed the association with female headship and the resulting demands for resources to be channelled to lone women as a threat to family values. Thus, we found ourselves going against the tide of the advocacy effort in rather unwholesome company.

Instrumentalism and opportunism

Activists, lobbyists and gender policy advocates working within institutions have adopted a variety of strategies to influence institutional agendas and bring about 'mainstreaming', often resorting to instrumental arguments to convince hard-ened bureaucrats of the need to address gender issues. Common instrumental arguments used are the need to invest in female education to serve population control and child welfare goals (see Jeffery and Jeffery, Chapter 11 in this volume), or the importance of women's participation in community organisations to improve service provision and assist anti-poverty efforts. Such arguments appear justified to get gender issues on the table in organisations whose mandate and goals do not embrace social justice or equity. The World Bank's recent policy doc-ument for Beijing, for example, makes the case for gender almost entirely on efficiency grounds, constructing a convergence between the interests of women and the promotion of economic liberalisation: 'Sound economic policies and well functioning markets are essential for growth, employment and the creation of an environment in which the returns to investing in women and girls can be fully realised' (World Bank, 1995: 5).

Instrumental arguments, while they may prove successful in raising gender issues, are problematic in that they often result in women or gender being simply a means to other ends. Further, they run the risk of being discredited. Tenuous evi-dence on the relationships between female education and fertility decline, or female education and productivity, can be easily challenged, weakening the justi-fication for addressing gender issues, with a danger that resources will be withdrawn. Finally, the use of instrumental arguments fails to recognise the gen-dered nature of institutions themselves: information or the right arguments will not in themselves produce change. Institutional structures, rule and cultures, including the ways in which information is collected, processed and prioritised, reflect dominant gender interests, so that the pursuit of gender equity must include demands for organisational change.

Mainstreaming: the depoliticisation of gender?

The ambivalence about – or even hostility towards – the GAD discourse expressed by some Southern women activists at Beijing perhaps reflects deeper anxieties about the imposition of what is perceived as an external agenda and about whose interests are served by the mainstreaming project. This is underlined by the lack of accountability of Northern development agencies to the Southern women in whose interests they claim to be acting. While Northern feminist groups can lobby their governments, albeit with limited effect, the responses of Southern women to policy decisions taken in Washington or London have not until recently formed part of the 'feedback loop' characteristic of pluralist politics (Jaquette and Staudt, 1988).[6]

The variety of ways in which 'gender' has come to be institutionalised and operationalised in the development arena presents a contradictory and ironic picture. There is a disjuncture between the feminist intent behind the term and the ways in which it is employed such as to minimise the political and contested character of relations between women and men. A problem with the concept of 'gender' is that it can be used in a very descriptive way and the question of power can easily be removed. In order to bring power back into gender, feminists need to move away from the idea of simple oppression and bring a gender critique into new theorising about power (Oldersma and Davis, 1991). More practically, we also need to challenge the privileging of certain kinds of information on women and as a consequence particular kinds of expertise within development bureaucracies.

It is ironic that a concept which was engineered to carry a political message can be so depoliticised in its use as to be rejected by some of the people most committed to gender-redistributive change, such as feminist development activists. This speaks not to a need to reject the concept of 'gender', but rather, to the need for much greater, and perhaps much more pragmatic and applied, dialogue between researchers and practitioners, to ensure that concepts developed for activist arenas are not developed in the isolation of theory. Theorists can never, of course, control what happens to concepts when they are taken up by activists, nor would that be desirable. But given that much of feminist academic research grounds its legitimacy on a claim to relevance to the struggles of contemporary women, the ways in which feminist concepts can be distorted, even by well-meaning newcomers and potential allies, deserves careful monitoring.

The second half of this chapter now turns to a virulent challenge to the concept of 'gender' which came from a very different direction in Beijing: conservative backlash politics. Whilst the first set of challenges related to concerns about the depoliticisation of gender relations, this contrasting challenge, ironically, related to a view that ideas behind the concept of 'gender' tend to over-politicise the relations between women and men. This backlash challenge demonised 'gender' as a code for the disruption of cherished certainties about human relations.

The bracketing of gender in the Platform for Action

We have to try to neutralise the tremendous amount of gender, gender perspectives, which are going to go directly against our families and against our children.

(Speaker on a panel of conservative women at the Fourth UN
Conference on Women, Beijing, fringe meeting, September 1995)

25

The Platform for Action agreed in September 1995 at the Fourth UN Conference on Women in Beijing was a more highly contested text than any of the other international statements agreed at recent international conferences – at one point two paragraphs of text alone had generated 31 pages of amendments. Unlike any of these other agreements, debate over the Platform for Action was unique in calling into question the conceptual foundation and subject matter of the conference itself – the concept of gender, and with it, notions of the injustice and mutability of gender relations. Was the conference to be about 'sex' or 'gender'? At the final Preparatory Committee meeting in March 1995 in New York, divergent views on this question emerged as country delegations took their last opportunity to signal their reservations over parts of the text prior to the Beijing meeting. Most dramatically, the representative from Honduras, backed by representatives from other Catholic countries, proposed the bracketing of the word 'gender' throughout the text. A working group eventually resolved on an acceptably broad definition of the term, but the tremendous anxieties over the meaning and implications of the 'gender perspective' illuminate an unexpected politicisation of the concept of 'gender', which expressed, in part, aspects of backlash reactions to contemporary feminism. The debates over the word 'gender' also shine light on some contradictions and inconsistencies in feminist theoretical and political distinctions between sex and gender.

It may be that the conservative opposition to the concept expressed a second-wind reaction after the failure to prevent agreement at the International Conference on Population and Development in Cairo in 1994 on a broad definition of women's reproductive health rights. Other factors explaining the conservative fixation on gender may include the perceived greater influence and presence of feminist NGOs, the greater visibility of lesbians in NGOs, and the inclusion, for the first time in the UN series of Conferences on Women, of very open language on sexual and reproductive rights.

The issue of the perceived influence of feminist NGOs became a particularly important target for conservative concern. The UN Conferences on Women over the last 20 years have set in place mechanisms for collaboration between feminist NGOs and multilaterals which are of a much more sophisticated nature than is conventional in these fora. In part, the growing importance of these NGOs in the UN Conferences on Women is a reflection of their relative weakness at the national level; international fora have become arenas where they can 'leap-frog' over the boundaries of state sovereignty to propose visions of women's liberation which national governments might not countenance – and for which there is often insufficient domestic support, even amongst women. As a consequence, there is a high degree of discursive familiarity between NGOs and multilaterals such as the UN on issues such as women's rights, or the meaning of 'gender', sometimes leaving individual states in the dark. This appears to have fanned conservative suspicions of a conspiracy by a minority of unrepresentative women in these NGOs to undermine national sovereignty and cultural self-determination.

The trouble with gender

The conservative challenge to the use of the concept of 'gender' raises issues central to feminist epistemology and politics. How is the body constituted in gendered identity formation? What is the relation between gender identities and political subjectivities? Does sensitivity to gender reveal a concern for equality or for a celebration of difference? Does a concern with equity risk assimilating women to the masculine mean? Would a celebration of difference play into the hands of a tradition which has used notions of 'biology is destiny' to explain and justify inequality? The trouble with gender is that it allows for considerable variation in the ways feminists interpret identity formation and the relationship between anatomy and culture. This variation has been seen as part of the richness and flexibility of feminism, but it has also meant the production of ambiguities, inconsistencies and contradictions which conservative groups exposed in attacks on feminism. On the one hand, the lingering essentialism or 'biological foundationalism' (Nicholson, 1994: 82) in feminist thought encourages romanticism about women's shared experiences and interests, and supports policy solutions which assume a relationship between female embodiment and representation of women's interests – such as the assumption that more women in decision-making will result in feminist decisions. This is incompatible with, on the other hand, the postmodern exposure of 'women' as a product of a masculine dominative logic, and the degendering of ontology, which so fundamentally denies a determinate meaning to both 'woman' and 'women' that it hardly makes sense to have a conference on 'women' at all.

Problems of universalism, essentialism, relativism and nihilism are not new to critical feminist theory or feminist practice. What is argued here is that the conservative reaction to 'gender' highlighted inconsistencies and areas of neglect in contemporary feminist approaches to the constitution of gender identity and political subjectivity, and that these are problems which stand in stark relief in an internationalist context like the Beijing Conference, which puts feminist claims to represent the meaning of women's experiences in all their heterogeneity to their starkest test. To develop this argument, a conservative polemic attacking feminist conceptions of gender which was circulated at the NGO Forum is analysed here, with a particular focus on its implications for feminist conceptions of the sex/gender relationship, and for conceptions of desire, motherhood, relationships to men, and the equality/difference tension.

'Gender, the deconstruction of women'

'Gender, the deconstruction of women', is a 29-page essay by Dale O'Leary which was widely circulated at the NGO Forum. O'Leary is a writer for the US conservative Catholic publication: *Hearth – Journal of the Authentic Catholic Woman*. It is not assumed here that her paper is representative of all conservative views or of fundamentalist religious perspectives in general. The paper does deserve some attention, however, in that of all the conservative documents available at the NGO Forum, it is the only one we are aware of which engages directly with feminist theory, and thus directly outlines some ways in which conservatives are politicising gender in reaction to feminism. The paper will not be analysed in terms of what it shows of a conservative position, but in terms of the issues it raises for the coherence of feminist approaches to gender.

To emphasise the problem of gender, though at the cost of any subtlety, O'Leary lumps together virtually all feminisms under the general title 'Gender Feminism'. The agenda of 'gender feminists' is presented through a translation of their 'code words' in the Platform for Action (this heightens the sense of conspiracy): 'free choice in reproduction' is explained to be a code for abortion on demand; 'lifestyle' a code for homosexuality (ibid.: 19).

The argument of O'Leary's paper runs as follows. If gender is defined as the social construction of roles and relationships between women and men, then sexuality can be fluid, the centrality of the family can be challenged, role assignments such as motherhood and male breadwinner are revealed as social constructs, and indeed the fixity or irreducibility of anatomical sex itself can be questioned. All of this of course has always been central to a feminist logic, though there has been less certainty about the last point, as will be suggested shortly. O'Leary's reaction to the feminist argument on social construction is to point out that there is no scientific proof for any of it, nor is there evidence that women do not freely choose traditional roles. On the contrary, science is showing that sexed behavioural characteristics and social choices are programmed genetically,[7] and surveys of women show that they do freely choose their roles and are not victims of 'false consciousness', and that even if they want equal opportunities, they do not necessarily desire a sex/gender revolution – they value their womanliness.

These views might be considered fairly typical of conservative reactions to feminism. The key reason for the panic in relation to the term gender, however, appears to be its implications for sexuality and reproduction, reflecting two major conservative bogeys – homosexuality and abortion. Interestingly, conservative positions on the naturalness of restricting women to mothering roles, or to secondary economic positions, and so on, are not particularly stressed in O'Leary's document, nor, by and large, in other conservative pamphlets available at the Forum. This reflects perhaps changes in the economic roles of women in conservative countries worldwide. Poverty and male unemployment globally have pushed more women into work and enhanced their role in supporting families, and few conservatives would suggest that women withdraw from work in the context of poverty (though they might defend men's privileged access to favoured labour market positions). Nor is any disapprobation expressed of women in public decision-making roles, and indeed, many conservative delegations, including the one from the Vatican, were led by women. This may reflect pressure from conservative women for more participation in decision-making, and a secular increase in women's education levels and participation in government in many developing countries.

Declaring war on women's natures?

Although the predominant concern with sexuality and reproduction reflects perennial conservative anxieties, it is also a direct reflection upon the implications of the gender argument for the way we think of the body. Implicit in O'Leary's document is an understanding that, taken to its logical extreme, the argument about social construction must eventually deconstruct the body. As Linda Nicholson points out, this understanding of the implications of gender thinking has come unevenly to feminists. She shows that there have been two trends in the ways feminists currently think of gender. First, there is the more familiar use of the term to stress the social construct in contrast to the biological given. Second, gender is increasingly used to refer to any social construction having to do with the male/female, as opposed to the masculine/feminine distinction (1994: 79). Nicholson quotes Scott to show how sex is subsumable under gender: 'gender is the knowledge that establishes meanings for bodily differences . . . We cannot see differences except as a function of our knowledge about the body, and that knowledge is not "pure", cannot be isolated from its implication in a broad range of discursive contexts' (Scott, 1988: 2).

Nicholson argues that the problem with the first definition is that it is self-contradictory and risks biological essentialism, because biological sex has to be invoked at the very moment that the influence of the biological is being challenged – in other words, 'woman' remains a given upon which characteristics are imposed through social reactions to the body (1994: 80–81). This first understanding of gender has grounded feminist cross-cultural work on women's status in the sense that sufficient physiological givens are assumed to be shared by all women to generate a common range of social constructions. The changeability of these social reactions across culture, the important exceptions, rescues this approach from complete biological essentialism, in stressing the mutability of sex identities. The cost of this approach has been a central dilemma and political schism within feminism, stemming from the underplaying of differences between women, across culture and race in particular, in the interests of maintaining a notion of universality in the cross-cultural feminine, a universality, moreover, which disguised its roots in the experiences of white Western women (Mohanty, 1991; Persram, 1994).

O'Leary's discussion of this first understanding of sex and gender illuminates familiar problems it poses for the ways we think about equality and difference. The notion of social construction can be interpreted as suggesting a fundamental equality and sameness between the sexes, and O'Leary touches on a problem with this. Bringing up the liberal feminist concern to see parity for women and men in all forms of employment, she argues that this will inevitably force women to conform to the male standard. She explains this, however, rather differently from feminists who point to structural pressures on women to become sociological males when they cross the public/private divide. Instead, she argues, the problem inheres in men's incapacity to become biological females: 'Trying to pretend that all the obvious differences are socially constructed and can therefore be changed, or that men and women can and should be the same, makes maleness the standard for women, because while women can enter the world of work, men cannot give birth' (1995: 14). This ignores, of course, the wide range of reproductive activities which men are perfectly capable of performing, but it does touch on a widely shared disappointment amongst women about the difficulty in winning social value for women's work rather than struggling for success in the public sphere, only to be found wanting by a male standard. O'Leary links this problem in the drive for equality with the obsession with generating gender-disaggregated statistics on women's representation of women in all public forms of employment or politics. Though she does not intend the point in this way, she is identifying a problem with the unreflective pursuit of formal equity. Not all statistical differences reflect discrimination. Nor does 50–50 statistical equality reflect genuine equality and a cultural change towards valuing women's interests – male–female equity in school enrolment levels, for instance, tells us little about gender bias in the curriculum.

The second account of gender, in which 'sex, by definition, will be shown to have been gender all along' (Butler, 1990: 8), is so sensitive to problems of essentialism that it rejects any account of sexual difference which invokes what is unique in female sexuality because this would re-cement the boundaries of gender identities. All associations with the term 'woman' are exposed as arbitrary meanings, and biology, rather than being something which women in all countries share, is instead a culturally specific set of ideas with little translatability across cultures. Now, the extreme postmodern unravelling of both 'woman' and 'women' is disconcerting enough to many feminists, whether academics or activists – it has often been pointed out that it may lead to a nihilistic conception of women (Persram, 1994: 287). As Nicholson observes: 'If those who call themselves feminists cannot even decide upon who women are, how can political demands be enacted in the name of women?' (1994: 102). To those espousing a conservative interpretation of women's roles,[8] this is not the issue, as they have never made the politically motivated assumption that women are socially constructed. Instead, the anxiety is over the challenge to the notion that 'biology is reality' (O'Leary, 1995: 14).

This second approach to understanding gender appears to have been identified more clearly by conservative groups than it has been, perhaps, by feminist activists – for instance, in the Gender and Development field it does not appear to have much currency. One strategy to bring out the implications of these notions of the fluidity of the body in an alarmist and trivialising way prior to the Beijing Conference was the mock horror expressed by conservatives in the US over a scientific paper about genital abnormalities. Anne Fausto Sterling's discussion: 'The five sexes: why male and female are not enough', showed that genital abnormalities produce 'herms' (hermaphrodites), 'ferms' (female hermaphrodites), and 'merms' (male pseudo hermaphrodites). Conservatives used this as a springboard for insisting on clarifying the status of 'sex' in the Platform for Action, demanding 'assurance that only two sexes would be recognised' (O'Leary, 1995: 6).

While these kinds of reactions and strategies can be and often are dismissed by feminists as distracting irritations, it is worth noting that feminists have not been consistent in the way notions of sex and gender, of biology and culture, ground their tactics. There is a tendency to use social constructivist arguments when convenient, and biologically essentialist ones at other times. At the Beijing Conference there were examples of policy arguments made on the basis of either sex or gender. Some lesbians invoked both in contradictory ways – for instance, it was widely maintained that the brackets around 'gender' in the Platform for Action directly signified homophobia, in that they expressed an attack on the notion of fluidity in the construction of the sexed body and of desire. Yet at the same time, a lesbian was reported as announcing, at one of the human rights tribunals, that she had been 'born a lesbian', insisting on a biologically grounded notion of her identity.[9]

The straw man of patriarchy – and other feminist universals

Everyone has a right to be listened [to] . . . and atheists and lesbians do not have the right to impose their views on the rest of us.
(Speaker from the floor at a meeting of conservative women at the Beijing conference)

O'Leary presents a crude version of feminism which bears little resemblance to the complexity of feminist thought. It is hard to imagine feminists today who would accuse happy mothers of suffering from false consciousness or dismiss women's subjective interpretations of meaning in their lives. However, her interpretation of feminism is probably not so different at a general level from popular understandings of feminism, and as such it points to certain 'sore points' – or neglected issues – within feminism which have alienated women and men, perhaps more than necessary. Not all feminists are 'atheists and lesbians', but if this is the popular perception of feminism, it suggests that feminists have undertheorised, or been dismissive of, a range of important aspects of women's lives. These include the role of women in many parts of the world in maintaining tradition, and the centrality of religion to their lives; women's joy in mothering and nurturing; and women's individual choices to make 'bargains with patriarchy' (Kandiyoti, 1988). Another neglected area is the great range of masculinities. This list may seem a reactionary set of concerns to some. Others may argue, and rightly, that feminists do deal with each of these areas, with masculinity perhaps more neglected than other areas because of the political imperative of addressing women's concerns first. Though feminists do deal with religion, motherhood, and so on, their analytical proclivities have been oriented primarily to critiquing not the subjective experience of motherhood or of worship or of partnership with men, but rather the conditions which are felt to strip freedom from women's choices in these situations – feminists critique the conditions of motherhood, not the value of parenting; they critique the gendered constraints of religion, not the value of

31

spirituality. These subtleties are lost, however, on most people, and unfortunately the negative language which is sometimes used – such as speaking of women's 'burden' of child care, or of the 'reproductive tax' (Palmer, 1991) – do not convince people that positive value in women's choices and identities is being recognised. Nowhere is this more so than in popular perceptions of the way feminists think about men and their relationship with women.

O'Leary brings this out rather wittily, charging feminists with creating a 'straw man of patriarchy': 'the proto-typical male chauvinist, patriarchal sexist oppressor who believes biology is destiny and wants women confined to the house, barefoot and pregnant, inferior, subordinate, second-class citizen'. She points out that if this person actually existed he would 'probably be confined to a maximum security facility as a sociopath' (O'Leary, 1995: 17). Feminists have always had trouble theorising patriarchy with enough subtlety to embrace historical and cultural variation (Nicholson, 1994: 91–2), let alone individual male subjectivities. Though they have not been quite as crude as O'Leary suggests, there is room for much more work in understanding masculinity and male domination. More critical, perhaps, is the need to move beyond the sharply dualistic confrontational categories in which western feminists have tended to place the relations between the sexes. Feminists from the South have pointed out that this male/female opposition may be more central to the constitution of gender identity of white middle-class Western women than women elsewhere (Trinh, 1987: 18). Postmodern feminists have pointed out that the very sharpness of this male/female dualism informing the concept of 'woman' actually undermines any meaning that 'woman' might have. Crowded 'with the overdeterminations of male supremacy, invoking in every formulation the limit, contrasting Other, or mediated self-reflection of a culture built on the control of females' (Alcoff, 1988: 504), 'woman' is emptied of any meaning of its own and is less useful for feminist politics. Feminists have argued for the need for a more plural interpretation of 'woman' which refuses to 'brace woman's mobility against the fixity of a petrified man' (Berg, 1982, in Persram, 1994: 286), but more plural interpretations of 'man' are needed also.

In the name of women

Given that feminists are indeed, as conservatives charge, a minority of women, and given that they are not in a position to legitimise their claims to represent the concerns of most women on the basis of democratic processes in social and political institutions which produce feminist representation, challenges to the relevance of feminist claims to women must be taken seriously. What is at stake is very clear in O'Leary's text – the relevance of feminism to women in developing countries:

> The success or failure of the Beijing conference depends on the delegates from developing countries . . . one senses their frustration with

the Gender Perspective. Most are pro-family, pro-religion, and basically pro-life. They know instinctively that Gender Perspective is not the perspective of women in their countries. On the other hand, they strongly support the advancement of women. . . . They are grateful for Gender Feminists' willingness to join with them in the battle against economic neo-colonialism. They do not want to appear to be opposing the equality of women.

(O'Leary, 1995: 28)

As O'Leary implies, feminism has an edge in the developing country context because of its tendency to take a structural approach to problems of women's poverty and oppression.[10] But to return to the subject of this chapter, a broader concern for feminists working in coalition the world over relates to the place of gender in theorising women's political subjectivity in cross-cultural contexts. Postmodernists argue that the only way to avoid generalising from an essentialised Western version of the feminine is to refuse to seek shared sex or gender characteristics, and to deny them political status. Cultural feminists propose instead a celebration of a multiplicity of feminine identities, but this can lead to a politically paralysed relativism (Goetz, 1991; Persram, 1994). The risk is that the reality of women's oppression can fall between the many stools of feminist anxieties over identity.

It seems possible to construct a feminist politics without insisting that the category of 'woman' or 'women' has a determinate meaning. The key, as Mohanty (1991) suggests, is to refuse to make an elision between 'women' as a socially constructed group, and 'women' as material subjects of their own history, in order that the material and ideological specificity of women's positions are appreciated, and generalisation about gender relations is avoided. According to Nicholson, this also means refusing to assume sisterhood on the basis of gender or sex, but to seek instead to construct coalitions which acknowledge difference (1994: 103). The creation of coalitions between groups with very different interests certainly seemed to be taking place in Beijing, with, for example, a broad alliance on reproductive rights between Northern and Southern women, which allowed for rather different interpretations of these rights – abortion rights concerns predominating amongst Northern women, and concerns for freedom from coerced abortions and contraception amongst Southern women. Similarly, coalitions concerned with economic crisis were formed between Southern women affected by structural adjustment, Western women dealing with social service cuts, and women in transitional economies dealing with high unemployment (Agarwal, 1995). As Agarwal notes, this was the expression of the emergence of a 'strategic sisterhood' to replace the 'romantic sisterhood' of the past (ibid.).

At some level, however, the appeal to coalitional politics as a replacement for appreciating the relevance of sex or even gender to feminist politics is unsatisfactory. Why then organise together as women at all? It is hard to find space in contemporary feminist theory for the genuine sense of connection *as women* of which so many women spoke in Huairou and Beijing, yet it seems dishonest not to bear testimony to the palpable sense of commonality in spite of great differences. It seems important not to confuse discursive constructions of 'woman' with the living talking real person who engaged with other women in the Forum and the conference. If we still find meaning in shared biology only because the world continues to behave and treat women as though this were their primary defining characteristic, this does not erase its meaningfulness as a point of connection between women. Acting as women in the name of women we will inevitably infuse 'sex' with meaning, but attention to the various paths by which we each come to be 'sexed' should help ensure that we avoid sinking back to reductive essentialisms. What seems critical, however, is that we are consistent in applying the politically motivated assumption that 'woman' is a socially constructed category to feminist activism and policy work. This will protect us from the dead end of essentialism, the cultural brutality of universalism, and will also allow us to broaden our base of allies beyond the boundaries of 'sex'.

Conclusion

So, where does this leave us, departing from Huairou clutching somewhat battered gender concepts and wondering how to reclaim their feminist content without alienating potential allies, particularly among Southern researchers and activists?

As Northern feminist researchers in gender and development, one role we can play is to track the redefinition of concepts as discourses become institutionalised and help to identify opportunities for advancing feminist ideas within this process, being aware that we are often complicit in it. An example is the current debate in donor circles about good governance and participation, which provides considerable scope for questioning the nature of participation and indeed politics from a feminist perspective and, concretely, the opportunity to push for greater accountability of donor agencies and wider institutions to women and their organisations.

It is also important that we engage in dialogue with colleagues who work on gender issues from outside a feminist perspective, to attempt to broaden the scope of their studies and to see how their findings can inform our own work and campaigns. Training workshops in feminist research methods might be one vehicle for such a dialogue. We also need to ensure that the pioneering contributions of feminist theorists and researchers are recognised as gender and development work moves into the mainstream and thus to convince funding agencies of the value of supporting non-quantitative, innovative and challenging research.

Finally, and perhaps most importantly, we need to look at whether and how GAD research serves those attempting to promote women's interests either in grassroots development work or through influencing policy. Some might claim that as academics it is not our business to determine how our research is used but this view is increasingly redundant in a world where much research is commissioned precisely to inform policy. At the very least, we need to maintain an open dialogue with feminist researchers and activists in the South, to listen to their critiques of current gender and development thinking, policy and practice, including our own, and to take on board their perspectives and priorities.

Notes

1 We were part of a team from several UK universities, comprising, apart from ourselves, Bridget Byrne, Lyla Mehta, Kirsty Milward and Sheelagh Stewart (IDS, University of Sussex); Cecile Jackson and Ruth Pearson of the University of East Anglia; Tina Wallace of the University of Birmingham and Ines Smyth formerly of the London School of Economics, now based at Oxfam. Tahera Yasmin Huque, who works for the Canadian International Development Agency in Bangladesh, was also involved in the UEA/IDS workshop: 'Breaking In; Speaking Out: Making Development Organisations Work for Women' (Stewart, 1995).

2 This is not the place for a detailed critique of this index: suffice to say that numerous questions could be raised about the validity of the measures chosen as indicators of 'empowerment'.

3 See Jackson's introduction for further discussion of this.

4 A few weeks before the conference, a senior policy advisor in a bilateral agency rang the Institute of Development Studies to enquire whether there was any evidence to support the 'two thirds' figure, since male colleagues had challenged her use of it. In a similar vein, a recent evaluation of the gender activities of the Canadian International Development Authority (CIDA), found that CIDA had not been able to convincingly back up its claim that failure to take on board gender will hinder the development process, such that this claim was now met with considerable scepticism (CIDA, 1993).

5 This questioning arises partly from the lack of conceptual clarity over what feminisation means, partly from the limitations of empirical evidence and partly from the implication that poor women should be the focus of our attention, rather than broader processes of gender discrimination.

6 Beijing provided an opportunity for strategic alliances between Northern and Southern activists to coalesce, notably the 'Women's Eyes on the World Bank' campaign. Since Beijing the Bank has set up a hand-picked 'External Consultative Group' composed of prominent Southern women activists, as a step towards greater accountability and increased legitimacy for its position on gender issues. The degree of influence, modalities and representativeness of this group, only recently formed, are not yet clear.

7 Interestingly, in the months following the Beijing Conference, many UK newspapers carried stories reviving socio-biological arguments and presenting new scientific evidence for gendered genetic programming.

8 Or as O'Leary puts it, women's 'vocations' (1995: 12).

9 I am grateful to Cecile Jackson for this example.

10 Interestingly, O'Leary's text refuses structural explanations for a whole range of oppressions women experience - like inner city poverty, domestic violence and lack of employment opportunities. However, she makes one exception, referring to women's poverty, lack of social rights, and poor labour market option, when explaining why some women become prostitutes (1995: 23)

References

Abzug, B. (1995) 'A message from NGO women to UN Member States, the Secretariat, and the Commission on the Status of Women', NGO statement, April 3, from the Internet.

Agarwal, B. (1995) 'From Mexico to Beijing', *Indian Express*, October 6.

Alcoff, L. (1988) 'Cultural feminism vs post-structuralism: the identity crisis in feminist theory', *Signs*, Vol. 13, No. 3, pp.405–436.

Appleton, S., Collier, P. and Horsnall, P. (1990), *Gender, Education and Employment in Côte d'Ivoire,*' Social Dimensions of Adjustment Working Paper, No. 8, Washington: World Bank.

Berg, E. (1982) 'The third woman', *Diacritics*, Vol. 12, No. 2.

Butler, J. (1990) *Gender Trouble: Feminism and the Subversion of Identity*, London: Routledge.

CIDA (1993) *Gender as a Cross-cutting Theme in Development Assistance: An Evaluation of CIDA's WID Policy and Activities, 1984–1992: Final Report,*' CIDA project no. 851/11109/S22564/139025/15/0103.

DAWN (1995) *Securing Our Gains and Moving Forward to the 21st Century: A Position Paper by DAWN for the Fourth World Conference on Women, Beijing, September 1995*, University of the West Indies, Barbados: DAWN.

Duley, M. I. and Edwards, M. I. (eds) (1986) *The Cross Cultural Study of Women: A Comprehensive Guide*, New York: Feminist Press.

Elson, D. (1995) 'Introduction,' in Çagatay, N. *et al.* (eds) (1995), *World Development*, Vol. 23, No. 11, Special Issue – 'Gender, Adjustment and Macroeconomics', Pergamon Press, November.

Goetz, A. M. (1991) 'Feminism and the claim to know: contradictions in feminist approaches to women in development', in R. Grant and K. Newland (eds) *Gender and International Relations*, Milton Keynes: Open University Press.

Goetz, A. M. (1994) 'From feminist knowledge to data for development: the bureaucratic management of information on women and development', *IDS Bulletin*, Vol. 25. No. 4, Brighton: Institute of Development Studies.

Goetz, A. M. (1995) *The Politics of Integrating Gender to State Development Processes: Trends, Opportunites and Constraints in Bangladesh, Chile, Jamaica, Mali, Morocco and Uganda*, UNRISD Occasional Paper for the Fourth World Conference on Women Beijing 1995, OP 2, Geneva: UNRISD/UNDP, May.

Haddad, L. (1991), 'Gender and adjustment: theory and evidence to date', Paper presented at the workshop on the Effects of Policies and Programmes on Women, January 16 1992, Washington, DC: International Food Policy Research Institute.

Interactive Information Services (1995) *Summary*, November 27, Internet.

Jackson, C. (1996) 'Rescuing gender from the poverty trap', *World Development*, Vol. 24, No. 3.

Jahan, R. (1995) *The Elusive Agenda: Mainstreaming Women in Development*, London: Zed Books.

Jaquette, J. and Staudt, K. (1988) 'Politics, population and gender: a feminist analysis of US population policy in the Third World', in K. Staudt, B. Jones and A. Jonasdottir (eds) *The Political Interests of Gender*, London: Sage.

Kabeer, N. (1994) *Reversed Realities: Gender Hierarchies in Development Thought*, London: Zed Press.

Kandiyoti, D. (1988) 'Bargaining with patriarchy', *Gender and Society*, Vol. 2, No. 3, pp.274–290.

Lockwood, M. (1992) *Engendering Adjustment or Adjusting Gender: Some New Approaches to Women and Development in Africa* (IDS Discussion Paper No. 315), Brighton: Institute of Development Studies.

Maguire, P. (1984) *Women in Development: An Alternative Analysis*, Amherst: Center for International Education, University of Massachusetts.

Makibaka (1995) *The Gender Trap: An Imperialist Scheme for Co-opting the World's Women: A Critique by the Revolutionary Women of the Philippines of the UN Draft Platform of Action, Beijing 1995*, Luzon, Philippines: Makibaka.

Mohanty, C.T. (1991) 'Under Western eyes: feminist scholarship and colonial discourses', in A. Mohanty, A. Russo and L. Torres (eds) *Third World Women and the Politics of Feminism*, Bloomingdale: Indiana University Press.

Nicholson, L. (1994) 'Interpreting *Gender*', *Signs*, Vol. 29, No. 1, pp.79–105.

Oldersma, J. and Davis, K. (1991) 'Introduction', in K. Davis, M. Leijenaar and J. Oldersma (eds) *The Gender of Power*, London: Sage.

O'Leary, D. (1995) 'Gender, the deconstruction of women', mimeo distributed at the NGO Forum of the Fourth World Conference on Women in China, September.

Palmer, I. (1991) *Gender and Population in the Adjustment of African Economies* (ILO Working Paper: Women, Work and Development, No. 19).

Persram, N. (1994) 'Politicising the *Feminine*, globalising the feminist', *Alternatives*, Vol. 19, pp.285–313.

Razavi, S. and Miller, C. (1995a) *From WID to GAD: Conceptual Shifts in the Women in Development Discourse* (UNRISD Occasional Paper for the Fourth World Conference on Women, Beijing 1995) OP 1, Geneva: UNRISD/UNDP, February.

Razavi, S. and Miller, C. (1995b) *Gender Mainstreaming: A Study of Efforts by the UNDP, The World Bank and the ILO to Institutionalise Gender Issues* (UNRISD Occasional Paper for the Fourth World Conference on Women, Beijing 1995) OP 1, Geneva: UNRISD/UNDP, August.

Scott, J. (1988) *Gender and the Politics of History*, New York: Columbia University Press.

Staudt, K. (1990) 'Gender politics in bureaucracy: theoretical issues in comparative perspective' in Staudt, K. (ed.) *Women, International Development and Politics: the Bureaucratic Mire*, Philadelphia: Temple University Press.

Sterling, A.F. (1993) 'The five sexes: why male and female are not enough', *The Sciences*, March/April.

Stewart, S. (1995) '"Breaking in: speaking out – making development organisations work for women", ODA funded workshop and research project on gender and development organisations, NGO Forum, Huairou, China, September 1995 (Draft report)', Brighton and Norwich: IDS/ODG.

Trinh, T. M.-H. (1987) 'Difference, identity, and racism', *Feminist Review*, Vol. 25, pp.5–22.

United Nations (1980) *Women 1980*, Conference Booklet for the World Conference of the United Nations Decade for Women, Copenhagen, 14–30 July, UN Division for Social and Economic Information.

United Nations (1995a) Draft Platform for Action, Fourth World Conference on Women, Beijing, China, 4–15 September, A/CONF.177/L.1, May 24, New York: United Nations.

United Nations (1995b) *The World's Women: Trends and Statistics*, New York: United Nations Statistical Office.

United Nations Development Programme (1995) *Human Development Report 1995*, New York: UNDP.

White, S. (1993) 'Gender and development: a review of key issues,' paper for JFS workshop, Edinburgh, July 5–7.

World Bank (1995) 'Toward gender equality: the role of public policy,' *Development in Practice*, Washington: World Bank.

Young, K., Wolkowitz, C. and McCullogh, R. (1981) *Of Marriage and the Market: Women's Subordination in International Perspective*, London: CSE Books.

2

RESCUING GENDER
FROM THE POVERTY TRAP

Cecile Jackson

Introduction

The New Poverty Agenda is seen as incorporating gender within a new broader concept of poverty (Lipton and Maxwell, 1992) capable of measuring, evaluating and redressing gender bias along with poverty reduction policies, based on labour intensive growth, targeted social services and safety nets. Multilateral positions on gender and development (GAD) for their part also stress the poverty of women as a primary justification for development interventions designed to improve the position of women. However, it is argued here that the concept of poverty cannot serve as a proxy for the subordination of women, that antipoverty policies cannot be expected to necessarily improve the position of women and that there is no substitute for a gender analysis, which transcends class divisions and material definitions of deprivation. The instrumental interest in women as the means to achieve development objectives such as poverty reduction may ultimately undermine GAD. Gender appears to have collapsed into a poverty trap; this essay raises a call for help, or at least a discussion about the relative benefits of captivity versus escape.

A retrospective on the past twenty years, since gender became a widespread development concern, would have to acknowledge that gender has been assimilated into development thinking in what appears to be a comprehensive way. Bilateral and multilateral development agencies have gender policies, priorities and strategies, gender units, gender specialists, gender reporting criteria and monitoring. If gender and development (GAD) has moved from the fringe to the mainstream of development, this should be cause for celebration rather than unease about what has been lost in translation. Gender has been assimilated into development thinking in a particular way (Jaquette, 1990), and the many strands of feminist thinking and varieties of gender analysis have not been equally absorbed by development agencies. Any evaluation of how far gender has become incorporated into development institutions needs to enquire not only about whether they have staff with gender responsibilities, how funds are allocated, whether policy documents exist; it also needs to examine the content of how development institutions understand gender issues. This chapter is about one characteristic of this assimilation process – the perception of gender issues in development as a variant of poverty problems. Twenty years ago Huntington

(1975) published a critique of Ester Boserup which expressed concern about the implications of abandoning the equality argument in favour of an efficiency justification, a concern which this chapter argues was well founded. The next section suggests some common and problematic themes in how most development agencies understand gender questions, the second section remarks on the main prescriptions of the New Poverty Agenda from a gender perspective as a prelude to the third section which discusses the problems with poverty concepts and measurement based upon 'outsider' definitions, and finally the last section extends the critique to subjective definitions of poverty.

Gender stances in multilaterals

Instrumentalism

Moser (1993: 66–9) describes what she calls an 'anti-poverty approach to women' as a strand in WID which sees women's poverty as the consequence of underdevelopment rather than of subordination, and she distinguishes this from the 'efficiency' approach to women, although it seems they have shared assumptions about the causes of, and remedies for, gender disadvantage. The poverty/efficiency approach has remained dominant in multilaterals for some years now, hence the World Bank WID Division focus on 'measures to include women in development that contribute to economic performance, poverty reduction, and other development objectives' (World Bank, 1989: iii) and statements such as '[i]nvesting in women can be a cost-effective route to economic efficiency' and '[e]xpanding women's choices in economic activity . . . can increase output and efficiency by enabling women to find their true comparative advantage, much as international trade can promote efficient specialisation and economic expansion among nations' (World Bank, 1989: iv–v). 'Investing in women is a major theme in the World Bank's two pronged strategy for poverty reduction' (World Bank, 1994: 8), i.e. to labour intensive growth and improved social services, and, furthermore, the Bank justifies concern with women's health on the grounds of the benefit to the family of healthy mothers and the cost effectiveness of women's health interventions.

An instrumental approach is evident in major development agencies like the World Bank where the justifications made for attention to gender are in terms of how this will facilitate other development objectives rather than being an end in itself. Gender issues have been taken on board insofar as they are consistent with other development concerns (including poverty) and insofar as women are seen to offer a means to these, other, ends. Gender concerns are, for the World Bank, justified with reference to economic growth and poverty reduction. Similarly, UNFPA justify gender in relation to population control and environmental agencies in terms of environmental management and conservation. Even women's 'empowerment' is instrumental – UNFPA expects empowered women to have smaller families. Thus women are now the means of controlling population, of achieving sustainable development, of poverty alleviation.

The concern with instrumentalism, however, could be said to be linked to a model of development policy, practice and outcomes which are linear, structuralist and oversimplified. There are at least two ways by which instrumentalist development policies and projects may be confounded. One is via unintended consequences which may not be related to any particular human agency, and the other is through the multitude of ways in which the instrument strikes back. Women as actors and agents have their own priorities and projects which they seek to further through participation in development activities or which emerge in the process of participation. Let us look at three examples. The British ODA funds a poverty-focused agricultural development project in the Chhotanagpur Plateau region of India, the Rainfed Farming Project, which has formed vegetable gardening groups of tribal and low caste women in Orissa. Over a few years they have spontaneously begun to collectively punish male domestic violence and act against alcohol abuse by destroying the equipment of village distillers. Thus an agricultural project distributing improved vegetable seeds to poor women has been enrolled by them in their project of collective action against domestic violence and alcohol related poverty and abuse. The project model of poverty as caused by the deficiencies of agricultural technology was subverted to add social welfare issues into the portfolio of activities undertaken by the groups.

A second example shows women using the vehicle of development interventions, in this case an income generating project, to capture state commitment and turn it to their own ends. A case study in northern Oman (Heath, 1995) demonstrates how, over a decade, rural Muslim women involved with a rather ineffective income generating weaving project, shaped and used the project to improve their gender relations within and beyond the household. These strategies were not based on improved financial independence through weaving but included the establishment of relations of patronage with the state, then used to deflect control by household men and to legitimise new freedoms in behaviour; the assertion by women of their creative identity as weavers, and their 'invention of tradition' (weaving was not a women's activity in the pre-project situation) around weaving and the representation of themselves as sustaining the cultural traditions of the nation; and the gendering of space in the weaving centres in ways which positively changed work legitimacy, veiling and seclusion practices.

A final example comes from the experiences of an NGO worker in rural Mexico observing the interface between a group of women beekeepers, with an initial self-image of themselves as rustic housewives (*mujeres pata rajada* i.e. women with cracked soles) pursuing beekeeping as a hobby, and government implementors of a WID initiative constituting them as entrepreneurs within a project (Villarreal, 1992). In this encounter the government agency sought to label the beekeeping women as needy victims, in line with government discourses on incorporation of peasant women into society whilst local male opinion denied any threat to the gender order by asserting the marginality of the women and the subordination of the beekeeping group to the *ejido*. Meanwhile, 'many of the women beekeepers learned the language of "subordination" in order to extract benefits from it, while

41

at the same time to some degree subverting this very ideology' (Villarreal, 1992: 260).

Studies such as these suggest the need for caution in linking policies and outcomes directly. The problem with the poverty trap is less the inevitable negative outcomes for women and more a 'political' one of the consequences for GAD of reliance on the poverty argument. The reasons for project 'misbehaviour' have been sought in the sociology of development organisations (Buvinic, 1986), institutional inertia, the gendered character of organisations and the marginal commitment to GAD by donors and governments (Staudt 1987; Goetz, 1992) but they also lie in the agency of women.

If women too are instrumental and the outcomes of actually existing development activities are a dynamic mixture of interlocking projects (Long and Long, 1992), then does instrumentalism as identified in feminist critiques matter? I think it does, because the 'projects' of actors do not interlock or overlap without struggle, negotiation and compromise, a process in which participants and officials are seldom equal. Where the policy and project objectives differ from those of participants, outcomes are likely to be closer to those of the more powerful bargaining partner, and the opportunities for subversion are uncertain. Goetz (1994: 24) shows why instrumentalism matters in the context of credit programmes (of the Grameen Bank and others) in Bangladesh which have been widely cited as examples of how to, synergistically, tackle gender and poverty issues simultaneously. In reporting evidence for the low level of loan control by women, she concludes that

> Donors' interests in seeing the development of financially self-sustaining rural development institutions has resulted in a preoccupation with cost recovery, to the degree that loan repayment rates have become the primary index of success, however much they obscure the important issue of the quality of loan use. . . . As poor women convincingly demonstrate a high repayment capacity, donors previously recalcitrant on the gender issue have pushed for the inclusion of women in credit programmes, not insensible to the obvious efficiency gains to be made.
>
> (Goetz, 1994: 30)

Thus although predominantly disbursed to women, loans arguably have limited benefits for women because the loans enter into gendered social relations in the household and women largely lose control of the loans. Goetz finds that a significant proportion of women's loans are directly invested by their male relatives, with 'women borrowers bearing the liability for repayment, though not necessarily directly benefiting from loan use' (1994: 1). Here an instrumental poverty programme offering capital to women has transformed many women into loan repayment officers, with uncertain long term consequences for gender relations. Money proves an inadequate currency for changing gender relations.

Synergism is a related feature of development discourses, i.e. the assertion of a positive, mutually beneficial, relationship between gender equity and other development objectives, and if instrumentalism casts women as the means to other ends, synergism implies that the means/ends distinction is irrelevant. However, this has not gone unquestioned. The antipathy of gender interests and population policy has been analysed by Hartmann (1987), for women's reproductive goals and interests do not necessarily conform with those of family planners. Furthermore, although it has been widely argued that the education of women is linked to declining fertility, and that thus the empowerment of women through education is consistent with population limitation policies, Patricia Jeffery (1994) argues that this link may speak less of empowerment and more of the impact of the nuclear family ideology embodied in the content of much educational material. The clash between women's interests and environmental conservation is another arena in which synergy is debated (Jackson, 1993; Green, 1994).

The entrapment of GAD by poverty reduction presents analogous problems, for the view that it is the concentration of women amongst the poor and vulnerable (the 'feminisation of poverty') which justifies gender and development activity has some policy implications. Does this mean that where poverty is not feminised then there is no justification for GAD? Are there no gender issues amongst those who are not the deserving poor? Must all GAD activity be focused on poor women? Will poverty alleviation improve the position of women? These are some of the questions which deserve wider debate. Part of the struggle against the increasingly instrumental approach to GAD in development agencies requires a demonstration of how gender analysis, interests and issues are distinct from, and sometimes contradictory to, poverty and class.

The arguments which show how women's subordination is not derived from poverty need to be excavated to demonstrate the (liberal) fallacy that poverty alleviation will lead to gender equity. Poverty and gender are not entirely separate social phenomena. Indeed, one of the main features of gender analysis is the insistence that gender identity patterns all social life and that therefore gender awareness is not about 'adding women' but about rethinking development concepts and practice as a whole, through a gender lens. This insight is one of many which appears to have been lost in translation. Thus, the unfortunate term 'the feminisation of poverty' has come to mean not (as gender analysis would suggest) that poverty is a gendered experience, but that the poor are mostly women.

The feminisation of poverty

The term 'feminisation of poverty' suggests that '[w]omen tend to be disproportionately represented among the poor ... the poorer the family the more likely it is to be headed by a woman' (World Bank, 1989: iv). Gender and development is frequently justified in terms of the poverty of female-headed households, for example the IFAD review on *The State of World Rural Poverty* in estimating the number of rural women below the poverty line in 114 countries makes the calculation on the basis of the number of households headed by women, added to the expected numbers of women in households classified as falling below the poverty line (Jazairy *et al.*, 1992: 274), i.e. it is assumed that all women-headed households are poor. This is not the case. Much depends upon the reason for female-headedness, those which are *de facto* household heads and receive remittances from migrant males may often be less poor than male-headed households (Kennedy and Peters 1992), whilst widows, divorced and separated women are indeed often amongst the poorest of rural people, with limited access to male income transfers and property rights. The study by Lloyd and Gage-Brandon (1993) of male- and female-headed households in Ghana is one example which shows that female-headedness is not associated with low incomes, whilst even for India where the heads of female-headed households are more uniformly elderly widows, the link with poverty is not generally strong (Agarwal, 1986: 187).

It is said that between 1965/70 and 1988 there was an increase of 47 per cent in women living below the poverty line compared to a 30 per cent increase for men (Jazairy *et al.*, 1992: 273). However, methodological queries cast doubt on these figures. As well as variability of poverty in female-headed households, the definition of female-headedness was debated, contested and redefined in the period in question. For the earlier dates (1965/70) women-headed households were generally defined in a *de jure* manner, whilst by 1988 gender scholarship in the 1970s and 1980s had been showing that numbers of women-headed households were underestimated because of the exclusion of *de facto* women-headed households. The changing definitions make comparisons over time invalid and what we now see is the belief that all female-headed households are poor combined with a now much more inclusive definition of female headship to suggest the feminisation of poverty. Combining *de facto* and *de jure* female-headed households created problems, one of which was the invalidity of time series comparisons such as those presented by IFAD, but also generated a category with little analytical use for poverty profiles as a result of high intra-group variation (Ahmad and Chalk, 1994: 185). Spurious averages, from populations including both these types of household, will be very misleading. Another methodological problem (Moore, 1994: 9) is that the use of percentage of income spent on food as an indicator of poverty may well also lead to an overestimation of the percentage of female-headed households among the poor since women-headed households seem to spend more on food even at higher income levels. It is arguable that the poverty of *de jure* women-headed households has been obscured by the inclination in GAD discourses to 'talk up' the numbers of women-headed households, and their poverty, to justify GAD in numerical terms.

One example of current poverty orthodoxy which displays some of the problems with assumptions about female-headed households is the World Bank country study on Uganda entitled *Growing out of Poverty* (1993a). This report insists that 'poorer households tend to be larger, have older and less educated household heads, and are more likely to be headed by a woman' (1993a: 5). This could be understood to mean that poorest households are more likely to be headed by a woman *than a man*, which is quite incorrect as Table 2.1 shows. The table reflects the very different meaning that poorest households are slightly more likely *than other households* to be headed by a woman.

Table 2.1 Selected characteristics of Ugandan households

Average	All Uganda	Non-poor	Poor	Poorest	Female-headed	Male-headed
Real per capita household						
expenditure	7,512	11,810	3,485	1,845	7,491	7,517
Household size	5.4	4.8	6.1	6.4	4.5	5.7
Dependency ratio (%)	44	38	51	52	45	44
Average age of household						
head	42	40	43	43	44	41
Female-headed households (%)	22	21	23	25	100	0
Household heads literate (%)	77	80	74	70	69	79
Percentage shares in total expenditure:						
Food	67	66	67	58	70	66
Drink and tobacco	5	6	5	3	2	6
Clothes	6	6	7	10	6	6
Rent	3	3	4	7	4	3
Fuel	2	2	2	3	2	2
Transport	0.3	0.4	0.2	0.2	0.1	0.3
Health	1	1	2	2	2	1
Education	1	1	1	2	1	1
Food expenditure, as share of total expenditure:						
Market purchases	26	30	23	19	29	26
Own production	40	36	44	39	41	40

Source: Adapted from World Bank (1993a), p.5.

Calculated from data for Household Budget Survey 1989/90 conducted by the Statistics Department of the Ministry of Finance and Economic Planning consisting of a stratified sample of 4,500 households across Uganda, except for eight districts in the North and East which were not sampled due to insecurity. Expenditures were calculated adding the value of purchased goods and the estimated value (at market prices) of the goods consumed out of own production.

The table also indicates other disjunctions between the classification by poverty and by gender of the household head; there are dramatic differences in per capita expenditure for categories of the poor, but virtually none for the gender of household head categories; the poor do indeed have larger households but the female-headed households are small and more similar to those of the non-poor; the dependency ratios across groups of the poor increases but that of households headed by women and men is remarkably similar. This table seems to suggest that female-headed households cannot all be assumed to be poor and that, whilst they are distinct from male-headed households in literacy, age (possibly, although no indication of significance is given) and some aspects of consumption these are not simply poverty differentials but speak of another axis of differentiation.

The meaning of female headship is highly contingent and cannot be used as a proxy for material deprivation (see Moore, 1994: 7–13, and Handa, 1994 for Jamaica). Apart from the important question of remittances and intra-household transfers which, as we discuss below, is a feature of women's incomes, the meaning of female headship is strongly related to age and life cycle as well as to cultural patterns such as the probability and acceptability of widow and divorcee remarriage and the levels of support from offspring and kin. Women-headed households are also seen as the victims of nucleation (Bruce, 1989) of extended families, divorce and fragmentation. The implication here is that women are better off in extended male-headed households. However, it is possible to see family fragmentation rather differently, since women-initiated divorce, for example, is often an indicator of relatively strong breakdown positions. Increasing divorce rates in Zimbabwe, the rise of informal unions and the phenomenon of single mothers are as much about the increasing viability of women as individuals as about their vulnerability and poverty (Jackson, 1994). Similarly the nucleation of households can be seen differently, as a process often stimulated by the increasing autonomy of younger women in extended households and their resistance to demands made on them by parents-in-law.[1] It often seems to be the case that women face a trade-off between material well-being, which may be greater in extended families, in conventional marriages, and under the wing of a male household head, and other aspects of well-being such as personal autonomy, independence and personhood.

The situation of female-headed households is extremely geographically variable and difficult to generalise about. There is little doubt that Indian widows, for example, are impoverished and vulnerable (Dreze, 1990) and insofar as they make up a major group of women-headed households in India there is possibly some validity in representing, and counting, such households as poor, but this is not a global truth. One implication of the focus on female-headed households is that it also rather implies that the feminisation of poverty only exists where there are many female-headed households, which is not everywhere. A table such as that in the IFAD study (Jazairy et al., 1992: 279) which states that the percentages of households headed by women in Asia and Sub-Saharan Africa are 9 per cent and 31 per cent respectively suggests, by the feminisation of poverty logic, that Africa has the greater problem, a view which I think would be hard to defend.

Finally, a poverty focus directs attention to female-headed households. But the emphasis on poor female-headed households avoids the more important, and more difficult area of intra-household poverty. The unitary conception of the household goes unchallenged: only the gender of its head has changed.

The combination of an instrumental interest in women as the means to the ends of poverty reduction, and the feminisation of poverty discourse has led to a damaging erosion of the differences between gender disadvantage and poverty. The next section briefly examines the prescriptions of the New Poverty Agenda to suggest that they are unlikely to be gender neutral in their effects and may indeed exacerbate gender differentials.

Poverty through a gender lens

The poverty consensus

The New Poverty Agenda of multilateral development agencies claims that the concept of poverty has 'been broadened, beyond the notions of inadequate private income or consumption, toward a more comprehensive perspective: absence of "a secure and sustainable livelihood" [which] allows us to measure and evaluate the *level* and *vulnerability* – and freedom from bias by gender and age – of individuals' access to privately and publicly provided goods and services and to common property' (Lipton and Maxwell, 1992: 10, original emphasis). This section queries whether the new poverty agenda can, or does in practice, deal with gender bias.

Labour intensive growth is the central prescription of the new consensus on poverty. Thus criticism is levelled by Lipton and Maxwell (1992) at the declining additional demand for labour in the HYVs (High Yielding Varieties) being developed currently (by comparison with the 1970s). For them, saving labour is unemploying labour. But is it reasonable to criticise labour saving technology in a static manner such as this? If labour saving technologies are more profitable and are therefore more widely adopted they may increase the absolute levels of employment. For example, in the Rainfed Farming Project (eastern India) described on p.41, the introduction of upland paddy varieties in villages of West Bengal, which tiller (send up multiple stalks) strongly and minimise weeding, has led to large areas of previously semi-cultivated upland being put under paddy. Here, labour saving paddy has been associated with increasing food production and rapidly rising upland land values (mostly owned by poor tribal and low caste farmers) as well as rising agricultural wage rates in the context of expanding labour markets. Labour conserving varieties are popular both with farming household women for reducing drudgery and with women wage workers for stimulating growth in labour markets.

It can also often be the case that increasing labour intensity in agriculture equals greater unpaid work for household women, and therefore a conflict of their interests with those of poor men and women in the labour force, who might gain from increased demand for wage labour. Much depends on the specific tasks in which labour is saved, the gender divisions of labour and the patterns of payment for tasks. Women are not a uniform group and the costs and benefits of labour saving technologies are class specific, but it is arguable that mechanisation has frequently been beneficial to women in relieving drudgery and that labour intensive agricultural growth is less clearly advantageous to rural women than to men.

The New Poverty Agenda also emphasises safety nets and targeted social welfare, although much of this discussion is about households rather than individuals. Targeting rather than universal benefits is seen as desirable because it allows resources to be concentrated on the needy (World Bank, 1993a, 1993b), but disadvantages include the high costs of administration for narrow targeting and most of the Bank's Program of Targeted Interventions have been broadly targeted

(1993b: 18). Means testing as a method of targeting is expensive, so the profiling of poverty aims to identify the characteristics of the poor to serve as a proxy (Ahmad and Chalk, 1994: 182), and this is the context in which the household categorisation by male/female headship has been used as a poverty marker.

Smart safety nets and self-targeted social welfare offer support at levels which are only attractive to the very poor, and the criteria for targeting is poverty, not gender. From a gender perspective one might wonder what poverty targeting will offer the high birth order girl child in a landed rural household in northern India, which may not be very poor but in which such a child may be very much at risk? Even where the targeted individual is a poor woman her gendered identity patterns the extent to which she may benefit from safety nets and social services. Besley and Kanbur (1993: 79) point out that a critical assumption in self-targeting such as workfare is that the opportunity cost of time is lower for target groups, an assumption which may not hold where the targeted individual bears household commitments such as child rearing that prevent them from giving up labour time in return for very low wages. A further objection is that where such work is highly energy intensive, as in construction projects, the health consequences for poorly nourished women may be serious. Kumar (1995) found that women's BMI (Body Mass Index) is negatively affected by participation in a food for work project in Ethiopia, unlike men's, and she suggests that this is because women are less able to substitute food for work labour for other household labour.

It is assumed that poor men and women will be able to respond similarly to safety net provision, but I argue below that the experience of poverty is profoundly different for men and women and that such an assumption may be misguided. Targets bear gender identities. Some people may slip through the safety net where gender norms, of propriety and self-respect for example, mediate responses to safety net provision. Thus in Bangladesh women have been unable to take up food for work opportunities because of disapproval by male kin, and after the Bangladesh floods in 1988 women were very reluctant to leave their rooftops for the relief camps where purdah was difficult to maintain: 'To be seen by strangers while washing, sleeping and especially eating (since a wife is defined as a provider, not a consumer, of food) caused them great shame' (Shaw, 1992: 212). Women refugees experience gendered problems of obtaining separate food rations if they are not attached to a male household and sexual harassment problems are widely documented for women in post-disaster situations. As Mary Douglas (1992) has pointed out, needs and wants are culturally defined and express gender ideologies, thus women consistently do not reliably identify, report and seek attention for their own ill-health. Self-targeting depends upon socially legitimised and individually recognised 'need' as the basis for participation. Where targeting refers to women, e.g. in education of girls, there is often an instrumental core (educated women have smaller families), and targeting of social services and safety nets relies on, in general, the identification of the especially poor. A central flaw with the poverty agenda is that it conceives of poor women as just like poor men, except poorer.

The emphasis in the New Poverty Agenda is now on 'secure and sustainable livelihoods' with less weight on income or consumption and more attention to the perceptions of poor people themselves. However, the livelihood concept, when stripped down for measurement, consists of familiar elements – poverty lines defining inadequate incomes, consumption, nutrition, health, life expectancy, assets – and thus the following discussion is structured around some of these poverty indicators. Poverty is defined in a number of different ways, e.g. the World Bank defines poverty as 'the inability to attain a minimal standard of living' (1990: 26), all of which, however, embody gender spin and distortion of various kinds, much of which relates to the use of the household as the unit of analysis. For example, the poverty reduction strategy of the World Bank is based upon the preparation of Poverty Assessments derived from poverty lines, poverty profiles and poverty indicators (Askwith, 1994). Poverty lines identify the proportion of the population with incomes below the level considered necessary to meet minimum nutrition and survival needs, and poverty indicators commonly include GDP per capita, mortality statistics, life expectancy and literacy statistics. The brief examination of poverty indicators below shows that poor women are disadvantaged by a different metric to poor men and that the populist alternative to poverty lines, the definition and assessment of poverty by the poor themselves, fails to transcend dominant gender ideologies which deny disadvantage.

Poverty observed

Food consumption

The poor are frequently defined as those who do not have enough to eat, and food bias against women is alleged. Are women especially poor because of food bias? The questions raised here are whether women are malnourished in relation to their specific needs and to men, and whether women are explicitly and consciously discriminated against in food consumption. Women are usually smaller than men, their physiology and metabolism differs from men's, their work differs and their nutritional needs are different (Harriss, 1990; Kynch, 1994). Studies of intra-household food allocation are beset with methodological problems but the view that adult women are discriminated against in access to food is now seriously questioned (for example see Gillespie and McNeill, 1992; Lipton and Payne, 1994; Svedberg, 1991). A review of nutrition studies in Sub-Saharan Africa found little evidence for food bias (Svedberg, 1991) and in south Asia the evidence for gender bias in anthropometric status of adults is contradictory and geographically limited (Harriss, 1990), whilst increases in mortality during famines affect men more than women (Dreze and Sen, 1989: 55), despite the ways families appear to prioritise male interests during crises, because women seem better able to survive famine conditions. Jocelyn Kynch's study of food and growth amongst the poor in Palanpur found that adult men were more wasted than adult women, and amongst adults the men who were thinnest in relation to their wives were concentrated in childbearing couples, they were 'provisioning men whose authority depends upon the ability to supply the household with food' (Kynch, 1994: 49). A gender analysis of the implications of male roles in Palanpur reveals the costs of the provisioning expectations of men in particular age groups. However, the picture for children was the reverse and girls were much more likely to be wasted and stunted than boys.

The terms 'food access' and 'food allocation' imply a rather mechanistic process whereby rights to food become actual consumption. But consumption is not simply determined by availability; there may be underconsumption without overt and explicit food discrimination, and adequate consumption despite it. Needs are culturally constructed and partly understood in relation to beliefs about work (its intensity and its perceived value) and well-being. In addition, where food is limited, the needs of other household members influence, to a variable degree, the level of consumption of any individual. For example, women within Asian households are socialised into an ideal of self-sacrifice, which begins with food denial, and in Bengal women fast for the welfare of their husbands whilst men do not reciprocate. As Harriss observes, 'male fasts [are] for individual spiritual purposes and female fasts [are] for the auspiciousness of the household collective (i.e. for husband, son or brother)' (1990: 359–60). Self-denial over food is not exclusive to women. Hampshire and Randall writing about Fulani pastoralists observe that 'the concept of Pulaaku – what it is to be a Fulani – involves eating to meet minimal requirements rather than to fill oneself up' (1994: 8), but it is certainly commonly bound up with altruism and prioritising the needs of others as a central element in many feminine identities. Thus food availability at the household level tells us little about the individual experience of food adequacy in either quantity or quality.

It seems paradoxical that at the same time as gender ideologies express gender bias in food access (e.g. in the commonly reported pattern of women eating last after the men and children) we find that in terms of outcomes, i.e. anthropometric measures of nutritional status and ability to survive famines, the evidence for discrimination against women is patchy and women not infrequently fare better than men. Is this partly a consequence of too ready an acceptance (see the World Bank Uganda study, 1993a: 10) by researchers of articulated nutritional norms as reflecting actual food access without any interrogation of how women's agency subverts norms, e.g. by snack food consumption, by eating during food preparation and by consumption of 'leftovers'? If poverty is understood as minimum access to food, and it emerges that women do not generally suffer food bias, then a logical conclusion is that women are not poor and do not suffer deprivation.

When the justification for gender policies in development rests on the poverty allegation, analyses such as these can seriously undermine the case, despite the fact that poverty here only refers to material deprivation. What can be lost from view is not only the food deprivation of some categories of women (in India, the very young and old, and those in the north) but also the myriad other forms of deprivation experienced by women. Kynch's (1994: 36–7) data on a northern Indian village studied in 1958, 1964, 1974 and 1984 found that for 0–5-year-olds the known deaths of male individuals surveyed fell from 22 per cent to 5 per cent whilst that of females remained at 17–19 per cent: i.e. overall mortality rates declined but the gap between male and female mortality widened.

How too does a Poverty Assessment account for the non-surviving girls and the costs of stunting? The situation of the girl child is particularly worrying for when son-preference damages the survival chances as substantially as occurs in northern India, mainly through unequal health care, what does it mean that surviving girls grow into adult women who do not suffer food bias?

Life expectancy

Life expectancy is another poverty indicator used as a summary measure of lifetime welfare to compare changing levels of well-being within and between countries. Yet in many developing countries women, despite being socially and economically disadvantaged, live longer than men and, notwithstanding high levels of maternal mortality, adult mortality of men outstrips that of women in all income groups (World Bank, 1990: 78). What gender differences in life expectancy tell us is not that most men are discriminated against, but that men and women experience different age-specific mortality risks related to both different physiologies and nutrition and to different divisions of labour, broadly defined. Whether these risks reflect gender inequity depends on how they are generated. For example, not all male mortality risks are the same and the health hazards faced by the wasted male providers in Kynch's study are very different from the health hazards of male overconsumption in the West. Gender analysis suggests that the quantity of life is not a good measure of well-being. As a recent review has pointed out, 'Because women live longer than men, the common belief is that they are healthier. In reality women are more likely to experience ill-health.' Much of this ill-health is women specific; for example 35 per cent of ill-health among women aged 15–44 years is accounted for by reproductive health problems, gender violence and rape (World Bank, 1994: 14). The evidence for gender violence against women spreads across all regions, classes, cultures and age groups and there are no grounds for believing that it is alleviated by increasing prosperity (Richters, 1994).

Assets

Poverty is also defined commonly in terms of household assets and resource access, land and livestock for example, but since patriliny is extremely common, women have widely different property relations to men. Thus, land ownership is seldom as defining of women's socio-economic position as it may be of men's. Patrilocal marriage also places a premium on mobile property for women, who may therefore have different strategies of asset accumulation to men; they may be excluded from land inheritance but accumulate gold. Possessions are often used to indicate poverty and prosperity as if they are gender neutral in their patterns of ownership, but most possessions indices are not relevant to assessing poverty of women, for they are based on typically male owned property. The problem goes beyond gender disaggregation of ownership of the same list of possessions, and requires a rethink of which indicators are used. It might be argued that men and women both benefit from 'household' assets, despite male ownership, and that therefore they are valid indicators of poverty. A woman married to a man with land, with a bicycle or with a radio is in some ways better off, but it is argued below that this may well not be the case.

Approaches to poverty which emphasise the transfer of assets to the poor (land reforms, social forestry, livestock) generally fail to recognise the differing relationship of women to property. Household ownership of land is not necessarily an unambiguous asset for household women. Settlement schemes in which women's labour becomes more deeply exploited abound: e.g. the Small Scale Commercial Farms and the Resettlement Areas of Zimbabwe where communal farmers and the landless have been given larger farms in which labour is scarce and women experience heavier workloads, and in which men recruit labour through extensive polygyny (Cheater, 1981; Jacobs, 1989). Furthermore, the disparity between the assets held by spouses may disadvantage women in bargaining by increasing the gap between the gains from cooperation (marriage) and the losses from breakdown. And of course, in the event of breakdown, few conjugal contracts uphold the rights of wives to a share of joint property (Goody, 1990). The endowing of men with land may adversely affect women's bargaining position within households. This is another poverty indicator which potentially distorts the understanding of gendered deprivation by use of a male yardstick.

Household income

Household income also tells us little about individual access to income and is therefore an unsatisfactory indicator of individual poverty (see Dwyer and Bruce, 1988); and 'there appears to be sufficient intra-household inequality to throw out standard estimates of overall inequality by an order of 30–40 per cent' (Kanbur and Haddad, 1994: 445). Household income is composed of a number of different streams; men and women cooperate in joint production and they engage in separate income earning activities, they consume jointly and as individuals. The variations in men's and women's incomes stem from a number of sources; women have generally poorer wages and lower levels of employment than men, they also have different kin and conjugal entitlements to transfers, different levels and forms of income access and control and different sets of expenditure obligations and responsibilities. The distinctive features of women's incomes affect, and limit, the degree to which household income can serve as an indicator of their well-being.

Despite the diversity and complexity of the work on incomes within households there is one point which has been made much of, and that is the evidence that women spend more of their money on children and household needs than men. This is becoming a much used argument justifying GAD on the grounds of child welfare. It may well be true that women prioritise children's needs, but there is a sense in which one might wish women to be a little less selfless and self-sacrificing. It is the sense that women have to be the 'deserving poor' to earn the attention of development agencies which disturbs. Some recent work (Hopkins *et al.*, 1994) has been investigating, and partly substantiating, the possibility that it is the particular characteristics of women's incomes (their seasonality and their regular nature) rather than women's altruism which explains gender differences in expenditure. One fears that if research shows that women's income expenditure is not as child welfare oriented as currently seems to be the case, the commitment to gender will wane. A real improvement in the position of women may indeed involve a shift to less altruism, yet paradoxically this could undermine the support of development agencies for GAD.

How does rising household income affect women within the household? Haddad and Kanbur's work (on a data set from the Philippines) on the intra-household Kuznets curve (1990) suggests that as household income rises, so too do levels of inequality (measured in this instance by calorie adequacy) amongst members, until relatively high incomes are reached. They conclude that 'it is not simply enough to increase the total resources of a household since, particularly for poor households, the accompanying increase in inequality may well undermine the beneficial effects on the poorest individuals of the total resource increase' (Haddad and Kanbur, 1990: 25).

There seems to be a considerable body of evidence for the argument that gender relations are more equitable in poor Indian households. Poor Indian women engage in labour markets more than wealthier women, they contribute more significantly to total household income, they have greater control over incomes and are less subject to restrictions on their physical mobility than the non-poor. Gender equity often appears to be inversely related to household income (Menscher, 1985; Agarwal, 1986), a situation with parallels in other Asian countries. Studies on women's experience of the green revolution have also shown a pattern of withdrawal of women's labour from farm work and increasing dependence of women on men as household incomes rise.

In reviewing village studies in India, Harriss (1992: 361–3) finds that the greatest excess mortality of girls occurs amongst poor landless groups in some studies, and amongst high caste landed groups in others. Some of the most severe discrimination against the girl child in India is found in high caste rural groups, characteristically also high income (Krishnaji, 1987; Jeffery *et al.*, 1989; Heyer, 1992). My research in Giridih district (1993–4) of rural south Bihar also found dramatic differences in the survival of girls among different caste/income groups: higher caste farmers had very few surviving daughters whilst the juvenile sex ratio in low caste and tribal households of the same village was much more balanced. This village is in a rainfed area where there has been no green revolution and where there is virtually no irrigated agriculture. A useful study over some years of fertility and mortality in a village of Uttar Pradesh found that in recent years the mortality of female children of the poor has now begun to rise dramatically, which has been related mainly to reduced employment for women as a result of crop changes (away from those demanding female labour) and mechanisation displacing women, and to rising dowry (Wadley, 1993). What seems to have happened is that as households have become more prosperous, in a context of green revolution generated growth, women have been withdrawn (or displaced) from wage work in order to conform with the strong purdah norms, and dowries have inflated to very high levels for the poor as well as the rich. Differential neglect and higher mortality of girls is thus related both directly and indirectly to the increasing dependence of women in upwardly mobile households where higher incomes bring with them deeper aversion to girl children.

This is not to suggest that women are better off poor, but that there can be something of a trade-off between women's material well-being and their autonomy, a situation which poor men do not seem to face. This is one way of looking at the limited degree to which poverty and gender development can be approached synergistically with the same policy instruments. If rising household income has a perverse effect on women's well-being then poverty reduction policies, even if successful, may well not increase women's well-being in the short run. There is great variation in the degree and manner by which women gain from raising male incomes and poverty reduction, but it seems clear that women within households may not necessarily benefit from higher male incomes; much depends on the transactions and transfers within the household.

The degree to which women benefit from higher personal incomes through, for example, income generating projects, also depends on intra-household transactions and the degree to which women can retain control of additional incomes. Conversely, project failure to reduce poverty through income generation does not signify an absence of change in gender relations. Heath (1995) shows how money earned in an income generating project may be largely irrelevant to changing gender relations, which derive as much from the non-financial leverage gained by women from project participation. Money is neither necessary nor sufficient for transforming gender relations.

Entitlements

Sen's idea of entitlements has been seen as an alternative approach to poverty lines, and these too vary for men and women in households. Naila Kabeer has pointed out, for Bangladesh, that the entitlements of women are 'embedded to a far greater degree than those of men within family and kinship structures. Even where women have independent entitlements, for instance through ownership of assets or sale of labour power, they may prefer to exercise them in ways which do not disrupt kinship-based entitlements, their primary source of survival and security' (1989: 9). Thus women (more than men) can be, and become, poor through both the condition and deterioration of household entitlements and the character and deterioration of the intra-household social relations upon which they depend. Kabeer calls for the use of more qualitative poverty indicators which recognise how, for example, marriage mediates the experience of poverty for women. Sen's capabilities framework (1987) offers a more flexible approach to well-being since capabilities may be formulated which reflect specifically gendered disadvantage, and include, for example, freedom from violence. However, this leaves the problem of the commensurability of men's and women's well-being and the invalidity of comparison.

The New Poverty Agenda claims to give more attention to the perceptions of poor people themselves, in line with participatory development approaches which acknowledge the rights, and value, of beneficiary involvement with development interventions. Do the perceptions and definitions of poverty elicited from the poor give more adequate representation to gender issues?

Poverty experienced

The turn to qualitative understandings of poverty has not generally been conducive to greater gender awareness and the approach which claims to be based on how the poor themselves define poverty (Chambers, 1988) is in ways even more gender blind than the head-count methods it criticises.[2] Here 'poor people' and 'the poor' are treated as an homogeneous group such that it is possible to speak of the 'knowledge of poor people' and the 'priorities' of poor people. Chambers calls for poor people themselves to be consulted about their own criteria for well-being and the use of Participatory Rural Appraisal (PRA) has been promoted as the relevant mechanism. PRA is no longer the preserve of small NGOs and is now used in poverty assessments by the World Bank (as 'Beneficiary Assessment') and by bilateral agencies (e.g. the Overseas Development Administration, 1995). Do the tools of PRA, such as wealth ranking, reveal critical gender variations in the experience of poverty?

Wealth ranking

Wealth ranking has a number of problematic features: it produces a single hierarchy yet there are multiple orderings reflecting the different dimensions of well-being, and it is static unlike poverty into which people move and escape, precipitated by particular events or simply as a consequence of domestic development cycles. There are at least two gender problems here. First, ranking of the household obscures the situation of women within it. Scoones (1995) has shown how in rural Zimbabwe men and women defined well-being differently and therefore classified people differently (women gave a greater weighting, than men or the research team, to cash incomes, remittances, women's incomes) and he acknowledges that 'Wealth ranking . . . associates wealth with a household, usually through the name of the oldest male resident. Yet "wealth" may be held and controlled by different individuals within the household' (Scoones, 1995: 85). A further objection arises around the gendered cultural internalisation of well-being expectations.

Gendered subjectivities

As Sen (1987) memorably reminds us, there are often large discrepancies between subjective perceptions of well-being and well-being as measured by 'objective' indicators such as some of those discussed. Chambers (1988: 23) illustrates this with reference to the studies of N.S. Jodha in Rajasthan which showed that the group of households who had experienced a fall in income (1964–84) also claimed to have experienced improvement in 37 of 38 aspects of well-being identified by themselves, over the same period. Clearly income is only one element of well-being, and it might be concluded that poverty lines underestimate well-being, but Sen insists that we do need objective measures of poverty as a counterpoint to perceptions which reflect the biases and prejudices inherent in all cultures. Populists such as Beck (1994) take issue with Sen's critique of 'mental-metricism', or subjective perceptions of poverty, on the grounds that it discredits the validity of what poor people say in general and he is at pains to defend the self-definitions of poverty by poor people and to assert solidarity and mutual support as features of poor communities. It is interesting that the example used by Sen to show the problem of mental-metricism is drawn from a 1944 study of the Bengal Famine of 1943 which reported that of widowers asked whether they were 'ill' or in 'indifferent' health 48.5 per cent of widowers said they were 'ill' and 45.6 per cent that they were in 'indifferent' health, whilst 2.5 per cent of widows asked the same question said they were 'ill' and none said they were in 'indifferent' health (Sen, 1987: 53). Beck's 'deconstruction' consists of the following: 'one wonders why a male academician should have chosen poor female famine sufferers as an example of "mental-metricism". Does this choice reveal "mental-metricism" on the part of Sen himself? . . . Could a comparative survey of the health of female and male academics who had just failed to get tenure, lost their house and car, and hadn't eaten for three days, be taken as an accurate reflection of their well-being or would we expect some "mental-metricism" to creep in?' (1994: 30).

Beck seems to have missed the point, the gender differences in perceptions of well-being, and instead has become angry about what he thinks is a slur against the truth of the perceptions of the disadvantaged, but perhaps what needs deconstructing is not Sen's 'mental-metricism' but Beck's populist outrage. In his study of villages in West Bengal, Beck does not confront the problem of his own representation of 'poor people's perceptions' despite the fact that his text repeatedly displays his own beliefs about the causes and nature of poverty (1994: 173–7). However, this apart, if we accepted Beck's version of poor peoples' views of poverty at face value what would it tell us about gender? Women appear as respondents, but they do not speak of gender, and nor do men. Thus, for example, Beck's discussion of violence is entirely in class terms (1994: 168) and says nothing about domestic violence, whilst Kabeer (1994: 149–50) cites a number of studies on the high levels of suicide, homicide, rape and prostitution amongst Bengali women, many of which implicated male kin, and domestic violence, which invariably did. This absence may therefore derive from the beliefs of the researchers, or may indeed be an absence in the views of 'the poor' because domestic violence is embodied in 'doxa' (Bourdieu, 1977) or because it is not spoken of for other reasons. In reviewing people's own concepts of poverty in India Barbara Harriss concludes '[t]hat people's own criteria [of poverty] do not include longer life, less disease, more freedom for women and makes one suspicious of what Sen (1985) calls "physical condition neglect" as well as outright gender bias in phenomenological enquiry' (1992: 372).[3] Anthropological work such as the Jefferys' extended work on childbearing in villages of Uttar Pradesh shows the (gendered) limits of subjective perceptions: '[G]irls' inferior chances of survival [are not] locally perceived. Yet they are manifest almost from birth in the maternity histories. For couples in Dharmnagri and Jhakri, however, it is primarily the unpredictability of sons' deaths that enters their calculations about family size' (Jeffery et al., 1989: 195).

Researchers blinded by populist sympathy for the poor easily overlook gender relations of inequality. There seems to be a strong connection between the view of mutual solidarity amongst the poor and the absence of gender analysis in work which claims to report the perceptions of the poor. According to Beck, 'poverty involves much more than lack of food, shelter and being subject to illness; it also involves the experience of being subordinated and oppressed, and resisting this where possible' (1994: 180). Being subordinated is not only related to poverty, it is also a consequence of being a woman, yet we are offered no discussion of resistance by poor women against poor men possibly because of the 'virtuous peasant' problem (Bernstein, 1990) characteristic of populism. Self-respect is a major feature in Beck's interviews and analysis yet he declines to comment on what this might mean for gender relations, specifically here the ways in which poor women observe purdah norms as an avenue to self-respect and the ways in which men's respect depends in large part upon the behaviour of their wives. There are many gains from moral conformity and observation of the 'patriarchal bargain' (Kandiyoti, 1988) but what are the intended and unintended consequences of such choices for women, in the short- and long-term, and therefore is it responsible to represent women's articulated perceptions as necessarily complete truths?

Cultural, including gender, ideologies pattern the entire business of communication upon which PRA depends. What women *can want*, what it is thinkable to desire, differs from what it is culturally thinkable for men to want; what women *can say*, what a muted 'vocabulary' allows, also differs and finally, what women *will say* in the context of a public PRA exercise bears a gender imprint. For women who are excluded from dominant worldviews and male vocabularies (Ardener, 1975) it is not wise to assume that they can, or will, simply express their priorities as PRA assumes. This is not to suggest that women are social automatons: clearly they actively subvert language and subordination, but only to point out that what all of us say is context dependent, contingent and to varying degrees constrained by identities. Some of the gendered politics of communication affecting PRA in my experience includes the construction of local knowledge in exogamous and patrilocal communities as the preserve of 'insiders' whilst women often appear as outsiders, and in local terminology even as 'strangers' despite their length of marital residence. Women can also be especially sensitive to allegations of gossip, yet PRA invites and requires opinions and information to be expressed publicly about others.

Although a more theorised perspective is developing in PRA and related methods (e.g. Cornwall *et al.*, 1993) there remains a curious paradox in the recognition that communications between researchers and researched are interactive, profoundly shaped by context, intra-community struggles, and the politics of (multiple) identities, and the simultaneous insistence that PRA tools are any better able than other methods to deal with these issues. David Mosse, writing from experience of using PRA on a British ODA agricultural development project in western India, states that 'PRA, far from providing a neutral vehicle for local knowledge, actually creates a context in which the selective presentation of opinion is likely to be exaggerated, and where minority or deviant views are likely to be suppressed' (1993: 11) and in this way the public PRA exercise can offer an avenue for the generalisation of personal, and gender specific, interests.

Whose perceptions and representations?

How does one evaluate the claims of Participatory Rural Appraisal (Mascarenhas *et al.*, 1991; Chambers, 1992) to give voice to the perceptions of local people by approaches which explicitly involve respondents as partners in research and which validate these perceptions and knowledges? Many of these approaches are based on group work, e.g. participatory mapping and modelling, diagramming, wealth ranking, transect walks and matrix ranking, and it is suggested that women are involved in either mixed or single sex groups depending on the context. At a practical level a number of objections can be raised about many of these techniques which claim to be open to all but for which, as always, participation makes certain demands. One is time to participate in lengthy exercises such as modelling, another is the mobility needed to participate in, for example, transect walks, when women are constrained by child care.

Assuming the researcher to be aware of a diversity of opinion within any community, the question of whose voice is represented arises. For example, Cornwall *et al.* recognise that the 'local community' consists of many different people with different power positions, different priorities and perceptions and they raise the question of which of these competing viewpoints are then privileged. For them, 'If truths are relative, choosing a version becomes more a matter of appropriateness or applicability' (1993: 28). Given that the choice of which truth to represent lies with the PRA researchers, who after all are in control of the external representation process, then how can it be claimed that PRA voices local perceptions?

PRA as practised assumes local knowledge to be complete and impartial, yet it seems to be neither. The reliance on PRA and the popularity of the approach in which the poor define their condition can conceal some major issues of inequality. In this regard there is something to be said for the older approaches to research, both long-term research and the much despised survey. Indeed, it was analysis of the Indian census which revealed the sex ratio problem in India (Miller, 1981).

Gender interests cannot be entirely equated with the articulated views of women. Women can be implicated in female foeticide and infanticide, in food and health biases within households, in exploitative relations with other women (e.g. as mothers-in-law) and in dowry deaths (Jeffery *et al.*, 1989: 30–1). Sen is justified in his concern about 'mental-metricism', not because it devalues the perceptions of the poor but because it insists that there is a role for other forms of knowledge than the self-perceptions of the poor.

One problem with measuring men and women by the same poverty yardstick, be it food, income, entitlements, or local perceptions of deprivation, is that it both exaggerates women's poverty in some directions and conceals it in others, for the causes and experience of poverty differ by gender. Another is that the poverty argument is precarious, being exposed to deconstruction and dissolution in its own terms, i.e. of both measured material deprivation as well as perceptions and representations of deprivation, and uncertain to deliver clear gains to women given the instrumentalism inherent in much of the commitment to GAD in development agencies.

Conclusions

This chapter has tried to make the case that gender justice is not a poverty issue and cannot be approached with poverty reduction policies, and that it is important to assert the distinction between gender and poverty in the face of the tendency in development organisations to collapse all forms of disadvantage into poverty. The influences which have resulted in gender issues being so closely identified with poverty are many. WID narratives were, in the 1970s, often constructed around women as victims of development, a trend which was sustained, despite protests from Southern feminists, in much of the critique of structural adjustment. Gender discourses also had to survive within development bureaucracies, which were themselves dominated by men, where it was easier to ring-fence gender issues as a problem of poverty, and to argue for the feminisation of poverty, than to admit a corrosive feminist view of gender disadvantage as crossing boundaries of class and ethnicity, denying the 'otherness' of the poor and directing attention to the gendered character of development agencies themselves.

The debates about targeting versus mainstreaming also possibly reflect these struggles. Special projects for women were the object of extensive GAD critique, on mostly legitimate grounds (e.g. McCarthy, 1984 on Bangladesh) and the anti-targeting stance was avidly taken up by development agencies. Thus the World

Bank WID Division states that '[w]omen are viewed too often as "targets" or "beneficiaries", and too rarely as effective "agents" or contributors' (1989: v) and advises that '[i]n general, do not design "women only" programs' (1989: vi).[4] However, one consequence of mainstreaming gender into 'every page of every project document' (as suggested by Chris Patten, the Minister for Overseas Development in Britain in the 1980s) may have been to depoliticise gender analysis and to expose it to the prevailing gender ideologies of project management, of which the most one could expect was the view of women as a resource in meeting other development goals, a position not always consistent with gender interests. It is arguable that mainstreaming has become assimilation in that the possibilities of developing distinct and autonomous GAD discourses have been limited by the absence of women-only activities and institutional bases, and the reduction of gender perspectives to conform with dominant views of deprivation as caused by poverty.

Rescuing gender from the poverty trap means we need poverty independent gender analyses and policies which recognise that poverty policies are not necessarily appropriate to tackling gender issues because the subordination of women is not caused by poverty. Even if smart safety nets are successfully provided for the materially deprived, non-poor women are of interest to GAD for a number of reasons. Women who are not poor, of course, experience subordination of different kinds: domestic violence, personal insecurity, limited opportunities, oppressive gender ideologies, and mortality risks which make them an important category in their own right. But in addition, the position of non-poor women is also relevant to poor women in both positive and negative ways. By changing societal perceptions of women's roles, identities and options the achievements of non-poor women can positively influence gender bargaining, ideologies and opportunities for poor women. Non-poor women also have negative influences on poor women, for example sanskritisation and the dowry problem in India, and it could be argued that tackling dowry practices among middle income groups may be the most important social issue to address in India today. A poverty focus misses the range of interconnected gender issues across classes and socio-economic strata and obscures both the problems of gender bias by women towards other women as well as the possibilities for solidarity across social boundaries.

Acknowledgements

I would like to thank Ruth Pearson for my title and shared ideas, and Anne Marie Goetz, Richard Palmer-Jones and Christine Okali for useful comments and support.

Notes

1 The conditions under which fragmentation occur are clearly significant: for example, the breakup of households under conditions of persistent and acute scarcity are discussed in Harriss, 1992.
2 The well-known critique of gender bias in census data needs no repetition.

3 'Sen (1985)' is the Sen 1987 in the reference list.
4 It is, incidentally, interesting that the term 'agent' is used here to refer to women as positive channels for development rather than to the capabilities of women for action which is not necessarily conducive to development as specified by development agents. Women's agency is, for many gender analysts, about their capacity for disruption, subversion and challenge to structural constraints.

References

Agarwal, B. (1986) 'Women, poverty and agricultural growth in India', *Journal of Peasant Studies*, Vol. 13, No. 4, pp.165–220.

Ahmad, E. and Chalk, N. (1994) 'On improving public policies for the poor: major informational requirements' in van der Hoeven, R. and Anker, R. (eds) *Poverty Monitoring: An International Concern* (London: Unicef, Macmillan), pp.173–90.

Ardener, E. (1975) 'Belief and the problem of women' in Ardener, S. (ed.) *Perceiving Women* (London: Malaby Press), pp.1–15.

Askwith, M. (1994) *Poverty Reduction and Sustainable Development: Semantics or Substance.* Discussion Paper 345 (Brighton, Sussex: Institute of Development Studies).

Beck, T. (1994) *The Experience of Poverty: Fighting for Respect and Resources in Village India* (London: Intermediate Technology Publications).

Bernstein, H. (1990) 'Taking the part of peasants?' in Bernstein, H., Crow, B., MacKintosh, M., and Martin, C. (eds) *The Food Question: Profits Versus People?* (London: Earthscan Publications).

Besley, T. and Kanbur, R. (1993) 'The principles of targeting' in Lipton, M. and van der Gaag, J. (eds) *Including the Poor.* Proceedings of a Symposium organised by the World Bank and the International Food Policy Institute (Washington, DC: IBRD), pp.67–83

Bourdieu, P. (1977) *Outline of a Theory of Practice* (Cambridge: Cambridge University Press).

Bruce, J. (1989) 'Homes divided', *World Development*, Vol. 17, No. 7, pp.979–91.

Buvinic, M. (1986) 'Projects for women in the Third World: explaining their misbehavior', *World Development*, Vol.14, No. 5, pp.653–64.

Chambers, R. (1988) *Poverty in India: Concepts, Research and Reality.* Discussion Paper 241 (Brighton, Sussex: Institute of Development Studies).

Chambers, R. (1992) *Rural Appraisal: Rapid, Relaxed and Participatory.* Discussion Paper 311 (Brighton, Sussex: Institute of Development Studies).

Cheater, A. (1981) 'Women and their participation in commercial agricultural production: the case of medium-scale freehold in Zimbabwe', *Development and Change*, Vol. 12, pp.349–77.

Cornwall, A., Guijit, I. and Welbourn, A. (1993) *Acknowledging Process: Challenges for Agricultural Research and Extension Methodology.* Discussion Paper 333 (Brighton, Sussex: Institute of Development Studies).

Douglas, M. (1992) *Risk and Blame: Essays in Cultural Theory* (London and New York: Routledge).

Dreze, J. (1990) *Widows in Rural India.* Development Economics and Public Research Programme, No. 26 (London School of Economics, Suntory-Toyota International Centre for Economics and Related Disciplines).

Dreze, J. and Sen, A. (1989) *Hunger and Public Action* (Oxford: Clarendon Press).

Dwyer, D. and Bruce, J. (eds) (1988) *A Home Divided: Women and Income in the Third World* (Stanford: Stanford University Press).

61

Gillespie, S. and McNeill, G. (1992) *Food, Health and Survival in India and Developing Countries* (Delhi: Oxford University Press).

Goetz, A. M. (1992) 'Gender and administration', *IDS Bulletin*, Vol. 23, No. 4, pp.6–17.

Goetz, A. M. (1994) 'From feminist knowledge to data for development: the bureaucratic management of information on women and development', *IDS Bulletin*, Vol. 25, No. 2, pp.27–36.

Goody, J. (1990) *The Oriental, the Ancient and the Primitive: Systems of Marriage and the Family in the Pre-industrial Societies of Eurasia* (Cambridge: Cambridge University Press).

Green, C. (1994) *Does 'Synergism' Work for Women?* Poverty, Population and Environment IDS Discussion Paper 343 (University of Sussex, Brighton: Institute of Development Studies).

Haddad, L. and Kanbur, R. (1990) *Is There an Intra-Household Kuznets Curve? Some Evidence from the Philippines.* Development Economics Research Centre, Discussion Paper 101 (University of Warwick).

Hampshire, K. and Randall, S. (1994) 'Migration and household structure: flexibility as a survival strategy for Sahelian agropastoralists'. Conference paper, Population and Environment Research Programme (University of Bradford, Development Project Planning Centre, 14–16 December).

Handa, S. (1994) 'Gender, headship and intra-household resource allocation', *World Development*, Vol. 22, No. 10, pp.1535–47.

Harriss, B. (1990) 'The intrafamily distribution of hunger in south Asia', in Dreze, J. and Sen, A. (eds) *The Political Economy of Hunger. Volume 1: Entitlement and Well-being* (Oxford: Clarendon Press), pp.351–424.

Harriss, B. (1992) 'Rural poverty in India: micro level evidence', in Harriss, B., Guhan, S. and Cassen, R., *Poverty in India. Research and Policy* (Bombay: Oxford University Press), pp.333–89.

Hartmann, B. (1987) *Reproductive Rights and Wrongs. The Global Politics of Population Control and Reproductive Choice* (New York: Harper and Row).

Heath, C. (1995) 'Hidden currencies: women, weaving and income generation in Oman'. PhD dissertation submitted to School of Development Studies, University of East Anglia, Norwich, UK.

Heyer, J. (1992) 'The role of dowries and daughters' marriages in the accumulation and distribution of capital in a south Indian community', *Journal of International Development*, Vol. 4, No. 4, pp.419–36.

Hopkins, J., Levin, C. and Haddad, L. (1994) 'Women's income and household expenditure patterns: gender or flow?' *American Journal of Agricultural Economics*, Vol. 76, pp.1219–25.

Huntington, S. (1975) 'Issues in women's role in economic development: critique and alternatives', *Journal of Marriage and the Family*, Vol. 37, No. 4, pp.1001–12.

Jackson, C. (1993) 'Questioning synergism: win-win with women in population and environment policies?' *Journal of International Development*, Vol. 5, No. 6, pp.651–68

Jackson, C. (1994) 'Changing conjugal contracts in rural Zimbabwean households'. Conference paper to the African Studies Association, UK Conference, Lancaster University, 5–7 September.

Jacobs, S. (1989) 'Zimbabwe: state, class, and gendered models of land resettlement', in Parpart, J. and Staudt, K. (eds) *Women and the State in Africa* (London and Boulder, Colorado: Lynne Rienner Publishers), pp.161-84.

Jaquette, J. (1990) 'Gender and justice in economic development', in Tinker, I. (ed.)

Persistent Inequalities: Women and World Development (Oxford: Oxford University Press), pp.54–69.

Jazairy, I., Alamgir, M. and Panuccio, T. (1992) *The State of World Rural Poverty: An Inquiry into its Causes and Consequences* (London: Intermediate Technology Publications).

Jeffery, P (1994) 'Education and population policy: the implications for women of the supposed relationship between girls' schooling and women's autonomy'. Paper presented at the Conference on Gender Research and Development: Looking Forward to Beijing, School of Development Studies, University of East Anglia, 9–10 September.

Jeffery, P., Jeffrey, R. and Lyon, A. (1989) *Labour Pains and Labour Power: Women and Childbearing in India* (London and New Jersey: Zed Books).

Kabeer, N. (1989) *Monitoring Poverty as if Gender Mattered: A Methodology for Rural Bangladesh.* Discussion Paper 255 (Brighton, Sussex: Institute of Development Studies).

Kabeer, N. (1994) *Reversed Realities: Gender Hierarchies in Development Thought* (London, New York: Verso).

Kanbur, R. and Haddad, L. (1994) 'Are better off households more unequal or less unequal?' *Oxford Economic Papers*, Vol. 46, pp.445–58.

Kandiyoti, D. (1988) 'Bargaining with patriarchy', *Gender and Society*, Vol. 2, No. 3, pp.274–90.

Kennedy, E. and Peters, P. (1992) 'Household food security and child nutrition: the interaction of income and gender of household head', *World Development*, Vol. 20, No. 8, pp.1077–85.

Krishnaji, N. (1987) 'Poverty and sex ratios', *Economic and Political Weekly*, Vol. 22, pp.892–97.

Kumar, S. (1995) 'Intra-household gender aspects of food and agricultural research' personal e-mail communication (7 July).

Kynch, J. (1994) *Food and Human Growth in Palanpur.* The Development Economics Research Programme No. 57 (London School of Economics, Suntory-Toyota International Centre for Economics and Related Disciplines).

Lipton, M. and Maxwell, S. (1992) *The New Poverty Agenda: an Overview.* Discussion Paper 306, (Brighton, Sussex: Institute of Development Studies).

Lipton, M. and Payne P. (1994) *How Third World Households Adapt to Dietary Energy Stress: The Evidence and the Issues* (Washington: International Food Policy Research Institute).

Lloyd, C. and Gage-Brandon, A. (1993) 'Women's role in maintaining households: family welfare and sexual inequality in Ghana', *Population Studies*, Vol. 47, pp.115–31.

Long, N. and Long, A. (eds) (1992) *Battlefields of Knowledge: Theory and Practice in Social Research and Development* (London: Routledge).

Mascarenhas, J., Shah, P., Joseph, S., Jayakaran, R., Devavaram, J., Ramachandran, V., Fernandez, A., Chambers, R. and Pretty, J. (1991) 'Participatory rural appraisal'. Proceedings of the February 1991 Bangalore PRA trainers workshop. RRA Notes No. 13 (London and Bangalore: International Institute for Environment and Development and MYRADA).

McCarthy, F. (1984) 'The target group: women in Bangladesh', in Clay, E. and Schaffer, B. (eds) *Room for Manoeuvre: An Exploration of Public Policy in Agriculture and Rural Development* (Cranbury, New Jersey: Associated University Presses), pp.49–58.

Menscher, J. P. (1985) 'Landless women agricultural laborers in India: some observations from Tamil Nadu, Kerala and West Bengal', in International Rice Research Institute (eds) *Women in Rice Farming* (Manilla), pp.351–71.

Miller, B. (1981) *The Endangered Sex: The Neglect of Female Children in Rural North India* (Ithaca: Cornell University Press).

Moore, H. (1994) *Is There a Crisis in the Family?* Occasional Paper No.3 (World Summit for Social Development, Geneva: United Nations Research Institute for Social Development).

Moser, C. O. N. (1993) *Gender Planning and Development: Theory, Practice and Training* (London: Routledge).

Mosse, D. (1993) *Authority, Gender and Knowledge: Theoretical Reflections on the Practice of Participatory Rural Appraisal.* ODI, Agricultural Administration (Research and Extension) Network Paper 44 (London: Overseas Development Institute).

Overseas Development Administration (1995) *A Guide to Social Analysis for Projects in Developing Countries* (London: HMSO).

Palmer-Jones, R. and Jackson, C. (1997) 'Work intensity, gender and sustainable development', *Food Policy*, Vol. 22, No. 1, pp.39–62.

Richters, A., (1994) *Women, Culture and Violence. A Development, Health and Human Rights Issue*, Women and Autonomy Series (Leiden: Leiden University, Women and Autonomy Centre).

Scoones, I. (1995) 'Investigating difference: applications of wealth ranking and household survey approaches among farming households in southern Zimbabwe', *Development and Change*, Vol. 26, No. 1, pp.67–88.

Sen, A. (1987) *Commodities and Capabilities* (Delhi: Oxford University Press).

Shaw, R. (1992) 'Nature, culture and disaster: floods and gender in Bangladesh', in Croll, E. and Parkin, D. (eds) *Bush Base: Forest Farm* (London and New York: Routledge).

Staudt, K. (1987) 'Women's programs, bureaucratic resistance and feminist organisations', in Boneparth, E. and Stoper, E. (eds) *Women, Power and Policy* (New York: Pergamon Press).

Svedberg, P. (1991) 'Undernutrition in Sub-Saharan Africa: is there a gender bias?', *Journal of Development Studies*, Vol. 26, No. 3, pp.469–86.

Villarreal, M. (1992) 'The poverty of practice: power, gender and intervention from an actor-oriented perspective', in Long, N. and Long, A. (eds) *Battlefields of Knowledge. The Interlocking of Theory and Practice in Social Research and Development* (London and New York: Routledge).

Wadley, S. (1993) 'Family composition strategies in rural north India', *Social Science and Medicine*, Vol. 37, No. 11, pp.1367–76.

World Bank (1989) *Women in Development: Issues for Economic and Sector Analysis.* WID Division Working Paper 269 (Washington, DC: World Bank).

World Bank (1990) *World Development Report 1990. Poverty: World Development Indicators* (Oxford and New York: Oxford University Press).

World Bank (1993a) *Uganda: Growing out of Poverty* (Washington, DC: World Bank).

World Bank (1993b) *Implementing the World Bank's Strategy to Reduce Poverty. Progress and Challenges* (Washington, DC: World Bank).

World Bank (1993c) *Poverty Reduction Handbook* (Washington, DC: World Bank).

World Bank (1994) *A New Agenda for Women's Health and Nutrition* (Washington, DC: World Bank).

3

ANALYSING WOMEN'S MOVEMENTS

Maxine Molyneux

Despite the appearance of an extensive literature on women's movements and the steady growth since the mid-1970s in works which offer a critical, feminist engagement with political theory,[1] discussion of the broader implications of women's politics remains a relatively unexamined aspect of the development literature. There have been some recent attempts to redress this absence,[2] yet it is as if the debate within feminist political theory and the field of development studies have pursued parallel paths with little real engagement with each other. This is all the more remarkable given the impact of women's movements on policy-making and politics in the developing world.

Meanwhile, the analysis of women's movements, both historically and cross-culturally, has demonstrated the range and diversity of the forms of solidarity women have engaged in, and has alerted us to the factors both structural and symbolic which are significant in particular cases.[3] Yet it could be said, without too much fear of exaggeration, that the attention devoted to women's movements has had two negative consequences. In the first place, it has tended to marginalise discussion and analysis of other political phenomena which are of at least as much significance both for what they have contributed to our thinking about institutional arenas for advancing women's interests, and for what they have achieved in practice.[4] Second, some of the dominant assumptions about women's movements found in the development literature remain quite problematic. In what follows I shall offer some thoughts on the ways in which contemporary debates about women's movements might be moved on to address the new context which gender politics confronts in the developing countries.

Women's movements and female collective action

The interest in women's movements has a long history. Its more recent origins go back more than twenty years, to the work of feminist historians such as Sheila Rowbotham, Louise Tilly and Olwen Hufton,[5] whose aim was to recover a 'hidden history' of female activism. This early work was not only concerned to establish that women were participants and not bystanders in the events of history, but it also suggested that women's political involvement was of a distinctive character and significance. As political actors women were seen to impart to their struggles, practices, strategies and goals certain gender-specific qualities. In subsequent and continuing debates these were variously explained as expressive of some essential feminine attribute or derivative of the specific social positioning of women as carers and as those responsible in the domestic sphere for the work of social reproduction.

This literature has been particularly concerned with two types of women's movement. On the one hand, there was an interest, coincident with the appearance since the 1970s of a reinvigorated and international feminist movement, in tracing the history of feminism and the work of feminist groups and organisations in various parts of the world. On the other hand, there was a parallel concern with the struggles of poor women over consumption needs, and their protests against social injustice. During the 1970s and 1980s these struggles gained a particular momentum in Latin America, India and some African and East Asian countries as the combined effects of political repression and economic recession took their toll.[6] In the 1980s during the period of economic recession, serious crisis and stabilisation policies, women's movements became an object of policy concern, as their potential as vehicles for the delivery of goods and services to those in need was realised. A third, more recent cluster of studies on women's movements has focused on the mobilisations of women within 'fundamentalist' movements, beginning with the analysis of the Iranian revolution.[7] These studies opened up a range of questions about female mobilisation which had remained on the margin of the earlier discussions and outside the scope of most of the comparative literature on women's movements.

While much of the work on women's movements in the development literature has been largely descriptive in character, there has also emerged a current of ongoing theoretical work. This has been concerned with three types of issue: first it has begun to examine the factors – historical, social and institutional – which condition both the emergence of female activism, and the specific, gendered forms of collective identity. A second form of enquiry, found more commonly in the planning and development literature, has engaged with questions of categorisation, in order to find adequate criteria for differentiating between the various types of women's movement that have come into existence. A third and more recent theme has been that of examining the relationship between women's movements and democracy, an issue which has become pre-eminent in the developing countries in the aftermath of authoritarian rule. We will review these three sets of issues in summary fashion below.

Why women's movements appear when they do

The comparative analysis of women's movements shows considerable variations between regions in their timing, character, influence and effectiveness. This suggests that the appearance of women's movements and of different forms of resistance and organisation have been contingent on five main factors: prevailing cultural configurations, family forms, political formations, the forms and degree of female solidarity, and more generally on the character of civil society in the regional and national context. One implication of this historical and comparative work is that women's movements are essentially modern phenomena. Although there have been forms of female collective action in pre-modern societies, these have tended to be either small-scale, or spasmodic eruptions of social protest. The mass, relatively sustained entry of women into the field of politics, the emergence of women's movements and of particularistic conceptions of women's interests and citizenship rights are developments which were associated both with the spread of Enlightenment ideas and institutions, and with the multiple processes of social and economic modernisation and the forms of political activity these entailed. Among the many effects of these processes can be instanced a redefinition both of the meaning of the public and of the private spheres and of women's lived relationship to each.

While women's movements in this sense first emerged in the political and social conditions of eighteenth-century Europe, it was in the nineteenth and early twentieth centuries that women in many other regions of the world began to organise against inequalities based on sex and to demand legal reforms aimed at removing patriarchal rights within the family and in society at large (Jayawardena, 1986). Modernising nationalisms and socialist thought played their part in these early claims on the polity, and self-proclaimed feminist movements sometimes achieved substantial legislative reforms. In other contexts, women's rights were handed down from above by liberal constitutionalists, by socialist states, or by populist regimes anxious to broaden their political base. They have sometimes resulted from the influence of colonial powers on subject states, and from dominant powers over defeated states. Finally, they have also been adopted as a result of more than half a century of UN advocacy in the international arena.

If women's movements have a historical association with the multiple processes of modernity both in its capitalist and socialist variants, they have not always expressed demands for full citizenship and equal rights. Some women's movements arose in opposition to what they saw as the corrosive trends of modernity and sought to defend women's emplacement within 'traditional society'. More recently the emergence of militant currents of religious 'fundamentalism' has seen the appearance of sizeable women's movements which seek to redefine women's rights in ways that challenge Enlightenment notions of equality and universal rights of citizenship.

Whatever form female mobilisation has taken, the twentieth century has been marked by the growing absorption of women by the public realm, not only education and employment, but also the particularly resilient realm of politics.[8] We see a steady progression in women's political involvement in the diverse range of political experiences from revolutionary upheavals, Fascist and populist regimes, Islamist movements, and in social movements more generally, while the number of women involved in liberal (and other) political processes as voters, candidates for election, members of parties and governments has continued to rise.[9] Yet women's entry into positions of power within formal, institutional politics every-where has been fraught with difficulty, and this is despite women's extensive incorporation into the public sphere as the century has progressed. While there have been some notable exceptions, the upper echelons of political power have remained a remarkably resilient bastion of male dominion if not exclusivity. This is true even in countries where other formal or structural constraints limiting women's access to the public realm have been considerably weakened, and where explicit formal structures and legislation have been put in place to support women's participation.

What are women's movements?

These are some of the background issues of history and politics which have helped to contextualise the extent and character of female mobilisation in given countries or regions. We turn now to look at the second set of analytic issues identified in the literature on women's movements, that of what factors are salient in differentiating between them. There have been numerous attempts at typologising women's move-ments and organisations (or practices within them), some of these within the development literature itself.[10] Needless to say, many of the underlying issues remain, and will remain, unresolved, given the differences in theoretical approach.

To start with, there are contrasting views as to what a women's movement is. On the one hand, there are clearly identifiable women's movements that, like those which mobilised to demand female suffrage, have a leadership, a membership, a broader following and a political programme. On the other hand, there are more diffuse forms of political activity which can also qualify as a movement, as distinct from other forms of solidarity such as those based on networks, clubs or groups. The definitional boundaries are complicated by the fact that networks or clubs sometimes develop into or form part of social movements. However it seems preferable to reserve the term 'movement' for something that involves more in size and effectivity than small-scale associations, if these are few in number and have little overall impact. But a large number of small associations, even with very diverse agendas, can in cumulative terms come to constitute a women's move-ment. Much of the literature on Peru during the 1980s speaks of a 'women's movement' made up of diverse currents, including grass-roots mobilisations organ-ised around basic needs. Tens of thousands of women were active in this way (Blondet, 1995; Vargas, 1991). Oduol and Kabira (1995) describe a similar devel-opment in Kenya in the last few decades where, again, thousands of women were engaged in intense activity aimed at 'improving their situation' in a variety of ways. While this kind of activism is not a women's movement in the terms noted above, in that it has no central co-ordination, and no agreed agenda, nonetheless the extent of participation and its overall significance suggests that popular women's movements often take this more diffuse and decentred form.

To speak of a movement then implies a social or political phenomenon of some significance, that significance being given both by its numerical strength and by its capacity to effect change in some way or another whether this is expressed in legal, cultural, social or political terms. A women's movement does not have to have a single organisational expression and may be characterised by a diversity of interests, forms of expression, and spatial location. Logically, it comprises a substantial majority of women, where it is not exclusively made up of women. Some authors have identified women's movements with particular organisational forms and goals. Sonia Alvarez suggests that women's movements: 'pursue women's gender interests . . . [and] . . . make claims on cultural and political systems on the basis of women's historically ascribed gender roles' (1990: 23). Wieringa identifies women's movements with resistance to 'the dominant system', and with a commitment to 'diminishing gender subordination' (Wieringa, 1995: 7). Alvarez adds the important rider that women's movements are also defined by their autonomy from control by other social groups. Thus excluded from this definition are all forms of, to quote Alvarez, 'state-linked mass organisations for women, women's branches of political parties, trade unions and other organisations of civil society that are not primarily organised to advance women's gender specific concerns' (ibid.).

These criteria however denote a particular *kind* of women's movement, and, while such movements have been significant in the development of feminism, they have not been the only kind, or even sometimes the most important kind. As Alvarez shows in her study of Brazil, many forms of female collective action are in effect marked by the absence of one or other of these criteria (Alvarez, 1990). Moreover, general treatments of women's movements have tended to exclude consideration of right wing mobilisations of women, even though there are by now some important studies of these.[11] Are Fascist mobilisations of women, or Islamist women's movements, *not* women's movements in *any sense*? And what do we do with the women's organisations and their sizeable memberships in the existing and ex-socialist states? These are usually excluded from consideration as women's movements on grounds of autonomy if not on grounds of interests. Yet they deserve consideration in order to evaluate their significance both as political phenomena and for what they signify for their participants.

We will examine these criteria in a moment, but suffice to note here that the definition of women's movements as autonomous and expressive of women's gender interests does not usually encompass what Sheila Rowbotham has called the phenomenon of 'women *in* movement', that is, women acting together in pursuit of common ends, be they 'feminist' or not (Rowbotham, 1992). Yet it is important to acknowledge that these other forms of female mobilisation, excluded from consideration as 'women's movements' nonetheless constitute a large proportion, possibly the greater part, of female solidarity in much of the modern world. Women have been an active if not always an acknowledged force in most of the political upheavals associated with modernity, as members of trade unions, political parties, reform and revolutionary organisations and nationalist movements. Such formal and informal relationships with political processes and institutions are significant for what they can tell us about the terms and character of women's incorporation into political life.

In order to recognise these diverse forms of female political action, we might rehabilitate a concept deployed in an literature on political movements, that of collective action. To paraphrase Charles Tilley, this connotes solidarity in pursuit of common goals (Tilly, 1978). This term can more easily encompass the variety of forms of female mobilisation that have accompanied the process of modernity. As far as women's movements are concerned, Alvarez' criteria involving the pursuit of women's interests and independent self-activity raise two issues which have tended to be conflated – that of organisational autonomy and 'women's interests'. However, it is at once evident that in analysing different forms of female collective action and interest representation, the question of how to define a women's movement is a more complex one than first appears, and the boundaries are less clear cut than is often implied. This is because both core definitional criteria, not only autonomy but also women's interests, remain problematic, as is evidenced by their contested histories.

Female collective action and types of institutionalised agency: the autonomy issue

From its inception as a social movement, feminism has been engaged in a long and unresolved debate over organisation. Two issues have been particularly emotive: that of autonomy, and that of what principles should govern internal organisation. From the earliest moments of women's political mobilisation, women activists in political parties, trade unions and social movements have argued that they needed a place within which to elaborate their own programmes of action, debate their own goals, tactics and strategy free from outside influence.[12] Flat, non-hierarchical organisational structures were also considered more appropriate ways of ensuring democratic principles and allowing greater debate and participation in the formulation of objectives. However, creditable though such principles may have been, the varied history of female activism reveals a considerable diversity of institutional arrangements, within which autonomy figures as only one of many possible forms, while genuinely non-hierarchical organisations have been the exception rather than the rule.[13] For many women's organisations the urgent problem was how to reconcile principles of democratic consultation with effective leadership, an issue which was increasingly felt to determine the success, even the survival, of the organisation concerned.

Underlying feminist concern with organisational structure, and expressed in the demand for autonomy, is the question of authority: more specifically, the question that is engaged is – from where does the authority to define women's goals, priorities and actions come? Here it may be useful to establish an initial set of distinctions between three ideal types[14] of 'direction' in the transmission of authority: these may be called *independent, associational* and *directed,* corresponding to the lines of authority which have crystallised in relation to female activism. We will briefly consider each in turn.

Independent movements

First are those referred to above as autonomous organisations, which are characterised by *independent* actions, where women organise on the basis of self-activity,
set their own goals and decide their own forms of organisation and forms of
struggle. Here the women's movement is defined as a self-governing community
which recognises no superior authority, nor is it subject to the governance of
other political agencies. Its authority resides in the community, and that community has, what Dahl (1982) calls 'final control over the agenda'. As we have seen,
this is the form that is most closely identified with feminist definitions of women's
movements.

It is often assumed that if collective actions by women issue from within an
autonomous organisation, then they must be expressive of women's real gender
interests. Yet this is a problematic assumption, since autonomous organisations of
women have been associated with a very diverse range of goals, demonstrating
apparently conflicting definitions of interests. These have ranged from self-help
activities of various kinds, to protest movements, to those associated with a self-
conscious feminism, to ones entailing the abrogation of women's existing rights
and envisioning the greater dependence of women on men and commitment to
family life. There have also been apparently spontaneous movements of women in
favour of practices such as *suttee* and female circumcision.

It is, moreover, important to note that there is an extensive record of female participation in independent collective actions in pursuit of universalistic goals, i.e. ones
which are *not* related directly to women's gender interests.[15] An example is provided
by some nationalist struggles, where women organise independently to help realise
the broader goals of nationalist or revolutionary forces, such as the women's clubs
which appeared in Cuba in the late nineteenth century supporting independence
from Spain (Stoner, 1988). Such forms of activism may have a special meaning and
clear implications for women (which accounts for why they gain their support), but
the goals of these movements are typically formulated in universalistic terms, and are
seen as indissolubly linked to national independence and development. Such movements are not therefore pursuing gender-specific interests, but they have involved
independent collectivities of women in the field of national politics.

Independent organisational forms are therefore compatible with a variety of different political positions and goals; and even when women do organise
autonomously, they do not always act collectively in pursuit of their gender interests. Women's interests cannot be 'read off' from the organisational form in which
they are expressed; the mere fact of an organisation's autonomy or internal organisational structure does not indicate that it is a privileged vehicle for the expression
of women's interests, or indeed that it is entirely free from authority, either
internally with respect to the organisation concerned or with regard to external
influence. The latter raises interesting questions concerning 'autonomy' in that an
autonomous movement typically designates some discourses and/or principles as
authoritative. Thus, while not recognising a 'higher authority' it might recognise *an*

71

authority in the form of a privileged interpretation of reality. The question then becomes one which has less to do with authority per se than with the values and purposes with which it is associated. Autonomous organisation does not exist in any necessary relationship with the content of the goals, or the interests which are articulated – or even with the identities of the actors involved. Furthermore, autonomous organisations do not *necessarily* lead to the empowerment of women: first because informal power structures can operate 'tyrannically' in the absence of formal limits or procedural rules governing the exercise of power. And second, because autonomy can in some contexts mean marginalisation and a reduced political effectiveness.[16]

Associational linkage

A second type of organisational principle and a different conception of authority is expressed in what we could call *associational* forms. These are ones in which independent women's organisations with their own goals and institutional autonomy choose to form alliances with other political organisations with which they are in agreement on a range of issues. These may be seen as *associative* in recognition of their quasi-independent status within an alliance of interests; their actions are not directed by a superior power, as women remain in control over their own organisation and set its agenda. In this situation women's associations may also choose to delegate power to outside agencies such as parties or public officials, an arrangement which, if it is to work, must be based on trust and established procedures of accountability. Power and authority in this model are negotiated, and cooperation is conditional on some or all of the women's demands being incorporated into the political organisation with which the alliance is made. Vargas (1996) notes in her reflections on women's movements in Latin America that this process of negotiation from an autonomous base is the key to democratic politics; it acknowledges that interests are diverse and sometimes conflictive, and that they cannot be defined in unitary terms and imposed from above'.[17]

This kind of associative linkage escapes the polar dilemma of 'autonomy or integration' which has long divided different currents within women's movements, and it has the potential to be an effective means of securing concrete agendas for reform. It does, however, run the risk of co-optation resulting in the women's organisation losing its capacity for agenda-setting. In order to minimise this danger, some autonomous women's movements have set conditions on organisations with which they are prepared to cooperate. In Brazil in the 1980s some feminist groups made it clear that they had no interest in legitimising any agency where criteria for participation were not based on democratic parameters, where resource issues were not resolved according to principles of transparency, and where the institution was 'not an ally of feminist causes' (Schumaher and Vargas, 1993: 459). Such conditionality, a necessary feature of this kind of arrangement, clearly depends as much on a conducive political environment for its realisation as on the effective capacity of women's movements to be in a strong bargaining position.

Directed mobilisations

A third ideal typical form is what could be called *directed* collective action. This applies to those cases where the authority and initiative clearly comes from outside and stands above the collectivity itself. The women's organisation or movement is therefore subject to a higher (institutional) authority, and is typically under the control of political organisations and/or governments. There is little, if any, room for genuine negotiation over goals. This means that either one or both of the following tend to occur: (1) that the goals of women's associations do not *specifically* concern women other than as instruments for the realisation of the higher authority's goals; and/or (2) that even if they do concern women, control and direction of the agenda does not lie with them as an identifiable social force. Female mobilisation is therefore directed, with the proviso that the degree of direction involved can vary substantially, as can the forms taken by the directing authority. However, there may be considerable fluidity in a given historical context; in one situation there may be a movement from direction to greater autonomy as the collective actors acquire more political resources and influence over the political process. In another situation the reverse could occur, with a once-independent movement coming increasingly under the control of a party or the government. A critical factor in the assessment of concrete cases of this directed form of collective action is the nature of the party or state concerned; Social Democratic governing parties with women's sections need only to be compared with the official women's organisations in state socialist variants to bring out the contrasts in the quality and type of direction involved.

While directed mobilisation of this kind represents the antithesis of independent women's organisations, it has in many parts of the world and for a substantial period of history constituted the principal form of female mobilisation. It is important, however, to establish some distinctions between the main forms that have arisen, three of which can be mentioned here. In the first type women are mobilised to help achieve a general goal, such as overthrowing the government, or bringing a party to power. In this case there is no explicit commitment to enhancing women's specific interests. For example, in Latin America the MNR, a left wing guerrilla organisation in Bolivia, managed in the 1970s to mobilise many thousands of women, and even had female commandos of armed militias. Yet according to one analyst 'there (was) not one single political or ideological document belonging to the MNR that address(ed) or propose(d) the matter of women's struggles'(Salinas, 1986: 143). In effect, women were used by the Party to repress popular discontent.

A second type of directed action is that which, while primarily concerned with securing broader political goals, nevertheless does express a commitment to advancing women's interests but within the context of a general commitment to social change. This is the case of those modernising nationalisms and socialist movements which sought to advance general goals, including the emancipation of women from traditional forms of oppression, and supported some conception of women's rights. Such movements aimed to mobilise women and encouraged them to promote their own interests through official women's organisations. Yet these interests were defined in advance by the party as the overarching authority, and no alternative definitions of interest or independent associations were permitted. In socialist conceptions women's interests were to be realised as a necessary part of the overall project of national development and social modernisation, formulated in opposition to 'traditional' forms of patriarchal oppression. They may indeed have had an emancipatory function in that they bestowed rights on women which were previously denied; however the point remains that women's organisations were subordinated to the authority of the state, and their actions were dictated by the Party.[18]

A third form of directed collective action is where women are mobilised for causes which may abrogate rights they already have in the name of collective, national or religious interests. Examples of the latter are those religiously inspired movements where some groups of women have been mobilised by political parties in support of redefining the 'gender regime' by rejecting liberal conceptions of gender equality in favour of more traditional notions of the 'patriarchal bargain' (Kandiyoti, 1988). This form of female collective action has been studied in relation to authoritarian regimes of various types, such as Nazi Germany or contemporary Iran, where it has been shown that such apparently 'irrational' mobilisations of women are not usefully seen in terms of 'false consciousness'. Rather, they suggest that there are marked variations in the ways women's interests and politics are defined. We will return to this point later.

These then, are different ways of identifying some preliminary distinctions with regard to women's movements and collective actions. We have seen that as far as women's interests are concerned, there is no necessary relationship between forms of organisation and interest articulation. While there are good reasons for the feminist emphasis on autonomy and non-hierarchical forms of practice, such principles, even when applied, cannot be seen as guarantors of some 'pure form' of women's movement expressive of 'women's interests'. Moreover there are cases where the agenda for women's associations is dictated from above and includes a commitment to enhancing women's interests. Finally there are cases where the agenda set by the organisational authority has little to offer women in terms of enhanced rights or greater political representation, yet it can succeed in mobilising substantial numbers of women. In other words women's gender interests are not always transparent, or even primary for women, any more than their gender identity is their sole identity.[19]

Women's interests

This takes us to a second area of analytic distinction employed in the discussion of women's movements, that of 'women's interests'. This issue came to occupy a place of considerable importance in the debate on gender and development, following the diffusion into planning contexts of some conceptual distinctions I elaborated in the mid-1980s (Molyneux, 1985). The history of the 'interest paradigm', as some have termed it, is a curious one; what began as an attempt to render the discussion of interests more sensitive to the complex issues at stake,[20] ended up as an over-simplified model which was sometimes applied in such a schematic way that the usefulness of thinking about women's interests at all was, for some, put in considerable doubt.[21]

All theories and concepts run the risk of being misapplied, but this is not usually reason enough to abandon them. The notion of interests has a long history in political theory and calculation, and, as Jonasdottir concludes in her critical evaluation of the concept, it is difficult to dispense with in accounts of politics, agency and collective action, let alone of political representation (Jonasdottir, 1988). What is needed, however, is some greater refinement in its treatment and caution in its deployment. Returning for a moment to the original conceptualisation, the aim here was to problematise the way in which women's interests were formulated. The 1975 article argued against certain constructions of women's interests and critiqued the notion that sex was a sufficient basis for assuming common interests. Instead, women's interests were seen as historically and culturally constituted, reflecting, but not reducible to, the specific social placement and priorities of particular groups of women; they were also seen as politically and discursively constructed. This allowed the possibility of questioning the ways in which interests are formulated and the uses to which arguments about interest are put, both by women themselves and by those seeking to mobilise them.

Two sets of heuristic distinctions were introduced: the first involved identifying a category of gender interests as distinct from what were generally referred to as 'women's interests'. This sought to distinguish between those general or specific interests which women's organisations may claim as their own but which are not identified with gender issues. *Gender* interests referred to those arising from the social relations and positioning of the sexes and therefore pertained, but in specific ways, to both men and women.[22]

A second, more contentious distinction identified two ways in which women's gender interests could be derived: these were termed respectively 'practical' interests, those based on the satisfaction of needs arising from women's placement within the sexual division of labour; and 'strategic' interests, i.e. those involving claims to transform social relations in order to enhance women's position and to secure a more lasting repositioning of women within the gender order and within society at large. The intrinsically political, potentially transformative nature of strategic interests needs re-emphasising. Kate Young suggests the notion of *transformatory potential* to indicate the 'capacity . . . for questioning, undermining or transforming gender relations and the structures of subordination'(Young, 1993: 156).

Before proceeding further it may be helpful to recall that my original discussion of women's interests was within a work of political sociology, in this case an analysis of the Nicaraguan revolution and its policies concerning women. Some later usages of these distinctions detached the categories from their explanatory context and adapted them in an effort to develop guidelines for the purpose of policy and planning.[23] These guidelines in turn were sometimes banalised in applications 'in the field', where they were treated, in the words of one practitioner, as a 'magic key' which would serve as a mechanical prescription for women's organisations to follow (Anderson, 1992). This is not to say that questions of interest have no pertinence for gender and development policy. The issue is what role they are designated in the planning process and by whom, and what relationship is established between the planning agency and the population with which it aims to work. This is as much an issue of good practice as of good theory.

If, in the evolution of the 'interest paradigm', some elements of the original analysis as well as the theoretical intent were misunderstood or lost in translation, two issues in particular could usefully be clarified: that of the way interests are conceptualised, and that of the relationship between interests and needs. In the first place some authors assume a conception of interest which is at variance with the original article. The latter began by acknowledging the impossibility of deriving women's interests from a generalised account of women's subordination, akin to Marx's theory of proletarian exploitation. Yet Kabeer and Wieringa in their critical discussions automatically assume a Marxist derivation, while Wieringa believes that interests are necessarily equivalent to 'objective interests' and are thus given *a priori* (Kabeer, 1992; Wieringa, 1994). The original formulation however explicitly rejects this conception because it rests on essentialist assumptions and 'explains collective action in terms of some intrinsic property of the actors and/or the relations within which they are inscribed' (1986: 253); this conception implies that women's interests are given in their structural positioning and simply need to be read as an effect of the division of labour, reproductive capacities or, more generally, from women's social/structural location.

This theory of interests has been criticised on a variety of other grounds both political and epistemological (Benton, 1981, 1982; Callinicos, 1987; Hindess, 1982; Scott, 1988). It presumes that interests can be identified irrespective of the subjective inclinations of agents, and thus opens up the possibility of outside agencies imposing their version of objective interests on subject peoples. Such conceptions presume that interests can be identified as in some way 'true', as in correspondence theories which posit a direct relationship between the agent's interests and reality. Such truth claims can be contested from a variety of positions, and there is consequently little support for such absolutist notions of truth in contemporary political debate. The formulation of interests and the struggles that arise in pursuing them are not usefully seen as an effect of some structural (or indeed biological) determination. While material needs or social positioning is important in explaining certain forms of mobilisation and resistance, their reductive deployment in terms of a 'structural effect' neglects the processes involved in the construction of meaning and hence of subjectivity itself. The formulation of interests whether strategic or practical is to some degree reliant on discursive elements, and is always linked to identity formation. This is especially true for women whose interests are often closely bound to those of the family or household. This suggests that claims about women's objective interests need to be framed within specific historical contexts since processes of interest formation and articulation are clearly subject to cultural, historical and political variation and cannot be known in advance.[24]

If reductive accounts of objective interests have their limitations, the solution is not to substitute a purely contingent and subjective construction of interests, as this has little explanatory power or political pertinence'.[25] Fierlbeck expresses the dilemma: 'to say that women . . . do have "objective" interests which must be addressed despite individual preferences devalues their own subjective articulation of what is important to them; while to admit only that women have "subjective" interests makes it all but impossible to address the disparities and attitudes that disadvantage women *qua* women' (Fierlbeck, 1995: 8). Jonasdottir (1988) suggests a compromise, arguing that any definition of interests must recognise agency and subjectivity, but they must also be understood to be formulated within determinate contexts which affect the way agency and choice are exercised. In this sense only subjective interests can be said to exist, but since these are formulated within specific, bounded, historical contexts and constraints, it is possible to see interests as socially defined in ways that allow the calculation, with due reflection on the particular context, of something like objective interests. Here, objective interests are deemed to correspond to the outcome which is of the most benefit to the agent concerned, and they should be pursued with the strategies most appropriate to their realisation.

These issues are pertinent to the distinction between strategic and practical interests, one which has been objected to on several grounds. Wieringa opposes the distinction because it privileges one form of demand-making over others as an appropriate basis for feminist strategy. She argues against distinctions of any kind as they contain 'hierarchical overtones', and she is against these in particular because she sees them as unhelpful 'binaries', which are an attempt to 'control and normalize reality'.[26] Yet we surely need distinctions as heuristic devices if only in order to reveal how much more complex reality is. This does not imply that they should be turned into dichotomous essences. Moreover in policy contexts such distinctions can have a dynamic role, if they are introduced as a way of stimulating debate and discussion. To argue against distinctions is surely to argue against theory itself, rather than to debate the uses to which theory can be put. Wieringa's position seems inconsistent; distinctions are hierarchical, yet practitioners are urged to carry out 'feminist activity' with 'feminist-informed analysis'. What is this other than a privileged theory and discourse? Wieringa at times seems to conflate the role of theory with that of practice. We can all agree that it would be bad practice in moral and instrumental terms to impose anything on an unwilling collectivity. But as Wieringa herself says, it would also be bad practice to avoid confronting difficult questions of politics and strategy on the grounds that what exists must be right.

With regard to the uses made of the strategic/practical distinction in planning contexts, the problem is that it has apparently been deployed in the form of a too rigid binary, with practical interests set against strategic in a static, hierarchised opposition. If this has occurred it is far from what was intended and contradicts the original intent. Clearly, practical interests can, at times should, be the basis for a political transformation. Indeed the evidence shows that this evolution has sometimes occurred in the process of struggles around practical interests, as in the case of 'popular feminism' in Peru (Blondet, 1995). Here poor women mobilising around practical gender interests have sometimes engaged in strategic struggles which simultaneously enhance their ability to satisfy their practical needs and their strategic interests. However it is equally important to stress that this transformation may not occur and that it is not simply given in the nature of struggles around practical interests. As many commentators have shown, such struggles more often than not do not proceed to demands which would challenge the structures of gender inequality, or enhance women's rights (Martinez, 1993). Whether they do or not is to a large degree contingent on political and discursive interventions which help to bring about the transformation of these struggles.

What purpose then is served by the distinction between practical and strategic? The distinction does differentiate between ways of reasoning about gender relations; in the formulation of practical interests there is the assumption that there is compliance with the existing gender order, while in the case of strategic interests there is an explicit questioning of that order and of the compliance of some women with it. Such a distinction between what Gramsci called a practical consciousness and what we could term a strategic vision, has always been important to politics, especially to emancipatory politics. How else, other than through what Foucault calls 'the critical labour of thought upon itself' could claims to think differently, and to see the world in different terms to that which is presented in conventional stories about social relations, occur? If in the formulation of practical interests women take inequality or male authority over them for granted, then this is a different way of seeing the world to that which evolves in the course of political discussion premised on alternative, egalitarian visions.[27] If feminism, like other forms of critical theory, insists on seeing this reality as containing oppressive relations and social injustices, and if its practice is concerned with challenging it and changing it, then it depends on some measure of critical, alternative, thought and hence on some means of making value judgements about the social order.[28] If such political and analytic distinctions are inevitable, they do not sanction practices which display arrogance, lack of respect for alternative views and ways of living. That is not only poor practice but self-defeating politics. The political *links* between practical and strategic interests can emerge only through dialogue, praxis and discussion.

Finally, in other usages of 'the paradigm', some, following Moser (1989), have preferred to interpret 'interests' as 'needs' because the latter does have a more direct applicability to planning and policy. The idea of need is a more categorical, less political and less fluid construct, even in the hands of those, like Fraser, who give it a more political meaning by emphasising how needs are discursively constructed (Fraser, 1989). Interests are conceptually different from needs, in that the former are more clearly intentional, belong within a political vocabulary, and are the product of a process of reasoning which assumes instrumental agency. In simple terms, needs are usually deemed to exist, while interests are willed. Jonasdottir has suggested that in some needs discourses the question of authority acquires a particular salience: needs tend to be defined by and acted upon by expert others – planners, the political elite – while interests imply some greater degree of agency. While I can agree that there is a difference in the application of the needs/interests discourses, the latter too can involve questions of external definition and authority. In any event, Jonasdottir is surely right to suggest that what is required for the purposes of political calculation is some way of combining a discourse of needs with that of interests. This is essential in the planning field. Moser in fact suggests that the planning process requires the identification of women's interests by women themselves so that they can be translated into planning needs (Moser, 1989). Needs and interests should therefore be closely related in the planning process, with the proviso that the caution that should be deployed in relation to interests is equally necessary in relation to needs. Fraser uses the term 'the politics of needs interpretation' to emphasise the contested, contextual and discursive character of needs, resulting from a political process of interpretation, much as has been said in relation to interests.

Democracy and interests

The identification of different kinds of interests raises other issues which are rarely considered in the development literature, namely, what is the *politics* (not just the power relations) involved in the articulation of women's diverse interests? It is evident that women's gender interests can be instrumentalised by political forces which claim to be promoting women's interests in general – as if this were self-evident, unproblematic and uncontested. In recent times appeals to women's practical interests have mobilised them into voluntary welfare work, and have been used to solicit their support for neo-conservative campaigns around 'responsibilising the family'. The point is not to deny that women might identify with these definitions of their interests but rather to ask questions about their broader political pertinence, and their longer term policy implications within specific contexts.

This question of broader political objectives is especially pertinent in the formulation of strategic interests, which implies a process of politicisation in which particular transformative visions and strategies are elaborated with the aim of enhancing women's position overall. Feminism has itself provided several kinds of strategic vision, each articulated within different political discourses – these include socialist, liberal, nationalist, radical, anarchist, communitarian and maternalist versions, to name but some. The context of my original discussion of interests was a socialist revolution, that of Nicaragua. It was concerned with the emancipatory politics of feminism and socialism and of their shared and conflicting theoretical universes. Within the Latin American context of the time, feminism was associated with general principles of equality and with the classic feminist programme which aimed to minimise the social differences between the sexes.[29] However, it has since become clear that other forms of strategic vision have been elaborated within women's movements, ones which are premised on different assumptions to 'equality feminism' and which sometimes depend upon radically opposed conceptions of gender relations. A critical distinction which can now be made is between women's movements which premise their strategic visions on the minimisation of difference between the sexes, and those which argue for the enhancement of women's place in society through an appreciation of the differences between the sexes.

The latter view finds expression in a variety of political strategies, some of which are opposed to classical feminist conceptions of autonomy and equality. Women's movements based on this kind of difference politics have included certain kinds of motherist movements and some strands of religious fundamentalism which attempt to retrieve a special place for women in the private sphere. In the latter case a distinctive conception of women's interests is at play: it sees protection by men and economic dependency on them as the necessary correlate of women's withdrawal or conditional presence within the public realm, and, as a consequence, their exclusion from institutional politics. A 'separation of the spheres' argument is an explicit component of women's interests conceived in this way.

Such conceptions of women's interests can be argued against on the grounds that they do not, nor cannot, enhance women's socio-economic and political status in the context of major, gendered social inequalities. This would be the 'equality' feminist view.[30] Yet sometimes these movements share some long-standing feminist preoccupations – a belief in women's informal power in the home and the need to valorise women's work in the domestic sphere and in those areas supposedly most suited to women's 'special attributes'. In some recent appropriations of this discourse there is an attempt to politicise these interests, to extend the realm of women's juridical rights in the home and empower women in this context.[31] When women's interests are formulated in this way as a vision of how to transform and enhance women's place in society, within terms of debate premised upon 'difference', then there may be grounds for speaking of them as being 'strategic' in character. However this question is resolved, it reveals that what is at stake is not only the difference between strategic and practical interests but between different conceptualisations of women's interests and the politics consequent upon them. In other words, the kind of strategic vision which animates women's politics crucially denotes the terrain of debate and intervention for feminism.

Do we need a theory of interests for women's politics? It has been objected by some analysts that the notion of interests derives from a masculine model, connoting male values of rational goal-oriented behaviour premised on utilitarian political assumptions. Women, it is argued, are animated by emotion, by values which are altruistic: women's love and care for others is not based on rational self-interest but on other, moral, imperatives (Elshtain, 1981). It is true that theories which conceive of interest in narrow utilitarian terms do not help in understanding the phenomenon of 'maternal altruism' but this is chiefly because they are premised on ideas of the individual as abstracted from social relations. If individuals are seen as *social* beings, it becomes easier to explain why women might identify their interests more closely with family and kinship. Yet while the embedded character of women's social positioning might make it more difficult to separate affect from interest, it does not mean that women's commitment to family and kin is purely moral and entirely without self-interest. The recognition of women's 'embeddedness' in the social is perhaps a more useful starting point than those essentialist notions of 'woman the carer'. Indeed, for many women the issue is not one of selfless altruism, of giving up their interests, but of how to reconcile the conflicting desires stimulated by affect and caring on the one hand and by self-fulfilment outside the home on the other.

So if interests can be adequately and acceptably defined within discussions of policy and politics, what is their broader significance for women's political practice? Can women's interests be a sufficient basis for politics? Or should we consider how, and indeed if, women's *gender* interests can be defined in relation to broader goals and political processes? We have already considered how women's movements have developed diverse forms of association with other political agencies; sometimes their gender interests have been defined and fought for by themselves, sometimes they have been defined, authorised and supported from above. In the same way, gender interests can be struggled for within a variety of different strategies. Two of these are particularly salient here: the pursuit of women's interests within the framework of particularistic demands; and the reframing of women's gender interests as part of a redefined general interest.

Feminism is often cited as an example of identity politics characterised by single issue and particularistic demands.[32] Yet this does not accurately describe the trajectory of modern feminism which has seen much overlapping of strategies and diversity of goals, many of them directed at achieving greater social equality and public provision. Within this diversity, particularistic demands have played an important part in the struggle for women's rights, most evidently in relation to such issues as reproductive choice and domestic violence. The pursuit of particularistic interests (the right to protection from abuse, the right to reproductive choice) is of course not necessarily at variance with strategies that pursue broader goals and interests and may be framed in terms of general principles (the right to protection from violence, the right to one's bodily integrity). Indeed, this framing of women's gender interests within a broader set of political and ethical principles has been an important component of women's struggles within liberal, socialist and nationalist states. Yet, as a tactic it is perhaps double-edged; it runs the risk that the specificity of women's situation and demands are crowded out by other claims and that principles of autonomy are sacrificed to expediency. But the process of taking women's interests out of the personal, private and non-political sphere into the public terrain of political demand-making and then of framing those demands in terms of a redefined general interest can be an effective way of giving feminist demands a more general salience, as well as according them a central place in discussions of how to incorporate women's interests into visions of a re-ordered, more just society. In this way interest-based politics does not have to be renounced altogether, as some have argued.[33] But if they are successfully incorporated within broader political visions, what then might these be in the conditions which prevail in the majority of the countries of the South?

Women's interests and strategic visions in the South

The context of the developing countries is, broadly, one in which feminism has not developed the kind of identity politics in which particularistic interests are paramount. Many feminist movements were founded by women who were formerly active in left political parties, and were disenchanted as much with their forms of organisation and practice as with their failure to take women's concerns seriously. The historical origins of these movements together with the different socio-economic and cultural contexts in which they arose have influenced their character as they have developed over time. Women's movements in the South, and feminist movements in particular, have been closely associated with agendas for social reform, involving both grass roots activism and making claims on the state for women's rights and social rights more generally.

The present conjuncture in much of the developing world is one marked by the ascendancy of neo-liberal values in the economic and political spheres. The 'double transition' to economic and political liberalism has been slow to deliver on its promise of greater prosperity for all; while inflation has fallen and growth has been stimulated; social inequalities have deepened and poverty levels are expected to increase in many countries. The female sex, over-represented among the least privileged groups, remains under-represented within policy-making arenas while continuing, in the main, to lack effective representative organisations. The process of economic restructuring, and the redefinition of state–society relations which has accompanied the demise of state-centred development, has rendered problematic the issue of social and economic rights. The trend towards deregulation and informalisation has brought legal changes, removing former labour rights and social entitlements, speeding up the process of casualisation within employment as women enter the workforce in unprecedented numbers. This context has challenged feminists to confront anew the possibilities and limitations of capitalist democracy and in so doing to contribute to the elaboration of a workable formula for the delivery of social justice. The new development agendas and discourses around welfare delivery and poverty alleviation threaten to depart from earlier notions of state responsibility, and to place the individual at the centre of new models of responsibilisation in which traditional family values have acquired a new salience. Yet while initially seen in largely negative terms, the 'rollback of the state' has also been associated with some positive effects, among them a greater role for civil society and social movements, a development upon which the vitality of democratic systems depends.

In this new national and international context, women's movements have been playing an important role, while women's interests are being re-conceptualised in a variety of different ways, often anchored within an overall project of democratisation and social justice. The definition of women's interests has come to include the demand for women to be acknowledged as full citizens – a vision which depends for its realisation on the attainment of social as well as civil and political rights and upon gaining institutional power. The fundamental shift in discussions of women's movements that has accompanied the processes outlined above is one which has seen a move away from a needs-based discourse to rights-based issues. This latter development forms part of a broad current of international and national politics, one which has received some impulsion from the human rights lobby whose efforts culminated in the Vienna conference in 1993. At the same time, within the context of contemporary political and theoretical debates the concept of citizenship has come to occupy a central place, because it signifies a way of problematising the politics and policies of the revitalised hegemonic order of liberal democracy.[34]

Yet the implications of this new political context for women's movements are not straightforward. The language of citizenship may have a broad appeal but it is a contested concept and differing notions of what is implied by struggles around issues of citizenship prescribe different political priorities and strategies. For some the priority is to establish international agreement on basic human rights; others challenge liberal individualist conceptions of citizenship through the revival of Marshallian concepts of social rights, or by republican conceptions of active citizenship, or through communitarian appeals to the moral society. Within feminism the citizenship debate has reframed earlier arguments about the appropriate sites of struggle, the desirability or otherwise of political alliances, and about whether principles of equality or difference should constitute the proper basis of political strategising.

Regional and cultural specificities necessarily pose different questions and elicit different political responses. The very *meaning* given to citizenship struggles is variable – in South Africa it is recast to deal with the continuing structures of racialised oppression in the post-apartheid state, while in parts of Latin America the emphasis has been on extending the rule of law and reforming the juridical apparatus in the wake of bloody dictatorships. What role does feminism have in these varied contexts, when it is itself far from having reached an 'ideal consensus' on the fundamental goals of the movement, let alone agreement over what principles should inform feminist conceptions of citizenship? The pervasive pluralism within women's movements, and within feminism itself, is evident in the reliance on different conceptions of women's strategic interests, each of which has its own implications for the chosen forms, sites and priorities of struggle.

The issue of women's strategic interests is therefore necessarily bound up with what broader political project women's organisations or movements are associated with. In the relatively new conditions presented by the return to democracy in many Third World states, feminists have been able to contemplate forms of association and alliance with other political forces and organisations with which they sympathise. This entails a shared commitment to an agenda which transcends while still encompassing particularistic interests, by reframing these where possible as part of a redefined social project. One of the most significant contributions of feminism has been the development of a new perspective on social and political life, one which not only reveals its profoundly unequal and gendered character, but which requires a reassessment of the priorities of states and of the normative social order. The critical insights of feminism have led to a gendered analysis of policies, and of their social consequences, evident in discussions of poverty and the impact of macro-economic policies on developing countries. Feminist theory has shown why the sphere of reproduction needs to be placed firmly within the planning process, not just to acknowledge *women's* invisible labour but to identify social needs more generally within conditions of racialised and gendered social inequalities. As was evident from the Beijing resolutions, for many feminists in the developing countries the important issue is how to develop a feminist politics which can also promote a general project of social justice. This implies some commitment to the principle of equality and to universal principles of citizenship, but in a way which does not presume an undifferentiated public with identical needs and interests.

(This paper first appeared in *Development and Change*, 1988, 29.2.)

Notes

1 See, for example, Pateman (1988), Coole (1993), Phillips (1991, 1993).
2 For some recent contributions see Jaquette (2nd edn. 1994), Jelin (1990), Waylen (1996), Wieringa (1995) Radcliffe and Westwood (1993), Safa (1993). Initiatives taken to address this absence within the development debate include the 1995 IDS conference entitled Getting Institutions Right for Women in Development (Sussex University) which focused on the ways that gender issues were reflected in institutional structures, including the much neglected issue of the state and public policy (papers published in Goetz, 1997).
3 See Rowbotham (1992) for a comparative account of women's movements and Threllfall (1996) for women's movements in the northern hemisphere. For more recent literature on women's movements in developing countries see note 2, also Alvarez (1990), Kandiyoti (1991), Tétrault (1994), Kumar (1992), and Basu (1992 and 1995).
4 Tarrés (1992) notes in relation to the Latin American literature a virtual absence in recent years of work on other forms of collective action, and little recognition in contemporary work on social movements of earlier contributions.
5 For early influential treatments see Hufton (1971), Rowbotham (1973), Croll (1978), Kaplan (1977), Bridenthal and Koonz (1977).
6 See Omvedt (1986), Jaquette (1994) and Jelin (1990), for comparative overviews and discussion.
7 Paidar (1995) is a comprehensive analysis of the role of women in the Iranian political process.
8 It is worth noting that the quantitative increase in women's participation has been accompanied by the absorption of women into formerly male preserves, none more so than the army. This however has not implied an erosion of gender roles as such; rather it required a redefinition of women's place within society as a whole, one

which added on to rather than eliminated their traditional gender responsibilities, while leaving men's largely untransformed.

9 'Other' includes state socialist attempts at legitimation through limited electoral processes.

10 Sen and Grown (1987) provide a useful typology for practitioners.

11 An important full length study of female support for Nazism was Koonz (1988).

12 For a classic record of the tensions between feminist demands for autonomous spaces and political parties see the exchange between Clara Zektin and Lenin in Zetkin (1934).

13 The participatory non-hierarchical model of doing politics has been criticised for allowing a 'tyranny of powerlessness', i.e. for failing to take account of forms of power which were exercised informally and not therefore subject to any regulation or control.

14 These are merely heuristic distinctions – 'idealisations' – which means that they do not have to correspond to reality; a great diversity of forms of female collective action have emerged over time, and there have been changes within given movements with overlapping forms, as between these three categories in given historical contexts.

15 Jean Franco has written: 'It is precisely Third World women who have insisted not only that there are differences *between* women but also that there are circumstances in which women's emancipation is bound up with the fate of the larger community' (Franco 1989: xi).

16 This point is made in the Latin American context by several authors; see for example Vargas (1996).

17 Here Vargas acknowledges Lechner's formulation (1990).

18 This case is explored in Molyneux (1996).

19 See Guzman *et al.* (1992) on this. Mouffe (1988) is also relevant in relation to the point that individuals generally occupy 'different subject positions' as a result of the complex process of identity formation.

20 For discussions and applications of the concepts see Moser (1989), Alvarez (1990), Young (1993), Kabeer (1992), Guzman *et al.* (1992), Safa (1990), García-Guadilla (1995), Nelson and Chowdhury (1994), Vargas (1993), Anderson (1992) and Wieringa (1994) among others.

21 See Anderson (1992) for a considered discussion of this trajectory.

22 The issue of men's interests is considered by New (1996) who suggests that many men have an interest in maintaining the oppressive gender order which works to their advantage; however, they also have an 'emancipatory interest' in equality and in ending the oppression of women. One could add that men's interest groups have formed in opposition to what are seen as women's unfair advantages in the sphere of positive discrimination and child custody. Sarah White (undated) has also written interestingly on men's gender interests in the development context.

23 The most thoroughgoing attempt at integrating the concepts within a framework for 'gender-aware planning' was that of Moser (1989).

24 Gina Vargas stresses the complex field of determination within which women's movements operate – 'with regard to their own contexts, subjectivities and concerns; in relation to different realities, experiences and influences, which reveal the complexity of the relationship between contradictions, contexts and subjectivities of women. The relationship between them is complex and tense, differences of class race ethnicity region are always present' (Vargas, 1993: 5).

25 Scott, like Callinicos, favours a view of interests as 'discursively produced', but abdicates an entirely relativist position in favour of politics and ethical positions which 'confront and change existing distributions of power' (1988: 6).

26 For a spirited critique of postmodernism's influence in development debates see Martha Nussbaum's essays in Nussbaum and Glover (1995).

27 Fierlbeck makes the important point that women's adaptation to subordination is too simply read as *consent*, which implies there was a real choice. In reality women's choices are often severely circumscribed, placing both consent and choice in doubt.

28 A measured defence of reason would, if space allowed, be proposed here. As Gillian Rose in *Love's Work* (1995) reminds us, there is no rationality without uncertain grounds, rationality relativises authority: 'yet this does not establish the authority of relativism, it opens reason to new claimants' (p.10). See also Lovibond's defence of rationality (Loribond, 1989).

29 Difference feminism does, however, have a long history in Latin America too, as well as an active presence within contemporary feminism.

30 As Scott and others have argued, the equality/difference distinction is unhelpful (another binary) when applied to politics and policy. Equality feminists recognise the importance of acknowledging difference for reasons of social justice in the legislative sphere (pensions, divorce settlements), as a way of redressing social injustice and hence furthering the aim of equality.

31 The German Mothers' Party, active in the 1980s, is a case in point: it called for *inter alia* wages for housework and increased rights to child custody.

32 Jonasdottir (1988) is surely right to say that women are not just another 'interest group', because they exist in a historically determined antagonistic and subordinate relationship to men. This has implications for issues of political representation.

33 See Mouffe (1992) and Dietz (1985) on why women's narrow self-interests should be transcended in the embrace of more general interests.

34 For a more detailed discussion see Molyneux (1998).

References

Alvarez, S. (1990) *Engendering Democracy in Brazil. Women's Movements in Transition Politics.* Princeton, New Jersey.

Anderson, J. (1992) *Intereses ó Justicia.* Entre Mujerres, Lima, Peru.

Basu, A. (1992) *Two Faces of Protest: Contrasting Modes of Women's Activism in India.* University of California Press, Berkeley.

Benton, E. (1981) 'Objective Interests and the Sociology of Power', *Sociology,* 15(2).

Blondet, C. (1995) 'Out of the Kitchens and onto the Streets' in A. Basu (ed.) *The Challenge of Local Feminisms.* Westview Press, Boulder, Colorado.

Bridentual, R. and Koonz, C. (1977) *Becoming Visible, Women in European History.* Houghton Mifflin Company, Boston.

Callinicos, A. (1987) *Making History.* Cambridge.

Coole, D. H. (1993) *Women in Political Theory: From Ancient Misogyny to Contemporary Feminism.* Wheatsheaf Books, Brighton.

Croll, E. (1978) *Feminism and Socialism in China.* Routledge and Kegan Paul, London.

Dahl, R. A. (1982) *Dilemmas of Pluralist Democracy.* Yale University Press, New Haven.

Dietz, M. G. (1985) 'Citizenship with a Feminist Face', *Political Theory,* 13(1) February: 19–37.

Dietz, M. G. (1987) 'Context is All: Feminism and Theories of Citizenship', *Daedelus,* 116(4): 1–24.

Elshtain, J. B. (1981) *Public Man, Private Woman.* Princeton University Press, Princeton, NJ.

Fierlbeck, K. (1995) 'Getting Representation Right for Women in Development: Accountability, Consent, and the Articulation of "Women's Interests"', *IDS Bulletin,* 26(3): 23–30.

Franco, J. (1989) *Plotting Women: Gender and Representation in Mexico.* Columbia University Press, New York.

Fraser, N. (1989) *Unruly Practices*. Polity, Oxford.

García-Guadilla, M. P. 'Gender, Environment, and Empowerment in Venezuela', in Blumberg *et al.* (1995) *Engendering Wealth and Well Being: Empowerment for Global Change*. Westview, Boulder, Colorado.

Goetz, A. M. (ed.) (1997) *Getting Institutions Right for Women in Development*. Zed Books, London.

Guzman, V. *et al.* (eds) (1992) *Una Nueva Lectura: Género en el Desarrollo*. Entre Mujeres/ Flora Tristán, Peru.

Hindess, B. (1982) 'Power, Interests and the Outcomes of Struggle', *Sociology*, 16(4)2: 498–511.

Hufton, O. (1971) 'Women in Revolution 1789–1796', *Past and Present*: 90–108 53, November:

Jaquette, J. (ed.) (1994) *The Women's Movement in Latin America*, 2nd edn. Westview, Boulder, Colorado.

Jayawardena, K. (1986) *Feminism and Nationalism in the Third World*. Zed Books, London.

Jelin, E. (1990) *Women and Social Change in Latin America*. Zed Books, London.

Jones, K. B. and Jonasdottir, A. G. (eds) (1988) *The Political Interests of Gender*. London, Sage.

Jonasdottir, A. G. (1988) 'On the Concept of Interests, Women's Interests, and the Limitations of Interest Theory' in K. B. Jones and A. G. Jonasdottir (eds) *The Political Interests of Gender*. pp.33–65.

Kabeer, N. (1992) *Triple Roles, Gender Roles, Social Relations: The Political Subtext of Gender Training*. IDS Discussion Paper 313, Brighton.

Kandiyoti, D. (1991) *Women, Islam and the State*. Macmillan, London.

Kandiyoti, D. (1988) 'Bargaining with Patriarchy', *Gender and Society*, 3: 274–90.

Kaplan, T. (1977) *Anarchists of Andalusia, 1868–1903*. Princeton University Press, Princeton, NJ.

Koonz, C. (1988) *Mothers in the Fatherland: Women, the Family and Nazi Politics*. London, Methuen.

Kumar, R. (1992) *A History of Doing. An Illustrated History of the Indian Women's Movement*. Kali for Women, New Delhi.

Lechner, N. (1990) *Los Patios Interiores de la Democracia*. Fondo de Cultura Economica FLACSO, Santiago, Chile.

Leon, M. (ed.) (1994) *Mujeres y Participación Politica*. TM Editores, Bogota.

Lovibond, S. (1989) 'Feminism and postmodernism', *New Left Review*, 178: 5–28.

Molyneux, M. (1985) 'Mobilisation without Emancipation? Women's Interests, the State and Revolution in Nicaragua', *Feminist Studies*, 11: 227–254, Summer.

Molyneux, M. (1998) 'Communitarismo, Moralidad y Politicas de Identidad' in *Gender and Citizenship*, E. Hola and A. M. Portugal (eds) *La Ciudadania*, ISIS Internacional, Ediciones de las Mujeres (25) Chile: 15–33.

Molyneux, M. (1996) *State, Gender and Institutional Change in Cuba's 'Special Period': The Federación de Mujeres Cubanas*. Institute of Latin American Studies, Research Paper (43).

Moser, C. O. N. (1989) 'Gender Planning in the Third World: Meeting Practical and Strategic Needs', *World Development*, 17(11): 1799–1825.

Mouffe, C. (1988) 'Towards a New Concept of Democracy', in C. Nelson and L. Grosberg (eds) *Marxism and the Interpretation of Culture*. University of Illinois Press, Urbana.

Mouffe, C. (ed.) (1992) *Dimensions of Radical Democracy*. Verso, London.

Nelson, B. and Chowdhury, J. (eds) (1994) *Women and Politics Worldwide*. Yale University Press, New Haven.

New, C. (1996) 'Man Bad, Woman Good? Essentialisms and Ecofeminisms', *New Left Review* 216 (March/April): 79–93.

Nussbaum, M. and Glover, J. (eds) (1995) *Women, Culture and Development.* Clarendon Press, Oxford.

Oduol, W. and Kabira, W. M. 'The Mother of Warriors and Her Daughters: The Women's Movement in Kenya', in Basu (1995): 187–208.

Omvedt, G. (1986) *Women in Popular Movements: India and Thailand during the Decade of Women.* UNRISD, Geneva.

Paidar, P. (1995) *Women and the Political Process in Twentieth-century Iran.* Cambridge University Press, Cambridge.

Pateman, C. (1988) *The Sexual Contract.* Polity, Cambridge.

Phillips, A. (1991) *Engendering Democracy.* Polity, Cambridge.

Phillips, A. (1993) *Democracy and Difference.* Polity, Cambridge.

Radcliffe, S. and Westwood S. (1993) *Viva: Women and Popular Protest in Latin America.* Routledge, London.

Rose, G. (1995) *Love's Work.* Chatto and Windus, London.

Rowbotham, S. (1973) *Hidden from History.* Pluto Press, London.

Rowbotham, S. (1992) *Women in Movement: Feminism and Social Action.* Routledge, New York and London.

Safa, H. I. (1990) 'Women's Social Movements in Latin America', *Gender and Society* 4 (3): 354–369.

Salinas, G. A. (1986) 'The Barzolas and the Housewives Committee', in J. Nash and H. Safa (eds) *Women and Change in Latin America.* Bergen and Garvey, South Hadley, Mass.

Schumaher, M. A. and Elisabeth Vargas (1993) 'Lugar no Governo: Alibi our Conquista?' *Estudes Feministas*, 1(2) Sao Paolo, Brazil.

Sen, G. and Grown, C. (1987) *Development Crises and Alternative Visions: Third World Women's Perspectives.* Earthscan, London.

Stoner, C. L. (1988) *From the House to the Streets. The Cuban Women's Movement for Legal Reform.* Duke University Press, Durham, NC.

Tarrés, M. L. (1992) 'Perspectivas analíticas en la sociología de la acción collectiva', *Estudios Sociológicos*, 10(30): 735–757.

Threllfall, M. (ed.) (1996) *Mapping Women's Movements.* Verso, London.

Tilly, C. (1978) *From Mobilization to Revolution.* Addison/Wesley, Reading, Mass.

Vargas, V. (1991) 'The Women's Movement in Peru: Streams, Spaces and Knots', *European Review of Latin American and Caribbean Studies*, 50 (June).

Vargas, V. (1993) 'Los Intereses de las Mujeres y los Procesos de Emancipacion'. Programa Universitario de Estudios de Genero, Universidad Nacional Autonomia de Mexico.

Vargas, V. (1996) 'Women's Movements in Peru: Rebellion into Action', in S. Wieringa (ed.) *Subversive Women.* Zed Books, London.

Waylen, G. (1996) *Gender in Third World Politics.* Open University Press, Milton Keynes.

White, S. (undated) *Making Men an Issue: Gender Planning for 'the Other Half'*, Mimeo, Institute of Development Studies, Sussex.

Wieringa, S. (1994) 'Women's Interests and Empowerment: Gender Planning Reconsidered', *Development and Change*, 25: 829–848, The Hague.

Wieringa, S. (ed.) (1995) *Sub-versive Women: Women's Movements in Africa, Asia, Latin America and the Caribbean.* Zed Books, London.

Young, K. (1993) *Planning Development with Women.* Macmillan, London.

Zetkin, C. (1934) *Reminiscences of Lenin.* International Publishers, New York.

Part II

HOUSEHOLDS AND INDUSTRY

4

JUMPING TO CONCLUSIONS?

Struggles over meaning and method in the study of household economics

Naila Kabeer

Clearly these assumptions do violence to reality. However, it is these models that are the most developed, that have seen the most rigorous empirical applications, and most importantly, provide a clear foundation on which to begin to develop a more comprehensive model of family behaviour.

(Rosenzweig, 1986: 233)

Causal explanations must be distinguished from storytelling. A genuine explanation accounts for what happened, as it happened. To tell a story is to account for what happened as it might have happened (and perhaps did happen). . . . By telling a story one can transform an issue from a metaphysical one to one that is amenable to empirical research. . . . At the same time, storytelling can be harmful if it is mistaken for the real thing.

(Elster, 1989: 7)

Introduction

Recent critiques of neo-classical economic theory have sought to re-present it as a particular form of 'story-telling' in order to draw attention to the value-laden foundations of what continues to be presented as an authoritative, dispassionate and detached methodological practice (McCloskey, 1990; Seiz, 1993; Strassmann and Polanyi, 1995). Feminist economists in particular have helped to highlight the paradox of a discipline which is premised on a fervent belief in self-interest as the primary motivating force for all areas of human endeavour but whose practitioners claim a stance of disinterested objectivity for themselves (Folbre, 1986a; Strassmann and Polanyi, 1995). In the first part of this chapter, I want to scrutinise in greater detail some of the *narrative devices* by which economists construct their stories in one particular field of research, that of the *household*. I want to show how these devices, in the shape of concepts, methods and argumentation, have framed the questions they asked, the methods through which they sought answers, the meanings they gave to these answers and in so doing, helped to maintain intact for a considerable period of time the claim that the neo-classical story was an acceptable rendition of what Elster terms 'the real thing'. In the latter half, I will describe some of the alternative approaches to the household which have emerged as the gap between fact and fiction in household economics became increasingly difficult to bridge.

Constructing the 'black box': the story of the unified household

The New Household Economics, till recently the dominant neo-classical model of the household, conceptualised household activity as the joint welfare maximisation of its members through the production of 'z-goods' – the direct objects of utility – by some combination of household labour, technology and purchased goods and services (Becker, 1965, 1976). Household decision-making was depicted as a two-stage process: the first entailed maximising the production of 'z-goods' by ensuring that marginal returns to productive inputs were equalised across uses; the second entailed maximising the joint welfare of household members by allocating 'z-goods' across the membership so as to maximise the aggregate sum of household utility. The allocation of labour within this model was treated as an extension of the allocation of other household resources. Labour was seen as primarily differentiated by productivity-related characteristics (e.g. skills and education) and allocated to different possible uses, such as market-related work, homebased production and leisure, on the basis of comparative advantage so as to equalise marginal returns to each unit of labour.

One problem posed by this conceptualisation was that whereas decision-making outcomes could be straightforwardly taken to 'reveal' subjectively determined preferences where the focus was on individual decision-making, there was no way of ascertaining whose preferences were revealed by household decision-making outcomes and hence no objective basis for determining that they did indeed maximise the aggregated utilities of individual members. This problem was dealt with through the ingenious ploy of *assuming* that it had occurred, either because of the altruism of family members or else through its imposition on household members by a dictatorial but benevolent (and male) household head. It is in this sense that the neo-classical household could be described as a 'black box': as long as observed outcomes of household decision-making could be reconciled with their account of what had happened, economists had no interest in actual decision-making processes.

In terms of intra-household relations, the neo-classical model had some clear-cut policy implications. It suggested that targeting welfare resources to 'vulnerable' household members would have no more effect on the intra-household distribution of welfare than a general rise in household income. In the first case, existing household resources would be redistributed by the altruistic head away from targeted members towards non-targeted members in order to regain the earlier welfare-maximising allocational equilibrium, while in the second case the increment in household income would be distributed among members in keeping with this welfare-maximising equilibrium. Similarly, it was irrelevant to intrahousehold distributional outcomes which member owned assets or earned income since all resources and income were pooled under the jurisdiction of the benevolent dictator to be re-allocated according to welfare-maximising principles. Thus, according to neo-classical predictions, the policy-maker might be able to influence the overall *level* of household welfare, but was impotent to alter its *distribution* within the household. Another important policy implication of the neo-classical household model, though one not generally taken note of by its adherents, was that the exercise of power by the household head was seen as essentially benevolent; the current concern with 'women's empowerment' could not have figured in the policy-making agenda generated by such an account.

However, the claims made by neoclassical economists for the analytical superiority of their models were not always borne out in the empirical domain. Indeed the constrast between theoretical claim and empirical performance is well-illustrated in Rozensweig's attempt to demonstrate the policy relevance of the household model (1986). Rosenzweig acknowledged its 'violence to reality', but claimed that the model's strength lay in its 'unified framework for describing and predicting important aspects of intra-household resource allocations' and hence the sound basis it offered for 'discerning what data to collect, what statistical techniques to use to learn something from that data . . . or what consequences to expect from policy interventions' (p.233) compared to the 'collections of 'precautions', 'insights' and/or examples' which apparently characterised alternative approaches. Unfortunately, because, like most neoclassical economists, he drew exclusively on a number of large, standardised data sets, collected by government departments and research bureaux as by-products of their own routine activities, rather than for the purpose of testing the specific hypotheses in question,[1] Rosenzweig's attempt to demonstrate this claim empirically was confined to a mixture of speculations, conjectures and enigmatic findings. For instance, it is difficult to know how policy-makers are to interpret and act on his finding that changes in the price of milk in Indonesia had no effect on the likelihood of illness among farm heads or their wives; that changes in the price of vegetables did have a significant, negative effect on illness among household heads but not their wives while changes in the price of fruit had a positive but statistically insignificant effect among farm wives but not their husbands. Indeed, it is difficult to make *theoretical* sense of such information within a neoclassical framework since it offers no rationale as to why gender might be linked to the individual propensity to consume milk, vegetables or fruit – although anthropologists might be able to offer sound reasons for such a link.

To be fair, Rosenzweig does conclude his paper by noting that the binding constraint on the development of knowledge in economics appeared to be the state of the existing data. However, it is equally fair to say that the underdeveloped state of existing data was itself a product of the dominant economic approach to method which held that the value of a model should be judged by the twin criteria of 'fruitfulness' and 'parsimony': in other words, by the power of its predictions to 'explain much by little' rather than by how realistic they were (see Friedman's classic exposition on this: 1953). The indifference to the complexities of social reality, which was one effect of this view of economic method, is well illustrated in the 'thinned down' representations of human behaviour which grace the pages of the mainstream economic journals.[2] A related effect has been the privileging of prediction over explanation: in Elster's terms, as long as the neoclassical story accounted for what happened as it *might* have happened, economists had little interest in finding out what *did* happen.

Neo-classical predictions and empirical anomalies: joint welfare maximisation and intra-household well-being differentials

The neoclassical story of the household came under critical scrutiny in the light of a range of empirical findings which appeared to be difficult to reconcile with its key predictions. One group of empirical anomalies related to the assumption of joint welfare maximisation within the household, and to the underlying assumptions of unified preferences and pooled resources on which it rested. For instance, studies particularly from the South Asian region began to document the existence of systematic intra-household inequalities in physical well-being, primarily along lines of age and gender, and traced them to discrimination against female household members in the distribution of health, food and other basic survival resources (Chen; Mahmud and Mahmud). Such findings appeared to challenge the central neoclassical premise of joint welfare maximisation within the household. In addition, anthropological studies challenged the notion that observed allocational outcomes within the household could be attributed to a unified decision-making process, based on rational choice, and suggested instead that such outcomes reflected differential obligations and interests among household members which led them to allocate resources within their jurisdiction in systematically different ways (see, for instance, the special issue of *Development and Change*, 1987; Bruce and Dwyer, 1988; Moore, 1988; also Whitehead, 1990). Anthropological findings of this kind were supported by quantitative evidence by economists which suggested that income and resources in the hands of women were spent very differently compared to men (Senauer, 1990; Haddad and Hoddinott, 1991) and that, by and large, women-controlled resources tended to have more beneficial effects in terms of meeting the family's basic needs to the extent that in some contexts the probability of child survival was twenty times greater when non-earned income accrued to women rather than men (Thomas, 1990).

Such evidence clearly contradicted the neoclassical prediction of the irrelevance

of who controlled resources within the household and of the impotence of the pol-
icymaker in intra-household welfare matters. This was also borne out by empirical
studies of policy interventions. For instance, a study from West Bengal by Sen and
Sen Gupta (1983) showed that gender discrimination among children in intra-
household food distribution appeared to be more effectively countered by a
feeding programme targeted at children than by the generalised increase in
household resources represented by land distribution. Studies of contract sugar
farming in Kenya found that increments in household income did not translate
into significant changes in the health of women and children because they were
controlled by men (Kennedy and Cogill, 1987; Kennedy, 1989). Schrijvers (1988)
also suggested that the anomalous discrepancy in rates of malnourishment among
pre-school children in an area where a massive irrigation project had been introduced to increase rice production (39 per cent) compared to the national average
(7 per cent) could be attributed to the project's negation of bilateral inheritance
practices and its distribution of newly irrigated land to men, thereby depriving
women of the resource capability to fulfil their traditional role of assuring household food security and children's nutritional needs.

The utilisation of economic method to defend the neoclassical story of the
household against these empirical challenges to it was spelt out in an exchange in
the pages of the *American Economic Review* in the early 1980s in relation to the growing evidence of systematic gender differentials in life expectancy among children
in Indian households. Rosenzweig and Schultz (1982) sought to demonstrate that
this apparent anomaly could be reconciled with the assumption of joint welfare
maximisation by taking account of productivity differentials among household
members. Gender differentials in children's survival chances could be seen as a
rational response by parents to gender discrimination in the marketplace. In
those areas of India where male children faced better employment prospects,
they were also like to receive a larger share of family resources and hence had a
greater propensity to survive. Ensuring the survival of higher-productivity members constituted a rational strategy for maximising the joint welfare of the
household. Consequently, the distribution of excess levels of female mortality
among children across India was related to the distribution of gender differentials
in the market place.

This interpretation was challenged by Folbre (1984a) on both conceptual and
methodological grounds. She suggested that while discrimination against female
children might be considered compatible with parental attempts at maximising
total household *income*, it was difficult to see how it could be equated with maximising total household *welfare*. Not only was the welfare of the non-surviving girl
child excluded from the equation, but the productivity of surviving daughters
was also undermined, perpetuating their future disadvantage in the market. She
put forward an alternative view of the household suggesting that power, rather
than altruism, characterised its decision-making process. She hypothesised that,
since mothers were commonly assisted by their daughters in domestic responsibilities, they were likely to have a greater stake in the survival of daughters than,

and hence different preferences from, fathers. However, if they did not participate on equal terms in decision-making, their preferences would not be reflected in household outcomes.

Rosenzweig and Schultz (1984) did not contest the plausibility of this alternative interpretation of the data but rejected it on the grounds that it failed to meet the criterion of parsimony. They suggested that progress in knowledge in this field required 'sharply focused conceptualisations and empirical research, not just the expression of dissatisfaction with the tractable simplicity of the joint family function or a distaste for its implications' (ibid: 522). Since individual preferences were not observable, and in the absence of any evidence to the contrary, the assumption that individual preferences could be aggregated into a joint household welfare function offered the more parsimonious route to hypothesis testing. The increase in complexity which the imposition of extra assumptions about differential preferences within the family would entail could only be justified if it generated additional or different predictions which would distinguish it clearly from the older unified preference model.[3]

Comparative advantage and gender-related inflexibilities in intra-household labour allocation

Another group of apparently anomalous findings thrown up by empirical research related to the intra-household allocation of labour. According to the neoclassical principle of comparative advantage which was supposed to govern labour allocation, changes in returns to a particular member's time in a particular activity would result in re-allocations of labour time among household members in response to this change along welfare maximising lines. Thus, for instance, households would respond to an increase in women's wages in the marketplace by increasing the supply of women's labour in market-related activities and re-assigning the equivalent amount of non-market work they may have been engaged in to other household members who were either idle or engaged in comparatively less productive uses of their time. A similar re-allocation would occur in response to a change in men's wages. However, the empirical data threw up evidence of systematic gender asymmetries in the effects of wage changes which appeared to contradict the neoclassical predictions.

In India and the Philippines, increases in adult women's wages led to a greater reduction in daughters' labour market participation – and increased involvement in domestic chores – than sons' while an increase in adult male wages led to higher school attendance among children in the Philippines and among sons in India (Rosenzweig, 1986). Other studies found that the major burden of adjusting to increased market participation by women was borne by women themselves. In the Philippines, Folbre (1984b) noted that increases in women's market participation were accommodated by reductions in their leisure time but their time devoted to domestic work and child care remained roughly the same. As Popkin noted, also on the basis of Philippine data, 'there is close to a one-to-one correspondence between an increase in maternal work time and the decrease in maternal leisure' (1983: 166). Men spent the same amount of time on child care regardless of family size; indeed in larger families they increased their leisure. Children appeared to reduce the overall workload of fathers, rather than mothers, even where they substituted for mothers' domestic labour.

Neo-classical attempts to reconcile these anomalous cross-wage effects with their models relied on voluntaristic explanations, often bordering on the tautological. Rosenzweig (1986), for instance, posited 'greater substitutability' between the labour time of mothers and daughters while Collier (1989) suggested a 'copying effect', with girls copying mothers and boys copying fathers. In fact, sociological and anthropological research had established the existence of powerful ideological forces buttressing the established gender division of labour far beyond any purely efficiency-based rationale, curtailing in particular men's willingness to undertake 'female' activities. In some cultural contexts, the reluctance of men to share in domestic chores, despite women's involvement in paid work, led to the phenomenon of the 'underemployed but overworked' woman, particularly among poorer households (Goldschmidt-Clermont, 1987). Sen and Sen (1985) found, for instance, that in the Indian context, poorer women were most likely to combine three categories of work: wages, expenditure-replacing and domestic chores. Specialisation in purely domestic work was largely the province of women from wealthier households. A study from Nepal noted that in all economic strata women worked longer hours in all three categories of work and had less time for leisure and social activities than men of an equivalent class (Bennett and Acharya, cited in Bardhan, 1987). The household literature from Sub-Saharan Africa also refuted the idea of substitutability in the intra-household allocation of labour (Haswell, 1981; Roberts, 1988; Whitehead, 1990; Palmer, 1991) and pointed out that women worked longer hours than men in much of this region because of their involvement in farm labour on their own fields, their non-reciprocal obligation to work on men's fields as well as their responsibility for domestic labour.

In other studies, cultural norms defining appropriate roles for women and men were found to constrain women's ability to take up paid work outside the home. Sender and Smith (1990) pointed to the operation of patriarchal constraints in Tanzanian households and highlighted the fact that, while manual agricultural labour was overwhelmingly performed by women, it was primarily as unpaid family labour. Even among the poorest Tanzanian households, male dominance within the household prevented the entry of women into waged labour, despite negligible access to non-waged income by the household, on the one hand, and the availability of waged labour and its potential for improving its situation, on the other. Only women from female-headed households, who were presumably free from such direct forms of patriarchal control, and women seeking to leave violent husbands, were able to take up such opportunities.

An illuminating example of neoclassical attempts to reconcile empirical anomalies and theoretical predictions is to be found in Khandker's analysis (1988) of the extremely low rates of female labour force participation recorded in rural

Bangladesh. He favours a rational choice explanation for this phenomenon over the non-neoclassical explanation put forward by Cain *et al.*, which he summarises in the following terms: 'powerful local norms of female seclusion due to "patriarchy" extend to the labor market, and this severely restricts women from working outside the family'. Unfortunately for a study which claims to be exploring the effects of female seclusion on women's outside work, Khandker collapses self-employment within the home and income-earning activities outside the home into the single category of 'market production'.[4] This does rather seem to miss the point of the exercise since Cain *et al.* do not suggest that female seclusion *rules out* women's participation in paid activities altogether, but rather that it *constrains* women to paid activities within the homestead or else within a narrow range of 'appropriate' occupations in female segments of the labour market. The female earning activities documented in Khandker's study are in precisely these 'appropriate' occupations: family-based enterprises, sewing, handicrafts and rice-husking are the main examples of women's home-based income-earning activities, while teaching and other salaried service, together with non-agricultural wage labour, are the main examples of outside employment.

Although Khandker claims that his hypothesis testing supports the neoclassical story of rational choice, in fact his findings lend themselves remarkably well to precisely the interpretation he is seeking to refute. His finding that household land holding, assets and husbands' estimated earnings are negatively associated with women's market activity is perfectly compatible with the suggestion in Cain *et al.* that wealthier households are better able to 'afford' female seclusion and indeed to provide women with a productive base at home. The fact that women's participation in market activity as well as the time that they allocate to such activity are both found to be positively related to their wages is uncontroversial, and compatible with both sets of explanations, as long as the gender segmentation of the labour market is kept in mind.

What is, however, harder to reconcile with the neoclassical story is Khandker's finding that it is the *husband's*, rather than the *wife's*, own education which has the statistically significant effect on women's work patterns by (a) increasing the likelihood that women take up earning activity, (b) increasing the hours of work they devote to it and (c) reducing the amount of time they put into unpaid work. Women's own education appears to play *no* significant role in their decision to take up paid work and the hours they put into it, but among non-working women it reduces hours devoted to such unpaid work. How does Khandker attempt to explain these apparently anomalous findings?

First of all, he suggests that women's education increases the productivity of women but *only* among those who specialise exclusively in unpaid labour; consequently, it is only among this group that education has the effect of reducing the amount of time necessary for domestic work and increasing ability to enjoy leisure. An alternative explanation, and it is not clear why Khandker does not consider it, would be that educated non-working women came from households which were wealthy enough to hire in female labour to undertake domestic chores. The unexpected significance of husbands' education, accompanied by the absence of any effect of women's own education on women's activities, is explained away in the following terms:

> The finding that a woman's time allocation is determined not by her own endowment but partially by her spouse's endowment does not necessarily reflect the fact that a husband functions as a 'patriarch' who determines exclusively his wife's time allocation in Bangladesh. To the extent that an educated woman is married to an educated man, this result may simply reflect a spouse selection bias due to the endogeneity of wife's and husband's education levels determined partially by the parental characteristics of the wife and husband.
>
> (1988: 123)

For a methodological tradition which values parsimony, this is a remarkably convoluted attempt to explain away an anomalous finding. Of course, it is true that the statistically dominant effect that male education has on women's behaviour does not *necessarily* reflect the presence of a patriarchal factor but, given that men's wages are controlled for, it is *possible* that male education is capturing a patriarchy-related effect: male education may have the direct effect of attenuating patriarchal discomfort at the idea of women earning or it may be an indirect measure of male occupations where the idea of a working wife is more acceptable.[5] The influence of patriarchal constraint does not have to be overstated but to completely discount it in the context of Bangladesh is not tenable.

Non-unified households: the emergence of alternative approaches in economics

However, not all economists have gone into denial in the face of the multiplicity of empirical challenges to the unified household story and alternative depictions of household behaviour are emerging which seek to achieve a closer approximation to empirical reality. These stories, which we will refer to 'nonunitary models',[6] share in common the assumption of possible divergence in preferences among household members but differ in their other assumptions (see Hart, 1996 for a more detailed discussion of these models). One group of non-unified models assumes efficiency (pareto-optimality) in household decision-making but is agnostic as to how this is achieved, relying on empirical analysis to establish the decision-making rules (Chiappori, 1992). A second variation of the non-unified approach applies a bargaining model to household decision-making. Here cooperation within the household is assumed to occur as long as the gains from cooperation outweigh the gains from separation (or divorce); a process of bargaining determines how the gains from this cooperation are allocated between the respective members. Allocational outcomes are likely to favour those with the greatest bargaining power, which in turn is posited to be a function of the minimum welfare level (the 'threat point') that individual members would enjoy, even if cooperation did not occur or were to break down. A third and more polar version of the household economy – the noncooperative model – assumes that individual members not only have differing preferences but may also operate as autonomous sub-economies – the 'separate spheres' model – so that each individual controls their own income and disposes of it according to their individual (non-pooled) resource constraint. Here the threat point from which bargaining proceeds is not divorce, which is external to the household, but a non-cooperative equilibrium within it. McElroy (1992) has suggested that these various models are not all mutually exclusive but that the unified preference model forms a sub-set of cooperative models while non-cooperative solutions can serve as threat points in cooperative models.

Aside from variations in the assumptions imposed on the household, collective models also vary in the extent to which they reproduce the economism and methodological individualism of orthodox household economics. As we noted, some retain an agnostic stance towards household decision-making rules and seek mainly to derive testable restrictions on household behaviour from their models so as to permit differentiation between unified versus collective models of the household. Some of the quantitative studies cited earlier concerning the extent to which income or resources in the hands of different household members – usually adult male and female members – significantly affect expenditure patterns fall within this category. Chiappori's (1992) suggestion that gender-differentiated expenditure patterns may reflect differences in the seasonality or other 'flow' characteristics of male and female income rather than the gender of the income earner has been explored for Niger households by Hopkins *et al.* (1994). They found that gender did matter in introducing differential patterns of total household, as well as seasonal food, expenditures.

Other economists working in the non-unified tradition have sought to integrate a concern with bargaining power in their models. While continuing to focus on differing individual preferences and on formal econometric modelling to test their hypotheses, formulations of the bargaining approach have now moved from an earlier conceptualisation of the 'threat-point' or fallback position in conventional economic terms, such as prices (including wages) and incomes, to the inclusion of structures and ideology. The earlier, more economistic version is exemplified by McElroy and Horney (1981) who explored the effect of husbands' and wives' non-wage income on the amount of leisure they enjoyed. In a unified preference model, the amount of leisure enjoyed by both husband and wife would have depended on total amount of non-wage income rather than on individual amounts. Their finding that there was in fact a positive relationship between individual non-wage income and amount of leisure enjoyed was taken as support for a bargaining model of the household, with non-labour income acting as a threat point.

Since then, however, the bargaining approach has opened out to a more structural analysis of intra-household inequalities since major differences in bargaining power were seen to derive from objective differences in the economic positions of men, women and children outside the household (Folbre, 1986a). The greater concern with the structural bases of bargaining power is evident in McElroy (1992), where bargaining power within marriage is made a function of 'extra-environmental parameters', or EEPS, which include sex ratios in the marriage market, laws concerning alimony settlements, and women's ability to return to their natal home in the event of marital breakdown. Sen's formulation emphasises the effects of ideological factors such as perceptions about the value of members' contribution to the household economy as well as individuals' perceptions of their own long-term interests. His story of the household depicts it as a site of 'cooperative conflict' within which unequal bargaining power of the different household members reflects inequalities in (a) their fall-back position (b) the perceived value of their contribution to the household (c) the perceived degree of convergence between their immediate well-being and their longer-term interests and (d) differences in the ability to exercise coercion, threat and outright violence (Sen, 1985, 1990).

Some of the differences in methodology and approach which persist among economists working within a shared framework of non-unified households are highlighted in a recent exchange between Chiappori (1988) and McElroy and Horney (1990) which, as Seiz (1993) points out, echoes the exchange cited earlier in this chapter between Folbre and Rosenzweig and Schultz in its laying out of conflicting approaches to questions of both method and relevance in economic analysis. Representing the interests of formal economic modelling, Chiaporri suggested that the bargaining model discussed in McElroy and Horney (1981) had not succeeded in generating testable hypotheses strong enough to merit rejection of the unified preference model. In their response, McElroy and Horney dealt with the technicalities of Chiaporri's critique but also invoked 'empirical relevance' in defence of their work. Citing a growing literature which did not normally find its way into the pages of technical economic journals, they pointed out that intra-household distributional issues in poorer parts of the world had life-and-death consequences and that the real value of the bargaining model lay not in whether or not restrictions on its demand system could be tested, but in whether by allowing for an enriched list of explanatory variables, it opened the door to the systematic exploration of many hitherto unexplored economic questions.

This invocation of both empirical reality and policy relevance as justificatory criteria for economic theorising suggests that some economists have begun to move away from the earlier stress on the fit between prediction and data as the determining criterion of the value of a model. The difference involved in terms of insights yielded when economic analysis is guided by a closer concern with 'actual' rather than 'modelled' reality, and with trying to answer life-and-death questions rather than the pursuit of greater technical sophistication, can be assessed by comparing recent analysis by Dreze and Sen (1995) of the excess female mortality in India with Rosenzweig and Schultz's treatment of the same question discussed earlier. Though Dreze and Sen do not reject the possibility that excess female mortality in the Indian context is related to gender differentials in returns to labour, the interpretation they bring to bear on this finding suggests that there is much more to the explanation than gender disadvantage in the marketplace. Both female labour force participation, as well as female literacy (far more than male literacy), are found to reduce the level of excess female mortality. The fact that female literacy has an independent, and even more significant, effect in reducing excess female mortality than does female labour force participation suggests that the possibility that it is proxying something other than economic returns to women's labour. Dreze and Sen suggest that this 'something' was the more intangible variable of women's agency: in other words, female literacy and, it could be argued, female labour force participation were both capturing the extent to which women were able to exercise voice and agency within intra-household decision-making processes. The fact that female literacy also had a negative and statistically significant impact on overall under-five mortality – female labour force participation and male literacy had no significant impact – as well as a larger effect on female under-five mortality than on male under-five mortality also testified to the importance of this factor in countering gender discrimination within the household.

However, an even more significant challenge in their analysis to narrowly economistic explanations of excess female mortality is the significantly lower levels of excess female mortality, as well as under-five mortality, which characterised the southern states of India compared to northern states (with states in the west and east occupying an intermediate position), a finding which lends support to more structuralist explanations of the geographical distribution of sex ratios in the subcontinent. It suggests that, over and above variations in female labour force participation and female literacy, variations in the broad *cluster* of ideological and material practices which constituted regionally specific gender relations in this part of the world have a powerful effect on the relative value attached to sons and daughters in specific regions, regardless of individual or household characteristics. A considerable body of research had already pointed to north–south differentials in family and kinship organisation, with correspondingly differential implications in gender relations and women's autonomy (Bardhan, 1974; Miller, 1981; Dyson and Moore, 1983; Agarwal, 1994). Broadly speaking, northern India was characterised far more than the south by the prevalence of female seclusion and the associated constraints on women's ability to work outside the confines of the homestead. Patrilineal kinship, whereby family name and property were transmitted through sons rather than daughers, was also more widespread in the north. The greater practice of kin, and generally village, exogamy meant that the labour and progeny of daughters are lost to their parents and come under the control of their husband and his kin while they are simultaneously cut off from the supportive network of their natal family. Furthermore, the practice of dowry payments by the bride's parents to the groom and his family, further intensifying the perceived economic liability of daughters to their parents, was also far more prevalent in the north. Consequently, observed gender asymmetries in employment prospects as well as in mortality rates could both be seen as manifestations of deeper asymmetries within society rather than in terms of simple causation.

Conclusion

This chapter has focused on different stories of household economics to *demonstrate* how the *standpoint of the storyteller* influences the questions asked about a particular phenomena, the methods by which answers are sought and interpretations given to these answers. Competing stories about the household have always implicitly been about competing stories of gender relations within the household and have differed according to whether the storyteller viewed the household as a site of altruism or of power. Although the consensus appears to be shifting to the view that intra-household relations are indeed characterised by power, the nature of this power and how it operates in this most intimate domain of our lives remains a deeply contested one. It is becoming increasingly clear that stories about power borrowed from other arenas do not transfer easily to the study of the household because of the difficulties of disentangling choice and power in a set of social relationships in which some of the most selfless examples of love and sacrifice and some of the most terrible forms of abuse and oppression have been documented. And since we are all, neoclassical economists as well as feminists, products of specific households and familial arrangements, the stories we tell about other people's households are likely to bear the unconscious imprint of our own experiences.

The very different interpretations that can be given to the same phenomenon, not just in the field of household research, but across the social sciences, makes the idea of 'objective' research deeply problematic, and well-founded critiques of the ideal of scientific detachment in the pursuit of knowledge by Marxists, feminists and now post-modernists have increasingly put quotation marks around such notions as 'reality' and the 'truth'. Yet policy is still made, research is still carried out and the stories we tell as a result of such research still matter and indeed can have powerful ramifications on the lives of those we are talking about. Commitment to critical research in the interests of social transformation does not imply that we totally abandon any attempt at objectivity but it does require us to remain aware of the biases and predispositions which shape our own stories, cautious of our claims to knowledge and educated about the methods and evidence by which alternative stories to our own have been constructed.

Notes

1 That this is standard practice among neoclassical economists is pointed out by Kenneth Arrow cited by Swedberg (1991).
2 E.g. *American Economic Review, Journal of Political Economy, Econometrica, International Review of Economics.*
3 A rather simpler and more candid response to the problems of aggregation in economics is to be found in Solow's comment (1957: 312): 'Either this kind of aggregate economics appeals or it doesn't. Personally I belong to both schools'.

4 His grounds for doing this is that in an earlier analysis of rural women's labour force participation he had shown that the transaction costs of switching from home-based earning to market-based earning were insignificant.

5 Given that education is certainly widely believed to be a measure of attitudes when it comes to other aspects of individual behaviour such as fertility and use of family planning, it is also plausible that it may be a proxy for men's 'tastes' in the matter of letting their wives work.

6 Although economists have opted for the label 'collective models' (see Alderman *et al.*, 1995), this nomenclature is somewhat confusing because treatment of the household as a heterogeneous collectivity rather than a homogeneous unity is in fact associated with a shift in analytical focus from collective to individual preferences.

References

Agarwal, B. (1994) *A Field of One's Own. Gender and Land Rights in South Asia*, Cambridge: Cambridge University Press.

Alderman, H., Chiappori, P., Haddad, L., Hoddinott, J. and Kanbur, R. (1995) 'Unitary versus collective models of the household: is it time to shift the burden of proof?', *The World Bank Research Observer*, 10(1): 1–19.

Bardhan, K. (1987) *Women Workers in South Asia*, ILO Asian Employment Programme Working Papers, New Delhi.

Bardhan, P. (1974) 'On life and death questions', *Economic and Political Weekly*, Special Issue 9(32–34): 1293–303.

Becker, G. (1965) 'A theory of the allocation of time', *Economic Journal*, LXXX (200): 493–517.

—— (1976) *The Economic Approach to Human Behaviour*, Chicago: University of Chicago Press.

Braun, J. von, Puetz, D. and Webb, P. (1989) *Irrigation Technology and Commercialisation of Rice in the Gambia: Effects on Income and Nutrition*, IFPRI Research Report No. 75. Washington: International Food Policy Research Institute.

Bruce, J. and Dwyer, D. (eds) (1988) *A Home Divided*, Stanford: Stanford University Press.

Cain, M., Khanam, S. R. and Nahar, S. (1979) 'Class, patriarchy and women's work in Bangladesh', *Population and Development Review*, 5(3): 405–38.

Carney, J. (1988) 'Struggles over land and crops in an irrigated rice scheme: The Gambia', in J. Davison (ed.), *Agriculture, Women and Land. The African Experience*, Boulder, Colorado: Westview.

Chen, L. C., Huq, E. and D'Souza, S. (1981) 'Sex bias in the family allocation of food and health care in rural Bangladesh', *Population and Development Review*, 7(3): 435–74.

Chiappori, P. (1988) 'Nash-bargained household decisions: a comment', *International Economic Review*, 29(4): 791–6.

—— (1992) 'Income sharing within the household'. Paper presented at the IFPRI–World Bank Conference on Intra-household Resource Allocation: Policy Issues and Research Methods. IFPRI, Washington.

Collier, P. (1988). *Women in Development. Defining the Issues.* World Bank Working Papers 129, Population and Human Resources Department. Washington: World Bank.

—— (1989) *Women and Structural Adjustment*, Unit for the Study of African Economies, Oxford University, Oxford, February 1989.

Development and Change (1987) 18(2).

Dreze, J. and Sen, A.-K. (1995) *India, Economic Development and Social Opportunity*, Oxford: Oxford University Press.

Dyson, T. and Moore, M. (1983) 'On kinship structure, female autonomy and demographic behaviour in India', *Population and Development Review*, 9(1): 35–60.

Elson, D. (1991) 'Male bias in macro-economics', in D. Elson (ed.), *Male Bias in the Development Process*, Manchester: Manchester University Press.

Elster, J. (1989) *Nuts and Bolts for the Social Sciences*, Cambridge: Cambridge University Press.

Folbre, N. (1984a) '"Market opportunities, genetic endowments and intra-family resource distribution": comment', *American Economic Review*, 74 (3): 518–20.

—— (1984b) 'Household production in the Philippines: a non-neoclassical approach', *Economic Development and Cultural Change*, 32(2): 303–30.

—— (1986a) 'Hearts and spades: paradigms of household economics', *World Development*, 14 (2): 245–55.

—— (1986b) 'Cleaning house: new perspectives on households and economic development', *Journal of Development Economics*, 22: 5–40.

Friedman, M. (1953) *Essays in Positive Economics*, Chicago: University of Chicago Press.

Garcia, M. and Senauer, B. (1992) 'Implications of intra-household analysis for the assessment of a food subsidy programme'. Paper presented at IFPRI/World Bank Conference on Intra-household Resource Allocation: Policy Issues and Research Methods, Washington, 12–14 February.

Goldschmidt-Clermont, L. (1987) *Economic Evaluations of Unpaid Household Work: Africa, Asia, Latin America and Oceania*, Geneva: ILO.

Guyer, J. (1986) 'Intra-household processes and farming systems research: perspectives from anthropology', in J. L. Moock (ed.), *Understanding Africa's Rural Households and Farming Systems*, Boulder, Colorado: Westview.

—— (1988) 'Dynamic approaches to domestic budgeting: cases and methods from Africa', in J. Bruce and D. Dwyer (eds), *A Home Divided*, Stanford: Stanford University Press.

Haddad, L. and Hoddinott, J. (1991) 'Gender aspects of household expenditure and resource allocation in the Côte d'Ivoire'. University of Oxford, mimeo.

Hart, G. (1996) 'Gender and household dynamics: recent theories and their implications' in M. G. Quibria (ed.), *Critical Issues in Asian Development: Theories, Experiences, Policies*, Oxford: Oxford University Press.

Haswell, M. (1981) *Energy for Subsistence*, London: Macmillan.

Hopkins, J., Levin, C. and Haddad, L. (1987) 'Women's income and household expenditure patterns: Gender or flow?', *American Journal of Agricultural Economics*, 76(194): 1219–25.

IDS Bulletin (1991) 22 (1).

Jones, C. (1986) 'Intra-household bargaining in response to the introduction of new crops: a case study of North Cameroon' in J. L. Moock (ed.), *Understanding Africa's Rural Households and Farming Systems*, Boulder, Colorado: Westview.

Kabeer, N. (1984) *Reversed Realities: Gender Hierarchies in Development Thought*, London: Verso.

Kennedy, E. (1989) *The Effects of Sugar Cane Production on Food Security, Health and Nutrition in Kenya: A Longitudinal Analysis*, Research Report, 78. Washington: IFPRI.

Kennedy, E. and Cogill, B. (1987) *Income and Nutritional Effects of the Commercialisation of Agriculture in South-Western Kenya*, Research Report, 63. Washington: IFPRI.

Khandker, S. R. (1988) 'Determinants of women's time allocation in rural Bangladesh',

Economic Development and Cultural Change, 4: 111–26.

Leslie, J. (1988) 'Women's work and child nutrition in the Third World', *World Development*, 16(11): 1341–62.

McCloskey, D. (1990) *If You Are So Smart: The Narrative of Economic Expertise*, Chicago: Chicago University Press.

McElroy, M. (1992) 'The policy implications of family bargaining and marriage markets'. Paper presented at the IFPRI–World Bank Conference on Intra-household Resource Allocation: Policy Issues and Research Methods. IFPRI, Washington.

McElroy, M. and Horney, M. J. (1981) 'Nash bargained household decisions: toward a generalisation of the theory of demand', *International Economic Review*, 22(2): 333–49.

McElroy, M. and Horney, M. J. (1990) 'Nash-bargained household decisions: reply', *International Economic Review*, 31(1): 237–42.

Mahmud, W. and Mahmud, S. (1985) 'Aspects of the food and nutritional problems in rural Bangladesh', ILO/WEP Research Working Paper 10–6/WP74.

Manser, M. and Brown, M. (1980) 'Marriage and household decision-making: a bargaining analysis', *International Economics Review*, 21: 31–44.

Miller, B. (1981) *The Endangered Sex*, Ithaca, NY: Cornell University Press.

Moore, H. (1988) *Feminism and Anthropology*, Cambridge: Polity Press.

Palmer, I. (1991) *Gender and Population in the Adjustment of African Economies: Planning for Change*, Women, Work and Development, 19. Geneva: ILO.

Popkin, B. (1983) 'Rural women, work and child welfare in the Philippines' in M. Buvinic, M. Lycette and W. P. McGreevey (eds), *Women and Poverty in the Third World*, Baltimore, Maryland: Johns Hopkins University Press.

Roberts, P. (1988) 'Rural women's access to labour in West Africa', in S. Strichter and J. Parpart (eds) *Patriarchy and Class: African Women in the Home and the Workforce*, Boulder, Colorado: Westview.

Rosenzweig, M. R. (1986) 'Program interventions, intra-household distribution and the welfare of individuals: modelling household behaviour', *American Economic Review*, 14(2): 233–43.

Rosenzweig, M. R. and Scultz, T. P. (1982) 'Market opportunities, genetic endowments and intra-family resource distribution: child survival in rural India', *American Economic Review*, 72(4): 803–15.

Rosenzweig, M. R. and Schultz, T. P. (1984) 'Market opportunities, genetic endowments and intra-household resource distribution: reply', *American Economic Review*, 74(3): 521–22.

Schrijvers, J. (1988) 'Blueprint for undernourishment: the Mahaweli River Development Scheme in Sri Lanka', in H. Afshar and B. Agarwal (eds), *Structures of Patriarchy: The State, Community and Household in Modernizing Asia*, London: Zed Books.

Seiz, J. (1993) 'Optimization and oppression: methodological issues for feminist economics'. Paper presented at the conference *Out of the Margin. Feminist Perspectives on Economic Theory*, Amsterdam, the Netherlands.

Sen, A. K. (1990) 'Gender and cooperative conflict', in I. Tinker (ed.), *Persistent Inequalities*, Oxford: Oxford University Press.

Sen, G. and Sen, C. (1985) 'Women's domestic work and economic activity', *Economic and Political Weekly*, 20(17): 49–56.

Sen, A. K. and Sen Gupta, S. (1983) 'Malnutrition of rural Indian children and the sex bias', *Economic and Political Weekly*, 18(19–21): 855–64.

Senauer, B. (1990) 'The impact of the value of women's time on food and nutrition', in

I. Tinker (ed.), *Persistent Inequalities*, Oxford: Oxford University Press.

Sender, J. and Smith, S. (1990) *Poverty, Class and Gender in Rural Africa. A Tanzanian Case Study*, Routledge: London.

Solow, R. M. (1957) 'Technical change and the aggregate production function', *Review of Economics and Statistics*, 39: 312–20.

Strassmann, D. and Polanyi, L. (1995) 'The economist as storyteller: what the texts reveal', in E. Kuiper and J. Sap (eds), *Out of the Margin. Feminist Perspectives on Economics*, London: Routledge.

Swedberg, R. (1991) *Economics and Sociology. Redefining their Boundaries*, Oxford: Oxford University Press.

Thomas, D. (1990) 'Intra-household resource allocation: an inferential approach', *Journal of Human Resources*,. 25(4): 635–64.

Whitehead, A. (1981) '"I'm hungry, mum", The politics of domestic budgeting', in K. Young, C. Wolkowitz and R. McCullagh (eds) *Of Marriage and Market: Women's Subordination in International Perspective*, London: CSE Books.

5

FAMINE AND TRANSFORMATIONS IN GENDER RELATIONS[1]

Jocelyn Kynch

Introduction

Famine analysis and famine policy have usually been conducted without considering how famine could affect gender relations. I define gender relations to be the social constructs of how men and women behave in relation to, and in transaction with, each other, and also signifiers of power relations between men and women (Young *et al.* 1981; Gallin and Ferguson, 1991: 4–7; Kabeer, 1994: 53–67). There has been some interest in gender within the literature on household food security, coping mechanisms and food production (for example, Corbett, 1988; Lieten *et al.*, 1989; Mackintosh, 1989; Whitehead, 1990; Davies, 1993; see also Koch Laier *et al.* 1996); however, these studies do not address the central argument of this chapter: that recurrent famine events introduce long term irreversible changes in relations between men and women.

Changes in gender relations leave evidence in differentials. The gender differentials in experiences and burdens of famine are documented in some studies (for example, Kynch, 1987; Vaughan, 1987; Agarwal, 1991, 1992; Brown, 1991; Mohanty, 1992).[2] Megan Vaughan emphasises the context of famine:

> The structure of famine, and in particular the pattern of gender differentiation within it, can only be understood when set in the context of longer-term economic and social change.
>
> (1987: 124)

She also argues that gender in famine is potentially important in terms of its policy implications: 'If gender does act as an independent variable, then in the construction of famine relief policies it needs to be taken into account' (1987: 147).

The context within which famines often occur and recur is that of economic restructuring or transition. Arnold (1988: 5) refers to famines as engines of change in the historical process, emphasising their potential to drive economic, political and social change; the economist Diane Elson (1992), writing about gender and structural adjustment, indicates that there are transformational possibilities inherent in crisis. One such possibility is that famine interacts with the emerging rules and patterns of behaviour which comprise institutional innovations and, for example, alters the institutional constraints on transformations of gender relations.[3]

Interactions between famine and induced institutional innovation are of obvious relevance to the present economic restructuring in African countries.[4] Platteau (1992) argues that induced institutional innovation through private property rights is central to this restructuring. One criticism of restructuring policies is that they are bereft of awareness about new gender relations which may become inbuilt (Whitehead, 1990; Elson, 1992; Geisler and Hansen, 1994),[5] and another is that, despite a potential for women's social emancipation and added social value, women remain over-represented among 'losers' and under-represented among 'winners' as a result of structural adjustment (Aslanbeigui et al., 1994: 2; Nussbaum, 1995: 33). A third criticism relevant to both emerging gender relations and gendered trade-offs, is that the role of famine as an engine of change is disregarded, although the development and aid agenda increasingly emphasise linkages between emergency relief and development (IDS, 1994).[6]

In the last two decades, the analysis of famine has been opened up dramatically by the political economist Amartya Sen (Sen, 1977, 1981, 1984a; Dreze and Sen, 1989), who has also made considerable contributions on gender (Sen, 1985, 1990; Kynch and Sen, 1983) and on inequality (Sen, 1992, 1995). Sen's entitlement approach (Sen, 1981) developed out of a critique of the pessimistic Malthusian hypothesis that famine is a natural disaster caused by food availability decline. Instead, Sen concentrated upon the relations between people and food, and how a collapse of a substantial group's command over food precipitates famine. This framework for famine analysis invites examination of how economic transformation affects the vulnerability of certain groups to food entitlement collapse (Sen, 1981: 173).

In order to understand how famine may affect gender relations in the context of socio-economic transformation, I shall consider what we may learn from the famine period between 1880 and 1920 in British India. Could famine, in interaction with famine relief policies, have distorted or levered changes in gender relations?

With Maureen Sibbons, I am investigating district data from British India between 1880 and 1940.[7] Coincidentally, 1880 was the year of publication of the Famine Commission Report upon which the Famine Codes (now Scarcity Codes) were based (Kynch, 1987; Dreze, 1988; Dreze and Sen, 1989: 122–6; Walker, 1989: 101–9). There were recurrent famines between 1880 and 1920 in many of the districts for which we have data.[8] This famine period was followed by a twenty-year period without widespread major famine, which was ended by the Bengal Famine in the early 1940s (for different interpretations, see Kynch and Sibbons, 1993; Patnaik, 1992).

The data (economic, public health, judicial) allow us to test for possible changes in outcomes of gender relations, such as: that excess mortality became more characteristic in certain age and gender groups; that 'coping strategies' became decisively gendered during famine; that 'unacceptable strategies' became part of quasi-legal gender relations; that new institutional 'fallback' positions emerged; that famine policies had implications for gender bias.

Before looking at some evidence, I shall first outline a simple model of how famines could alter gender relations. I shall then review advantages to be gained from using an entitlement approach for analysis of gender in famine, because it offers a methodology based upon disaggregation of people into groups, and also because food entitlement is affected by the institutional context (spatial and temporal). However, the entitlement approach to famine has limitations with respect to dynamic socio-economic relations such as gender, and I consider how a wider analytical framework (Sen, 1984b: 496–500, 520–9; Dreze and Sen, 1989: 9–14; Agarwal, 1991, 1992) may take us further.

Next I shall consider evidence from India in three parts. The policy environment of changing gender relations is the first part, in which the discourses about famine relief policy (especially the changes in access given to women), public health and epidemics, and how they brought about constraints on transformations, are considered. I argue that the recurrent famines around the turn of the century were a turning point in women's agency and perceived advantage in adopting a reproductive role in India. The second part offers evidence on gender and mortality in selected British Indian districts between 1880 and 1940, concluding that the gender impact of famine which most affected gender relations was upon young adults. In the third present-day nutritional outcomes in one of the districts illustrate that institutional constraints on gender relations have outcomes which are dysfunctional and inefficient. This chapter therefore supports the critique of the 'new institutional economics' that institutions need not be functional or efficient (Sen, 1990; Folbre, 1994; Bardhan, 1989; Vanberg, 1994).

Developing an approach to gender and famine

Figure 5.1 is one possible illustration of how famine events could exert 'leverage' on transformations in gender relations. Famine is occurring during a process of partly exogenous economic change, itself causally related to the incidence of famine. One set of gender relations (G_0) is evolving towards another set (G_1).[9]

G_0 represents the sum of possible gender relations within the socio-economic structure. The limits of G_0 are that any set of gender relations will fall within the dominant norms. The relations are realised as specific male–female roles in, for example, the gender divisions of labour, and male–female outcomes in, for example, human growth and health, longevity, education, participation. Observers of a set of gender relations may, of course, disagree about the wider injustice of either the relations or their outcomes – for example, if extreme sex-bias or brutality occurs.

G_s are gender relations in coping or survival strategies which people adopt during crises. These overlap with G_0 because they include both coping behaviours within the prevailing rules, and some survival strategies which cannot be

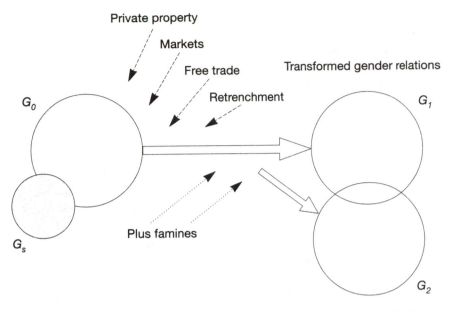

Figure 5.1   A model of famine leverage on gender relations

accommodated within the dominant norms of the socio-economic structure. These latter are represented by the shaded area, and it is my argument that famine strategies, as a sub-group of survival strategies, frequently fall into this area. Disapproval is shared by the actors but not necessarily by outsiders. For example, gender roles including women's independent access to the labour market may be regarded by outsiders (including development experts) as a positive influence on well-being even if disapproved locally; abandonment of dependants or exclusion is often regarded as negative as well as being disapproved. A problem for relief and development agents is whether to support local gendered strategies or not.

It is interesting to consider whether G_0 (or G_s) falls within the other rules and behaviours of societies, or what is sometimes referred to as the fundamental institutions of property and constitutional rights of individuals. A mismatch would cause disputes and tension, and therefore result in evolution or adaptation.

The transformation of G_0 to G_1 is affected by other processes as well as the structure of property relations; for example, economic restructuring, retrenchment by the state, the penetration of markets, individuation. Examples of these multiple, and partly exogenous, economic forces occurring together with famines are found in Africa since the 1980s, and in India around the turn of the century – both continents have experience of recurrent famine and induced innovation (Platteau, 1992; Bhatia, 1967; Kumar, 1982). One interpretation of the importance of social as well as economic institutional innovation in structural adjustment is that a

111

process of social institutionalisation counteracts the instability induced by structural adjustment towards a global economy.

What happens when famine occurs? Some people survive by behaving in ways that are so abnormal that they incur high social costs. If this occurs, and they gain an advantage in terms of survival or household reproduction even when incurring social disapproval or exclusion, then it is possible for a small discrete shift in the transformation of G_0 to occur. If famine recurs, then a 'memory' of gain or loss reinforces the shift, and in the long term exerts leverage on gender relations. In Figure 5.1 this is shown by G_2. G_2 is a famine-levered version of G_1, the latter being the evolved socially valued gender relations. Simultaneously, relief policy is interactive with famine leverage and can reduce or capture its impact. The gender relations in G_0, G_1 or G_2 are different, but if we wish to rank them, the exercise requires a constructive critique of inegalitarian norms which can meet strong cultural opposition (see, for example, Okin, 1995).

In this chapter I shall examine gender roles and their outcomes (for example, in selective excess mortality) in order to establish whether there is evidence that recurrent famines in British India exerted leverage, and shall also consider the embedding of gender bias in policy.

The entitlement approach and gender

Attention to the specific economic, social and political context of famine is a well recognised strength of the entitlement approach (Vaughan, 1987). The entitlement approach to famine analysis applies to essentially economic, legal, preventable, events.[10]

Sen argues that famines are essentially economic in their causes: it is the collapse in food entitlements of a substantial number of people in an occupation group, in particular in their exchange entitlement, which precipitates famine. For example, the rural labourers in Bengal 1943 and Bangladesh in 1974, farmers in Wollo in 1973, and pastoralists in Harerghe in 1974, suffered exchange entitlement shifts (Sen, 1981: 163). The important divisions upon which the entitlement approach rests are economic.

'Famines', Sen (1991) writes, 'are divisive phenomena'. They affect a small proportion (5 to 10 per cent) of the population and concern 'power to command food on the part of particular occupation groups . . . Divisiveness has two aspects – economic and political. The *immediate links of famines are with economic divisions*' (Sen, 1991: 6, added emphasis). Sen is here writing about war and famines, and he goes on to consider the political and legal moderations or corrections of divisiveness.

In analysing a famine, we should first identify the vulnerable occupation group or groups. Gender divisions will, of course, affect some of these; for example, as Agarwal (1991) points out, paddy husking was one of the worst-affected occupations in Bengal in 1943 and women were doubly hit: first they lost a traditional 'fallback' occupation when displaced by destitute agricultural labourers, and secondly their earnings were depressed by the increased entrants.[11]

Applications of the entitlement approach have often concentrated too exclusively on the production unit which tends to be delineated by the men and asset ownership. There is a pragmatic reason, which Dreze and Sen summarise when they write that *currently*, because famines are occurring in Sub-Saharan Africa, discrimination 'only supplements in a relatively small way the enormous destructive forces that come into play in African famines' (1989: 56). This is a powerful point, but need not deter us from asking about the impact of famine on gender relations, especially if these may influence non-famine gender relations.

The entitlement approach actually invites consideration of alternative aggregations of individuals, and draws attention to the discriminatory impact of famine on social groups (Arnold, 1988). We should expect discriminatory impact if men and women experience famine differently (Vaughan, 1987; Arnold, 1988: 86–91; Dreze and Sen, 1989: 55–6; Brown, 1991; Agarwal, 1992). In her analysis of famine in Malawi, Vaughan (1987) suggests that women did indeed experience famine differently, and that weak external links to other ecological zones and to the labour market were a source of some women's greater vulnerability relative to men (see also Mohanty, 1992).

Individuation specially affects women. During famine, Vaughan (1987: 124) argues, 'The scarcer the food, the smaller became the units of consumption. Beyond a certain point the advantages of co-residence with kin ceased to be so apparent, and women were left increasingly dependent on their husbands (if they had any) or themselves.' Furthermore, famine may reinforce other processes of individuation which are already taking place within households, and expose intrahousehold relations: as Agarwal (1992: 192) writes about the disintegrating family: 'Famine poses in the most stark terms the economic and moral dilemmas relating to intrahousehold food sharing and mirrors intrafamily relations that few other contexts can.'

In Bengal in British India, Agarwal argues that it was a husband who was likely to eject his spouse (Agarwal, 1991: 173–4). The outcomes of individuation depend upon gender relations, and in both Africa and India an important food entitlement of women is through dependency on husband or kin. Protection for women through raising consumption by food doles fails to challenge their weak links to non-household employment or dependency upon men.

Therefore, although the cause of famine is the collapse of food entitlement of an occupation group, aversion or relief policy needs to protect the entitlements of the individual or social groups, and not just the production units of an occupation group.[12]

A second aspect of Sen's entitlement approach is its legal framework – the approach is usually developed within a dominant private property framework (Sen, 1981: 2–3). This poses problems of male bias in visibility in reports and records. Breman and Daniel concur that many women labourers existed invisibly in the countryside, and discuss the notion of the female coolie as 'incomplete' and immoral, or at best as a woman labourer 'perennially on trial' (1992: 283–8; see also Kynch, 1987). Labour regulations reinforced women's invisibility and restricted access to public space (Kumar in Krishnamurty, 1989: 148; Kynch and Sibbons, forthcoming), and constrained participation in decisions about entitlement.

Analytically, Gasper (1993) points out that it is not always clear how the approach can be legitimately extended. Further, the role of violence in engendering responses to famine, such as different migration patterns of young men and women, may be underestimated (Keen, 1994: 87–9; see also de Waal, 1989). Many gender relations fall into the quasi-legal rather than legal domain, and furthermore may not be respected even if legally attainable.

Sen developed his conceptual framework for the analysis of gender (Sen, 1990, 1995) going beyond the entitlement approach. Indeed, he argues that entitlements, which are about commodities, are only 'instrumentally important' in addressing the primary concern with sex bias in capabilities – what a person can be, or do. Gender divisions are the outcomes of cooperative conflicts. Cooperative conflict is 'the presence of strong elements of conflict embedded in a situation in which there are mutual gains to be made by cooperation' and is 'endemic in social relations' and 'a pervasive feature of social living' (Dreze and Sen, 1989: 48–9). Three important factors affect the outcome of a cooperative conflict: the 'fallback' or 'breakdown' position of the person if cooperation fails; the perception of a person's contribution, and their agency. These are central to the cooperative conflicts which affect the well-being of women, and which Kabeer (1991, 1994) takes as a starting point for household analysis.

Agarwal's (1991, 1992) innovative exploration of extended entitlements within a bargaining approach to gender in households offers insights on famine and gender. Agarwal extends the entitlement framework to include common property resources and social support systems of patronage, kinship and friendship. Famine involves stretching and breaking social security mechanisms which typically burden and benefit men and women differently, and this involves a rupturing of the 'moral economy'. The definition of legality in these extensions is complex.[13]

The third aspect of Sen's work which is relevant to an entitlement approach to gender and famine is that famine is conceptualised as an event rather than a process (Curry, 1992). Watts (1991), drawing on Rangasami's (1985) and de Waal's (1989) criticisms, argues that entitlement approaches have neglected both '"forces" of deepening intensity' in a hunger process and the 'architecture of responses to famine' (1991: 17–20). The research into relief and development (IDS, 1994) is concerned with famine as process. Dreze and Sen (1989) address this through the distinction between protection and promotion of food entitlement, and emphasise the linkages (and feedbacks) between protection and promotion of food entitlement: short term, famine aversion is about protection.

Much of the analysis of gender and hunger has emphasised hunger processes and a continuum of 'coping strategies' which stretch to 'famine' strategies for some people even in normal times, in seasonal food shortages or in micro-famines (Watts, 1983, 1991; Rangasami, 1985; Corbett, 1988; Ryan 1990; Maxwell, 1991; Beneria and Feldman, 1992). This literature suggests a sequencing of strategies with the severity of crisis, commitment of domestic resources, increasing social costs and irreversibility of the outcomes of 'famine' strategies, and informs, for example, Osmani's (1995) argument that there are long-run irreversible consequences of famine, which pertain to the endowment set of the household, nutritional status of the individual, structure of the family and structure of the moral economy (1995: 33). However, it is unclear that 'famine' strategies belong in a continuum, or if they are as legitimate or institutional as other strategies.

Davies (1993) develops an alternative and more complex analysis which challenges this consensus on sequential responses when repeated shocks occur to a transitional economy, and draws distinctions between *coping* (a 'short-term response to an immediate and inhabitual decline in access to food') and *adapting* ('a permanent change in the mix of ways in which food is acquired'), and between coping within existing rules and adapting the rules themselves (1993: 378–9).

In fact, many of the terms used in describing famine refer to exceptions, rule-waiving and negotiation of abnormal conduct. For example, on relief works in India, it was reported that *rules were waived* by *some* engineers who were in charge, in order to allow pregnant women to receive a higher digger's wage. *Some* police tended to be *tolerant* of petty thieving by local people during famine, but arrested migrants for trespass (for which *some* magistrates gave the emaciated a sentence of flogging) (Kynch, 1987, 1988). Prostitution was *shocking* but tolerable.[14] Gore (1993) argues that even coping strategies are pursued under an existing set of rules which may have to be confronted and negotiated. We could say that the discourse between authorities and people over famine strategies and relief is around a line – which I depicted in Figure 5.1 as the crossing into the shaded area of G_s. The depiction of a continuum is untenable if there is a break between coping and famine strategies.

In British Indian provinces, it can be shown that there were empirical distinctions between famine and other times (which include 'normal' and 'hardship' periods (Kynch, 1988; Kynch and Sibbons, 1995)). Famine and hardships are ranked in a descending order of severity as famine, economic distress, epidemics and scarcity. The significant indicators of famine also had strong regional associations – not unlike sex or female mortality ratios (Kynch and Sen, 1983; Kishor, 1993). In some provinces of British India the dominant types of indicators were price or wage entitlement to food (Bengal, Central Provinces), in others age-specific or urban death rates (Punjab, Bombay, Madras) often with evidence of migration or increased admission to jail. These regional indicators are reminders that famine leverage will have a region-specific content. With respect to women, access to employment and property, support of kin or seclusion differ provincially and this will affect transformations or leverage of gender relations.

In summary, the entitlement approach has benefits in understanding the institutional context of famine, but also some limitations with respect to gender. The approach is useful in understanding people's current relation to food, but not necessarily predictive of the longer-term consequences of particular entitlement protection policies. In encompassing gender relations, the framework of

115

capabilities and cooperative conflicts will take us beyond the economic emphasis of the entitlement approach to famine. The problem of whether famine relief should go beyond entitlement protection, and consider the effects of famine strategies or famine relief operations on capabilities, is illustrated by British Indian policies in the famine period.

Colonial policy background to gender relations

I shall now look at key elements in the policy environment of gender relations in north and central British India, which influenced or reinforced famine leverage on gender relations. Two policy areas were of particular importance: famine relief, the principles of which were laid down in the Indian Famine Commission Report 1880, and public health which covered the monitoring and policies on the condition of the people and epidemics. Famines and epidemics were often conflated, and the most vulnerable groups were required to enter public spaces where they were affected by public policy.

Dreze (1988) argues that certain essentials of the Famine Commission's analysis in 1880 were similar to the entitlement approach, and that the successes in averting famine rest upon the extent of correct analysis. The central strategy was provision of unskilled manual employment at subsistence wages for all the able-bodied who came to public works, complemented by gratuitous relief – discretionary charitable doles – to those unable to work. As far as gender relations were concerned, this strategy was potentially innovatory, for relief work was, theoretically, available to individuals at rates determined by the price of staple cereals. Furthermore, contract work and piece-work were initially proscribed because of their discriminatory effects upon women and upon weak or inefficient workers (Kynch, forthcoming).

In principle, able-bodied women were only differentiated from men by a sex-distinction in tasks: the tests of need were self-acting on relief works, and the efficacy of the test of manual work has remained robust (Dreze, 1988: 31). However, *purdanishin* women were one of the categories exempted from self-presentation on works (special classes included village servants, weavers and the 'respectable proud'), and were selectively given spinning or other piece-work in their homes. Purdah was not challenged in the principles of famine relief, but the meaning of the social institution became more secular and widely spread. Occupational purdah (Chen, 1995) is now broader than the category of respectable *purdanishin* to be relieved by home-working in the Famine Codes.

The principle of giving women individual access to relief employment was an important innovation, the implications of which would have been far-reaching, had it also been incorporated in the emerging labour markets. As I argue below, this innovation was never completely implemented or built upon, because British and Indian men began to undermine its practice in the famines of the 1890s and 1900s. Nevertheless, in spite of its unpopularity, there is some evidence that the principle of treating able-bodied women as individual wage-earners in relief employment had some impacts, both in terms of the relative wages of men and women, and upon the demand for relief work. The principle of individualised tasks and wages on relief works had a measurable impact on relative wages. Although famine relief wages were often low, the relative wages of men and women were at least as favourable, and often more equal, than those on non-relief work (Kynch, 1987: 140). It is difficult to assess if more equal wages increased the likelihood of women presenting themselves at relief works, because individualised task and payment systems were widely opposed, as I argue below. The Famine Commission of 1880 (para. 133) expected that women would present themselves on relief works in large numbers, on the basis of past famine experience: for example, percentages of men: women: children were reported as 42: 47: 11 (Moradabad poorhouse employment 1860–1), 25: 50: 25 (Bijnor relief gangs 1869), women made up three-quarters of workers in Jhansie in 1869, and commonly half of relief workers in Madras in 1877. Under the Famine Codes, women remained the largest group of workers, with an average relief gang having 43 per cent women (Bengal 1896–7), women making up 45 per cent of relief workers in United Provinces (1907), 50 per cent (United Provinces 1913–14) and 70 per cent in Bihar and Orissa (1916–17).[15] The persistence of a high proportion of women workers on relief was evidence of the burden of famine.

It is curious that this high proportion of women has left little memory trace (see, for example, Chen, 1995). One reason is that the innovation of individual women's access to employment did not fall within the dominant norms of gender relations. At the time, both policy administrators and labourers were pragmatic in their opposition to individual women's control of access to, and payment for, relief work. In practice, tasks were often set and payments were made for gangs, frequently based on familial groups because this smoothed and lowered supervision costs. Some works supervisors refused to allow women on works, except as dependants. The negotiation and exceptions noted on p.114 indicated humanitarian concern and not empowerment. The disparity between principle and practice was not widely challenged because policy increasingly favoured cost-effective reduction of famine mortality as a criterion of good relief organisation (Bhatia, 1967: 271–2; Kynch, forthcoming). A summary of criteria and indicators of successful relief operations by the turn of the century is shown in Figure 5.2. In the pursuit of cost-effective relief, discourses between famine administrators, relief works organisers, professional labour and respectable Indian society harmonised social prejudices against women working independently outside the home, especially for higher wages. For example, the report on famine in Bengal 1896–7 claimed that 'the methods adopted for relieving distress, the cost, and in a large degree the moral effects on the people' had greatly improved. The operation was certainly leaner and fitter, and was argued to release public funds for development of roads, railways, irrigation and conservancy.

After the extremely cheap famine operations of 1896–7 and 1899–1900, the 1901 Famine Code shifted relief from individuals to the 'family'. The argument was that it was the 'custom' for male workers to earn and for the family to be dependent. It was also cheaper because it prevented dual-earning units. The bar-

---

Prevent deaths from starvation
(no or few reported deaths from starvation)

Saving of human life (at reasonable cost)
(no increase in mortality;
estimated costs of relief not exceeded;
self-acting test of distress and enforcement of task)

No government interference with free trade
(no government import, or ban on export, of grains etc.,
information or advances to help private trade)

Work to be of permanent utility
(conversion of existing District Board works; completion)

Relief of employment works not to compete with private works
(restrict wages; loans and grants to individuals)

Bold = criterion; *italics = indicators or actions*

Figure 5.2   Criteria for famine relief operations

riers against women workers on relief works were now confirmed. The more equal wages available on relief works (and absence of piece-work) were also said to be not 'customary'. The provincial Famine Codes thus became more sensitive to local institutions, and brutally safeguarded society against state sponsorship of women controlling their own labour even as a survival strategy. Contemporary documents acknowledge the trade-off between more economical relief and disadvantaging women and the weak (Indian Famine Commission 1880: para. 133; Government of Bengal 1898: 45; various Famine Codes; Kynch, forthcoming). The blatant contradiction between avoiding the dependency of men (Hall-Matthews, forthcoming), but exhorting that of women remained unremarked.

Turning now to public health, the Sanitary Commissioners (from 1919 Directors of Public Health), who were the officials responsible for public health, became increasingly concerned at female ill-health and welfare. Some engaged in a dialogue about poverty, famine, health and economic well-being with Governors who praised their diligence but often wished they would write at less length and keep to their terms of reference. Gradually, an identification of women's health with fertility concerns replaced the wider investigations. Even as late as the 1920s, Commissioners viewed population falls as lamentable and symptomatic of economic and social decline, and associated rises with economic welfare.[16] However, concern at persistent female illhealth combined with the emergence of the eugenics movement to redefine high fertility as a problem and female illhealth as reproductive illhealth. From the turn of the century, public health measures included the introduction of lady health visitors, training of midwives and maternal and child welfare clinics. Voluntarist organisations and legal restrictions on women's work helped reinforce the perception of women as primarily reproductive.

The Sanitary Commissioners oversaw the control of epidemics, which were a major cause of famine mortality. Sibbons (1995) considers the conflation of famine and cholera epidemics. She argues that

> cholera was a disease which affected certain groups of people at particular times: the poor throughout India particularly at times of famine or scarcity and in relation to their migration in search of work or food, with subsequent crowding into relief camps or urban areas; the poor during economic transition and in response to the labour market signals; . . . other large social gatherings; and British troops during the earlier period in cholera's dissemination throughout India.
>
> (1995: 1)

Gender roles – in this case men's behaviour when searching for work or markets – increased men's exposure to infection (Sibbons, 1995: 21–7). However, blame fell upon individuals labelled as 'cultural others', rather than on the insanitary conditions in which they gathered together or lived.[17]

Plague, which arrived in 1896 and spread through north India, was termed a 'disease of the home', being associated with women's domestic tasks such as grain preparation. Some measures against villagers were extraordinarily harsh and harshly implemented: these included evacuation, exclusion and forced disinfection and decontamination. Relative to men, mortality of females from both plague and influenza, but not usually from cholera, was high. The extreme was in Punjab, where the Punjab Sanitary Commissioner's Report of 1901 records 40–60 per cent excess female deaths over male deaths from plague, but only 1 per cent excess from all causes. By 1907, this plague excess was reduced to 15 per cent. On the one hand, the Sanitary Commissioner in the Punjab emphasised the limits of compulsory measures and the need for measures to be acceptable to the people. In 1912 and 1913, the Lieutenant-Governor of Punjab remarked that the treatment of other sicknesses by plague staff was popular and was 'bringing them in closer touch with the people'. This quickly changed in 1914 to 'the ultimate solution of the plague problem seems to be the education of women in domestic hygiene'. On the other hand, it was acknowledged that, even before being targeted with domestic hygiene education, women seemed to have learned 'by bitter experience to take better care in protecting themselves' in the first decade of plague in Punjab (Sanitary Commissioner's Report of 1905), and the fall in the preponderance of female mortality was not attributed to policy.

Famines and associated epidemics forced people into survival strategies to which policy responded within a broadly free market framework (see Figure 5.2). However, policy also embedded perceptions of 'custom' in the emerging British Indian policy and institutional framework, constraining the possibility of rural women gaining control of their own labour or opportunities outside reproduction. This is a tale of lost opportunities for poor men, too, because their entrenched provisioning role constrained their health and activity.

In fact, famine relief operations captured malevolent aspects of gender in famine survival strategies during a period of socio-economic transformation: introducing a new form of labour, piece-work in purdah, reducing destitute women of 'lower class' to greater dependency on men in emerging labour markets. The public policy response to epidemics reinforced women's caring role in 'healthy' households, but subordinated their knowledge to that of outside experts.

Gender and mortality in some British Indian districts

The first objective of famine relief policy was the minimisation of starvation deaths (see Figure 5.2 on p.118). Death from starvation is notoriously difficult to authenticate, but patterns of deaths during famine, whatever the proximate cause, reveal the burdens of the crisis in their starkest form.[18] What are the general features of gender and deaths, and can we relate these to the occurrence of famine?

I have looked at 22 districts of Punjab, Bombay, Central Provinces (as in Sibbons, 1995), together with a district of western United Provinces (Moradabad, see below) in order to evaluate mortality with respect to famine.

First, taking the total of 1,239 district years between 1880 and 1940 in which data were available, the distribution of mortality between males and females remains very constant. The mean value of the percentage of female deaths in the total deaths in the population in each district year was 47.9 per cent (standard deviation 1.65), and there were no remarkable 'outliers' (no standard deviation or Z-score, was greater than +/–3). There was just one Z-score value of over 2, in the influenza-distressed year of 1918. Three-quarters of the district-year proportion of female deaths were between 47 and 49 per cent (see also FDEAD column in Table 5.1). We therefore have evidence of an overall constancy of the proportion of reported male or female deaths – and this confirms Sen's observations about the proportions being exaggerated uniformly across sexes during the Bengal famine (Sen, 1981).

There is, however, a tendency for deviations from the trend line to become more frequently positive after 1900, except in distress years such as 1905 and 1920–2. In part, this could be because registration of female deaths improved. However, it is not a sufficient explanation: indeed, it was used at the time to explain both high and low deaths.

What happens when we consider selected age groups? Some of the results, together with total deaths, are shown in Table 5.1. The numbers of male deaths in each district were roughly 12–15,000, and it can be seen from looking at the lower half of the table that the absolute differences (F–M) were often small numbers for young adults: this is to be expected since young adults normally have low mortality rates.

As Table 5.1 suggests, the proportion of infant and old female deaths was gen-

120

Table 5.1 Percentage of female deaths to total deaths, and number of excess female deaths in selected districts of Punjab, Bombay and Central Provinces in British India

Province	All deaths FDEAD (%)	Infants INFFDEAD (%)	Young adult YWDEAD (%)	Old OWDEAD (%)
Punjab	47.7	47.6	50.8	45.8
Bombay	48.6	47.7	54.0	49.2
Central Provinces	47.2	46.9	50.9	49.3
	(F–M)	*(F–M)*	*(F–M)*	*(F–M)*
Punjab	–1028	–489	+ 46	–522
Bombay	– 748	–511	+197	– 74
Central Provinces	–1428	–780	+ 16	– 43

Source: Author's data extracted from Sanitary Commissioner/Director of Public Health Reports, 1880–1940

Note: FDEAD number of female deaths relative to total deaths; INFFDEAD number of female infants dead relative to all infant deaths (ages 0–4); YWDEAD number of young women dead relative to all young adult deaths (ages 20–30); OWDEAD number of old women dead relative to all old people's deaths (ages 50 plus); (F–M) excess (+) or deficit (–) of female deaths per district year.

erally lower than young women's deaths. Overall, the proportions were: infant females (INFFDEAD) 47.50 per cent (standard deviation 1.76, 1,173 district years); young women (YWDEAD) 52.12 per cent (sd 4.12, 1,184 district years); old women (OWDEAD) 48.07 per cent (sd 3.10, 1182 district years). We need to bear in mind that absolute numbers of deaths of young people and the old were smaller than those for infants. Nevertheless, there does appear to be a valid question about whether young women suffered higher and more variable mortality relative to men than was the case for other age groups. In the districts and years which I am considering here, three-quarters of values of YWDEAD lay between 49.4 and 57.3 per cent – a wide range of 8 per cent.

Agarwal (1991, 1992) suggests that, by the time of the 1943 Bengal famine, women's bargaining position was crucially undermined in the childbearing ages because of a lack of a fallback position outside the family. In distress, childbearing women were the group most at risk of being actively abandonned. The evidence of mortality across northern India is that childbearing women were a group at risk, but we need to look more closely at household bargaining and fallbacks in each district to ascertain how this came about.

Other factors would undermine young women's agency to alter their weak position. For example, there is evidence of fall in births early in a famine, the explanation of which is very under-researched. It could be because men or women reject pregnancy (for example by induced miscarriage, abortion or abstinence) or because women do not become pregnant (for example, amenorrhoea). In either case, young women's immediate value as childbearers is sharply reduced.

Relating a bargaining approach to mortality of young women in famine is complex. First, we have to consider the availability of a fallback in terms of access to common property resources, state transfers or relief and opportunities to migrate to towns, relief works or other kin. Second, we have to look at advantages and disadvantages from the reduced birthrates associated with famine. We also have to look at the districts' particular institutions which affected food entitlement in order to decide how the fallback position could influence a 'switch' towards behaviours such as abandonment or deliberate neglect which would normally carry social costs.

Finally, there is strong evidence that bias against women in general was regional in nature – and is today (Kishor, 1993). At the extremes, in Punjab over half (53 per cent) of all episodes of surplus deaths over births, which were not necessarily in famine years, were also biased against females, while in Central Provinces there was very little bias (6 per cent of episodes) (Kynch and Sibbons, 1993).

To summarise, in the 22 districts of Punjab, Central Provinces and Bombay, the proportion of young women's deaths (YWDEAD) was over half of all young deaths between 1880 and 1940. These years cover a famine period (up to 1920) and a non-famine period (1920–40). Taking our argument further, if we are to investigate the possibility that the situation changed for young women during the period of recurrent famine, then we should look for significant differences between the two periods.

For example, the decade of 1890–1900 was one of widespread economic distress and included two famines in 1896–7 and 1899–1900 which covered Bombay, Central Provinces and Punjab. By contrast, 1920–30 was characterised by retrenchment and political activity, with distress being much more localised.

Although the proportion of total female deaths remained similar in both decades, (47.6 per cent in the 1890's, 47.8 per cent in the 1920s), the proportion of young women's deaths rose significantly (51.1 per cent, 53.7 per cent). There are several possible reasons for this: first, the change in the pattern and severity of epidemics has been used to argue that the burden of famine fell most heavily upon men. As noted earlier, cholera was associated with famine and with higher male deaths (data on case mortality or age incidence by sex are not available). Plague and influenza were associated with higher female deaths in later famines. For each disease, however, the distribution of deaths during famines is better explained by the abnormal behaviour of men and women – in relation to employment search and to domestic work – than by biological sex differences. Selective aspects of behaviour in famine, especially the aimless wandering of men which threatened social disorder but also brought risks of disease, were reduced by relief operations. The relief operations effectively reduced the epidemic deaths of men, but in ways which were consistent with gendered behaviour and roles which further constrained women.

A second reason could be that the socio-economic transformations towards a market economy, or modern India (Sarkar, 1983), which increased the vulnerability of agricultural labour to food entitlement collapse in the famine period, thereafter contributed to improved standards of living, better nutrition, and a fall in mortality. This was the expectation of cost-effective relief (see Figure 5.2). However, famine and relief operations may have increased the rigidity of gender divisions and gender roles towards provisioning-reproductive, as I have suggested, which relatively increased risks to reproductive women. An example from present-day India is now given.

Gender outcomes in present-day agricultural households

I begin with some conclusions which I reached from a study of nutritional outcomes of agricultural households in a village in Moradabad district of western Uttar Pradesh (Kynch, 1994). As in most of northern India, gender divisions were rigid: they could be interpreted as a bargain between male provisioners who were the producers, and female reproducers with limited decision-making power (Kabeer, 1991). The outcomes can be summarised as follows:

1   Men (especially in childbearing couples) were so wasted that they risked ill-health and arguably poor ability to work.
2   Women were so stunted that they risked reproductive failure (higher risk of underweight babies and maternal depletion syndrome).
3   There was cumulative evidence of bias in the growth of very young girls.

Wasting refers to thinness or the effects of acute hunger. Stunting refers to the failure to achieve potential growth, or the effects of chronic hunger in childhood. The risks and the seriousness of risks from wasting and stunting vary across different age groups and with activity, and are difficult to compare (see Kynch, 1994 for details).

In a poor environment, and if we assume that the village has a local normative idea of good nutrition based upon appearance or degree of wasting, the evidence pointed towards a prioritisation of reproduction over production. In village terms, whether these met international reference standards or not, children and child-bearing women were protected relative to men in the agricultural households. This does not imply that any individual's needs were met.

Indeed, the results were worrying. While it has been argued that very wasted people can carry out agricultural tasks satisfactorily, they still risk being ill, and arguably lose potential to do different or non-farm work – we can say that the agriculturalists were inefficient producers. The women's stunting makes them inefficient childbearers, and female children suffered poor growth (ACC/SCN, 1994).

In north India, women are more vulnerable to poverty in the absence of a fit adult male than men are in the absence of a fit adult female (Dreze, 1990). Also, survivors in a household without adult sons are at risk of 'substantial economic decline' (Cain, 1986). In Palanpur, it was in the interests of men (in order to avoid expenditure and ensure the household's future) and women (to secure access to commodities) to avoid reproductive failure and to protect the growth of boys. Concerning the latter, given the general poor environment into which stunted women are more likely to bear low-birthweight babies needing to catch up on growth, passive neglect of catch-up in baby girls could be sufficient to make the gendered nutritional outcomes sustainable.[19]

The behaviour which relates to nutritional outcomes in Palanpur is strongly institutional: that is, having rules of behaviour and social interaction which society values (see Bardhan, 1989; Fowler, 1992). Bardhan writes: 'Institutions are the social rules, conventions, and other elements of the structural framework of social interaction' (1989: 3), while Fowler (1992: 14) attempts to clarify a confused area: 'Institutions are stable patterns of behaviour that are recognised and valued by society' and quotes Uphoff: 'Institutions, whether organisations or not, *are complexes of norms and behaviours that persist over time by serving collectively valued purposes*' (emphasis in original). The rules can be deduced from behavioural routines: there is a village standard of thinness which households should observe for all members, that children should be less thin than adults, that the growth of boys should be protected. It is an institution with dysfunctional outcomes for efficient production and reproduction in a poor village environment. Indeed, if the surface of social approval is scratched, the outcomes are obviously also regarded by villagers as unpleasant (Jeffery *et al.*, 1989: Appendix 1; Kynch 1994: 37). Earlier I suggested that recurrent famine was a turning point which entrenched or embedded these behaviours within the structure of social interaction in north India.

Table 5.2 Deaths in famine years, Moradabad district

| Year | | All deaths | | Young adults |
	(F–M)	%FDEAD	(F–M)	%YWDEAD
1896	– 3909	46	– 212	47
1897	– 1785	48	+ 24	50
1905	+ 133	50	+ 381	55
1907	+ 1609	51	+ 584	55
1908	+ 838	51	+ 301	53
1913	– 3472	46	– 267	46
1914	– 3887	47	– 397	46
1918	+ 898	51	+1353	55
1919	– 2625	47	+ 53	51
1929	– 1066	49	+ 406	58
1930	– 719	49	+ 617	61

Source: Author's data extracted from Sanitary Commissioner/Director of Public Health Reports for United Provinces

Note: FDEAD number of female deaths relative to total deaths; INFFDEAD number of female infants dead relative to all infant deaths (ages 0–4); YWDEAD number of young women dead relative to all young adult deaths (ages 20–30); OWDEAD number of old women dead relative to all old people's deaths (ages 50 plus); (F–M) excess (+) or deficit (–) of female deaths per district year.

The district of Moradabad was affected by famine in the years 1896–7, 1905–7, 1913–14, 1918–19 and 1929–30 – there were also scarcities. The reported deaths in these years by excess of female and proportion of female deaths, are shown in Table 5.2. In general, males suffered higher numbers of deaths than females in famines. An excess of female deaths was recorded only in 1905–8 (famine and distress, plague) and 1918 (influenza epidemic). Bhatia (1967: 268–9) praises the relief of the 1907–8 famine in the United Provinces, but this operation coincided with excess female deaths in Moradabad. Provincially high demand for labour and rising wages existed, so that only the weak or disabled needed public help (1967: 277).

Data on annual deaths from the whole period indicate a slight upward drift of the percentage of registered female deaths in total deaths over time ($R^2 = 0.24$, significance 90 per cent). The proportions of infant and old female deaths remain, like female proportion of total deaths, remarkably constant.

In the case of young adults, the picture is quite different. The upward trend of the percentage of deaths of young women (aged 20–30) to all young people's deaths is strong ($R^2 = 0.57$) and highly significant (99.99 per cent).[20] Furthermore, as Table 5.2 illustrates, this was the only age group in which female deaths regularly exceeded male in famine years or showed a significant trend over time. This is consistent with the argument above (pp.120–1).

The exception of the famine of 1913–14, however, requires explanation. The Government of United Provinces' *Final Report on Working of the Famine Relief Operations in United Provinces of Agra and Oudh for the Years 1913 and 1914* shows that in 1913 and 1914 Moradabad suffered from drought, and that crop outturns were down to one-third of normal; there was also a fodder shortage and cattle were given relief. Parts of Moradabad were famine-affected and 0.6 per cent of the population relieved on village government-aided works. Low-caste labourers were joined, reluctantly, by Muslims and higher castes together with women, especially widows. Gratuitous relief was given early and was 'intentionally generous'. In the wider region, women made up 50 per cent of building and road workers, and 49 per cent of irrigation workers, and the woman's task was raised to three-quarters of the man's (because women were said to be as sturdy as men). Women were reported to be sent to the works while men migrated or stayed in villages to keep cattle alive. It is sometimes argued that if women increase their workload, children may suffer. In most two-year famines in Moradabad, child mortality rose, and more unusually in 1897 and 1908, females were reported dead more often than males in the 0–1 and 1–5-year age groups, but this did not occur in 1913–14. In terms of mortality, and relief working, these appear to be exceptional years, after which entrenched deaths of young women continued to dominate. There is no evidence that men lost control of their cattle or their women.

Discussion and conclusions

I have examined some evidence on outcomes of gender relations and the potential of famine to affect transformations of gender relations. Famine was presented as a cause of leverage on transformations: first, because of the existence of famine strategies which tend to fall outside the dominant norms of behaviour (in Figure 5.1, within G_s but outside G_0) unlike coping strategies (within both G_s and G_0); second, because famine strategies become, through recurrence, embedded in new norms of gender relations (G_2).

The relations of poor men and women to food – or their food entitlements – can be differentiated primarily by linkages to the labour market and by the degree of individual control, specifically men's control of women's entitlement. Entitlements of women are more likely to be quasi-legal, involving common property resources and social support systems which characteristically break down in famine. The analyses of famine by Agarwal (1991, 1992) and of cooperative conflicts in provisioning and reproduction in poor households (Kabeer, 1991, 1994) help develop a framework for analysing gender and entitlements in recurrent famine.

Broad conclusions can be drawn about the legacy of famine policy formulation and implementation in British India, from epidemic control, and from the experiences of mortality of young men *vis-à-vis* young women.

First, the famine relief initially (1880–1901) offered more equal access to employment and wages than existed previously or on non-famine works. This both protected food entitlements of vulnerable individuals, and introduced gender relations of greater equality but outside the dominant norm. In Osmani's (1995) terms, this was, potentially, a 'benevolent irreversibility'. If realised, it promoted an efficient, non-discriminatory, response to an emerging labour market.

However, legal sex distinctions always operated, and pragmatic cost-effective criteria were applied to relief operations, which led to a capturing of unequal gender relations by restricting women's access to employment and therefore their wage-entitlement to food except through men, and this was introduced incrementally as famines recurred. The extension of the meaning of purdah to include occupational seclusion added further constraints on women. The terms on which women entered relief work had changed from individual wage labour to forced entry (Chen, 1995) under the control of the productive unit.

Second, the control of epidemics favoured biodeterministic explanations of sex differentials in susceptibility to disease. This both subordinated women's knowledge to that of experts, and defined women's illhealth as reproductive – although there was a sustained interest in the nutrition–infection synergism in Sanitary Commissioners' reports.

Concerning the entrenchment of excess mortality, there is some evidence that young women suffered relatively more than young men in British India, and that this became more significant over time. Osmani (1995) offers an alternative, but reconcilable, explanation of the long-term effects of famine mortality patterns. He argues that, because men's mortality is higher than women's during famine in many societies (a fact open to dispute), this reversal

> actually causes an irreversible setback for the longer-term well-being of women themselves. As men die proportionately more, the proportion of female-headed households inevitably rises, a tendency that is further exacerbated by the fact that the rate of divorce tends to increase at times of famine . . . The point is simply that in a society where women face severe constraints in their access to productive activity, any phenomenon that leaves more women to fend for themselves without at the same time removing those constraints cannot be good for them.
>
> (Osmani, 1995: 28)

Higher male mortality in famine was not always found in the districts or provinces of British India, although Osmani is correct to say that this was generally believed. I have argued that gender relations in famine survival strategies actually levered the constraints more tightly, even on relief works.

Indeed, I noted that women working during famines can leave little memory trace, and that the dominant perception in northern India is that women do not work outside the home. For example, Martha Chen writes about the Bangladesh famine in 1974 that:

> Bangladesh [formerly part of Bengal] has a long history of food-for-work programmes . . . but the participation of women was a new phenomenon . . . Conditioned by tradition to believe women should not seek outside gainful employment, local officials regularly turned women back. Where they were recruited, women faced problems related to the work and payment norms.
>
> (Chen, 1995: 41)

This is not a new phenomenon: indeed, the reasons for opposition to women workers are almost identical to those given by famine officials (supported by male professional labour) seven decades earlier (see also Kynch, 1996).

Part of the evolution of Indian famine relief has been its increased capacity to build upon earlier successes and failures, but this has not been the case with respect to gender relations, or the effect on women's food entitlement, concerning which relief was malevolent even if it saved lives. This particular effect of relief in India should not be overgeneralised, for a colonial state could be socially innovative, as Deborah Bryceson (1981) quotes from a District Report of 1935 from Tanganyika:

> During the recent famine many young natives left the district altogether leaving their wives and young children to the care of the government, and the latter would have starved if they had not received assistance. To overcome a recurrence of this, an endeavour was made which has been fairly successful, to get the women to plant their own shambas. This scheme has only one drawback and that is, when the young man returns,

in many cases, he expects to live on his wife both for his food and his tax.

(Bryceson, 1981: 101)

In India, women rarely gained such autonomy, although men's opportunistic behaviour was more universal, which perhaps explains a relief administrator's patronising fondness for male Bhils as he wrote:

[The Bhil men] confidentially told me that if they had had the remotest idea that they were going to be asked to work they would never have come. At last we came to a compromise. They said 'All right Bapjii (father), take the women and children' and there the matter rested . . .

. . . to do justice to the men I must say that nearly always the man was leaner, feebler and nearer death than his wife and children . . .

[By July] my friend, the Bhil, walks about his fields moving his atten-tuated limbs in quite a jaunty manner. He still makes Mrs Bhil do most of the work, but that is how he is built, and she is no new woman with fan-tastic ideas about the rights and wrongs of life.

(from Mewar, 1897 in Indian Charitable Relief Fund Report, 1901)

Inclusion of famine strategies and changes in relief policy can also undermine an already weak fallback position in household bargaining, prompting abandon-ment, or reinforce negative perceptions of women outside the reproductive role. A preliminary conclusion from British Indian data is that famine-levered changes in young people's fallback positions in intra-household bargaining are important in determining gender relations.

Migration of young people epitomises the desperation, destitution and social upheaval of famines, and studies from east and western British India (Orissa by Mohanty, 1992; Bombay by McAlpin, 1983) of migration and famine concur with evidence from Africa (Malawi by Vaughan, 1987; Tanganyika by Bryceson, 1981) that external, non-household factors such as access to labouring opportunities may be crucial to survival, although the incentives and constraints on men and women differ greatly between, and within, Africa and India.

The current dominant theory of induced institutional innovation has often been uncritical of transformation or outcomes of institutions, or the benefits of institution-building. To some extent this can be derived from the 'neo-classical economic imperialism' which has gained ascendancy over more sociological approaches which include dysfunctional or socially costly institutions. Bardhan (1989) is an exception; writing on the economic theory of rural institutions, he rightly warns of dysfunction and path-dependency.

Famine events play a role in altering both the state's and people's perceptions of behaviour and socially valued interactions, which become embedded in the non-famine framework of economic and social relations, including gender.

Notes

1 This chapter uses findings from research by Jocelyn Kynch and Maureen Sibbons on the analysis of Indian famine data, funded by the Leverhulme Trust (F391D), and a study by Jocelyn Kynch and Mike Maguire into nutrition in a north Indian village, funded by ESCOR (R3907). I am specially grateful to Maureen Sibbons, Cecile Jackson, Des Gasper, Simon Maxwell, Diane Elson and Nancy Folbre for valuable comments on earlier drafts.

2 See also see Maddox (1991); Bairagi (1986); Dreze and Sen (1989: 55–6); Dreze (1988: 97–8).

3 Chen (1995: 37) draws attention to the predicament of poor women in crises when 'they must break with tradition and act independently because they lack the security the tradition is supposed to offer'.

4 On induced institutional innovation see Ruttan and Hayami (1984); Ruttan (1986), also Bardhan (1989). Boyce (1987: 25–30) examines the theory of institutional innovation in the Indian context.

5 Two influences deserve attention: the first is what Vanberg (1994) notes is 'misleadingly' sometimes called 'economic imperialism' in institutional analysis, which has allowed a neglect of tensions between rational choice and rule-following (i.e., economic versus sociological analyses); the second is the related point that, in the dominant neo-classical model, gender relations are assumed to be biologically determined (Folbre, 1994).

6 As elsewhere, a higher proportion of the UK aid programme now goes on emergency relief, and this is explained both by the high level of need and because 'providing such aid "is something the United Kingdom is particularly good at"', in part because relief organisation tends to have 'military or certainly semi-military aspects' (House of Commons, 1994: 54–5). A high-tech image (air-lifts, lorry convoys and men with big shoulders) also reinforces the masculinity of the development agenda (Buchanan-Smith and Maxwell in IDS, 1994; Kynch 1987).

7 Kynch (1987, 1988, forthcoming); Kynch and Sibbons (1993, forthcoming); Sibbons (1995).

8 The districts illustrate various transformations, for example from foodgrain-exporting to famine-proneness, or from famine-proneness to robustness.

9 In social or economic theories which take gender to be biologically determined, it can be argued that G_0 and G_1 are in fact identical: this would not alter the potential of famine to lever a change.

10 For important debates about the entitlement approach see, for example, de Waal (1987, 1989, 1991); Vaughan (1987); Gasper (1993); Gore (1993); Keen (1994).

11 Although rice-husking was, with transport, the only rural profession to increase in 1943, Mukherjee in Krishnamurty (1989) suggests that mechanisation had reduced the important role of hand-husking, which may have employed as many as 25 per cent of women aged 15–59 in 1910.

12 In fact, the relief policy usually advocated protects the productive unit while offering only 'safety net' provision for those outside such units (often the abandonned or destitute).

13 Platteau (1991) equates the 'moral economy' with hunger insurance mechanisms, the characteristic breaking of which leads to demands for welfarist legislation which recent evaluation suggests benefits women over their life cycle (Hills et al., 1993).

14 Ballhatchet (1980: 20) observes that in British India military dilemmas over prostitutes were affected by a recognition that 'religious attitudes were less rigid in India than in England, though social structures were more rigid: prostitutes were not denounced as sinners, but society permitted them no alternative occupation'. Perhaps 10–20 per cent of women in military brothels 'came as a result of socio-economic hardship' although the authorities distinguished respectable professionals from 'disorderly vagrants, who infested shadowy haunts at night and tempted unwary

soldiers to destruction' (1980: 162–3).

15 J. C. Geddes, *Administrative Experience Recorded in Former Famines* (1874: 137,111,110); Bengal Famine Code 1913, Appendix II: 24; Government of United Provinces, *Final Report on the Working of Famine Relief Operations* (1918); Government of Bihar and Orissa, Revenue Department No.1418/11–F–5 of 1918.

16 This goes against the received wisdom that policy incorporated a Malthusian perspective: officials often held other views. Later, the role of the eugenics movement does seem crucial to me.

17 An extreme example is when cholera in Bogra, Bengal 'was traced to fakirs and it disappeared as soon as a few of them were prosecuted' (Public Health Report of 1929).

18 I should clarify why I have used numbers and not rates of death in this chapter. First, my interest is in relative male and female deaths, so that rates are of no advantage. Second, errors in both registered deaths and census data are undoubtedly present, perhaps more so in famine or epidemic years, and the use of rates based upon an estimate of population added to data problems.

19 Passivity of neglect adds cultural acceptability to economic explanation. Gender discrimination cannot be explained without reference to non-economic factors (Kynch and Sen, 1983, Kishor, 1993).

20 Whether the trend is in fact linear, or we should investigate for 'breaks' or non-linearity, remains a matter for research.

References

ACC/SCN (1994) *SCN News*, Number 11, Mid-1994. UN Administrative Committee on Coordination, Sub-Committee on Nutrition.

Agarwal, B. (1991) 'Social security and the family,' in Ahmad *et al.* (1991).

Agarwal, B. (1992) 'Gender relations and food security: coping with seasonality, drought and famine in South Asia', in Beneria and Feldman (1992).

Ahmad, E., J. Dreze, J. Hills and A. Sen (eds) (1991) *Social Security in Developing Countries*, WIDER Studies in Development Economics, Oxford: Clarendon Press.

Arnold, D. (1988) *Famine: Social Crisis and Historical Change*, Oxford: Basil Blackwell.

Aslanbeigui, N., S. Pressman and G. Summerfield (eds) (1994) *Women in the Age of Economic Transformation*, London: Routledge.

Bairagi, R. (1986) 'Food crisis, nutrition and female children in rural Bangladesh', *Population and Development Review*, 12: 2, 307–15.

Ballhatchet, K. (1980) *Race, Sex and Class Under the Raj: Imperial Attitudes and Policies and their Critics, 1793–1905*, London: Weidenfeld and Nicolson.

Bardhan, P. K. (1989) 'Alternative approaches to the theory of institutions in economic development' in Bardhan (ed.) *The Economic Theory of Agrarian Institutions*, Oxford: Clarendon Press.

Beneria, L. and S. Feldman (eds) (1992) *Unequal Burden: Economic Crises, Persistent Poverty and Women's Work*, Oxford and Boulder, Colorado: Westview Press.

Bhatia, B. M. (1967) *Famines in India 1860–1965*, 2nd Edition, Bombay: Asia Publishing House.

Boyce, J. (1987) *Agrarian Impasses in Bengal: Institutional Constraints to Technological Change*, Oxford: Oxford University Press.

Breman, J. and E. V. Daniel (1992) 'Conclusion: the making of a coolie', *Journal of Peasant Studies*, 19(3/4): 268–95.

Brown, E. P. (1991) 'Sex and starvation: famine in three Chadian societies' in R. E. Downs, D. O. Kerner and S. P. Reyna (eds) *The Political Economy of African Famine*, Philadelphia, Penn.: Gordon and Breach Science Publishers.

Bryceson, D. (1981) 'Colonial famine responses: the Bagamoyo district of Tanganyika, 1920–61', *Food Policy*, 6(2): 91–104.

Cain, M. (1986) 'The consequences of reproductive failure: dependence, mobility and mortality among the elderly of rural South Asia', *Population Studies*, 40: 375–88.

Chen, M. (1995) 'A matter of survival: women's right to employment in India and Bangladesh', in Nussbaum and Glover (1995).

Corbett, J. (1988) 'Famine and household coping strategies', *World Development*, 16(9): 1099–112.

Curry, B. (1992) 'Is famine a discrete event?' *Disasters*, 16(2): 138–44.

Davies, S. (1993) 'Versatile livelihoods: strategic adaptation to food insecurity in the Malian Sahel', mimeo, Institute of Development Studies, University of Sussex; published (1996) *Adaptable Livelihoods*, Basingstoke: Macmillan Press and New York: St Martin's Press.

De Waal, A. (1987) 'The perception of poverty and famines', *International Journal of Moral and Social Studies*, 2(3): 251–62.

De Waal, A. (1989) *Famine that Kills: Darfur, Sudan, 1984–1985*, Oxford: Clarendon Press.

De Waal, A. (1991) 'Logic and application: a reply to S. R. Osmani', *Development and Change*, 22.

Dreze, J. (1988) *Famine Prevention in India*, Development Economics Research Programme DEP/3, STICERD, London School of Economics.

Dreze, J. (1990) *Widows in Rural India*, Development Economics Research Programme DEP/26, STICERD, London School of Economics.

Dreze, J. and A. Sen (1989) *Hunger and Public Action*, Oxford: Clarendon Press.

Elson, D. (1992) 'From survival strategies to transformation strategies: women's needs and structural adjustment', in Beneria and Feldman (1992).

Folbre, N. (1994) *Who Pays for the Kids? Gender and the Structures of Constraint*, London and New York: Routledge.

Fowler, A. (1992) *Institutional Development and NGOs in Africa*, INTRAC/NOVIB.

Gallin, R. S. and A. Ferguson (1991) 'Conceptualising difference: gender, class and action', in Gallin and Ferguson (eds) *Women and International Development Annual, Volume 2*, Boulder, Colorado: Westview Press.

Gasper, D. (1993) 'Entitlements analysis: relating concepts and contexts', *Development and Change*, 24: 679–718.

Geisler, G. and K. T. Hansen (1994) 'Structural adjustment, the rural–urban interface and gender relations in Zambia', in Aslanbeigui *et al.* (1994).

Gore, C. (1993) 'Entitlement relations and "unruly" social practices: a comment on the work of Amartya Sen', *Journal of Development Studies*, 29(3): 429–60.

Government of Bengal (1898) *Final Resolution No. 385 on the Famine in Bengal of 1896–97*, Revenue Department, Agriculture (Famine), Bengal Secretariat Press, Calcutta.

Hall-Matthews, D. (forthcoming) 'Historical roots of famine relief paradigms: ideas on free trade and dependency in India in the 1870s', in Toye and O'Neill (eds) *A World Without Famine*, London: Macmillan.

Hills, J., H. Glennester and J. Le Grand (1993) *Investigating Welfare: Final Report of the ESRC Welfare Research Programme*, Welfare State Programme Discussion Paper WSP/92, STICERD, London School of Economics.

House of Commons (1994) *Second Report: Public Expenditure: Spending Plans of the Foreign and Commonwealth Office and the Overseas Development Administration*, London: Foreign Affairs Committee.

IDS (1994) 'Linking relief and development', *IDS Bulletin*, 24(4) Institute of Development Studies, University of Sussex.

Indian Famine Commission (1880) *Report of the Indian Famine Commission*, Part I: Famine Relief and Appendix I: Miscellaneous Papers, HMSO, Calcutta and London.

Jeffery, P., R. Jeffery and A. Lyon (1989) *Labour Pains and Labour Power: Women and Childbearing in India*, London: Zed Books.

Kabeer, N. (1991) *Gender, Production and Well-being: Rethinking the Household Economy*, Discussion Paper 288, Institute of Development Studies, University of Sussex.

Kabeer, N. (1994) *Reversed Realities: Gender Hierarchies in Development Thought*, London: Verso.

Keen, D. (1994) *The Benefits of Famine: A Political Economy of Famine and Relief in Southwestern Sudan 1983–1989*, Princeton, New Jersey: Princeton University Press.

Kishor, S. (1993) '"May God give sons to all": gender and child mortality in India', *American Sociological Review*, 58 (April): 247–65.

Koch Laier, J., S. Davies, K. Milward and J. Kennan (1996) *Gender, Household Food Security and Coping Strategies: an Annotated Bibliography*, Development Bibliography 14, Institute of Development Studies, University of Sussex.

Krishnamurty, J. (ed.) (1989) *Women in Colonial India: Essays on Survival, Work and the State*, Delhi: Oxford University Press.

Kumar, D. (ed.) (1982) *The Cambridge Economic History of India, Volume II*, Cambridge: Cambridge University Press.

Kynch, J. (1987) 'Some state responses to male and female need in British India', in H. Afshar (ed.) *Women, State and Ideology*, London: Macmillan.

Kynch, J. (1988) 'Scarcities, distress and crime in British India'. Paper presented to 7th World Congress of Rural Sociology, Bologna, Italy.

Kynch, J. (1994) *Food and Human Growth in Palanpur*, Development Economics Research Programme DEP/57, STICERD, London School of Economics.

Kynch, J. with M. Sibbons (forthcoming) 'Famine relief, piece-work and women workers: experiences in British India', in Toye and O'Neill (eds) *A World without Famine*, London: Macmillan.

Kynch, J. and A. Sen (1983) 'Indian women: well-being and survival', *Cambridge Journal of Economics*, 7: 363–80.

Kynch, J. and M. Sibbons (1993) *Famine in British India: Learning from Longitudinal Data*, Papers in International Development 9, Centre for Development Studies, University of Wales Swansea.

Kynch J. and M. Sibbons (forthcoming) 'Women dying, women working: disempowerment in British India', in H. Afshar (ed.) *Women and Empowerment*, London: Routledge.

Lieten, G. K., O. Nieuwenhuys and L. S. Sandbergen (eds) (1989) *Women, Migrants and Tribals: Survival Strategies in Asia*, New Delhi: Manohar Publications.

McAlpin, M. (1983) *Subject to Famine: Food Crises and Economic Change in Western India, 1860–1920*, Princeton, New Jersey: Princeton University Press.

Mackintosh, M (1989) *Gender, Class and Rural Transition: Agribusiness and Food Crisis in Senegal*, London and New Jersey: Zed Books.

Maddox, G. (1991) 'Famine, impoverishment and the creation of a labor reserve in

Central Tanzania', *Disasters*, 15(1): 35–42.

Maxwell, S. (ed.) (1991) *To Cure All Hunger: Food Policy and Food Security in Sudan*, London: Intermediate Technology Publications.

Mohanty, B. (1992) 'Migration, famines and sex ratios in Orissa division between 1881 and 1921', *Indian Economic and Social History Review*, Oct.–Dec. 29(4).

Nussbaum, M. (1995) 'Introduction', in Nussbaum and Glover (1995).

Nussbaum, M. and J. Glover (eds) (1995) *Women, Culture and Development: A Study of Human Capabilities*, Oxford: Clarendon Press.

Okin, S. M. (1995) 'Inequalities between the sexes in different cultural Contexts', in Nussbaum and Glover (1995).

Osmani, S. R. (1995) 'Famine, demography and endemic poverty', mimeo, Development Studies Association Annual Conference, Dublin.

Patnaik, U. (1992) 'Why food availability and famine: a longer view', *Journal of Peasant Studies*, 19(1): 1–25.

Platteau, J-P. (1991) 'Traditional systems of social security and hunger insurance: past achievements and modern challenges', in Ahmad *et al.* (1991).

Platteau, J-P. (1992) *Formalization and Privatization of Land Rights in Sub-Saharan Africa: A Critique of Current Orthodoxies and Structural Adjustment Programmes*, Development Economics Research Programme DEP/34, STICERD, London School of Economics.

Rangasami, A. (1985) 'Failure of exchange entitlement theory of famine: a response', *Economic and Political Weekly*, 20(12 and 19 October): 1747–52, 1797–1801.

Ruttan, V. W. (1986) 'Induced institutional innovation', in G. E. Schuh (ed.) *Technology, Human Capital and the World Food Problem*, Miscellaneous Publications 37, Department of Agricultural and Applied Economics, University of Minnesota.

Ruttan, V. W. and Y. Hayami (1984) 'Towards a theory of induced institutional innovation', *Journal of Development Studies*, 20: 203–23.

Ryan, R. W. (1990) 'Comparisons of traditional and modern food rationing systems in response to famine', *Social Science Information*, 29(4): 785–804.

Sarkar, S. (1983) *Modern India 1885–1947*, Madras: Macmillan India.

Sen, A. (1977) 'Starvation and exchange entitlement: a general approach and its application to the Great Bengal Famine', *Cambridge Journal of Economics*, 1: 33–59.

Sen, A. (1981) *Poverty and Famines: An Essay in Entitlement and Deprivation*, Oxford: Clarendon Press.

Sen, A. (1984a) 'Food battles: conflicts in the access to food', *Food and Nutrition*, 10(1): 81–9.

Sen, A. (1984b) *Resources, Values and Development*, Oxford: Basil Blackwell.

Sen, A. (1985) 'Women, technology and sexual divisions,' *Trade and Development*, 6: 195–223.

Sen, A. (1990) 'Gender and cooperative conflicts', in I. Tinker (ed.) *Persistent Inequalities*, New York: Oxford University Press, pp.23–49.

Sen, A. (1991) *War and Famines: On Divisions and Incentives*, Development Economics Research Programme DEP/33, STICERD, London School of Economics.

Sen, A. (1992) *Inequality Reexamined*, Oxford: Clarendon Press and New York: Russell Sage Foundation.

Sen, A. (1995) 'Gender inequality and theories of justice', in Nussbaum and Glover (1995).

Sibbons, M. with J. Kynch (1995) *Cholera and Famine in British India 1870–1930*, Papers in International Development 14, Centre for Development Studies, University of Wales Swansea.

Vanberg, V. J. (1994) *Rules and Choice in Economics*, London: Routledge.

Vaughan, M. (1987) *The Story of an African Famine: Hunger, Gender and Politics in Malawi*, Cambridge: Cambridge University Press.

Walker, P. (1989) *Famine Early Warning Systems: Victims and Destitution*, London: Earthscan.

Watts, M. (1983) *Silent Violence: Food, Famine and Peasantry in Northern Nigeria*, Berkeley: University of California Press.

Watts, M. (1991) 'Entitlement or empowerment? Famine and starvation in Africa', *Review of African Political Economy*, 51: 9–26.

Whitehead, A. (1990) 'Rural women and food production in Sub-Saharan Africa', in J. Dreze and A. Sen (eds) *The Political Economy of Hunger, Volume 1: Entitlement and Well-Being*, Oxford: Clarendon Press.

Young, K., C. Wolkowitz and R. McCullagh (eds) (1981) *Of Marriage and the Market: Women's Subordination in International Perspective*, London: CSE Books.

6

GENDER, POWER AND
CONTESTATION

'Rethinking bargaining with patriarchy'

Deniz Kandiyoti

Over the last decade, preoccupations with the effects of gender inequality were articulated with increasing analytic rigour in exchanges between economists, anthropologists and feminist critics of both disciplines. Not surprisingly, these exchanges focused primarily upon conceptualisations of the household and of intra-household allocational practices (Guyer, 1981; Harris, 1981; Whitehead, 1981; Sen, 1983, 1990; Folbre, 1984, 1986; Jones, 1986; Guyer and Peters 1987; Dwyer and Bruce, 1988; Evans, 1989; Agarwal, 1990; Standing, 1991; Moore, 1992). This was not simply due to the fact that households could be readily identified as important sites for the reproduction of gendered identities and inequalities but also because of the differing policy consequences implicit in varying conceptions of the household. As Dwyer and Bruce (1988) pointed out, the model of the unified household seemed a particularly convenient policy tool and policy-makers in both industrialised and developing countries chose to direct resource flows and benefits to the household as a unit or to the nominal household head. It was mainly left to anthropologists, especially those working in sub-Saharan Africa where less corporate forms of householding are in evidence, not only to demonstrate the fallacy of income-pooling assumptions inherent in a unitary model but to point to policy failures flowing therefrom.[1] As a result, a new consensus appears to have emerged which Moore (1994) characterises as a *rapprochement* between feminist analyses of the household and mainstream models in anthropology and economics. This consensus presents 'a view of the household which sees it as a locus of competing interests, rights, obligations and resources, where household members are often involved in bargaining, negotiation and possibly even conflict' (Moore, 1994: 87).

The emphasis on bargaining highlighted that one of the crucial issues to be explained is what influences relative bargaining power both within and beyond the household and, just as importantly, the question of what constitutes agency. I endeavoured to address these issues in 'Bargaining with Patriarchy' (1988) by means of an attempt at institutional analysis based on a number of simplifying assumptions. I argued that bargaining always takes place in the context of 'rules of the game' implicit in different systems of kinship defining the nature of conjugal contracts (Whitehead, 1981), residence and inheritance rules. I utilised two ideal-typical models of householding; the less corporate forms prevalent in some parts of sub-Saharan Africa contrasted to more corporate forms found in the Middle East, East and parts of South Asia.[2] These rules, whilst subject to change and rede-finition, may nonetheless provide a relatively enduring framework for human transactions which economists tend to relegate to a residual category labelled 'culture' (whose effects may sometimes be expressed as a set of variables). I also proposed that these rules informed both women's rational choices and the less conscious aspects of their gendered subjectivities predisposing them to favour differing strategies of resistance and/or collusion in different contexts. By so doing, I was both presenting women as rational actors deploying a range of strate-gies intelligible within their normative universe *and* pointing to the essentially circumscribed nature of the same strategies; in other words, whilst endorsing James Scott's version of resistance I was attempting to eat my Gramscian cake at the same time by arguing that women were nonetheless operating within the parameters of dominant gender ideologies.[3]

In this chapter I would like to offer a critique of this approach and argue that our formulations of power and resistance, which often draw upon frameworks pri-marily geared to elucidating issues of class struggle and consciousness, may be problematic when applied to gender relations. In what follows, I shall examine how our notions of bargaining have evolved and how these inevitably rest upon often implicit assumptions about consciousness, personhood and subjectivity. I shall conclude with an evaluation of the possibilities and limitations of our current conceptual frameworks in accounting for gendered experiences of power, subor-dination and resistance.

Battles over the household

The debates over economic models of the household will not be dealt with here as they have been covered extensively elsewhere (Evans, 1989; Ellis, 1993; Agarwal, 1994; Kabeer, 1994). I shall concentrate, instead, on Hart's (1995) incisive survey of more recent developments because it provides an excellent illustration of the difficulties of theorising power relations manifested through gendered forms of hierarchy.

Until recently, the debate was cast exclusively in terms of unitary versus bar-gaining models of the household. The former are typically characterised by the aggregation of the preferences of all household members into a joint utility func-tion so that the household is treated as a single decision-making unit, whereas the latter consider the household as a site of both cooperation and conflict where intra-household allocation is the outcome of a bargaining process. The debate has shifted again with the emergence of a neoclassical critique of the unitary model which proposes a return to the individual as a unit of analysis and the requirement that each individual should be characterised by his/her own preferences. Collective models thus describe the household as a group of individuals with their own preferences among whom collective decision processes take place. This approach remains totally agnostic about the actual forms that intra-household relations may take. These are treated as an entirely empirical question which can only be derived from the data and the unitary approach is criticised for arbitrarily imposing *ad hoc* institutional assumptions. However, assuming that one can unproblematically 'recover' sharing rules from aggregate survey data, which typically requires predefined categories and assumptions about underlying relations, is quite naive and reveals, in Hart's view, the limits of economism. 'A basic dilemma confronting collective modelers is that the data that they need to follow through with their analysis requires a prior understanding of precisely the institutional rules they are seeking to recover from those data' (1995: 53). It is ironic that the solution proposed to remedy models found deficient precisely because of their inability to adequately conceptualise *relationships* should be a further retreat into a methodological individualism which abandons any attempt at institutional analysis. Non-cooperative models of the household such as the Carter–Katz model (Carter and Katz, 1993), on the other hand, do take institutional analysis seriously and attempt to formalise the insights gained from in-depth ethnographic studies by invoking categories such as 'degrees of patriarchy'. However, these models also sit uneasily with a conceptualisation of gender which entails struggles not only over resources and labour but also over socially constructed meanings and definitions which are often multiple, contradictory, fluid and contested. In other words, a focus on gender should entail a 'reconceptualisation of "the household" in relational terms and an analytical as well as empirical focus on the gendered micropolitics of negotiation, cooperation and contestation in different but intersecting institutional arenas' (Hart, 1995: 61).

Moore (1994) elaborates further upon the notion that bargaining in the household is never simply determined by economic factors by suggesting that gender ideologies are not merely cultural beliefs and attitudes which are somehow attached to economic and political processes but are actually *constitutive of them.* Local ideologies about the appropriate behaviour of women and men can be shown to have material consequences. Thus, the ideology of female domesticity may lock Indian lacemakers into very poorly remunerated work since other employment alternatives cannot be entertained for women of their caste (Mies, 1982), while homebased piece-workers in Turkey may 'euphemise' their paid employment and their relationships to employers using the idiom of kinship and reciprocity (White, 1994).[4] Drawing upon Fraser's (1989) conceptualisation of rights and needs as an arena of struggle over their establishment, interpretation and satisfaction, Moore suggests that conventional understandings of who gets what through what sort of work may act as 'local theories of entitlement'. These are not presented as norms that fully determine negotiated outcomes but as resources that may be drawn upon in the process of bargaining and negotiation.

One of the more fruitful suggestions flowing from this approach is that the outcome of negotiations may also be affected by supra-local discourses 'about the rights and needs of particular kinds of persons which might be made manifest through the targeted provision of advice and/or credit provided by extension services or local development projects, or through such things as state legislation on school attendance and the provision of pensions' (Moore, 1994: 106). Thus, the explicit or implicit assumptions inherent in development interventions may get translated into material and symbolic resources which may be capitalised upon by some local actors, sometimes to the detriment of others. In the same way that it was not lost on Mandinka male farmers in the irrigated rice scheme in Gambia analysed by Carney (1988) that the project was channelling inputs directly to them on the assumption that Mandinka households operate as a joint utility function, NGOs and development agencies delivering 'Women in Development' assistance programmes which define women as appropriate recipients of training and credit may articulate a different agenda which may also enter the field of negotiation as a resource.

The problem is, of course, that alternative gender ideologies, such as those implicit in different development interventions, do not enter a level playing field but one in which certain discourses appear as hegemonic, sanctioned and authorised whilst others are marginalised, disqualified and discounted. Goetz and Gupta's (1996) detailed study of loan use in rural credit programmes for women in Bangladesh illustrates this point graphically. These authors question the empowerment contribution of credit to rural women in the context of high degrees of male control over loans, undermining women's capacity to determine the way a loan is invested or its profits used. This may postpone the positive social externalities expected from increasing women's control over household income and, in the case of bad investments by men, may force women to mobilise repayment funds from resources which could be used for consumption and savings purposes. In some instances, loan transfers may even act to exacerbate gender-related tensions within rural households. These findings caution us against adopting quantitative indicators such as repayment rates as an index of women's empowerment and show how existing gender ideologies may exert their influence in new institutional contexts. This introduces a seemingly intractable question, namely, how do forms of resistance which may force a reinterpretation of local theories of entitlement in favour of the less powerful, become possible at all? The answer to this question necessarily entails a consideration of the capacity of disadvantaged groups to achieve a degree of articulation of their interests and to acquire the means to act in their furtherance. This is where notions of subjectivity are inevitably invoked in ways that presuppose implicit, and often contradictory, assumptions about personhood.

Contests over subjectivity

I would like to illustrate the contention above in relation to a series of exchanges concerning the influential work of Amartya Sen (1990). Sen proposed that differences in bargaining power in the household are a function of the range of options available to different household members (the fallback position or what Sen terms the 'breakdown well-being' response), the extent to which members identify their self-interest with their personal well-being (the 'perceived interest' response) and the perceived significance of their contribution to the household (or the 'perceived contribution' response). He claims that women may sometimes define their interests differently from what would be expected from 'an objective measure of self-interest'. Furthermore:

> the lack of perception of personal interest combined with a great concern for family welfare is, of course, just the kind of attitude that helps to sustain the traditional inequalities. There is much evidence in history that acute inequalities often survive precisely by making allies of the deprived. The underdog comes to accept the legitimacy of the unequal order and becomes an implicit accomplice . . . It can be a serious error to take the absence of protest and questioning of inequality as evidence of the absence of that inequality (or of the nonviability of the question.)
>
> (Sen, 1990: 126)

Agarwal (1994) takes issue with this imputation of false consciousness to women and favours, instead, a position that is closer to James Scott's which presents subordinates as conscious actors generally capable of penetrating the ideological fabric woven by the privileged. The obstacles that stand in the way of women do not have the shape of an inadequate apprehension of their own needs and rights but of the material impossibility of realising them. Thus, in explaining intra-household gender inequalities Agarwal prefers to place 'much less emphasis than Sen does on women's perceptions of their self-interest and much more on the external constraints to their acting on those interests. Or, to put it in another way, what may be needed is less a sharpening of women's sense of self-interest than an 'improvement in their ability to pursue that interest, including by strengthening their bargaining power' (1994: 57).

Women emerge from this account as rational beings with an adequately developed sense of where their best interests lie. Indeed, even instances where women appear to sacrifice their short-term welfare for the benefit of their families and kin could be reinterpreted as an investment towards their future security, which 'would be perfectly in keeping with self-interested behaviour, and need not imply a gap between women's "objective" well-being and their perception of their well-being' (p.435).

Apffel-Marglin and Simon (1994) are even more critical of Sen but from a totally different, indeed opposite, perspective. They target the same quote by Sen to argue that this exemplifies the imposition of women-in-development discourse, the direct heir of Victorian colonial feminism, to the distinct realities of Third World women:

When women's own self-perception concerning their well-being is not that of the independent self, but rather a self embedded in kinship (and other social) webs, as well as in the local landscape, the women-in-development logic leads to invalidating these perceptions as not true to reality.

(1994: 33)

What appears to be at stake here is not degrees of consciousness about self-interest but a radically *different* sense of one's selfhood expressed through a fundamentally different set of values and priorities. These authors argue that the emergence of the unitary and proprietary self, the self that Western liberalism and liberal feminism speak of, is the product of 'the enclosure of the commons and the industrial mode of production'. To this they contrast so-called commons (non-enclosed) regimes where 'the self is not bounded by skin, but is rather embedded in relationships to others and to the non-human world' (p.36).[5]

I will refrain from a discussion of the analytic utility and political wisdom of allocating Third World women (rural Indian women, in this particular case) to a world of radical 'otherness' that forecloses comparisons and makes any discussion of inequality, understood in Sen's and Agarwal's sense, both irrelevant and meaningless. I would like to concentrate, instead, on the difficulty of conceptualizing gendered identities and subjectivities in a manner that avoids both essentialism and the unproblematic assumption of the self-determining individual. This difficulty is not peculiar to gender but manifests itself more broadly in relation to attempts to theorise subjectivity in terms of class, caste, race or any other potential marker of subordinate identities. This dilemma is illustrated, for instance, by the *Subaltern Studies* project, an attempt to write South Asian history from a perspective which rejects both neo-colonialist and neo-nationalist economistic modes of historiography and focuses upon the dispossessed of the periphery, articulating their submerged but nonetheless distinct perspectives. In an incisive review, O'Hanlon draws our attention to 'the tension between the desire to find a resistant presence, and the necessity of preserving difference and otherness in the figure of the subaltern' (1988: 191). She points to the paradox inherent in the simultaneous recuperation of the self-originating, self-determining individual of Western humanism, in the person of the 'subaltern', at the very moment when Western historicity is brought under assault. She also draws explicit parallels between attempts at recuperating the experiences of the 'subaltern' and feminists' attempts at salvaging a 'feminine' subject from the mystifications imposed by phallocentric discourse, seeing in both enterprises a potential for a slide into essentialism.

There are, furthermore, additional specificities inherent to forms of marginalisation operating in the case of women. Gender identities – while ubiquitous and seemingly grounded in the ontological primacy of sexual difference – are always cross-cut by and inscribed in other forms of inequality based on class, race and ethnicity. The salience of women's gender interests at any given point in time and in different localities begs the question and may not simply be assumed to inform

140

strategies of resistance or forms of solidarity. This was an important point raised by Molyneux (1985) who made a distinction between women's interests – a much broader category which may give rise to a wide range of mobilizations – and women's gender interests. The popularity of the distinction between women's practical and strategic gender needs as a tool for planning (Moser, 1993) has rather overshadowed the more important prior observation that mobilization by women does not necessarily presuppose an expression of gender interests.[6] Even when we concede that gender interests may, under certain circumstances, act as vehicles for mobilization we would still be left with the unresolved problem of trying to theorise forms of domination, subordination and resistance based on gender with analytic tools primarily developed to account for forms of peasant, slave, working-class or 'subaltern' resistance and consciousnesses. Although all of the above require an understanding of the operations of power, their objects are not interchangeable.[7]

Power and resistance: conceptual conundrums

The particular appeal that Scott's framework on 'everyday forms of resistance' (1985) and 'hidden transcripts' (1990) held for some feminists, the present author included, deserves some comment. This appeal was based on diverse and potentially contradictory sources of influence. 'Female-sphere' theorists (Jaquette, 1982) increasingly produced accounts of 'women's worlds' as sites of solidarity, strength and alternative values resulting in a valorisation of the so-called 'private' sphere.[8] Evidence of the cultural autonomy of women meant that they were no longer treated as passive victims but construed as active agents. Despite the potential for essentialism implicit in some of these positions (see Fraser and Nicholson, 1988), this meshed in well with post-Foucauldian notions about both the pervasiveness and the limits of the exercise of power and the potential for subversion and contestation in the interstices of established orders. The fact that resistance did not necessarily have to take overt and organised forms but could be expressed through covert and indirect forms of bargaining was particularly well suited to women's contestations of domestic power structures involving as they do face-to-face relations with intimates such as husbands, mothers-in-law, sons and daughters rather than encounters with the more impersonal workings of bureaucracies and state apparatuses. The ethnographic evidence, comprehensively surveyed by Agarwal (1994) indeed points to numerous examples of women's covert resistance involving both daily activities such as diversion of food and income resources from the control of the male household head to more symbolic contestations of male power through song, dance and parody.[9]

However, what is frequently overlooked in discussions of Scott is the extent to which resistance itself is framed by the terms of an already existing contract rather than with reference to some future utopian arrangement. In other words, it is with reference to a feudalistic peasant–landlord relationship that Malaysian peasants in Scott's study were attempting to stem the encroachments of capitalist relations into their lifeworlds. They typically did so by inviting power holders to honour their traditional obligations or suffer shame and loss of face through gossip and moral censure. This implies that both the powerful and the dominated are, up to a point, bound by the same normative constraints. However, as Hart (1991) rightly points out it was primarily men who were enmeshed in subservient political patronage relations, relations from which women were excluded leaving them much freer to express resistance in more militant and overt ways. The absence of a gender perspective in Scott's work had concealed from view that class consciousness and forms of contestation may differentiate along gender-specific lines. Nonetheless, the central idea that systems of dominance do operate within certain normative boundaries holds a certain appeal. This was behind my own suggestion that gender orders also involve mutually binding constraints which I had labelled, for want of a better term, 'patriarchal bargains'. However, the powerful are much better placed to change the rules of the game unilaterally, at which point attempts by subordinates to call their bluff may emerge as rather pitiful and ineffectual forms of rearguard action. This is precisely what Mitchell's (1990) cogent critique of Scott demonstrates. He argues that by invoking subordinates' rational decision to conform rather than rebel with reference to their recognition that any other course of action is 'impractical' or 'dangerous' Scott is, in fact, concealing the evidence of hegemony by relabelling its effects, merely acknowledging 'limits' to peasant resistance without making them part of his analysis.[10]

This also corresponds to one of the central weaknesses of my earlier work where the invocation of patterns of householding and kinship, quite apart from simplifying a much more complex reality, resulted in positing these as entities 'out there', as somehow 'prior' and automatically generative of frameworks within which either acquiescence or contestation could take place. In addition, the possible outcomes of contestation are almost built into the structures through which they are enacted and although charges of determinism are evaded by pointing out that only *some* out of a possible range of strategies are analysed it is hard to see how and under what conditions other alternatives might materialise. Against such a background, some acts of resistance may indeed, as White (1986) suggests, contribute to false consciousness since they may blind people to the extent of their powerlessness by creating a space where mainly cathartic and expressive needs are fulfilled. Indeed, acts of resistance may, in some instances, be interpreted as part and parcel of the maintenance of systems of domination in that they provide spaces where subordinates may legitimately 'let off steam' and acquire a breathing space. This is particularly evident when women utilise culturally sanctioned forms of temporary disability, such as spirit possession.[11] This type of action does not normally or necessarily lead to a renegotiation of conjugal or labour contracts but produces relief within them. Okely's (1991) useful evocation of moments of defiance and rebellion as not necessarily indicative of absence of subordination points in a similar direction.

If forms of class domination, which are based upon a set of arbitrary arrangements, are made to appear as 'natural' and morally sanctioned, this is all the more so in the case of gender relations where kinship and marriage arrangements appear to be founded on the biological bedrock of procreation, the care of bodies and the perpetuation of lineages. Thus, even within women's acts of open contestation it is possible to detect the limits set by the 'naturalisation' of certain social practices. Agarwal presents useful evidence of these limits in the context of a discussion of successful collective action in the Bodhgaya struggle in Bihar where women were able to press for individual land rights. On the question of whether this could produce a longer-term, intergenerational change in favour of women, the author voices some doubts: 'The reluctance to endow daughters with land because of the norms of patrilocality and village exogamy, and the difficulties of management that women face when they own land in one village and are married into another, are not easy problems to resolve, especially if land is distributed in the names of individual women' (1994: 454). It is therefore quite conceivable that for these women, even as they pressed for their rights in land, certain other features of their lives simply appeared as 'givens', in this particular case, certain rules of post-marital residence and inheritance. In a very different context, Humphrey, who analyzed the substantial changes in domestic organisation and interpersonal relations among the Buryats under the Soviet regime, also comments that these 'had curiously little effect on the patrilineal lineage as a kinship *concept*' (1983: 287).

How are we to explain this apparent tenacity? Some scholars have invoked Bourdieu's notion of 'doxa' (most particularly, Risseeuw, 1988), which refers to unquestioned, self-evident and common-sense assumptions about social life, in contrast to orthodoxy and heterodoxy which imply the possibility of different or antagonistic beliefs. To the extent that doxa does not even entertain a reality outside itself, it is endowed with a primal innocence which is never fully recaptured by orthodoxy. The dominant classes have a stake in defending the integrity of doxa, or at least establishing the poor substitute of a form of orthodoxy that will actively censor or limit the universe of possible discourse. The dominated classes, on the other hand, have an interest in pushing back its limits, attempting to narrow the field of what is beyond question.

This undoubtedly powerful framework should work best to explain relations between social actors whose relative privilege or disadvantage *vis-à-vis* one another appears to be endowed with a certain degree of stability and permanence (such as landless peasants *vis-à-vis* landlords).[12] This does not necessarily characterise gender relations, which fluctuate throughout the life cycle and present varied and changing possibilities for power and autonomy even for the relatively disadvantaged. Thus, women's attachment to and stake in certain forms of patriarchal arrangements may derive neither from false consciousness, nor from conscious collusion but from an actual stake in certain positions of power available to them. For instance, women's life cycle in the virilocally extended household may be such that the deprivation and hardships they experience as young brides is eventually superseded by the control and authority they enjoy over their sons' wives. The cyclical nature of women's power in the household and their anticipation of inheriting the authority of senior women encourages a specific kind of identification with this system of hierarchy. This does not necessarily imply that all women will accede to this position of power but merely that it is culturally available to them; some may not bear sons, others, even more unfortunate, may remain childless. However, so long as this version of women's life cycle carries normative weight and cultural legitimacy, those most likely to attempt to push back the limits of 'doxa' may be younger women encouraging their husbands to set up separate households (although this represents no guarantee that these same younger women will not nurture exactly the same expectations of future cohabitation with their own married sons). Nor are the differences of interest pitting younger against older women in certain circumstances fixed or permanent. Under a different regime, where the position of mother-in-law is emptied of the matriarchal power conferred upon it by a particular form of domestic arrangement, young brides may welcome cohabitation with older women as a source of help with child care and household maintenance. This illustrates one of the more vexed aspects of trying to 'fit' gender relations into frameworks best suited to explicate hierarchical relations between differently constituted social categories. Experiences of gendered power are not merely fractured by class, race and ethnicity but by the complicated emotional (and material) calculus implied by different organisations of the domestic realm through women's and men's unfolding life cycles.[13]

It is not easy to assimilate the effects of kinship practices and gender ideologies to those of cultural hegemony or hegemonic control understood in the Gramscian sense either. Approaches that problematise the gender division itself and present certain versions of gendered identity (such as heterosexual macho masculinity) as 'hegemonic' both in the sense of being endowed with cultural legitimacy and being bolstered by a multiplicity of social institutions (the state, the Church, the schooling system, the media) appear to come close to such an articulation (Connell, 1987). Connell makes useful suggestions concerning the ways in which gender is reproduced in different institutional arenas and how these constructions of gender can be contradictory and conflictual as well as complementary. Poststructuralist feminists go furthest by arguing that it is the gender division itself which is generative of oppression, by marking out certain gendered identities as subordinate, rather than the institutionalised privileges of men over women *per se.* The principal form of false consciousness, in this case, would reside in taking these divisions at face value (as 'foundational') rather than seeing through them as the effects of a particular kind of discursive formation. The only viable feminist politics would, then, appear to consist of practices that unsettle or subvert the binary oppositions (sex/gender, male/female, masculine/feminine, equality/difference) that lie at the heart of this discourse (see for instance, Butler and Scott, 1992). Indeed, Butler puts before us as the central task of feminism 'to interrogate what the theoretical move that establishes foundations *authorises*, and what precisely it excludes or forecloses' (1992: 7). Thus, the category of 'sex' itself imposes a duality and a uniformity on bodies in order to maintain reproductive sexuality as a compulsory order. Butler suggests that 'this kind of categorisation can be

called a violent one, a forceful one, and that this discursive ordering and production of bodies in accord with the category of sex is itself material violence'
(1992: 17).

Joan Scott's definition of gender involves two interrelated but analytically distinct parts. Gender is 'a constitutive element of social relationships based on
perceived differences between the sexes, and *a primary way of signifying relationships
of power*' (1988: 42, emphasis mine). This definition has far-reaching implications.
Power does not merely manifest itself in and through gender relations but gender
is constitutive of power itself insofar as relations which may not always literally be
about gender utilise the language of sexual difference to signify and legitimise
power differentials. This goes much further than a mere acknowledgement that
women and men do not constitute homogeneous categories and that these are
riven by multiple differences (which may imply possibilities for antagonism as
well as coalition building). It points, among other things, to the contingency of the
association of gender with this or that sexed body and to the gendered nature of
all power relations. This represents an exhilaratingly liberating proposal which
extends the reach of gender analysis well beyond a consideration of systems of
institutionalised inequality between men and women. However, it is the very
broadness of this claim which may introduce some limitations and explain why the
gender and development literature tends to confine itself to the first part of the
definition, namely that of gender as a social relation. I have argued throughout
this chapter that the concepts we employ to designate the workings of power and
domination never seem to fully capture the specificity of their manifestations
through historically and culturally contextualised forms of gender relations. In
short, gender appears to resist an unproblematic incorporation into frameworks
which are meant to explicate the reproduction and maintenance of other forms of
social hierarchy such as those based on race and class. The task of gender analysis
is, admittedly, to reveal how all forms of social hierarchy are ultimately gendered
but this only provides an imperfect guide to issues of subjectivity and consciousness as well as resistance which are necessarily complex, contradictory and
context-specific.

Having set aside concepts such as male dominance and patriarchy, with their
overtones of universality, and opted for gender we may now discover that this
latter may be put to a variety of uses. There is, in particular, a marked divergence
in the usage of gender by post-structuralist feminists and feminists working on
development issues. The conceptualisation of gender implicit in most current
writing on development endorses the multiple, contested and contradictory meanings associated with the male/female distinction but remains committed to a
social relations approach which analyses how this distinction reproduces inequalities between men and women at every institutional level. It therefore authorises
the marking out of certain social categories – namely women – as relatively disadvantaged and talks about their empowerment without undue concern about
essentialism, the reinscription of the gender distinction, the freezing of multiple
identities and the consequent expression of feminism as identity politics. As a

result, there is a continual slippage between the categories of 'gender' and 'women', indicative of a continuing gap between conceptual frameworks, which recognize the relational and contingent nature of gender, and the tools utilised in development practice, which tend to take existing societal demarcations and divisions of labour at face value. The approaches used (such as participatory methodologies) tend to favour phenomenological rather than deconstructive goals and aim for an adequate grasp and representation of how men, women and children map out their social worlds in specific contexts without necessarily interrogating or aiming to destabilise these categories themselves (such as those of male or female elders, juniors or marginals). Taking 'naturalised' categories at face value may enhance adequate communication and promote so-called 'bottom-up' approaches to development which are sensitive to local constructions of gender, but it does not necessarily further the goal of putting them into question. Moreover, a deconstructive move which is intended to be enabling and radical at the theoretical level may turn out to be not only debilitating but also patronising and dismissive of local understandings when it is enacted in a development context. There remains a gap apparently difficult to bridge between the forms of theoretical practice advocated by post-structuralist feminists and the tactical essentialisms of gender and development practitioners who have to deal with the world as if it were actually constituted by the categories presented as self-evident by members of the communities in which they work (however internally varied the interpretations of such categories may be). This latter tendency may nonetheless still be preferable to the blinkering and distortion that may result from the importation of Western feminist concerns and units of analysis into gender and development writing. Bryceson (1995) provides excellent illustrations of how the superimposition of such concerns may seriously distort perceptions of rural Africa and result in lop-sided policies with limited viability. Ultimately, we may have to remain agnostic over the relevance and utility of the category of gender itself if it lessens our alertness and sensitivity to the myriad forms which social organization and hierarchy may take and if it results in extracting men and women as social categories from the contexts in which they are embedded.

Conclusion

I have argued throughout this chapter that the various conceptual frameworks we employ to talk about power and contestation present us with specific problems when applied to gender relations. Although the task of gender analysis ought, precisely, to be forcing a revision of androcentric frameworks this does not in and of itself provide us with a language to talk about gendered subjectivities and forms of consciousness. Approaches emphasising bargaining and negotiation have undoubtedly refined our understanding of household dynamics and gender relations but often rest upon unexamined assumptions about subjectivity and consciousness. Explaining resistance has often relied on the notion of the autonomous, self-determining individual, the main area of contention revolving around subordinates' capacity to see through the mystificatory discourses of the dominant or, on the contrary, their tendency to fall prey to false consciousness. 'Bargaining with patriarchy' represented an uneasy compromise since it suggested that contestation and resistance were possible but always circumscribed by the limits of the culturally conceivable. In that respect, it suffered from the same limitations as James Scott's analysis of peasant resistance where the evidence of hegemony remains concealed because its effects are relabelled and kept out of the analysis (Mitchell, 1990). Yet talking about hegemony in the case of gender relations is helpful only up to a point and mainly by way of analogy. True, the constriction of discursive universe produced by the equation of masculinity or femininity with some of its socially dominant variants and of sexual relations with heterosexuality bespeaks a powerful dominant ideology. However, analyses that problematise the gender division itself (and treat it as an originary act of discursive violence) are generally able to do just that, and do it repeatedly, in different textual, historical or institutional contexts. This need not automatically further our intimate understandings of the specific social relations or institutional frameworks that reproduce gendered inequalities. Yet this is the currency which gender and development approaches normally have to deal in. There seems to be no obvious way to bridge the gap between theories of gender and feminist social practice, especially in the field of gender and development. A suspension of judgement about our most central assumptions, renewed each time we encounter a new social context, may be salutary: gender may or may not be a salient category for an explanation of contestation and resistance, the self-determining, autonomous individual may or may not be a useful starting point for analysis, 'women' may or may not emerge as a social category around which an articulation of interests takes place and resisting subjects may be both rational actors and unable to think beyond the 'naturalised' givens of their communities. This may be another way of saying that the messiness of social reality has always exceeded the explanatory power of our conceptual frameworks and that this is all the more so in the area of gender.

Acknowledgements

I would like to thank Gill Hart, Bina Agarwal, Jens Lerche and Ruth Pearson for their stimulating comments on earlier drafts of this chapter.

Notes

1 There is, however, considerable variation in the importance accorded to conjugality in African households. See, for instance, the contrast between O'Laughlin (1995) who highlights the centrality of conjugality and male/female interdependence in explaining access to resources and Ekejiuba (1995) who presents the woman-centred hearth-hold as the primary unit of consumption and production, the male-headed household being defined as a more volatile entity due to the vagaries of multiple marriages, separation and divorce.

147

2 Kabeer (1994) utilises this typology which she elaborates with additional illustrations.

3 James Scott (1985) in his study of a rice-growing village in northern Malaysia invoked the concept of everyday forms of resistance to denote modest and covert forms of struggle (such as dissimulation, false compliance, pilfering, foot-dragging, etc.) which whilst stopping short of collective and outright defiance nonetheless served to limit and undermine the domination of more powerful groups. He went even further by suggesting that the presence of such struggles provides proof that ruling groups are unable to exert cultural domination over subordinates. He took Gramsci and his followers to task for their insistence upon the notion of cultural hegemony since he presents the effects of domination as constraints imposed by the coercive capabilities of dominant groups, constraints which do not extend into the domains of culture and ideology. Whilst I am in sympathy with the notion of everyday forms of resistance, I have serious problems with Scott's limited understanding of the concept of hegemony and find a model which invokes external coercion to ensure compliance particularly ill-suited to an understanding of gender relations and gendered forms of power.

4 The notion of 'euphemisation' is drawn from the work of Pierre Bourdieu (1977) who in his analysis of patterns of exchange and generosity, which are constitutive of patterns of political authority among Kabyle peasants in Algeria, suggests that for domination to be exerted in a lasting and credible fashion it has to disguise itself as a set of moral relations. Domination is therefore based on *misrecognition* whereby strategies of subordination become transformed into relationships of kinship, loyalty, generosity, etc. Gender ideologies may be effectively deployed to produce these effects.

5 While economists seem particularly wedded to the autonomous individual as their unit of analysis, some anthropologists suffer from a different but equally pernicious bias; salvaging islands of uncorrupted alterity where pre-capitalist forms of community and subjectivity somehow remain immune to global trends of commodification.

6 Some have argued that women's identities *qua* women are necessarily implicated in whatever forms of struggle (such as nationalism) they may be engaged in by virtue of their different social positioning from their male counterparts. This is a separate issue which cannot be dealt with here.

7 This is partly what accounts for the remarkable resilience of the term 'patriarchy' despite the problematic nature of this concept. It is a matter of continuing debate whether 'gender' fully captures the power dynamics implied by the former term.

8 This tendency takes various forms in different disciplines, ranging from 'hidden power' approaches in anthropology (see for instance Susan Carol Rogers, 1975) to 'maternalist' theories in political science (Elshtain, 1981; Ruddick, 1989) and 'female ethics' theories in psychology (Gilligan, 1982).

9 This does not exhaust all possible forms of resistance, however, since the same author points to distinctions between individual covert/individual overt forms of protest as well as group covert/group overt forms.

10 These 'limits' were varied, ranging from the piecemeal and isolating nature of the economic changes that had taken place in the village to the sheer fear of organised state repression, which were not themselves analysed as modes of domination. More significantly, Mitchell argues that the fact that a legally enforced system of private property appears as a 'natural fact' for villagers is something quite different from a rational understanding of the impracticality of challenging this arrangement.

11 Ong's (1987) work on spirit possession among Malaysian women factory workers illustrates this point well. El-Kholy (1996) makes similar observations concerning the *zar* among Egyptian women.

12 I am grateful to Jens Lerche for pointing out that possibilities for mobility and exit options (such as migrating out of an oppressive relationship) exist even in the most seemingly rigid class and caste relations. I, nonetheless, feel that the fact that power

positions in gender relations are so intimately tied to life-cycle changes creates immense additional complications from the point of view of the subjective apprehension of inequalities.

13 This creates a deeply paradoxical situation. When we look at men's and women's access to certain critical resources (such as education, income and even nutrition) categorially (or from the vantage point of the census taker who collates data using binary sex categories) we come up against a picture of inequality as stark and rigid as that of any other system of discrimination. However, the reality and experience of this discrimination is not necessarily *lived* categorially (as in us the poor, the landless, etc.) but mediated by alternative cross-cutting axes of loyalty (such as my family, my tribe) which are constantly refashioned throughout the life cycle.

References

Agarwal, B. (1990) 'Social Security and the Family: Coping with Seasonality and Calamity in Rural India', *Journal of Peasant Studies* 17(3): 341–412.

—— (1994) *A Field of One's Own: Gender and Land Rights in South Asia* Cambridge: Cambridge University Press.

Apffel-Marglin, F. and Simon, S. (1994) 'Feminist Orientalism and Development', in W. Harcourt (ed.) *Feminist Perspectives on Sustainable Development* London: Zed Books.

Bourdieu, P. (1977) *An Outline of A Theory of Practice* Cambridge: Cambridge University Press.

Bryceson, D. H. (ed.) (1995) *Women Wielding the Hoe* Oxford and Washington: Berg Publishers.

Butler, J. (1992) 'Contingent Foundations: Feminism and the Question of "Postmodernism",' in J. Butler and J. Scott *Feminists Theorize and Political.*

Butler, J. and Scott, J. (eds) (1992) *Feminists Theorize the Political* London and New York: Routledge.

Carney, J. (1988) 'Struggles Over Land and Crops in an Irrigated Rice Scheme: The Gambia', in J. Davison (ed.) *Agriculture, Women and Land: The African Experience* Boulder, Colorado: Westview Press.

Carter, M. and Katz, E. (1993) 'Separate Spheres and the Conjugal Contract: Understanding the Impact of Gender-Biased Development', in L. Haddad *et al.* (eds) *Intrahousehold Resource Allocation in Developing Countries: Methods, Models and Policy.*

Connell, R. W. (1987) *Gender and Power* Cambridge: Polity Press.

Dwyer, D. and Bruce, J. (eds) (1988) *A Home Divided: Women and Income in the Third World* Stanford, California: Stanford University Press.

Ekejiuba, F. I. (1995) 'Down to Fundamentals: Women-centered Hearth-holds in Rural West Africa' in D. Bryceson, *Women Wielding the Hoe.*

El-Kholy, H. (1996) 'I Do Not Want to Have Sex with My Husband: Spirit Possession as a Discourse of Resistance in Low-income Cairo'. Paper presented at the International Middle East Association Conference, Amman, 4–8 April.

Ellis, F. (1993) *Peasant Economics: Farm Households and Agrarian Development* Cambridge: Cambridge University Press, 2nd edition.

Elshtain, J. B. (1981) *Public Man, Private Woman* Princeton: Princeton University Press.

Evans, A. (1989) *Gender Issues in Rural Household Economics*, IDS Discussion Paper No. 254, Institute of Development Studies, University of Sussex, Brighton.

Folbre, N. (1984) 'Market Opportunities, Genetic Endowments and Intrafamily Resource Distribution: Comment', *American Economic Review* 74: 518–20.

—— (1986) 'Hearts and Spades: Paradigms of Household Economics', *World Development* 14: 245–55.

Fraser, N. (1989) *Unruly Practices: Power, Discourse and Gender in Contemporary Social Theory* Minneapolis: University of Minnesota Press.

Fraser, N. and Nicholson, L. (1988) 'Social Criticism without Philosophy: An Encounter between Feminism and Postmodernism', *Theory, Culture and Society* 5 (2–3): 373–94.

Gilligan, C. (1982) *In a Different Voice* Cambridge, Mass.: Harvard University Press.

Goetz, A. M. and Sen Gupta, R. (1996) 'Who Takes the Credit? Gender, Power and Control over Loan Use in Rural Credit Programs in Bangladesh', *World Development* 24(1): 45–63.

Guyer, J. (1981) 'Household and Community in African Studies', *African Studies Review* 24(2/3): 87–137.

Guyer, J. and Peters, P. (eds) (1987) 'Conceptualizing the Household: Issues of Theory and Policy in Africa', *Development and Change* 18(2): 197–214.

Harris, O. (1981) 'Households as Natural Units', in K. Young, C. Wolkowitz and R. McCullagh (eds) *Of Marriage and the Market* London: CSE Books.

Hart, G. (1991) 'Engendering Everyday Resistance: Gender, Patronage and Production Politics in Rural Malaysia', *Journal of Peasant Studies* 19(1): 93–121.

—— (1995) 'Gender and Household Dynamics: Recent Theories and their Implications', in M. G. Quibria (ed.) *Critical Issues in Asian Development* Hong Kong: Oxford University Press.

Humphrey, C. (1983) *Karl Marx Collective: Economy, Society and Religion in a Siberian Collective Farm* Cambridge: Cambridge University Press.

Jaquette, J. (1982) 'Women and Modernization Theory: A Decade of Feminist Criticism', *World Politics* 34(2): 267–84.

Jones, C. (1986) 'Intra-Household Bargaining in Response to the Introduction of New Crops: A Case Study from North Cameroon', in J. Moock (ed.) *Understanding Africa's Rural Households and Farming Systems* Boulder, Colorado: Westview Press.

Kabeer, N. (1994) *Reversed Realities* London: Verso.

Kandiyoti, D. (1988) 'Bargaining with Patriarchy', *Gender and Society* 2(3): 274–90.

Mies, M. (1982) 'The Dynamics of Sexual Division of Labour and the Integration of Women into the World Market', in L. Beneria (ed.) *The Sexual Division of Labour in Rural Societies* New York: Praeger.

Mitchell, T. (1990) 'Everyday Metaphors of Power', *Theory and Society* 19: 545–77.

Molyneux, M. (1985) 'Mobilization without Emancipation? Women's Interests, the State and Revolution in Nicaragua', *Feminist Studies* 11: 227–54.

Moore, H. (1992) 'Households and Gender Relations: The Modelling of the Economy', in S. Ortiz and S. Lees (eds) *Understanding Economic Process* New York: University Press of America.

—— (1994) *A Passion for Difference* Cambridge: Policy Press.

Moser, C. O. (1993) *Gender, Planning and Development: Theory, Practice and Training* London: Routledge.

O'Hanlon, R. (1988) 'Recovering the Subject: Subaltern Studies and Histories of Resistance in Colonial South Asia', *Modern Asian Studies* 22(1): 189–224.

Okely, J. (1991) 'Defiant Moments: Gender, Resistance and Individuals', *Man* 26: 3–22.

O'Laughlin (1995) 'Myth of the African Family in the World of Development', in D. Bryceson, *Women Wielding the Hoe.*

Ong, A. (1987) *Spirits of Resistance and Capitalist Discipline: Factory Women in Malaysia* Albany: State University of New York Press.

Risseeuw, C. (1988) *The Fish Don't Talk about the Water: Gender Transformation, Power and Resistance among Women in Sri Lanka* Leiden: E. J. Brill.

Rogers, S. C. (1975) 'Female Forms of Power and the Myth of Male Dominance: A Model of Male–Female Interaction in a Peasant Society,' *American Ethnologist* 11: 727–56.

Ruddick, S. (1989) *Maternal Thinking* London: Verso.

Scott, J. (1985) *Weapons of the Weak: Everyday Forms of Peasant Resistance* New Haven: Yale University Press.

—— (1990) *Domination and the Arts of Resistance* New Haven: Yale University Press.

Scott, J. W. (1988) *Gender and the Politics of History* New York: Columbia University Press.

Sen, A. K. (1983) 'Economics and the Family', *Asian Development Review* 1 (2): 599–634.

—— (1990) 'Gender and Cooperative Conflicts', in I. Tinker (ed.) *Persistent Inequalities: Women and World Development* New York: Oxford University Press.

Standing, H. (1991) *Dependence and Autonomy: Women's Employment and the Family in Calcutta* London: Routledge.

White, C. (1986) 'Everyday Resistance, Socialist Revolution and Rural Development: the Vietnamese Case', *Journal of Peasant Studies* 13 (2): 49–63.

White, J. B. (1994) *Money Makes Us Relatives: Women's Labour in Urban Turkey* Austin: University of Texas Press.

Whitehead, A. (1981) 'I'm Hungry, Mum: The Politics of Domestic Bargaining', in K. Young, C. Wolkowitz and R. McCullagh (eds) *Of Marriage and the Market* London: CSE Books.

Part III

MONEY AND MARKETS

7

TALKING TO THE BOYS

Gender and economic growth models

Diane Elson

Introduction

The last ten years have seen a blossoming of critical research on gender and macro-economic processes, theories and policies; the next ten years present us with the challenge of building on this to try to start transforming practice and move towards the use of macro-economic policy as an instrument for empowering rather than burdening women. This will not be easy. There will be obstruction from gender based coalitions of men, intent on blocking changes, even though greater gender equality promises benefits for society as a whole (Folbre, 1994, 1995). There will be obstruction from class-based coalitions of men and women, intent on preventing any active use of macro-economic policy to change the out-come of market processes. There will be a need to tackle the international dimensions of macro-economic policy, and to work simultaneously on national and international levels, in order to contest the constraints that international bond markets currently place on macro-economic policy.

We shall have to work simultaneously on improving conceptual understanding, improving our empirical knowledge, and constructing a process of institutional change. This chapter is written in the belief that in doing all these things we shall have to act both 'in' and 'against' the established modes of macro-economic theory, empirical enquiry and policy processes. If we only work on the 'inside' we run the risk of merely achieving small improvements in the formulation of models or collection of statistics which do not actually transform women's lives.

If we only work on the 'outside', we run the risk of simply communicating with those who already share our viewpoint, and of not engaging with actual processes of macro-economic policy making. A great deal can be done at the grassroots level in terms of transforming women's livelihoods through the creation of new economic institutions that have gender-aware principles of operation. But macro-economic processes and policies are national and international processes and policies – and require intervention at that level. This requires some kind of engagement with those on the 'inside', to show both where we think they are wrong, and also what we think should be done instead. It requires some willing-ness to get to know and speak the language of the 'insiders' – economists,

155

statisticians, Ministries of Finance and Governors of Central Banks. There is always a danger with this kind of engagement that one gets incorporated, and becomes an 'insider' oneself. From talking to the boys (most people involved in the macro-economic analysis and policy formulation are male), one may become oneself 'one of the boys'.

A way of guarding against this is to emphasise ways of transforming the conceptual tools rather than the integration of women into the existing paradigm; and to emphasise the democratic transformation of public debate and policy processes and not simply the incorporation of new forms of expertise.

This chapter explores these issues with respect to the most basic macro-economic growth model. It is couched in non-technical language in the sense of not using complex mathematical or diagrammatical notation, in order to communicate to the wide readership of this book. It could be expressed in more technical language for the economics profession, if that seemed likely to improve the chances of communicating with that audience, though in fact the gist of the argument can be expressed without using either complex maths or diagrams. What maths and diagrams do is make more precise the limits to outcomes and policy options, and the trade-offs we may face. This precision is, of course, only precision within the confines of a particular set of assumptions, and will be a spurious precision if the assumptions are an inadequate representation of the processes we wish to investigate. All models are by their nature abstractions – but this is their strength, not their weakness. The weakness comes not from making abstractions *per se* but from making inappropriate abstractions.

Formal economic models whether stemming from neo-classical, structuralist or Marxist versions of economics, are closed systems. They, by their very nature, set bounds. Because of this, they can be misused to suggest that there are no alternatives to some particular policy. But they can only properly be used to investigate the implications of accepting a particular set of assumptions about variables, parameters, behaviour and technology. Their very boundedness is useful in forcing us to think clearly about which parameters we need to change in order for different policies and different outcomes to be feasible.

The coherence of formal models is a one-sided abstraction, because economic processes do not jump cleanly from one equilibrium to another. But by making us think hard about limitations and priorities, they can help us avoid macro-economic policies that are unsustainable and lead to economic crises, which disempower women as much as do badly designed adjustment policies.

Some people may query the usefulness of discussing growth models at all. Shouldn't we be criticising economic growth rather than modelling it, they may say? To which I would reply that the two things are not incompatible. Moreover, it is useful to engage with simple growth models because they form the conceptual framework of many medium-term macro-economic policies. This does not mean an endorsement of aggregate growth of national output as the only important macro-economic objective; nor an endorsement of any and every pattern of growth. Indeed, growth models themselves may generate a critical understanding of growth processes. Harrod's original purpose in devising his widely used model of growth was to develop a critique of the assumption that a full employment balanced growth path can be taken for granted (Walters, 1995). He was concerned about the problem of what the most recent *Human Development Report* called 'jobless growth' (UNDP, 1996: 2).

That same *Human Development Report* identifies four other undesirable types of growth: ruthless growth, where the fruits of economic growth mainly benefit the rich; voiceless growth where growth is not accompanied by an extension of democracy or empowerment; rootless growth, which causes peoples' cultural identity to wither; futureless growth, where the present generation squanders resources needed by future generations. Nevertheless, the Report concludes that more economic growth, not less, will generally be needed in the next century. But it will need to be directed to supporting human development, reducing poverty, protecting the environment and ensuring sustainability (UNDP, 1996: 1).

Here we shall focus on simple growth models not because we are assuming that growth of aggregate national output is a good thing irrespective of the pattern of growth, but because such models crystallise in a simple form some influential ways of thinking about savings, investment, productivity and output and employment. We shall look at ways of making use of such models as a departure point in order to raise potentially transformatory questions about economies as gendered structures, and about the interaction of production and social reproduction. We shall also identify an agenda for empirical research arising out of this discussion.

The Harrod–Domar growth model: basic considerations

The most simple model of growth, which every student of development studies generally comes across in one form or another, is the Harrod–Domar model. This is a synthesis of work originally undertaken separately by Harrod (1939, 1948) and Domar (1946) to create a model which can be used to answer questions such as – if the policy objective is to achieve a rate of growth of national output of 5 per cent a year, how much will the country need to save and invest? The model suggests that the answer depends on the productivity of investment. Its reasoning is summed up in the conclusion that the annual growth of output is equal to the annual share of savings in national output divided by the incremental capital–output ratio (which measures the amount of output produced by a given addition to the capital stock in a year). To raise the rate of growth it is necessary to raise the rate of saving and/or to raise the productivity of capital. This is based on the assumption that all savings are invested and result in additions to the capital stock, and that the capital stock is fully utilised. It also assumes that there is no shortage of labour to utilise the capital stock, and no large-scale unemployment which might lead to hesitation in the investment of savings by depressing demand expectations.

The basic version of the model was modified to introduce exports, imports and foreign sources of saving by Chenery and Strout (1966). This resulted in what is generally known as the 'two gap' model, which is used as the basis for evaluations of the foreign aid requirements of a country by national governments and donor agencies, (see for example, Ministry of Foreign Affairs, Netherlands, 1994). The 'two gap' model forms the basis of the Revised Minimum Standard Model used by the World Bank to make projections of growth and balance of payments deficits for countries undergoing structural adjustment (Tarp, 1993). In this chapter, however, we shall confine our attention to the basic version of the Harrod–Domar model, as expounded in textbooks such as Gillis *et al.* (1992), in order to highlight a number of issues which arise irrespective of whether the national economy is relatively 'closed' or relatively 'open' to the international economy. These are issues to do with savings, investment and productivity, issues which as Amartya Sen has argued, were at the heart of development economics when it was first constructed as a separate discourse in the 1940s and 1950s (Sen, 1983); and which continue to be urgent and unresolved issues, despite the attempts of the neo-classical counter-revolution in development economics to shift the emphasis from the macro analysis of capital accumulation to the micro analysis of prices (Toye, 1987).

The Harrod–Domar model is constructed at a high level of abstraction and does not specify the pattern of ownership of the capital stock; or the processes through which savings are mobilised, investments are made, and capital stock is used in production; or the distribution of the output provided. Domar, in fact, constructed his version of the model with a planned economy in mind, whereas Harrod had in mind a market economy, with savings and investment and production largely in the private sector. The assumption of full capacity utilisation on which the synthetic version of the model is built is in fact more plausible for a 'mixed' economy with a large public sector and a 'Keynesian' public policy or for a centrally planned socialist economy; because in these types of economy there is less likely to be a deficiency in aggregate demand. Those making investment decisions in such an economy do not have to worry too much about the risk of lack of demand because there is a relatively soft budget constraint, and a state which stands ready to act as buyer of last resort. (However, such economies may well be prone to other problems such as inflation or low productivity.)

Many criticisms may be made of the Harrod–Domar model as a basis for development policy (for an early and effective example, see Streeten, 1968). For instance, as well as ignoring problems of deficient demand, it ignores problems of inter-sectoral input–output relations, and problems of lack of sufficient skilled labour. However, these last two deficiencies can in principle be remedied by disaggregating the model, using an input–output table; and by extending the concept of investment to include investment in health, nutrition and education to develop the skills and capacities of workers. Here, we shall focus on the gender blindness of the Harrod–Domar model. As with all aggregate growth models, the Harrod–Domar model pays no attention to gender relations (Walters, 1995). However, thus gender blindness is not a benign gender neutrality, because the omission of consideration of gender relations in relation to saving, investment, productivity and growth serves to consolidate and perpetuate gender inequality. In the next two sections we discuss strategies for introducing an awareness of gender into the model.

Gender disaggregation

It may seem that the way to introduce gender into the basic growth model is by disaggregating the economy into a male economy and a female economy, with male and female streams of savings, investment and output. Certainly from the perspective of neo-classical economics, gender disaggregation is the obvious move to make. This is the procedure advocated by Collier (1990, 1994) in dealing with a different type of model – the small dependent economy model of structural adjustment, in which resources are switched from non-tradables to tradables. Collier sets out his reasons as follows:

> Gender is one of many ways in which data can be disaggregated and the rationale for doing this is twofold. First, in earning income, women often face different constraints, from men. Since structural adjustment is largely about changing constraints, if those facing women and men are sufficiently different, it is illuminating to treat the genders as distinct groups rather than studying gender-undifferentiated averages. Second, women and men often have radically different propensities to consume particular public services and so budgetary changes can have powerfully gender-differentiated effects. It should be stressed that gender is not a topic in itself but rather a possible disaggregation to be borne in mind when studying a topic. Sometimes gender disaggregation will not add enough to be worthwhile. However, for some topics it will be useful and for others essential. A corollary of this rationale for an analysis which distinguishes between women and men is that, generally, there is not a small, self-contained set of 'women's issues' which can be appended to an otherwise unaltered analysis. Rather, the claim is that many standard issues in resource allocation become better illuminated when the analysis is dissaggregated by gender.
>
> (Collier, 1990: 149–50)

Walters (1995) writing from a Keynesian perspective is not so sure that disaggregation is the best way of proceeding:

> Of course, disaggregation is possible. At the simplest level, representative agents in different economic circumstances would carry different parameter values within a disaggregated model. However, a mechanical disaggregation based on the fact that all economic agents are biologically male or female would be inappropriate. Gender disaggregation should correspond to our understanding of how gender relations impose

constraints on the overall behaviour of macro models; the analogy is dis-aggregation by class. In Keynesian macro-economic models, based on class, the models are driven by the aggregate level of spending which becomes a function of the distribution of income between workers and capitalists. This is a structural, rather than an individualist disaggregation. It is based on the different economic functions of workers and capitalists and corresponds to the institutional division between firms and house-holds. Any disaggregation by gender should be based on a similar understanding of the way in which gender as a social institution impinges on or constrains the behaviour of the macroeconomy.

(Walters, 1995: 1870)

The caution displayed by Walters seems justified when one considers how gender is understood in the gender-disaggregation analysis conducted by Collier (1988, 1990, 1994; Collier *et al.*, 1991). This analysis locates gender primarily in terms of the 'physiological asymmetry of reproduction' and the impulse of boys to copy men and girls to copy women. Biology and preferences are the ultimate foundations of gender inequality.

The basic problem with disaggregation is that it focuses on the separate char-acteristics of men or women (whether individuals or groups) rather than the social institutions of gender as a power relation. It can thus lead to the analysis of women in isolation from men (and vice versa); or the female economy in isolation from the male economy. The danger is that it does not draw sufficient attention to the reciprocal determination of the characteristics of women and men as eco-nomic agents; and the reciprocal determination of the characteristics of male or female sectors of production. Nevertheless there is much to be gained in empiri-cal research in a multisectoral framework in distinguishing between male-intensive and female-intensive sectors of the economy. A greater empirical understanding of the comparative sectoral pattern of the employment of men and of women is extremely useful for any analysis of inter-sectoral resource transfers, such as are implied by structural adjustment (Elson *et al.*, 1997).

The strategy of gender disaggregation does not however do very much to trans-form perceptions of how a national economy functions. It would be useful to consider strategies which pose the issue of the economy itself as a gendered struc-ture, rather than as a gender-neutral structure within which men and women undertake different activities.

Gendered parameters

One strategy for doing this at the abstract level of a simple growth model is to con-ceptualise the parameters of the model as 'bearers of gender'. This entails recognising the matrix of gender relations as an intervening variable in all eco-nomic activities, whether undertaken by men or women, in male-intensive or female-intensive sectors of the economy. In the context of the simple

Harrod–Domar growth model, this means introducing gender relations as an intervening variable that can influence the productivity of investment and the propensity to save. Unequal gender relations could operate to reduce the productivity of investment – in technical terms to raise the potential value of ICORs (Incremental Capital Output Ratios) above the level that would prevail with more egalitarian gender relations.

There is certainly a wealth of evidence which demonstrates male bias in the use of productive resources. Male bias disadvantages women in access to and control of credit and land; in the creation and dissemination of new technologies; and in the acquisition of health, strength and skills. Male bias disadvantages women in credit, labour and product markets and intra-firm labour processes, marginalising women from decision-making processes; in access to and control of infrastructural services (energy, water, transport, buildings) and in intra-household arrangements for the organisation of both production of commodities and the social reproduction of people. Male bias excludes women's voices from the policy processes in which public expenditure patterns are determined. There is a large literature on all these forms of male bias which leaves no doubt that they are widespread and have significant impact on women's well-being (Agarwal, 1988; Tinker, 1990; Birdsall and Sabot, 1991; Young, 1993; Kabeer, 1994; Elson *et al.*, 1997). But in addition, gender inequality, just like class inequality, is likely to be a barrier to the most effective and productive use of human resources to meet human needs.

Quantitative evidence can be cited to illustrate this point with respect to control over the use of resources by small-scale producers. For example, Ongaro (1988) looked at the adoption of new farming technology in maize production in Kenya in the 1980s and investigated the impact of gender relations on the use of technology by comparing the effect of weeding on yields in female-headed households and male-headed households. It was found that in female-headed households the weeding undertaken raised yields by 56 per cent, whereas in male-headed households the increase in yield was only 15 per cent. After controlling for other differences between the two types of household, the study concluded that the most likely explanation was a systematic difference in effort due to differential entitlement structures, with women in female-headed households having more incentive to weed more effectively because they controlled the proceeds of their own work whereas the women in male-headed households did not.

Output is also lost because women small-scale producers do not have the same access as men to productive inputs, including education. For instance, Moock's (1976) investigation of the efficiency of women as farm managers in Kenya found that their performance compared very well with that of men, but that their access to resources was more restricted. On the basis of the coefficients in Moock's study, it has been calculated that if the woman farmers had the same access to inputs and education as the men farmers in the sample, yields could be increased by between 7 and 9 per cent. Another study covering beans and cowpeas as well as maize suggests even bigger increases in yields, of around 22 per cent, would be possible if women farmers had the same access to inputs and education as men farmers (Saito *et al.*, 1994). Similar results have been found for Burkino Faso, where a recent study suggests that the intra-household reallocation of resources from men to women could increase the value of household output by 10–20 per cent (Alderman *et al.*, 1995).

Similar findings are reported in a study of small-scale urban retailers in Peru (Smith and Stelcher, 1990). This established that women were as effective managers of resources as men. However, firms with a smaller amount of capital tended to have much higher returns to capital, and a much higher proportion of female-owned firms had low amounts of capital. Directing increments of capital (via reforms of credit) to female-owned firms would therefore tend to raise the overall rate of return to capital (and *ipso facto* reduce the investment required to achieve any given rate of growth).

Similar arguments can be made with respect to eliminating discrimination against women in labour markets. Such discrimination has been treated in economic analysis mainly as an equity issue, but can also be seen as socially inefficient. A pioneering study by Tzannatos (1992: part 1,15) has demonstrated that if gender discrimination in patterns of occupation and pay in Latin America were eliminated not only could women's wages rise by about 50 per cent, but national output could rise by 5 per cent.

In counterpoint to this, it is certainly possible to construct scenarios in which gender inequality might lead to increased profitability of investment through extracting more effort from women. There are cases where such tendencies can be discerned. A study of gender and industrial reform in Bangladesh has found that between 1983 and 1990, the average weekly hours worked in urban formal sector manufacturing by women workers increased from 41.3 to 55.9. For men, the increase was from 48.9 to 53.2, so that by 1990 women were working on average longer hours than men despite having more unpaid work in social reproduction than men (Zohir, 1996). However, such long hours of work for women are likely to reduce labour productivity through ill-health and stress. Exploitation of women workers certainly leads to a bias in the distribution of income against women and towards employers (who are usually men). But profitability and productivity are not the same thing. It is possible for lower profitability to be combined with higher productivity. If women's hours of work were reduced and discrimination against women ended, the social return in terms of output per unit of investment would tend to be higher, but the private returns to owners of capital might tend to fall. The latter would then have an interest in perpetuating gender inequality even though there would be gains in terms of final output.

Societies may be temporarily locked into a particular path-dependent set of unequal gender and class relations which are conducive to the persistence of behaviour patterns that create adverse trade-offs between equality and productivity. There are clearly parallels here with the debates on productivity and democratic or participatory economic institutions (see for instance Bowles *et al.*, 1993). Much depends on whether people's preferences and institutional structures are believed to be exogenous or endogenous. Insofar as preferences and institutions are endogenous, then there is much more scope for dynamic institutional transformations which can move societies out of vicious circles into virtuous circles in which equality and efficiency are mutually reinforcing rather than at odds; and production is organised through cooperative rather than exploitative institutions. The key issue then is how such dynamic transformations can be accomplished. The view taken here is that what is required is not 'investment *in* women' but investment *with* women in institutional changes which change preferences, perceptions, norms and rights. In considering the costs of this investment it must be remembered that perpetuating gender inequality is also costly, requiring expenditures that buttress male power without enhancing productivity, a point we return to below.

We still lack macro-level studies which gather and review available micro evidence on gender inequality and the productivity of investment for a particular country and attempt to synthesise the findings to produce some estimate of the implications of failure to reduce male bias for the country's rate of growth: and to indicate which forms of male bias have greatest quantitative significance for the value of the rate of growth. This is likely to depend on economic structure, with male bias in labour markets being a more significant factor in reducing the return to investment in countries whose production is largely organised through wage employment in private and public sector corporations: and male bias in credit and produce markets being more significant in countries where self-employment and small businesses account for a larger share of output.

Besides the ICOR, the other important parameter in the Harrod–Domar model is the savings propensity. Studies providing direct evidence linking the degree of gender inequality with the value of this parameter are hard to find. Most studies at household level seem to focus more on expenditure patterns than on savings. There is a need for some comparative studies to explore the hypothesis that a greater degree of female control over household budgeting is conducive to a higher rate of saving; and that where women and men have separate income streams, women have a greater propensity to save out of income under their control than do men. The reason for setting up the hypothesis in this form is the intuition that women's responsibilities and obligations in the sphere of social reproduction may lead them to take a longer view, and that women, for cultural reasons, have a greater tendency than men to derive satisfaction and well-being from activities which are less commodity intensive. Some household-level studies which have probed leisure activities have found that women spend their leisure in visiting friends and relatives, going to church, and playing with their children, while men go to football matches and bars and cafes (e.g. Kanji, 1993). This is an area where more research is needed. However, there is plenty of evidence suggesting that a more equal gender distribution of income would be conducive to spending patterns that contribute to higher growth rates in the long term in ways that promote human development. To bring this evidence to bear, we need to extend the model to incorporate social reproduction.

Extending the model to incorporate social reproduction

The simple Harrod–Domar model (like most growth models) takes labour for granted and treats it as a non-purchased input into production that does not constrain growth (Walters, 1995). However, there is now widespread recognition that the productivity of investment depends on the capabilities of the people who use it in production, especially their health and skills.

Mainstream economics recognises this in the concept of 'human capital' and endogenous growth theory gives formal expression to the idea that investment in 'human capital' can overcome the tendency for diminishing returns to investment in physical equipment and infrastructure, and thereby raise the rate of growth (Walters, 1995). However, mainstream analysis only recognises investment in the acquisition and acceptance of human capacities through adult individuals investing their own time and money in acquiring additional qualifications and through social investment by governments in education and health facilities. What is left out of account is the process of social reproduction in which women invest time and money in the education and socialisation of children; and in nutrition and healthcare for both children and adults. Feminist analysis emphasises the importance of looking at economies through women's eyes, so that social reproduction is brought into the picture as well as production (Picchio, 1992; Sen, G., 1995; Folbre, 1994).

Given the prevailing structures of gender relations, household investment in the nutrition, health and education of children tends to be more the responsibility of women than of men. There is a great deal of evidence from all over the world to suggest that there is incomplete pooling of income within households, and that there are significant differences between expenditure from female-controlled income and expenditure from male-controlled income. Women attach a higher priority to expenditure on family nutrition, health and education-related goods (e.g. school uniforms) than do men. Men are much more likely than women to spend part of their income on purely personal consumption of commodities such as alcohol, cigarettes, gambling, higher status consumer durables, and female companionship.

Among the important sociological and anthropological studies to have established this are Kumar (1979), Guyer (1980), Tripp (1981), Pahl (1983) and Dwyer and Bruce (1988). More recently their findings have been corroborated by econometric studies based on a new class of household models which do not assume a single household utility function. For instance, a positive relationship was found between the proportion of cereals produced under women's control and household consumption of calories in Gambian households by von Braun (1988). Similarly, a study in the Philippines found that raising the share of income accruing to wives increased acquisition of calories and proteins (Garcia, 1990). Particularly revealing is a study of households in the Côte d'Ivoire which found that doubling women's share of cash income raised the budget share of food and lowered the budget shares of alcohol and cigarettes (Hoddinott and Haddad, 1995).

Within the context of an extension of the Harrod–Domar model to include human resources as determinants of growth, this evidence could be interpreted as indicating a greater propensity on the part of women than on the part of men to invest in maintenance and enhancement of human capacities. This gendered difference in expenditure patterns may be partly the result of a greater incidence of maternal than paternal altruism. It may be partly the result of information asymmetries – since men are not so involved in the day to day care of children, they are not so well informed about the needs of children. It is also likely to be determined by efforts to preserve existing sources of power and advantage. One of the few sources of power and advantage to women in many countries is privileged access to their children, especially sons. Women invest in their children to gain and maintain access to this resource. A source of power and advantage to men in many countries is privileged access to an autonomous public sphere life outside the family. Much of their 'leisure' expenditure may be interpreted as expenditure to gain and maintain their access to this sphere, and the alternative to family life that it offers. (Among poor men, this public sphere in which they have 'free time' may also serve to reconcile them to their lack of power in relation to richer men). In both cases an analogy may be made with what economists call rent-seeking behaviour, understood as expenditure to create and retain some position of advantage; but in the case of women's expenditure on their children, much of the expenditure is directly productive; whereas in the case of men's expenditure on leisure commodities, a considerable proportion of it is directly unproductive (e.g. excessive consumption of alcohol, tobacco, gambling), leading to a depletion rather than an enhancement of human capacities, particularly since it is also often associated with violence against women (Elson, 1992). It would be interesting to explore the possibilities of estimating the scale of loss of productive output in relation to GDP that arises from the diversion of resources to these forms of activity that serve to buttress male power and at the same time deplete human resources.

The co-ordination of production and social reproduction in the growth process

The simple Harrod–Domar model assumes away any problems of co-ordination between the spheres of production and social reproduction. It is a full-employment, full-capacity utilisation model. Harrod's original model is more Keynesian in spirit than this and focuses on the issue of what, if any, mechanisms exist to produce a full employment balanced growth path. It results in the conclusion that this will only happen by chance and there is no mechanism which will be sure to bring it about. Subsequent developments in neo-classical growth theory assume away this problem by assuming first that there is a wide array of production technologies, so that labour and machinery can always be substituted for one another; and second that markets will operate so as to price people into jobs (Walters, 1995).

The problem with assuming that flexible technology and smoothly functioning markets will serve to co-ordinate production and social reproduction is that social reproduction is not organised along commercial principles. While it would be over-romantic to assume that women work at social reproduction entirely for love, it would be crass to assume that social reproduction can be modelled on the same principle as livestock production. Women and men do not on the whole regard their children as just another crop, to be left to rot with equanimity if the risk of tending them becomes too high. As Humphries and Rubery (1984) put it, social reproduction is relatively autonomous. It has its own norms, procedures, patterns of compulsion and choice which interact with and respond to but are not reducible to those of the market-orientated production of commodities. It is not surprising that if co-ordination is left to the market, the outcomes are likely to be dysfunctional growth patterns identified in the *Human Development Report* (UNDP, 1996). The strength of Harrod's growth model is that it recognised this co-ordination problem; but (as Walters, 1995 shows), its weakness is that the only method it allows for resolving the problem is via policies which impact on the market demand expectations of investors. That is because Harrod sets up the co-ordination problem as a problem of equating the warranted rate of growth with the natural rate of growth. The warranted rate of growth is that growth rate at which the market demand expectations upon which firms base their investment decisions are confirmed, or warranted, by the spending decisions of consumers. The natural rate of growth is defined as the maximum rate of growth allowed by population, accumulation of capital, technological improvement and work/leisure preference schedule, supposing that there is always full employment (Harrod, 1939: 30). The natural rate of growth is treated as exogenously given (which is equivalent to treating social reproduction as fully, not relatively, autonomous). Policy could influence the warranted rate of growth via measures to raise investors' expectations of future market demand – such as the institutionalisation of the state as 'buyer of last resort' through the pursuit of Keynesian macro-economic policies; and industrial planning and information sharing about private sector plans and expectations through corporatist institutions such as business/government/trade union economic councils. Critics of Keynesian approaches have stressed the dangers of inflation inherent in such an approach. But they have ignored the problems posed by the unequal gender division of labour in both production and social reproduction.

Increasing the aggregate demand for labour through planned development is not guaranteed to produce a balanced distribution between men and women of paid work in production and paid work in social reproduction. Instead, depending upon the composition of aggregate demand for goods and services, it may produce overwork for women as they increase their participation in paid work in production, while continuing to do most of the unpaid work of social reproduction; and at the same time leave men in a debilitating idleness or underemployment as they fail to find 'men's jobs' in paid production but are culturally constrained from undertaking 'women's work' in either production or social reproduction. A fully adequate co-ordination of production and social reproduction will require a transformation of the norms about what is 'women's work' and 'men's work' and a transformation of investors' expectations not only about the future rate of growth of consumer demand, but also about the ways in which the sphere of production relates to the sphere of social reproduction. In down to earth terms, this means that firms will need to be transformed so that they do not penalise employees for undertaking domestic responsibilities and there will have to be social investment in providing the infrastructure and services required to reduce the burdens of social reproduction.

Of course, in the late twentieth century, Keynesian policies and development planning have largely been abandoned, and policy makers are urged to rely on deflationary policies and market prices to co-ordinate production and social reproduction. The shortcomings of this approach have been documented in the wealth of research on stabilisation and adjustment policies. In effect, whereas the Harrod–Domar approach to growth assumes that policy makers can manipulate production so as to meet the needs of social reproduction, the World Bank approach to growth assumes that social reproduction will always accommodate itself to the savings and investment decisions made in the productive economy. This is apparent in the formulation of the World Bank's growth model, the Revised Minimum Standard Model, which is used to produce assessments of the aid required to achieve growth targets on the assumption that the level of consumption is residually determined (Tarp, 1993). This amounts to assuming that social reproduction can be accomplished with whatever is left over after investment needs have been met. This implies that social reproduction has no autonomy in the growth process, something that can only be taken for granted if people can live on fresh air or women's unpaid labour is available in unlimited supplies (Elson, 1991, 1995).

We need more empirical studies of how production and social reproduction interact in mutually determining ways in the growth process, shedding light on the scope and limits of the relative autonomy of social reproduction, and the ways in which gendered norms and institutions are reinforced, decomposed or recomposed. Feminist contemporary economic history (as undertaken by Folbre, 1994) has much to contribute here.

Conclusions

The arguments and evidence put forward here point towards the conclusion that measures to restructure gender relations can be a powerful force for producing a growth path which supports human development and balances work in production and social reproduction. We have suggested that gender analysis can deconstruct and reconstruct thinking about savings, investment, productivity, output and employment. Aggregate levels of savings, investment, output and employment can be seen as the outcome of gendered structures. The parameters of simple growth models can be linked to gendered patterns of control over resources. The adequacy of growth models in relation to human development objectives can be linked to the way in which growth models treat the interaction of production and social reproduction. We have been engaged in an exercise in challenging and changing the discourse of the economic theory of growth. Along the way, we have identified an empirical research agenda for the next few years. We need more comparative empirical case studies of gender equality and productive efficiency; and gender equality and savings, followed by 'scaling up' of micro-level evidence to reveal the macro-level implications; and more contemporary feminist economic history that looks at the interactions of production and social reproduction and the decomposition and recomposition of gender over the last five decades of development.

If this change in discourse and this new empirical research is to make a real difference it will have to be translated into new policies, and that will require public action both to mobilise women outside the policy process and to build coalitions with sympathetic insiders. But that, as they say, is another story, beyond the scope of the present volume.

References

Agarwal, B. (ed.) (1988) *Structures of Patriarchy*, New Delhi: Kali for Women; London: Zed Books.

Alderman, H., Hoddinott, J., Haddad, L. and Udry, C. (1995) *Gender Differentials in Farm Productivity: Implications for Household Efficiency and Agricultural Policy*, Food Consumption and Nutrition Division Paper 7, Washington, DC: International Food Policy Research Institute.

Birdsall, N. and Sabot, R. (eds) (1991) *Unfair Advantage: Labour Market Discrimination in Developing Countries*, Washington, DC: World Bank.

Bowles, S., Gintis, H. and Gustafsson, B. (eds) (1993) *Markets and Democracy*, Cambridge: Cambridge University Press.

Chenery, H. B. and Strout, A. M. (1966) 'Foreign Assistance and Economic Development', *American Economic Review*, 56, 4: 679–733.

Collier, P. (1988) *Women in Development – Defining the Issues*, Policy, Planning and Research Working Paper, 129, Washington, DC: World Bank.

Collier, P. (1990) 'The Impact of Adjustment on Women', in World Bank, *Analysis Plan for Understanding the Social Dimensions of Adjustment*, Washington DC: World Bank.

Collier, P. (1994) 'Gender Aspects of Labor Allocation during Structural Adjustment – A Theoretical Framework and the African Experience', in Susan Horton, Ravi Kanbar and Dipak Mazumdar (eds) *Labor Markets in an Era of Adjustment*, Vol. 1, Washington, DC: World Bank.

Collier, P., Appleton, S., Devon, D. L., Burger, K., Dunning, J.W., Haddad, L. and Hoddinott, G. (1991) 'Public Services and Household Allocation in Africa: Does Gender Matter?', mimeo, Oxford: Centre for Study of African Economies.

Domar, E. (1946) 'Capital Expansion Rate of Growth and Employment', *Econometrica*, 14: 137–47.

Dwyer, D. and Bruce, J. (eds.) (1988) *A Home Divided: Women and Income in the Third World*, Stanford: Stanford University Press.

Elson, D. (1991) 'Male Bias in Macro-economics: The Case of Structural Adjustment', in D. Elson (ed.) *Male Bias in the Development Process*, Manchester: Manchester University Press.

Elson, D. (1992) 'From Survival Strategies to Transformation Strategies: Women's Needs and Structural Adjustment', in L. Beneria and S. Feldman (eds.) *Economic Crises, Persistent Poverty and Women's Work*, Boulder: Westview Press.

Elson, D. (1997) 'Gender Awareness in Modelling Structural Adjustment', *World Development*, 23, 11: 1851–68.

Elson, D., Evers, B. and Gideon, J. (1997) 'Concepts and Sources', *Gender Aware Country Economic Reports, Working Paper No. 1.*, GENECON Unit, Graduate School of Social Sciences, University of Manchester, Manchester.

Folbre, N. (1994) *Who Pays for the Kids? Gender and the Structures of Constraint*, London: Routledge.

Folbre, N. (1995) 'Engendering Economics: New Perspectives on Woman, Work and Demographic Change'. Paper presented at World Bank Annual Conference on Development Economics. Washington, DC.

Garcia, M. (1990) 'Resource Allocation and Household Welfare: A Study of the Impact of Personal Sources of Income on Food Consumption, Nutrition and Health in the Philippines', PhD thesis, The Hague: Institute of Social Studies.

Gillis, M., Perkins, D., Roemer, M. and Snodgrass, D. (1992) *Economics of Development* 4th Edition, New York: Norton.

Guyer, J. (1980) *Household Budgets and Women's Incomes*, African Studies Centre Working Paper 28, Boston, Mass: Boston University.

Harrod, R. F. (1939) 'An Essay in Dynamic Theory', *Economic Journal*, 49: 14–33.

Harrod, R. F. (1948) *Towards a Dynamic Economics*, London: Macmillan.

Hoddinott, J. and Haddad, L. (1995) 'Does Female Income Share Influence Household Expenditures? Evidence from Cote d'Ivoire', *Oxford Bulletin of Economics and Statistics*, 57: 77–96.

Humphries, J. and Rubery, J. (1984) 'The Reconstitution of the Supply Side of the Labour Market: The Relative Autonomy of Social Reproduction', *Cambridge Journal of Economics*, 8, 4: 331–46.

Kabeer, N. (1994) *Reversed Realities – Gender Hierarchies in Development Thought*, London: Verso.

Kanji, N. (1993) 'Gender and Structural Adjustment Policies: A Case Study of Harare, Zimbabwe', Phd thesis, London: London School of Economics.

Kumar, S. (1979) *Impact of Subsidised Rice on Food Consumption and Nutrition in Kerala*, Research Report 5, Washington, DC: IFPRI.

Ministry of Foreign Affairs, Netherlands (1994) *Guidelines on Programme Aid*, The Hague.

Moock, P. (1976) 'The Efficiency of Women as Farm Managers: Kenya', *American Journal of Agricultural Economics*, 58: 831–5.

Ongaro, W. A. (1988) 'Adoption of New Farming Technology: A Case Study of Maize Production in Western Kenya', PhD thesis, Gothenberg: University of Gothenberg.

Pahl, J. (1983) 'The Allocation of Money within Marriage', *Sociological Review*, 32: 237–64.

Picchio, A. (1992) *Social Reproduction – The Political Economy of the Labour Market*, Cambridge: Cambridge University Press.

Saito, K., Mekonnen, H. and Spurling, D. (1994) *Raising the Productivity of Women Farmers in Sub-Saharan Africa*, Discussion Paper 230, Washington, DC: World Bank.

Sen, A. K. (1983) 'Development: Which Way Now?', *Economic Journal*, 93: 745–62.

Sen, G. (1995) 'Alternative Economics from a Gender Perspective', *Development*, 1: 10–13.

Smith, J. B. and Stelcher, M. (1990) *Modelling Economic Behaviour in Peru's Informal Urban Retail Sector*, PHRD Working Paper 469, Washington, DC: World Bank.

Streeten, P. (1968) 'Economic Models and their Usefulness for Planning in South Asia', Appendix 3 in G. Myrdal, *Asian Drama*, Harmondsworth: Penguin Books.

Tarp, F. (1993) *Stabilization and Structural Adjustment*, London: Routledge.

Tinker, I. (ed.) (1990) *Persistent Inequalities: Women and World Development*, Oxford: Oxford University Press.

Toye, J. (1987) *Dilemmas of Development*, Oxford: Blackwell.

Tripp, R. (1981) 'Farmers and Traders: Some Economic Determinants of Nutritional Status in Northern Ghana', *Journal of Tropical Pediatrics*, Vol. 27.

Tzannatos, Z. (1992) 'Potential Gains from the Elimination of Labor Market Differentials', in *Women's Employment and Pay in Latin America, Part 1 Overview and Methodology*', Regional Studies Program Report 10. Washington, DC: World Bank.

UNDP (1996) *Human Development Report*, New York: United Nations.

Von Braun, J. (1988) 'Effects of Technological Change in Agriculture on Food Consumption and Nutrition: Rice in a West African Setting', *World Development* 16, 9: 1083–98.

Walters, B. (1995) 'Engendering Macroeconomics: A Reconsideration of Growth Theory', *World Development*, 23, 11: 1869–80.

Young, K. (1993) *Planning Development with Women*, London: Macmillan.

Zohir, S. (1996) 'Gender Implications of Industrial Reforms in Bangladesh', Draft PhD, University of Manchester.

8

'NIMBLE FINGERS' REVISITED

Reflections on women and Third World industrialisation in the late twentieth century

Ruth Pearson

This chapter seeks to review and reassess some of the debates concerning the experience and interpretation of women's incorporation into the waged labour force at a time when industrial production, particularly for export, has become one of the most successful strategies for developing countries seeking to achieve economic growth and development. In this connection I deal with some of the responses to earlier work by myself and Diane Elson based on strongly articulated accusations that we presented a 'stereotypical' view of women workers 'which is remarkably homogenous and generally negative' (Lim, 1990: 111).

'Nimble fingers' revisited: a response to the critics

feminists who see patriarchy and gender subordination as critical underpinnings and inevitable consequences of all capitalism refuse to recognise any benefits to women in the Third World from employment in export factories, insisting that such employment intensifies rather than alleviates their gender subordination. The works of Elson and Pearson are popular with this group.

(Lim, 1990: 111)

This quotation reflects the way in which discussion of women and industrialisation has become, and perhaps always was, a *signifier* meant to represent a notion of women's equality or economic importance rather than either part of the analysis of the industrialisation process in development or a context for understanding the impact of development on gender relations.

By the 1970s it was impossible to ignore women's role in the new industrial map of the world. Dramatic changes in the location of manufacturing production meant that an increasing proportion of the world's production of key consumer goods – textiles and garments, and new goods and components based on electronics components – was being manufactured or assembled in certain low wage economies of the developing world. This represented a break with the traditional international division of labour in which the advanced countries produced high value added manufactured goods and developing countries exported raw materials and food products for processing in the industrial centres of Europe and North America.

Whilst there were predictions that women would continue to be excluded from the new economic structures of post-independence Asia, Sub-Saharan Africa and Latin America, it was clear that women were very a part of this 'new' phase of industrialisation. When in 1978 we first raised the question as to what was the significance for gender relations, and thus for the women employed in so-called 'world market factories' (Fröbel *et al.*, 1980), of women's growing share in these sectors of export industry, we were calling into question what had been a shared assumption – in both the neoclassical tradition and the Marxist tradition[1] – the notion that provision of jobs for women was an important way of 'integrating women into the development process'. We noted that

> the idea that women's subordination stems from a lack of job opportunities and can be ended by the provision of sufficient job opportunities is deeply rooted and held by a wide spectrum of opinion from international development agencies, government bureaux, mainstream marxists to many women's organisations.
>
> (Elson and Pearson, 1981a: 143)

However, we chose to take not the *absence* of employment but instead the *availability of* job opportunities as our starting point to interrogate the relations through which women were being incorporated into the development process and to explore industrial employment 'from the point of view of the new possibilities and the new problems which they raise for Third World women who work in them' (ibid.: 144).

Industrialisation and women: from the margins to the centre

In making the experience of women in the new phase of export-led industrialisation our point of departure we were implicitly deviating from a long-held consensus concerning the impact of development on women's industrial employment – again from all shades of the political spectrum.

The classic consensus about women and industrialisation, which was current until the 1970s, was that industrialisation was a process which marginalised women, in the sense of excluding women from industrial employment. This position was held both by the 'modernisation' school of development, epitomised by Esther Boserup who argued in her path-breaking book published in 1970 that women's labour is displaced as production is transferred from the household to the factory and that since men are the decision makers both in the family and in the labour market, are better educated and trained than women and are less burdened with family obligations, they are much more likely to draw benefit (from the increasing specialisation of labour and hierarchisation of the labour force) than women, who end up at the bottom of the labour market hierarchy.

(Boserup, 1987: iii)

Dependency theorists, writing from the experience of earlier industrialisation in Latin America, also concluded that industrialisation marginalised women:

contrary to general belief, industrial development did not bring about a substantial increase in the employment of female labour. Although there was an increase in the absolute number of women employed in the . . . major (industrial) sectors, the increase in the number of men was substantially greater.

(Saffioti, 1978: 124)

Saffioti attributed the lack of opportunities for women to 'dependent capitalism' which

accelerated the expulsion of women from directly economic roles . . . this marginalisation of female labour, which is often explained almost exclusively in terms of prejudice, the vestiges of 'traditional society' and the low level of economic development turns out to be a consequence of the full development of capitalist production.

(Saffioti, 1978: 124)

However, the rapid incorporation of women into the new export manufacturing sectors from the mid-1970s onwards necessitated a rejection of this position. As evidence emerged of the high female share of the labour force in the new industries which emerged in South East Asia and Central America from the mid-1970s there was a re-evaluation of the role of women in industrialisation. Export-led industrialisation, based on labour-intensive processing or manufacturing of goods designated for export to First World markets relied on the comparative advantage of poor economies in the developing world: cheap labour. And as countless studies and analyses have demonstrated, when 'cheap' labour is deconstructed beyond the absolute wage levels to include employee protection, employers' contribution to the social wage, taxation, investment and working conditions in combination with non-militancy, docility, manual dexterity and conscientious application to often monotonous production process, women are almost invariably the preferred labour force. The combination of high productivity and low wages offers the lowest cost per unit of production demanded by rational management following commercial rather than sexist or discriminatory logic (see Elson and Pearson, 1981a).

173

The new consensus concerning women and industrialisation was rapidly incorporated into development analysis orthodoxy; male economists who had remained curiously immune to discussion of gender issues in development assimilated the information that the bulk of the industrial labour force in NICs (Newly Industrialised Countries) was female as the key indicator of the importance of gender in policy analysis. This new consensus was succinctly described by Joekes.

> Exports of manufactures from developing countries have been made up in the main by female labour: industrialisation in the post-war period has been as much *female* led as *export* led.
>
> (Joekes, 1987: 81)

Certainly over the last two decades women's share of industrial employment has been paramount as export-oriented industrialisation has spread from its initial bases in Mexico and the four Asian tigers (Hong Kong, South Korea, Taiwan and Singapore). By the late 1990s rapid industrial growth has also taken place in many Asian countries, with limited expansion in Latin America and Sub-Saharan Africa.

In Asia this expansion has been most marked, though it is still far from universal; in South Asia only in Bangladesh has export-led industrialisation really taken off, while Nepal, Pakistan and most of India remain outside the export-led industrialising project. In East Asia expansion beyond the original 'tigers' has seen extensive growth of industrialisation in Malaysia, Indonesia, Thailand and the Philippines (Horton, 1996; Chant and McIlwaine, 1995); as yet factory-based production for export is not a feature of the emerging economy in Vietnam but there has been a dramatic expansion of export manufacturing in the Republic of China since the 1980s (Summerfield, 1994).

In Latin America Mexico was the prime location for US manufacturers and importers wishing to take advantage of the proximity and cheapness of the labour force (Pearson, 1991). But although production for export is significant in various small economies of Central America and the Caribbean (particularly the Dominican Republic, Jamaica, Guatemala and Costa Rica), none of the other large economies have successfully pursued this route of economic growth in the 1980s and 1990s (Morawetz, 1981; Pearson, 1986).

No other country in Sub-Saharan Africa has yet matched the stunning example of Mauritius (Hein, 1986; McQueen, 1990) where employment in manufactures for export grew in the 1980s from 9,700 to 106,000 in seven years. Although there are abundant resources of 'cheap' women's labour in African countries, political instability and relative underdevelopment of the infrastructure have precluded the location of manufacturing production for export in this region. The problems go beyond the lack of physical infrastructure, including not just factory buildings, roads and telecommunications or even ports of entry and exit but also an underdeveloped social infrastructure (education, transportation system) inadequate to deliver a productive wage labour force for two or three shifts a day in conditions conducive to maximising productivity.

The view that contemporary industrialisation is as much female-led as export-led was widely supported by empirical work by socialist feminist economists on employment patterns and the sexual division of labour in Third World economies. While women in the 'overdeveloped' economies were deployed as 'housewives' to consume the burgeoning world production of consumer goods, Third World women's role was as producers of these commodities. There was,

> an increasing convergence of the sexual and the international division of labour . . . men defined as 'free' wage labourers, women as non-free housewives – and a division between producers (mainly in the colonies and mainly in the countryside) and consumers (mainly in the rich countries or the cities). Within this division there is also the division between women mainly as producers – in the colonies – and as consumers – mainly in the West.
>
> (Mies, 1986: 116)

In contrast, the empirical research and published case studies were at pains to map the gendered landscape of the new international division of labour; the women workers in the expanding export manufacturing industries in the Third World were mainly young (between 14 and 25 and single, or at least childless). The first generation of women factory workers were either rural migrants or from migrant households but as industrialisation expanded over time there were larger reserves of urban workers. The higher the proportion of urban workers, the higher the educational level of the workers. So rather than depicting women workers in Third World export factories as a homogeneous undifferentiated group of cheap and exploitable labour, much of the research tracked the varied and changing structure of the female industrial labour force from the late 1970s onwards. It became clear that the construction of a 'cheap' female labour force depended on the specificities of gender relations and practices in the local labour market.

While Mies saw women's attraction to international capital as deriving from the fact that being bound to domestic and reproductive work women were not free labour able to organise and resist as men were, our analysis indicated that capital and management had to release women's productive labour in a form as unfettered as possible for the demands of reproductive labour. Thus very often young women were targeted before they took on the responsibilities of marriage and maternity; but in situations where this was not possible – for example in the Caribbean where historically the age of first child bearing is relatively low and women often complete their families by their early thirties – the average age of women workers was ten to fifteen years higher than in Mexico or South East Asia. In this case women were targeted *after* rather than *before* their productivity was compromised by biological and social reproductive activities (Pearson, 1986).

There is broad agreement that this form of Third World industrialisation generally implies a very high female share of the industrial labour force, and

175

often a rapid increase in women employed in industry; however, there is a fierce debate about the implications of such employment for the women concerned (Lim, 1990). While Lim insists on restricting her discussion to the positive impact of waged employment for women, many have questioned the working conditions, insecurity, lack of training and promotion, health hazards, low wages and absence of social security benefits (Edgren, 1982). Many socialist feminists have focused on the exploitation often involved in such employment, ignoring the Engelian heritage which welcomes wage employment for women as an opportunity for equality and struggle with the rest of the proletariat. Other studies have highlighted the contradictory nature of this employment trend. In some situations young women are pressured into working in factories by parents and other family members, sometimes sacrificing their own futures to support members of their natal families (Kung, 1983; Greenhalgh, 1985; Salaff, 1990). In others daughters choose factory employment in the face of strong parental opposition seeing it as a route to personal liberation (Wolf, 1992). And as export production has become well established in various countries, growing numbers of women have continued their employment through their thirties and forties, veterans of production downsizing and technological change: they have taken on new roles in production processes which are less labour intensive and more technologically sophisticated.

More recently a new consensus has replaced the view that industrialisation is necessarily based on the employment of women. Reflecting the common characterisation of the flexible labour in a global economy, Standing (1989: 1077) argues that

> The 1980s might be labelled the decade of deregulation. It has also marked a renewed surge of feminisation of labor activity . . . the types of work, labor relations, income, and insecurity associated with 'women's work' have been spreading, resulting not only in a notable rise in female labour force participation but in a fall in men's employment as well as a transformation – or feminisation – of many jobs traditionally held by men.

This position, the *global feminisation of labour*, not only highlights the fact that women's share of industrial employment has increased because of the reorganisation of the geography of global manufacturing; it also contends that women have replaced men under conditions of 'flexible' and deregulated employment. Rather than suggesting that industrialisation relies primarily on the employment of women it is postulated that industrialisation depends on the conversion of all industrial employment to the (inferior) conditions endured by female labour.

In fact all the trends described in these three positions are discernible in different situations; whilst there are regional, national and/or sectoral trends there are also variations within specific countries in both the process of industrialisation and the role and effect of women's participation.

Women and industrialisation: deconstructing diverse trends

As the empirical case study work has indicated, women's experience of industrial employment – marginality, inclusion and exploitation – is as varied as the trajectory of industrialisation in different parts of the third world. Even though the dominant paradigm in macro economic theory has been the restructuring of less developed economies towards trading in the world market this has not meant for all countries the growth of a thriving export manufacturing sector.

In fact it is becoming clear that as industrialisation proceeds and diversifies in different 'theatres of accumulation'[2] the process of deconstruction and change in the gendering of the industrial labour force is in a constant state of flux. While the 1980s witnessed the spread of industrial employment to a greater number of Asian countries (see Horton, 1996; Heyzer 1988) in other countries various factors, including technological change and geopolitical readjustment, have caused the *decline* of women's industrial employment and/or women's share of industrial employment in countries which once exemplified the strong correlation between export-led industrialisation strategies and women's employment.

In Mexico, for example, the share of women in the *maquiladora* workforce began to decline after 1982 even though the total rates of employment were growing significantly (Brannon and Lucker, 1990). There were many factors which accounted for increasing masculinisation of production in Mexico's export manufacturing factories – including a shift in the sectoral balance of production, labour displacing technological change, the shortage of appropriate productivity, changes in the organisation of production, the need for higher levels of training and trends towards certification (Pearson, 1991, 1993).

In Hong Kong, on the other hand, the decline in women's employment is also the result of changing political circumstances, as more and more foreign and regional capital relocated to the Special Economic Zones (SEZs) in the Republic of China, established after 1979 in areas adjacent to the major communication and trading ports of Hong Kong and Taiwan (Summerfield, 1994; Ho, 1995).

Nor are trends themselves linear or unidirectional. The case of South Korea is instructive. In the early 1990s it was evident that women were being displaced from their share in the industrial workforce partly because of the upgrading of the level of technology involved and the reduction in the labour intensity of production. The other reason given was the absorption of women after marriage into domestic and reproductive work including childcare and elderly care (Phongpaichit, 1988).[3] Figures for the changing share of women in industrial labour forces can also mislead because they fail to capture the relocation of industrial processes and production between the factory and domestic-based production. Kim (1996) points out that many Korean women, particularly mothers of young children, are involved in industrial homeworking, carrying out manual operations as subcontracted workers for a range of manufacturing firms.

However, as industrialisation has progressed some women have retained their position in the labour force in spite of production fluctuations, technological change and international relocation. In Mexico changes in the technology of production and in management practices have meant that some women are emerging as multi-skilled workers crucial to the new flexible and just-in-time production cultures, particularly in the electronics and garments sectors.

> the female labour force has accumulated experience in the *maquiladora* industries over the last twenty-five years and a new type of woman worker is emerging on the basis of flexible systems of organisation of production and labour. At the present time there are groups of older women who have worked here for at least ten years, as well as married women and women with children . . . they have a higher level of education and employment experience and the evidence indicates that their wage is an essential component of the family budget.
>
> (Barajas Escamilla and Rodríguez Carillo, 1990, author's translation)

From the vantage point of twenty years on it could be argued that the focus on women's employment continued to reflect an implicit assumption of the direct correlation between women's waged employment and the diminution of oppression and subordination of women, in spite of the dialectical manner in which we posited the potential outcomes of women's waged employment:

> we would like to distinguish three tendencies in the relation between factory work and the subordination of women as a gender: a tendency to *intensify* the existing forms of gender subordination; a tendency to *decompose* existing forms of gender subordination; and a tendency to *recompose* new forms of gender subordination. We are not suggesting that these are mutually exclusive tendencies . . . they are . . . not categories which can be aggregated to produce a uni-dimensional conclusion that the position of women is getting worse or better. Rather they are suggested as ways of analysing particular conjunctions shaping women's lives, in the hope that this will help clarify the strategic possibilities facing women in those situations.
>
> (Elson and Pearson, 1981: 31)

Much of the debate and discussion which followed has focused on the key variable – are women getting access to waged work in industrial factories? The rapid increase and spread of labour intensive industrialisation not only made women's work in industrialising economies very visible, it has also reinforced the focus on waged work as the key to women's emancipation. Although there was much discussion of the gendered experience of employment for women – lower wages, unstable and short-term employment contracts, intensive supervision, manipulation of images and identities of women and femininity[4] – it could rightly be charged that we failed to deconstruct the model of man as the standard worker and women's experience as other – that is, our analysis constantly reverted to

178

comparison with men as industrial workers: Do women earn more or less? Do women have a higher or lower share of industrial employment? Is women's employment growing faster or slower than men's? Are women retrenched more readily than men? This constant comparison with the experience of men in industrial employment reflected our conclusion that 'for women, unlike men, the question of gender is never absent' (ibid.: 26).

Gender then in this analysis was constructed as prior and constant, a relation of subordination which follows women into the labour market: not because of ascriptive gender relations which assign a particular position to women – they can either be excluded from the labour force, or assigned to particular positions – but because the way in which they are integrated into the labour force reflects the fact that

> women do not do 'unskilled' jobs because they are the bearers of inferior labour; rather the jobs they do are 'unskilled' because women enter them already determined as inferior bearers of labour.
>
> (ibid.: 24)

In part this analysis can be said to have broken new ground. Veronica Beechey (1983), reviewing a number of studies on women's employment in the late 1970s and early 1980s, complained that 'the literature on sexual divisions within the labour market is quite sharply divided between those which emphasise employers' demands for different types of labour power and who therefore lay stress on the demand for labour, and those which emphasise labour supply'. Our analysis captured the important *connections* between the constitution of women as a subordinate gender in society and the experience of women workers within the waged economy:

> the recruitment of women workers in new industrial situations – either new sectors and processes or parts of the world new to given kinds of industrial processes – does not itself provide capital with suitable labour power. This labour has to be constituted, taking into account the pre-existing sexual division of labour. It is constructed directly by the recruitment, selection, management and personnel policies of individual companies and indirectly by the intervention of the State and negotiation within traditional modes of gender control.
>
> (Pearson, 1988: 463)

However, we were dealing primarily with a production situation which by and large offered specific employment categories – labour-intensive processing involving high degrees of manual dexterity performed at speed and under controlled production conditions – only to women. Thus while we were able to interrogate the processes which reproduced or modified women's primary social subordination within the workplace – through recruitment, selection, management practices, discriminatory remuneration and contracting – we

179

focused only in passing on the 'processes of gender construction within the labour process itself' (Beechey, 1983: 158).

Such an analysis may in many ways seem simplistic, if not essentialist when examined through the lens of time. Although constantly asserting the fact that the construction of a female labour force was the result of the interplay of capitalist relations and demands of accumulation with local and specific dynamics of gender relations, we left unproblematised the construction and modification of gender relations themselves.

The consequences of this were possibly quite important. We have been at pains to challenge stereotypes of Third World women workers (Elson, 1983; Pearson, 1986) to deconstruct the different modalities in which women in different places and/or at different stages in their domestic and reproductive lifestyle become incorporated into the industrial labour force, and have accumulated a wealth of case study material detailing the specific nature of employment conditions and labour force supply in different parts of the world.[5]

Nevertheless we became quite attached to an undifferentiated category of women which – whilst not universal or representative – became the unit on which we could base our theoretical analysis of the significance of women's employment in Third World industrialisation.[6] Lim's continuing refrain (1990) that the benefits of factory employment to women have been ignored by feminist analysts whose interest is not the specific perspectives of the women workers but a theoretical analysis of the interaction of capitalist accumulation and gender deserves to be considered. However, this does not mean agreeing that the analysis reviewed above was designed to continuously represent Third World women as unambiguously disadvantaged by being involved in industrial employment. However, in our desire to pursue the implications for gender positioning of the new geography of women's labour we were ignoring the ways in which that experience continually reformulated specific women's gender identities and the ways in which women were active agents in the interaction between capital accumulation and traditional forms of gender identities. Our eagerness to examine the processes which connect the 'modern' experience of industrial employment with 'traditional' modes of gender control allowed us to posit for heuristic purposes an uncontested and undifferentiated notion of traditional gender identities and controls, and an experience of interaction which was structurally determined by capital and patriarchy rather than open to negotiation and reconstitution by women workers themselves.

Indeed the notion of 'traditional modes of gender control' is too static to throw light on the complex process of the construction of a docile labour force, in spite of our invocation of Fanon as a way of explaining the apparent passivity of women factory workers (Elson and Pearson, 1981b). Reliance on secondary data and summarised case studies precludes an examination of the forms of collective and individual agency deployed by women constrained by specific modes of gender subordination (see Kandiyoti, Chapter 6 in this volume).

Many scholars still continue to confine their gender analysis of industrialisation

180

to a discussion of the rise and fall of the demand for women production workers, though it should be said that there is increasing awareness of the role of home based and other non-factory workers (Safa, 1995). Such analyses take as their basis the model of global restructuring based on flexibility of labour and the global feminisation of labour articulated by Standing (1989), with the explicit assumption that such employment opportunities may not be in women's best interests. But such a view tends to accept a linear notion of industrialisation, and resort to a constrained understanding of the complexities of the process of decomposition and recomposition of gender relations catalysed by the changing role of different women as industrial production expands, contracts and is modified in different countries of the world. Elson (1996) specifically challenges the new consensus that 'flexibility' and 'feminisation' should not necessarily be interpreted either by the substitution of women in jobs previously carried out by men, or by the continuing erosion of workers' rights and entitlements caused by the international mobility and competition of capital for lower and lower-cost labour. While recognising the reality of such processes Elson rightly points out two crucial trends: first that the growth of women's share of industrial employment often reflects the decline of jobs previously done by men, rather than the substitution of 'cheaper' women in men's jobs;[7] and second that there is nothing intrinsic to the increasing flexibility of employment which leads to an erosion of workers' rights. Because the process of flexibilisation has taken place in an economic and political climate where the prevailing orthodoxy has been for states and employers to eschew responsibility for worker's well-being in the name of eliminating market distortions, in many situations there may well be a trade-off for workers between maintaining employment opportunity and defending rights and conditions (see Elson, 1996: 42–8). Given that the process of industrial restructuring will be constantly negotiated between the competing perceived interests of capital and labour, the bargaining power of women in the labour force, like women in the household (see Sen, 1990; Kabeer and Kandiyoti, Chapters 4 and 6 in this volume), will be influenced by alternative income-generating opportunities as well as the differentially gendered power of women to assert their conditions in the bargain. It is because in the current global economy women's social subordination coincides with the absence of economic alternatives that the employment of women in industrial factories has been accompanied by the deregulation of labour protection. This does not imply that this is inevitable or eternal. It does point to the need for an organisational strategy based on conjunctural analysis of the particular dynamics of industrialisation and gender relations.

Gender and industrialisation: strategies for action

Recognising the intrinsic links between the experience of women industrial workers and the dynamics of gender relations outside the factory has stimulated increased attention to political and organisational strategies which link workplace issues with gender issues pursued by other groups. Chhachhi and Pittin (1996: 123–4), on the basis of an examination of some dozen case studies of successful and less successful organisational experiences led by women industrial workers, conclude that women workers should develop '*coalescing strategies* . . . i.e. the formulation of demands which overcome divisions such as factory and household, wage work and domestic labour, private and public'. Their analysis stresses that redress for the gendered experience of women workers cannot be achieved without simultaneously tackling issues such as the sexual division of labour, the declining value of the real wage in the context of inflation and structural adjustment, and issues surrounding reproduction in the domestic and social spheres.

It is important to constantly record that the proportion of Third World women who are engaged with industrial production – whether it is in factories producing for export or for domestic consumption, or home-based workshops or sweatshops in the informal sector – is tiny: perhaps only 5–10 per cent of all women economically active worldwide. But it should also be remembered that the phase of international economic change we have just lived through has provided formal sector waged employment for women in developing countries on a scale unprecedented in history. Part of the significance for gender relations of this extension of the opportunity of wage employment to new groups of women is the implication for women in different contexts of earning a wage. Most of the debate assumes that women will utilise this wage to contribute to the income of the households in which they are daughters or wives, thus enhancing their bargaining power.[8] However, as is argued for Taiwan and Hong Kong in the 1960s and 1970s, young women's wages may also be appropriated by other family members, e.g. to support brothers' education or marriage, to the detriment of the women's own futures. But in the enthusiasm for placing women in income-generating projects exercised by many development agencies there has been little agonising about the assumed connections between women's earned income and empowerment. In much of the academic and policy discussions women's interests are defined purely in terms of their ability to ensure the survival of their households, particularly in households which are not (adequately) supported by male 'breadwinners'. The possibility that women might seek waged employment or other forms of income generation to *liberate* themselves from their families, to pursue alternative futures – education and training, migration – or to establish alternative households has had little consideration. Even in the current enthusiasm for micro-credit as a route for improving women's earning potential women are generally located within a spousal household in which their potential entrepreneurial activities can enhance their bargaining power or alternatively intensify the control by male family members (Goetz and Sen Gupta, 1996), echoing the decomposition or recomposition of gender relations discussed above. As Blumberg *et al.* (1995: 5) state

> a growing body of research . . . suggests that increased income under women's control enhances (1) their self confidence, (2) their say in household decision making in the areas of fertility, economic decisions

(such as buying and selling, or allocating major resources), and domestic decisions (such as the education of sons and daughters), and (3) their say over other 'life options' (such as marriage, divorce, and freedom of movement.

Nevertheless we should acknowledge that the past twenty years have witnessed the development of innovative strategies by women workers to organise in defence of their interests both as women and as workers. Too often such organisation has been in opposition to – or at best without the support of – male-led labour unions which either ignore the demands of women workers or consider them as divisive, irrelevant and marginal to the interests of the 'real working class'.

Also as Lim (1990) and others have documented, employment in factories, like participation in income-generating projects, credit schemes for small businesses or collective action around health or environmental issues (García-Guadilla, 1995), can provide the basis for collective action, giving women experience of re-moulding the conditions of their livelihoods and lives rather than reacting to pre-existing structures.

This was the basis of our argument in 1980 that

> the main lesson . . . is that struggle at the level of the factory cannot be judged solely in terms of its effect on pay and conditions of work. It has to be judged not simply as an instrument for making economic gains, but as a way of developing the capacities of those involved in it, particularly the capacity for self-organisation. In this context, participation in collective action in the factory itself, even of a sporadic and spontaneous character is more important than purely formal membership of a trade union.
>
> (Elson and Pearson, 1981b: 163)

Certainly, as Chhachhi and Pittin (1996) demonstrate, the last twenty years have witnessed a range of innovatory and effective organisational strategies by women workers in many parts of the Third World, taking up issues of wages, working conditions, health and safety, sexual harassment and workplace and domestic violence, reproductive rights, civil and political participation, consumer issues and education and training.

However, our recognition of the politicising nature of workplace collective action was not matched by any extensive discussion of the significance for women of their incorporation into the waged labour force itself. Women's economic contribution has long been invisibilised and unrecognised, hence no doubt the 'surprise' of many that women have played such a key role in late twentieth-century industrialisation strategies. The direct and extensive participation in the public economy meant not only that women's economic contribution was made visible and recognised but also that for the women involved their consciousness has been shaped by the experience of collective production, as well as collective struggle. Even as women change their occupation according to their life cycle and the changing nature of economic accumulation, the experience of work affirms their sense of participation in the civil and public spheres of their society. While we acknowledged early on that gender relations were socially constructed and fluid we gave less attention to the potentially liberating implications of collective action in the public sphere, even though many of the more radical development approaches to women's emancipation stress collective action as a key element in 'empowering women'.[9]

Although, as we rightly pointed out, employment for women in export industries is unstable, often short lived and undertaken in exploitative working conditions for lower than subsistence wages, factory work because of its collective nature inevitably provides a location for a different kind of gendered experience, offering the possibility of alternative versions of gender roles and expectations. Indeed as Chhachhi and Pittin (1996: 121) remind us:

> women's waged labour did change in form and locus, but . . . women retained, wherever possible, their state and involvement in, and earnings from waged labour. Thus, for example, Rosie the Riveter may have been forced out of heavy industry, but she moved into the office, the shop, the café.[10]

The challenge now is to ensure that washing the world's dishes is remunerated at a rate which will enable her to eat out when she wishes and only cook the family meals when she chooses. OK, Rosie?

Notes

1 The shared approach to gender issues in economic theory is not confined to the discussion on access to employment by women (See Pearson, 1994). Folbre (1986) reveals the 'black box' approach of both Marxist and neoclassical theory to the division of labour within the household, in spite of the intense feminist deconstruction of categories of domestic labour and housework which occupied much of the 1970s (see Molyneux, 1979).

2 This phrase is used by Armstrong and McGee (1985) to talk about the ways in which similar economic trends, namely industrialisation and urbanisation, have diverse implications in Asia and Latin America in comparison with industrialised countries.

3 According to Thamh-Dam Trong (personal communication) the government of South Korea is currently evaluating a range of social policies designed to facilitate married women maintaining their role in the labour force.

4 One of the most interesting examples of the ways in which women's gender identity can be manipulated is demonstrated by studies of women industrial workers in Malaysia. From the mid-1970s till the early 1980s there was much discussion about the ways in which (mainly US-owned) firms used management methods which emphasised the connection between modern and Westernised notions of femininity and the opportunities to work in modern hi-tech factories making electronics components (Cardosa Khoo and Khoo (1989), Grossman (1979)). Since the mid-1980s, a new generation of Muslim Malay women have been recruited into the factories leading different management strategies to respond to the very different social and cultural

aspirations of these workers who have developed an alternative (some would say resistant) Malay female identity based on religious propriety, constructed in opposition to 'Immoral Western' femininity (Scott, 1989).

5 A useful source for information of published work on women and industrialisation is Elson and Wright (1996). Additional sources include Heyzer (1988) and Horton (1996).

6 See Hirshman (1995) for a parallel critique of Sen and Grown's (1987) attempt to provide a critique in *Development, Crises and Alternatives Visions: Third World Women's Perspectives*.

7 This is not to say that there are *never* instances where women are directly substituted for male workers in order to reduce costs. This was the case with Humphrey's study (1987) of factory work in São Paulo, Brazil in the early 1980s. However, to claim that this is always the case is analogous to claiming that *all* Third World export production – in say electronics, sports wear, garments, etc. – directly replaces production which has to be literally relocated from Europe or North America. In the 1970s, this may well have been the situation in specific contexts – see Fröbel *et al.* (1980) who detailed the relocation of textile and garments industries to Asia and Latin America. But with the expansion of global communications and production facilities, changing technologies and competitive infrastructure in many NICs and other developing countries, by the 1990s the majority of such production facilities carry out production processes which never had a material existence in industrialised countries.

8 Sen's analysis of cooperative conflict assumes that a wage increases women's perceived contribution to the household, and thus improves their bargaining power as well as raising their fallback position (see Sen, 1990).

9 Even where NGOs or governments saw income generating projects for women solely in terms of providing access to monetary resources, women often used the opportunity to redefine their relationship with the public sphere. See Heath (1996) for a discussion of income generating weaving projects in Oman.

10 *Rosie the Riveter* is the title of a significant documentary film made in the USA after the second world war. Using footage from cine newsreels as well as interviews with women involved, it traces women's participation in various sectors of heavy industry (including shipbuilding) during the war in spite of constant efforts to present such activity as an extension of women's domestic activities. Women welding sheet steel onto the hulls of warships were only doing an activity similar to ironing clothes, according to the commentator.

References

Armstrong, W. and McGee, T. G. (1985) *Theatres of Accumulation: Studies in Asian and Latin American Urbanization.* Methuen, London and New York.

Barajas Escamilla, R. and Rodríguez Carillo, C. (1990) 'La mujer ante la recoversión productiva: el caso de la maquila electrónica', in Gonzáles-Aréchiga, B. and Carlos Ramírez, J. (eds).

Beechey, V. (1983) 'What's So Special about Women's Employment? A Review of Some Recent Studies of Women's Paid Work', *Feminist Review* Winter.

Blumberg, R. L. (1995) 'Introduction: Engendering Wealth and Well-Being in an Era of Economic Transformation', in R. L. Blumberg *et al.* (eds).

Blumberg, R. L., Rakowski, C. A., Tinker, I. and Monteón, M. (1995) *EnGENDERing Wealth and Well-Being: Empowerment for Global Change.* Westview Press, Boulder, San Francisco and Oxford.

Boserup, E. (1987) *Women's Role in Economic Development,* 2nd edition. Gower Press,

Aldershot (first published 1970).

Brannon, J. and Lucker, W. (1990) 'The Impacts of Mexico's Economic Crisis on the Demographic Composition of the Labour Force', in Gonzáles-Aréchiga, B. and Carlos Ramírez, J. (eds.).

Cardosa-Khoo, J. and Khoo Khay, J. (1989) 'Work and Consciousness: Women Workers in the Electronics Industry in Malaysia', in K. Young (ed.) *Serving Two Masters*. Allied Publishers Ltd, Bombay.

Chant, S. and McIlwaine, C. (1995) *Women of a Lesser Cost: Female Labour, Foreign Exchange and Philippine Development*. Pluto Press, London.

Chhachhi, A. and Pittin, R. (eds) (1995) *Multiple Identities: Women's Organisational Strategies*. Macmillan, Basingstoke.

Chhachhi, A. and Pittin, R. (eds) (1996) *Confronting State, Capital and Patriarchy: Women Organising in the Process of Industrialization*. Macmillan Press, Basingstoke.

Edgren, G. (1982) 'Spearheads of Industrialisation or Sweatshops in the Sun?', in E. Lee (ed.) *Export Processing Zones and Industrial Employment in Asia*. ILO, Bangkok.

Elson, D. (1983) 'Nimble Fingers and Other Fables', in W. Chapkis and C. Enloe (eds) *Of Common Cloth: Women in the Global Textile Industry*. Transnational Institute, Amsterdam and Washington, DC.

Elson, D. (1996) 'Appraising Recent Developments in the World Market for Nimble Fingers', in Chhachhi and Pittin (eds) 1996: 35–55.

Elson, D., and Pearson, R. (1981a) 'Nimble Fingers Make Cheap Workers', *Feminist Review* No. 7 (Spring): 87–107.

Elson, D. and Pearson, R. (1981b) 'The Subordination of Women and the Internationalization of Factory Production', in K. Young *et al.* (eds) *Of Marriage and the Market: Women's Subordination in International Perspective*. London, CSE Books.

Elson, D. and Wright, C. (1996) 'Gender Issues in Contemporary Industrialization: An Annotated Bibliography', *Labour Studies* Working Paper No. 10, Centre for Comparative Labour Studies, University of Warwick.

Folbre, N. (1986) 'Hearts and Spades: Paradigms of Household Economics', *World Development* Vol. 14 No. 2: 245–55.

Fröbel, F., Heinrichs, J. and Kreye, O. (1980) *The New International Division of Labour*. Cambridge University Press, Cambridge.

García-Guadilla, M. P. (1995) 'Gender, Environment and Empowerment in Venezuela', in Blumberg *et al.* (eds).

Goetz, A. M. and Sen Gupta, R. (1996) 'Who Takes the Credit? Gender, Power and Control over Loan Use in Rural Credit Programmes in Bangladesh', *World Development* Vol. 24 No. 1: 45–63.

Gonzáles-Aréchiga, B. and Carlos Ramírez, J. (eds) (1990) *Subcontractión y empresas transnacionales: Apertura y restructuración en la maquiladora*. El Colegio de la frontera Norte, Fundación Friedrich Ebert, Mexico.

Greenhalgh, S. (1985) 'Sexual Stratification: The Other Side of "Growth with Equity" in East Asia', *Population and Development Review* Vol. 11 No. 2: 265–314.

Grossman, R. (1979) 'Women's Place in the Integrated Circuit', *South East Asian Chronicle* No. 66. Jan.-Feb.: 2–17.

Heath, C. (1996) 'Hidden Currencies'. Unpublished PhD thesis, School of Development Studies, University of East Anglia.

Hein, C. (1986) 'The Feminisation of Industrial Employment in Mauritius: A Case Study of Sex Segregation', in R. Anker and C. Hein (eds) *Sex Inequalities in Urban Employment*.

Macmillan, London.

Heyzer, N. (1988) *Daughters in Industry: World Skills and Consciousness of Women Workers in Asia*. Asian and Pacific Development Centre, Kuala Lumpur.

Hirshman, M. (1995) 'Women and Development: A Critique', in J. Parpart and M. Marchand (eds) *Feminism Postmodernism Development*. Routledge, London.

Ho, C. (1995) 'Women and Unemployment in Hong Kong'. Paper given in IAFFE Session on Women and Economic Transition, NGO Forum of Fourth UN World Conference on Women, Hiarou, China, September.

Horton S. (ed.) (1996) *Women and Industrialization in Asia*. Routledge, London and New York.

Joekes, S. (1987) *Women in the World Economy*. Oxford University Press, Oxford.

Kim, Y.-O. (1996) 'Homeworking in South Korea', in Chhachhi and Pittin (eds) 1996: 307–309.

Kung, L. (1983) *Factory Women in Taiwan*. University of Michigan Press, Ann Arbor.

Lim, L. (1990) 'Women's Work in Export Factories: The Politics of a Cause', in I. Tinker (ed.) *Persistent Inequalities*. Oxford University Press, Oxford.

McEwan S. A. (1986) 'Urban Women in LDCs: Examining the Female Marginalisation Thesis', *Journal of Development Studies* July.

McQueen, M. (1990) *APC Export Diversification: the Case of Mauritius*. Overseas Development Institute Working Paper No. 41. London.

Mies, M. (1986) *Patriarchy and Accumulation on a World Scale: Women in the International Division on Labour*. Zed Press, London.

Molyneux, M. (1979) 'Beyond the Domestic Labour Debate', *New Left Review* No. 116 (Jul.–Aug.): 3–27.

Morawetz, D. (1981) *Why the Emperor's New Clothes Are Not Made in Colombia*. Published for the World Bank, Oxford University Press, New York.

Pearson, R. (1986) 'Female Workers in the First and Third Worlds: the Greening of Women's Labour', in K. Purcell *et al.* (eds) *The Changing Experience of Employment: Restructuring and Recession*. Reprinted in R. Pahl (ed.) *On Work*. Blackwell, Oxford, 1988.

Pearson, R. (1988) 'Multinational Companies and Women Workers', in R. Pahl (ed.) *On Work*. Blackwell, Oxford.

Pearson, R. (1991) 'Male Bias and Women's Work in Mexico's Border Industries', in D. Elson (ed.) *Male Bias and the Development Process*. Manchester University Press, Manchester.

Pearson, R. (1992) 'Gender Issues in Industrialisation', in T. Hewitt *et al.* (eds) *Industrialisation and Development*. Oxford University Press, Oxford.

Pearson, R. (1993) 'The Rise and Rise of the Maquiladora Industry: A Gendered Perspective'. Paper presented to the Institute of Latin American Studies Seminar on Mexico, University of London, Spring.

Pearson, R. (1994) 'Gender Relations, Capitalism and Third World Industrialization', in L. Sklair (ed.) *Capitalism and Development*. Routledge, London and New York.

Phongpaichit, P. (1988) 'Two Roads to the Factory: Industrialisation Strategies and Women's Employment in S.E. Asia', in B. Agarwal (ed.) *Structures of Patriarchy: The State, the Community and the Household*. Zed Press, London.

Safa, H. (1995) 'Gender Implications of Industrialization', in Blumberg *et al.*

Saffioti, H. (1978) *Women in Class Society*. Monthly Review Press, New York and London.

Salaff, J. (1990) 'Women, the Family and the State: Hong Kong, Taiwan and Singapore – Newly Industrialised Countries in Asia', in Stichter and Parpart.

187

Scott, M. (1989) 'Brave New World', *Far Eastern Economic Review* 21 December: 32–4.

Sen, A. (1990) 'Gender and Cooperative Conflicts', in Tinker, I. (ed.) *Persistent Inequalities: Women and World Development*. Oxford University Press, Oxford.

Sen, G. and Grown, C. (1987) *Development Crises and Alternative Visions: Third World Women's Perspectives*. Monthly Review Press, New York.

Standing, G. (1989) 'Global Feminization through Flexible Labour', *World Development* Vol. 17 No. 7.

Summerfield, G. (1994) 'Chinese Women and the Post-Mao Economic Reforms', in N. Aslanbeigui, S. Pressman and G. Summerfield (eds) *Women in the Age of Transformation: Gender Impact of Reforms in Post-Socialist and Developing Countries*. Routledge, London and New York.

Wolf, D. (1992) *Factory Daughters: Gender, Household Dynamics and Rural Industrialisation in Java*. University of California Press, Los Angeles, and Oxford University Press, Los Angeles and Oxford.

9

FEMALE AND MALE GRAIN MARKETING SYSTEMS

Analytical and policy issues for West Africa and India

Barbara Harriss-White

The study of markets cannot be scientific unless studied in the context of their relevant institutions.

(Penny, 1985: 101)

Gender is constructed by a plurality of oppressions.

(Bardhan, 1993: 147)

This chapter concerns gender and one aspect of micro-economic relations which seems understood as being endowed with many adverse implications for gender-political change.[1] The material subordination of women has been most richly researched in two institutional sites. The first is within the household where gender divisions of task have been explained in relation to the opportunity costs of male and female labour on stylised markets outside the household (as developed in the new home economics: see Haddad *et al.*, 1997). Implicit in this market driven theory of intrahousehold divisions of labour is a social process of decision making. While some have seen patriarchal authority at work (whether despotic or benign: Folbre, 1986), others have stylised the process as one of bargaining (Kandiyoti, 1988; Sen, 1990). The consequences of gender differentials in fall-back positions and unequal conjugal contracts have been invoked to explain gender asymmetries in command not only over decision making but also over resources, autonomy and welfare. Further, the operation of rules of property ownership and control and its transfer at inheritance and marriage have been found to deprive women of resources and thereby of access qualifications for many aspects of public participation (Agarwal, 1995). The second well researched institutional site of material subordination is the process of production. This is almost invariably analysed in terms of the operation of labour markets and labour relations since so little property is controlled by women. Here, life cycle vulnerabilities, employment probabilities, skill acquisition and differentials in remuneration, income and their security (differentials not justified by productivity or by demand and supply) are stacked against women.[2] In this chapter, the gendering of a third area, markets in commodities other than labour, will be explored in a preliminary way, taking staple foods as examples, since almost everywhere they form the basis of social reproduction and are thus a useful 'prism'. Such markets have been comparatively less researched than other gendered interfaces (as is the fate of market behaviour more generally despite its centrality to a wide range of economic theory).[3] Three analytical issues suggest themselves:

1 the gender construction of non-labour, commodity markets;
2 market relations as ambivalent processes of gender emancipation and sub-ordination;
3 the impact of women's participation in marketplace exchange on economic relations within the household.

From these, four 'policy issues' appear to follow:

1 technical change in rural marketing and its impact on livelihoods;
2 liberalisation, the expansion and integration of national markets and the masculinisation of control over trade;
3 the efficiency of gender divisions;
4 political organisation within marketing systems.

First, however, it is necessary to clarify the nature of markets.

Markets as institutions

The 'market' is conventionally seen as an atomistic realm of impersonal economic exchange of homogeneous goods carried out by means of voluntary transactions. These are mediated on an equal basis by large numbers of autonomous, fully informed entities with profit maximising behavioural motivations able to enter and leave freely. The market is thus the supreme medium for the expression of individual choice (Hodgson, 1988: 178). Much more often than not it is assumed to be perfectly competitive. Models of other stylised market structures (monopoly, oligopoly) alter certain criteria, retain others and predict the consequences for prices and quantities.

The abstractions leave us shorn of means whereby to understand not only how supply is supplied and demand is demanded, but also the structure and behaviour of real market systems which relate demand and supply. For exactly the reason that real markets are highly diverse and complex socio-economic phenomena, real markets have indeed proved awkward to define.

A restrictive definition of market exchange in which voluntarism, egalitarianism and informational availability are stressed has been offered by Pandya and Dholakia: 'the simultaneous transaction of valued goods and services between

190

two parties [who are] capable of accepting or rejecting the value offered . . . and [who are] uncoerced . . . and capable of communication and delivery' (1992: 24). Markets are then efficient mechanisms of resource allocation, resulting in an expansion of productivity.

By contrast, Fourie sees a real market as 'an economically qualified, purposeful interchange of commodities on the basis of *quid pro quo* obligations at a mutually agreed upon exchange rate . . . in a cluster of exchange and rivalry relations' (1991: 43, 48). Here, the social relations unique to market exchange require the combination of 'horizontal' and adversarial competition between populations of buyers (and populations of sellers) on the one hand and a mass of 'vertical', exclusive, mutualistic, bilateral transactions between one buyer and one seller on the other. The implications of this definition (*pace* the voluntarist definition) are that exchange rates mutually agreed on may not always be mutually beneficial, that vertical contractual arrangements may prevail over horizontal competition and that purposeful bargaining and the obligations resulting from it may rest on and reinforce a highly unequal base or fall-back position. Without wishing to be reductionist, it would seem that market exchange will be a site of exploitation as well as of allocation. It has the capacity to be a site of ethnic and/or gender subordination as well as of liberation.

Much exchange which would fall within Fourie's definition of market would fall outside that of Pandya and Dholakia – repeated, relational contracting, the socially consensual determination of prices (Jorion, 1994; Guerrien, 1994) coercive interlocked contracts (Bhaduri, 1986). The extent of such non-market marketing will affect the pace at which markets react to deregulation and other policy levers normally considered to provide incentives.

Systems of non-market exchange have been recognised to comprise two principal sorts: redistribution and reciprocity. Polanyi contrasted such non-market exchange with that of a stylised modern society where commercial logic rules and an unembedded pricemaking market dominates economic life (Polanyi, 1957/1985). But, as Braudel has observed, it is too easy to reduce one phenomenon to sociology and another to economics (1985: 227). John Davis is the most recent of many to argue against Polanyi's dualistic schema on the empirical grounds *not* that reciprocity and redistribution did or do not characterise underdeveloped exchange, but that they are deeply pervasive in what he calls OECD economies (Davis, 1992) where he has identified over 50 different types of exchange. Market and non-market exchange jostle together. With reference to markets for agricultural products with which we shall be principally concerned here, it is likely that both redistribution and reciprocity are of quantitative importance themselves. Further, when market relations are entered into in order to acquire an input to a relation of reciprocity (e.g. grain for gifting; procurement for a state-administered public distribution system), it is the logics of reciprocity or redistribution not the profit or utility maximising market logic that is the motivation for marketing.

Fourie's kind of market is conventionally distinguished from other types of

191

economic activity, for example that within firms. Although some theorists have depicted firms as clusters of individual market-like contractual relationships, firms can also be seen as 'a command economy in microcosm' (Folbre, 1994: 45). Their internal structure of authority is understood by some primarily to minimise trans-actions costs and by others primarily as a coercive mechanism. Upon empirical scrutiny, it is apparent that firms cannot be reduced to bundles of micro-markets. Firms are a distinct type of economic institution. A conventional characterisation contrasts institutions/firms with markets. If that contrast is accepted, then markets would have to be understood as *'not-institutions'* (see Folbre, 1994: 24 for one example).

But markets cannot exist in a deinstitutionalised form: no economic phenom-ena do. It is only possible to construct supply and demand schedules on the assumption that buyers and sellers react as though any price could be the equi-librium price. Prices are thus formed in logical time as if expectations had vanished and memories were eliminated but as if complete information existed about other prices at the moment of price formation. This is a necessary condition for perfect competition. But perfect competition not only does not exist, it would not be viable for long if it did exist because entry, exit, investment and disinvest-ment depend in the actual world upon the belief or the fact that information regarding opportunities is restricted. Two central tenets of the neoclassical project are incompatible: the 'methodological individualism' involving voluntarist, indi-vidualist subjective preference; and instrumental rationality on the one hand, and the market (as an actually existing bundle of 'legal, customary, political and other social arrangements': Hodgson, 1988: 174) on the other. Markets are institutions.

'Institution' is a notion used in at least three rather loose ways. The first is soci-ological. Any behavioural regularity is the manifestation of an institution (Fourie, 1991: 52). Thus a conference is an institution, but so also is the way in which bio-logical sex becomes social gender, or norms of justice and other aspects of ideology and social rules are developed and reproduce. Exchange processes are constituted by, and constitute in turn, a wide set of social institutions: state, local-ity, class, ethnic group, age and gender. It is one thing to state this but quite another to examine these complex relationships empirically. Yet, since all social institutions are specific to time and place, since they change over time and place, and since the social configurations of markets vary in significant ways, there can be no escape from empirical enquiry. The further two senses in which the idea of 'institution' is understood also involve behavioural regularities. Thus the first soci-ological usage can be argued to be all encompassing. Economists, however, distance their use of the concept from that of sociologists by carving out two fur-ther distinct territories for 'institution'. Thus the second is micro-economic. Institutions are understood in 'special case' terms. North (1990) would have us recognise organisations as distinct from (social normative) institutions and exam-ine the tensions between them. Organisations are groups of individuals bound by some common purpose to achieve objectives (North 1990: 5). The organisations or micro-economic institutions of interest to economists are those concerned with production: firms and contracts. The third sense of institution is macro-economic and legal, encompassing the definition of rights, the scope of economic behaviour, the mechanisms to protect exchange, penalise miscreants and through taxation ensure state legitimacy (Giddens, 1992; Shaffer, 1979).

In her recent book, Folbre (1994) has convincingly sustained her hypothesis that production and reproduction are shaped by a variety of types of institution of collective action. These institutions can be ascribed (e.g. caste), acquired (e.g. 'Lionesses'), multiple, not coordinated (patriarchal behaviour, for instance, may be in direct conflict with egalitarian developmental beliefs; families are sites of both cooperation and conflict) and not monitored. *Pace* the new home economics, returns to participation in such social institutions are not consciously calculated, nor is it likely that they are calculable with a precision making economic sense.

Social institutions can be of two types: first, social groups (e.g. family, caste and ethnic group in all of which patriarchy may tilt the distribution of resource control in male favour); second, social norms, ideologies and conventions (e.g. patriarchy as a cultural construct). These are Kalpana Bardhan's 'plurality of oppressions' (1993). We will look here principally (though not exclusively) at the intersection of two social institutions: gender and class in which markets for staple foods are embedded.

The gender construction of staple food markets

Marketplaces and staple food markets are highly gendered complexes of social institutions. But (although there are no textual religious proscriptions of women from trading) gender works in these markets in ways differing radically from society to society. The central questions concern institutional autonomy: whether the social institutions of production, household reproduction and the reproduction of gender ideologies 'enable' certain kinds of female participation in such markets and 'constrain' others, and if so how and why.

For Boserup, gender divisions of labour in production were related straightforwardly to those in markets (1970: 87–92). The gendering of property ownership or usufructuary rights over land was reflected in those over products. Female farming systems had female traders. Male farming systems, male traders. Empirical analysis shows that this is not, nor was it at the time, an accurate generalisation.

In West Africa, for instance, while agricultural production may be controlled by women as well as by men, local trade in basic consumption goods has been widely observed to be a public domain for women in which not only can competition be fierce, but also accumulation not entirely unknown.[4] Even so, women are portrayed as tending to occupy particular niches in female grain marketing systems,[5] more often than not defined by:

- commodity (staple food, cooked food, beer) perhaps because access to, or production of, these goods can be carried out domestically; these goods may also be a female gendered subset where commodities are gendered according to notions of rank, status and purity (where female goods are inferior);

- points in the market system (small-scale processing and retailing perhaps because of highly gendered concepts of the 'strenuous work' required by other marketing activities or because of the prior requirements of the reproductive burden);

- organisational forms (individuated) and forms of reproduction of the firm (simple/oriented to subsistence, perhaps the result of gendered inheritance customs and access to capital and of gendered constraints on spatial mobility);

- motivation (household subsistence/target incomes, perhaps because of the gendered division of intrahousehold expenditure responsibilities and gender-specific norms of ostentation in private consumption, savings and investment);

- territoriality and spatial mobility (local, non-mobile because of male gendered transport ownership and gendered notions of propriety in the public territories of marketplaces);

- season (most active in, if not fully confined to, the post-harvest months with a rapid turnover time and lower capital requirements). The irresistible implication is that other forms of local trade will tend not to be controlled by women, even in 'female' marketing systems.

Pujo has thoughtfully reviewed speculation about the female gendering of West African trade (1997: 41–4). All the explanations put forward are problematical. One materialist hypothesis – of 'residualisation' – stresses the role of land scarcity under conditions of rapid commercialisation which results in production's becoming increasingly dominated by men. Women then turn to the control of commercialisation and the sphere of distribution, giving them a domain independent of men.[6] But for this there is little empirical support. In particular, the division by gender of male production and female distribution is not rigid in any society and trade is far from a residual activity, being capable of generating comparatively great wealth. A second hypothesis – that of 'compatibility' – rehearses the idea that trade is easy to combine with household activities (which are understood as prior claims on female labour). Where social reproduction requires market exchange as well as labour within the household, then women are found in markets. Again, this is toppled by empirical evidence. A third 'cultural' argument sees female identity as involving both fertility and independence. Thus trading and the separate budget associated with it are just as much required of women as a large number of children. But not all women trade and marketplaces and processes are not so simply arranged.[7] A general explanation has not proved possible. As with so many social phenomena (the regional patterns of the sex ratio spring to mind) the explanations for patterns of gendering will be both specific and complex. To reveal how social institutions and economic behaviour interact it is useful to be able to examine gender ideologies and then the contrariness of their outcomes in the 'actual' observable gendering of tasks, control over technologies and capital in markets, and their impact on structural aspects of markets: entry, concentration, competition and information and thus on perfor-mance. To my knowledge, Pujo's work in the forest interior of Guinee in 1992 is the only study that has succeeded in looking systematically at the rice market any-where in this way. Performance has even been specified in gendered industrial organisation terms:[8] the gendered distribution of returns to trade, employment and comparative productive efficiency (Pujo, 1997: 239–74).

While the labour process in rice production in Guinee Forestière is mostly gender-sequential, that of marketing is gender-segregated. 'The idea that pro-cessing transforms "male" paddy into "female" rice is used by many peasant women to obtain access to the output' (Pujo, 1997: 182) . But from then onwards the rice market is segmented by gender, operational scale and technology. The vast bulk of trading firms are individuated. In 1992, 80 per cent of firms in Guinee Forestière were run by women and all of them were individuated. The classifica-tion of activity in the marketing system therefore corresponds with types of firm (which is not the case in India). The gender division of labour is summarised in Figure 9.1. In practice it coincides closely with the ideologies of appropriate activ-ity. Marketplace trade is indeed female. These women traders are relatively younger than male traders (average age 37 versus 50) and their firms are smaller (average 32 tonnes versus 134). Female traders tend to operate through person-alised 'network' trading contracts and are price takers. By contrast, shop-based trade is controlled by men. Men control all derived markets (e.g. the rental mar-kets for transport and storage) and all materially productive activity (mechanical milling). They are price makers and can and do practise collusive price formation. Quite exclusive proscriptions prevent women from being mill mechanics. Trading capital and skills result from gender-specific social relations. While young men acquire capital and skill by labouring (seasonally) in the firms of relatives and/or by commercial loans, young women (when released from reproductive chores) watch female relatives in the marketplace but their access to trading capital depends entirely on loans from parents, siblings or husbands. These loans are more restricted in size than those to men. Further, they carry with them the oblig-ation to share the returns from trade – on average half of their earnings.

Thus the gender construction of trade limits the access of women to capital and causes an unequal distribution of costs, returns and obligations. Gender intersects with other social institutions:

- class: found to be particularly awkward. Though the commoditisation of labour is at an incipient stage, males dominate capital accumulation; the household is a site of exploitation through exchange; dependent women traders can also be exploited by means of usurious interest on credit from male wholesalers. Indeed, in these circumstances gender has been argued to be *the* class division (Pujo, 1997: 291–4);
- locality (information and access to capital is heavily urban biased);
- ethnic group (the historically trading *ethnies* put up barriers to entry to interregional trade);

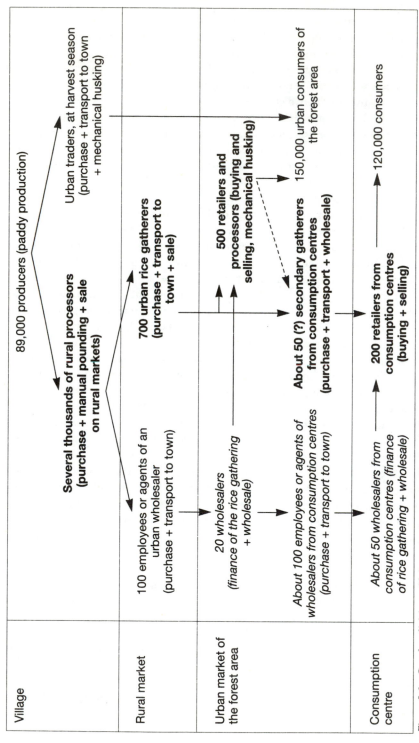

Figure 9.1 Gender division of labour in the market for local rice

Source: Pujo, 1997: 191.
Note: Bold letters represent women, italics represent men and roman type represents both men and women.

- religion (allegiance to which consolidates network transactions and may also lead to forms of contract which mask interest payments);
- family (marriage patterns affect entry to marketing systems);
- age (women gain independence with age and can accumulate at a faster pace; however, the great majority of women stop trading altogether when their dependants leave the households);
- the state (whose political oppression provoked the emigration of (male) traders and encouraged accumulation through smuggling and where current new entrants to the large-scale wholesale trade in rice are male officials who have often derived their starting capital from bribery) (Pujo, 1997: 291–301).

So not only can certain men be far poorer than certain women (in the Kissi region, male peasants are universally poorer than female bulkers of rice), but female traders are themselves far from being a homogeneous category. In Guinee, the returns to female traders are more highly unequal than those to men (differing by a factor of four between female retailers and wholesalers in Gueckedou: 253). At the other extremity in Hausa Nigeria, though the grain trade is dominated by men, and women are generally secluded, there is very considerable economic differentiation among female traders (Robson, forthcoming).

In South Asia, by contrast, local staple food markets would appear to be much more highly commercialised and economically differentiated. Depending on location, private wholesaling firms are up to 100 times larger in terms of gross output than their counterparts in Guinee. There is a significant wage labour force in the marketing systems (working for the owners of firms and in gangs in marketplaces) which is absent in the accounts of Guinee Forestière or of Hausaland. The classification of activity in markets does not correspond with types of firm. Firms can be very much bigger and more internally differentiated with tendencies towards uniqueness in the complex combinations of activities that each performs (Harriss-White, 1996). The patriarchal labour process in grain marketing is complex in ways different from that in West Africa. And female *traders* in India are much more homogeneous than their counterparts in West Africa.

Our evidence from West Bengal in the north-east (in 1990) and Tamil Nadu in the south-east (in 1980 and 1993–5) shows that in a typical firm owned by the males of a joint family and practising a diversity of trading and transformation activities, there are multiple relations of male labour. Male family labour (up to 13 members have been encountered) whose work is loosely specified, may work part-time or seasonally or as part of a multiple occupational profile. Permanent workers (averaging three but up to seven, whose task specification may be quite refined but whose terms and conditions are vague) may work at the simultaneous performance of more than one activity within the firm or on own account. Rates of pay are unsystematised, and accentuated by both patronage and debt bondage. Male casual labour (averaging 9 but up to 40) may be permanently attached to a trading firm but employed on a daily, weekly, seasonal, group contract or piece-rate basis for manual work. While tasks are highly specified, contracts, terms and conditions, and rates of pay vary greatly. Lastly, male child labour is underestimated,[9] used at key points in the grain marketing system (messages, carrying food and drink for negotiations, cleaning), and may be paid secure though very low wages. For some children, such work is an apprenticeship (though there is no reason why such apprenticeships should replace formal school because the children of rich traders participate in both activities).

Labour 'markets' in grain marketing are heavily structured by the assets distribution and by networks of gender, caste and locality. Markets are segmented spatially and socially. Large differences in contractual forms, in modes and levels of payment can obtain over short distances such that the very notion of a market in the restricted definition of Pandya and Dholakia is challenged.

Women participate in this grain trade in four ways, according to their caste and class position:

1   Directly (as in West Africa, but from a more restricted and poorer population segment), women from pauperised, female-headed and/or low caste households are confined to petty and often seasonal operation, to subsistence orientation and simple reproduction, to particular positions and activities within the system (especially processing and retailing), local territorial linkages, weekly marketplace sites and unlicensed and/or illegal transactions in cash. Their participation is conditioned by the life cycle, and when children are no longer dependent, these women tend to stop trading.

2   Female casual wage workers from the assetless class form the large substratum of labour in grain milling and pre-milling processing. Marketing systems rest on the backs of these women. The average mill employs 15, but up to 70 have been encountered.[10] Outcaste women are allowed to turn paddy on the large drying yards because the kernel is still protected from ritual pollution by its husk. As in Guinee and Hausaland women are debarred from being mill mechanics and it is unusual to find them handling heavy consignments of scalding paddy during the parboiling process. Female 'coolie' is prevalently but incorrectly regarded by mill owners as a household supplement for their employees.[11] Wage differentials of two thirds to a half that of male wages in rice mills in no way reflect productivity (which in any case would be tantamount to impossible to measure accurately since the division of tasks in milling is sex sequential). Female mill work is deliberately casualised and I have never encountered a unionised female labour force. The sexual exploitation of the mill workforce by management is not unknown.

3   In the recent past in smaller family firms, unwaged female family members have provided that part of the wage to labour in trading firms which takes the form of prepared food (though with the commercialisation of labour, this practice of payment in tea and meals is dying, or itself being commercialised). Female labour will then subsidise the firm. It has to be added that a large rice milling and trading firm will almost certainly 'subsidise' some of the costs of

reproduction of their male labour force such that the social reproduction of male labour is not entirely borne by female labour within working-class households. Accidents on site are usually compensated and medical expenses often paid at times of sickness. Both male and female labour receive at least one month's extra pay at a major festival. Often this is given in kind as cloth. It can also be argued, however, that such payments both retard the formation of labour markets (because of their informational opacity) and reflect 'backward' relationships of patronage rather than market exchange (by dint of their discretionary element).

4   Women in accumulating firm-families are used for the caste-based reproduction and expansion of firms first by means of their dowries on marriage and second through the (rare) practice of fictitious 'benami' registration of a trading company in a woman's name generally for the purposes of tax avoidance. In the first case, the higher education of such women is a good example of the economic inefficiency of gender institutions. For such women, education is a status good and leads neither to economic participation nor to control over assets or over major economic decision.[12] Educated mothers are thought better to educate their own children; but the structure of ownership of large mercantile companies, framed by the pre-emption of tax laws, frequently requires strong male control of young male adults and discourages migration for advanced education, so there exist constraints to education other than gender and other than its costs.

So the South Asian grains trade is also seen to be highly gendered. In turn, gender intersects with caste and class position. The lack of ownership or control over property, or any means of circulation (which determines creditworthiness), makes the economic role of women belonging to the accumulating oligopolies somewhat indirect, in contrast to the role of poor women in petty trade and the casual labour force.

Thus male marketing systems are dynamised by female wage labour and female marketing systems have male traders at their power points even if they also have a profusion of apparently independent female traders. The classification of marketing systems as male or female might be appealing but it is inaccurate as a generalisation and it obscures increasingly common characteristics of grain markets in these two regions. Both types of marketing system provide more livelihoods to women than they do to men, but women's livelihoods are on the whole relatively humble. We now turn to the thorny question of whether even these humble livelihoods can be emancipating.

Markets and gender subordination

Class societies which specialise, reproduce themselves through exchange. Just as social reproduction takes place within households so it takes place in markets. We have seen how marketplaces in certain parts of the world have been identified as female domains, as sites for the exercise of female autonomy. But equally, we have seen that market exchange is both complex and inherently riddled with ambiguity. It does not follow that processes of commodity marketing either ensure female autonomy and emancipation (within either the marketing system or the domestic unit) or remove the shackles from female property ownership or accumulation. Just as the household is a site for relationships which subordinate women so also, with subtlety, is the 'market' for wage labour and for grain.

In West African *rural* markets, despite the fame of the 'market queens', 'mama benz' or 'market mammies' and despite the undoubted greater freedom to trade and autonomous control over the returns to trade than in India, it seems the upward economic mobility of women is rarely achieved. Robson's work in Nigerian Hausaland rams home the point that, there, men do not share their control of agricultural production. Men have over the recent past come to engulf and to dominate periodic marketplace trade and even to share the village market with secluded women traders. The latter, for reasons of inheritance custom, access to capital and periodic taboos on trading based on life cycle events, are unable to accumulate (Robson, forthcoming).

In Guinee, the access of women to marketplaces and to commerce is restricted more often than not by the decisions of men about market supplies, which are frequently generated out of production processes centring upon the household. Women in marketplace trade may thus be prevented from buying and selling and constrained to selling. While market information is segmented by gender (and women are socialised and 'apprenticed' from childhood to appreciate better than men the subtle conventions surrounding volumetric measurements),[13] the economic resources necessary for the spatial and social mobility to amass wholesale consignments, command transport and/or own processing facilities are in the hands of men.

Inheritance down the female line is not possible, so the intergenerational transfer of commercial resources from mother to daughter has to be made early in the latter's maturity. Only petty quantities can be transferred in this way. The average capital of male traders is 27 times that of female traders. In Pujo's study only one woman trader gained returns greater than any male traders.

Once entry into trade is achieved, then gender-stratified access to technology and money means that processing costs for women are double those for men. Women's wholesale trading costs are 12 per cent higher than those of men; their transport costs are 55 per cent higher per unit distance; their storage costs are greater by a factor of three. Even the way trade is taxed disadvantages women in Guinee, the mechanism being gender specific because of the gender-geography of trade. On men tax is levied at a fixed rate per shop. On average it amounts to about 1 per cent of income. Women, by contrast, pay a tax every day they occupy a site in a marketplace – amounting to about 5 per cent of earnings. As a result male traders in Guekedou make $3,500 per annum to a weighted average of $820 for women (Pujo, 1997: 74).

Men exert other kinds of indirect control over female trading. In the forest interior of Guinee, rotating credit associations among women traders facilitate accumulation and yet women traders' investments in cattle, houses and jewellery, and their savings, are still frequently controlled by men. The extent of economic and functional differentiation means that it is not to be assumed that women traders have any particular collective interest on account of their gender.

In South Asia, the same phenomena are writ large and much more intensely, it would seem. Roles within market systems are structured by non-market criteria. Control over capital is exclusively male while 55 per cent of the casual livelihoods comprising the physical work of marketing and post-harvest transformation are held by women. Casual female labour gets take-home pay based on piece rates which is on average about two thirds that of casual male labour. The subordination of women is extremely crude depending on the type and class of commercial firm. Petty trade admits low caste and poor women. Their 'independent' returns are rarely much more than can be got by wage labour in commercial firms and are on the poverty line: 2 per cent of the estimated average returns of a rice wholesale firm. But gender constrains entry into the permanent wage labour force where take-home wages including perks in kind average 20 to 300 per cent higher than earnings in the casual female labour segments.

Gender also constraints accumulation which is by men. In elite firms, the role of women is very rarely productive or managerial. Nor are women family members deployed in the firm. Instead women are constructed socially as vehicles for the transfer of commercial resources between kinship groups. The exploitation of low-paid casual female labour by this commercial class not only fuels capitalist profits but also in turn reproduces the educated, somewhat secluded, leisured state of women in the households of the 'rurban' elite. Indian grain markets reflect in vivid ways the gender subordination characteristic of Indian society as a whole. Resistance to these arrangements is rare and meets intense male hostility. The issue of resistance will be revisited in the concluding discussion of political organisation.

Not only is gender far from being a homogeneous category, but the extent to which gender divisions and ideologies structure and constrain individual or collective agency varies. While it looks as though what Folbre terms the 'structures of constraint' are less fortified in rural and 'rurban' West Africa, they are formidable in India. There, businesswomen and female entrepreneurs can be found. But (a) rarely in rural or even 'rurban' areas and (b) rarely in the grain trade.

The impact of market participation in domestic reproduction

It is a matter of debate whether intrahousehold activity is structured (and household resources are allocated) primarily by patriarchy without reference to markets (Baud, 1983) or by markets without reference to patriarchy (Haddad *et al.*, 1997) or whether the two interact. If it is the latter, the debate proceeds to tackle the question of whether household labour responds to labour markets or livelihood opportunities such as marketplace trade, where low wages or returns are gender neutral and reflect the low productivity of women, the terms and conditions of market participation of whom are conditioned by patriarchally determined work burdens within households. Or whether marketplace remuneration is independently patriarchally determined so that wages and incomes for women are low irrespective of their supply and their productivity.

Returns from trade, involving more or less autonomous action in public marketplaces (West Africa) or wage labouring in trading firms (India), insofar as it brings exchangeable income is argued to be empowering (Batliwala, 1993). By now it must be realised that if women are empowered or emancipated by the act of trading in the social arena of the marketplace, it is despite the fact that they face higher costs and lower returns and that gender ideologies compound female disadvantage by preventing challenge to the commanding heights of the wholesale trade. For women's income to empower them in the social arena of the household, their income has to remain in their control. Further, the consequences of this control have to matter to other household members. As Robson argues it is not control *per se* which denotes empowerment. Female earnings which release male income to enhance male private expenditure are disempowering (Robson, forthcoming, quoting Pahl, 1980: 322). Empowerment within the household also requires control over negotiations, discussions and decisions about the disposal and use of income (which means examining types and purposes of expenditure, savings, investment and transfers). Empowerment requires changes in the ideologies shaping norms and motivation, increased capacities to renegotiate the terms of market participation and the allocation of the burden of unremunerated, less-perceived and appreciated productive and reproductive work.

In the conventional model of a single stylised household, the possibility that gender relations within the household and in the market are class, regionally or ethnically specific is ignored. In focusing on one institution of culture and material economy (gender), the others have inevitably been put on hold. In Guinee, Pujo has found that the disposition of the returns from commercial activity of women traders with the same size of commercial enterprise will depend on the class position occupied by their husbands. The elasticity of relations of household reproduction (which may condition marketplace participation rather than be conditioned by it) is also a matter for empirical research. There is fragmentary evidence in South India that reproductive roles such as child care are not gender-rigid and that the elderly – even elderly males – may play an important reproductive role and condition the availability of adult women for remunerated economic activity (Gillespie and McNeill, 1992).

Although there is fragmentary research in this area, it would be cowardly not to summarise what is known (and not known) about the reproductive consequences of the gendering of trade. In Guinee, Hausaland and India, women are very rarely allowed land rights or ownership of tools or cattle.[14] So income from commodity trading is one of the restricted opportunities other than wage labour by means of which women may enhance a household's income. In Guinee and India decisions on the disposal, household use or purchase of grain may be made by men (usually), by women and jointly (both much more rarely).

In West Africa there is significant variation between local regions in gender roles and burdens within households. The impact of female income from trade is added to the impact on the gendered control of the product of the labour process in production. In the Kissi region of Guinee women put in 40 per cent of the total labour in production but control 28 per cent of the product and perform all the reproductive labour, therefore having far less residual leisure than men. Even so women may sometimes be allowed to *manage* the granaries whose contents they do not *control*. Women traders keep separate accounts of expenditure and savings. But their lower returns and continual pressures by males to negotiate the appropriation of women's capital and the shedding of male expenditure responsibilities threatens this separate sphere. Further, the average income of a woman trader roughly equals her individual reproduction costs so, since women have obligations and dependants, they themselves are almost invariably thrown into relations of economic dependency (Pujo, 1997: 155–70, 209, 252).

In Zarewa village in Hausaland about one third of secluded women prepare and market cooked food. Women's incomes from grain and food marketing together with diverse other activities amount to about 13 per cent of household income: clearly much less than what men bring in and also much more unstable as a stream. While 85 per cent of household decisions are made by men, according to them, women reckon that 69 per cent are! One third of women's income goes on expenditure for the rest of the household, most of which is on food. Women spend less on themselves than do men and a smaller fraction of women than men reckon they have decision-making autonomy over matters of work, food or health expenditure (Robson, forthcoming).

From four pieces of field research into poor agrarian localities in Rajasthan (where female disadvantage is acute) in tribal Andhra Pradesh and in northern Tamil Nadu (where until recently female status has been relatively better: Agnihotri, 1996), it has been confirmed beyond doubt that female economic participation and the income derived from it does not by itself translate into greater decision-making power for women within their households, *except amongst the very poorest*. In labouring households the relationship is quite consistent.[15] For the rest, economic participation by itself does not enable a transformation of domestic control over resources and decisions. It does not lead inexorably to a change in the social relations of consumption inside the household (via the allocation of food) or outside it (via consumption expenditure). Within the household the significance of such earnings may be trivialised as 'pin money' or 'pocket money', appropriated or exchanged on more or less adverse 'terms of trade'. Independent female income may be a necessary condition for empowerment within the household but it is not sufficient. Other factors such as male outmigration, the consciousness-raising of an NGO, the extent of nuclear as opposed to joint/extended family forms, the particularities of joint family size and composition which affect relative status and the extent to which food needs were got from subsistence production were found to catalyse female income into female domestic power. In any case, neither resources nor decisions are to be assumed to be invariably in male hands. Resources may be controlled by one gender and decisions about their use by another gender or by joint negotiation. The degree of male control over expenditure decisions differs across commodity or type: health and agricultural inputs tend to be very male areas, food decisions tend to be much more female. But the degree of female control over household resources and decisions or even the intensity of female economic participation does not necessarily affect the political and social status of women in the public social territory outside the household.

With relevance to commodity market participation (though originally set out in relation to labour markets) Palmer has suggested four main considerations for the analysis of the intra-household impact of the participation of women in markets (1991: 11–15). By implication such factors may (individually or in combination) explain the varied relations already observed but they are not complete and their relative importance and role cannot be generalised:

1   the gender distribution of access to the means of production and distribution;
2   additional tasks faced by women in household reproduction and family maintenance and their gender elasticity);
3   the nature of the markets between the genders within the household (reflecting *inter alia* the extent to which a household is unitary or segmented);
4   norms governing the disposition of incomes between investment, savings and consumption between the genders and generations.

Palmer excludes from her list the crucial point of Sen (1990) that perceived contributions are as important as observable practices in the determination of relative status and welfare within households: that it is the relational quality of gender that counts as well as the material results of gendered transactions.

Despite the existence of returns from trading activity, gendered economic relations leading to subordinate status for *most* women and for *most* of their lives are associated with the subordinate status of women in marketing systems for staple foods – vividly in male marketing systems and even to be observed in female marketing systems. But with the evidence available it is just as plausible that both domestic and commercial relations are structured by the overarching forces of patriarchy. While commodity trading does not enhance the status of women within their households in any deterministic way, this does not mean that lack of independent income necessarily denotes low social or micro-political status within the household either. In Hausaland, for instance, age bears respect: 'women gain status with age' (Robson, forthcoming).[16]

Marketing systems show a certain idiosyncratic institutional autonomy, not only with respect to gender but in relation to most other social institutions, even including the social configuration of production over its spatial territory (Harriss-White, 1996). However, if, as Polanyi argued, markets destroy other forms of exchange and replace social embeddedness and socially constituted forms of distribution by a cold commercial logic, we find that they carry out this historic mission over a very long time scale. What we observe commonly is that market exchange 'simply' reworks the social institutions through which it is constituted and that where forms of exchange moving towards a 'cold commercial logic' are found, they are on a very small scale indeed and they daub more complexity onto already highly institutionally complex relations of exchange. As with gender, so with caste in India and ethnic groups in Guinee, grain markets are reinforcing institutional inequalities and social territorialisation. Although sites and social arenas so generative of livelihoods for women lead the watcher to expect a politics of struggle, it is because marketing systems are quite remarkably *not* observed by field workers to be the site of individual, iconoclastic gender-agency, collective gender-struggle or social transformation that we now need to address 'policy'.

Policy issues

It is irresponsible to list 'policy issues' residually, as is conventionally done, as 'impediments to be removed' (caricatured by Rodgers, 1989: 1) by an equally analytically residualised state or policy process. The nature of the public policy process and all significant interests threatened by it need analytical specification in every case where the search for room for manoeuvre, for strategy and tactics for policy change is serious.

Here, instead of endogenising policy processes and situating policy advocacy, I shall restrict the discussion to a small set of social problems for women which arise from the conditions described earlier and which are relevant to the agenda-forming component of the policy process. These are principally relevant to the male marketing systems of South Asia but gain urgency from their bearing on the female marketing system of West Africa.

Technical change and livelihoods

Staple food marketing systems, even as they tend to subordinate women, nevertheless provide huge numbers of livelihoods. Eighty per cent of firms in Guinee Forestière were run by women. One hundred and forty-nine agrocommercial firms studied in South India generated jobs for 5,500 adults, of whom 72 per cent, or, 3,960, were for women (Harriss-White, 1996). That proportion would be higher if the invisible and unvalorised role of women from the families of elite firms were included.

Technical change in foodgrains (rice and oil) processing has involved (1) foreign imports of technology developed for the radically different 'factor endowments and ratios' of the US and Japan, (2) foreign technical assistance, the quality of whose scientific advice left a great deal to be desired and (3) protective domestic legislation outlawing the 'indigenous' technologies (Harriss and Kelly, 1982). Adoption of such imported packages was pressed on state institutions (co-operatives and parastatals) which were isolated from the other state and private institutions of finance, pricing, procurement and logistics upon which the package depended. Low capacity utilisation and higher per unit marketing and processing costs have resulted in chronic state subsidisation. 'The market' has resisted technical change in package form (a rational response) but has over the years adopted techniques in stages. This has resulted in economies of scale and accentuated the structural concentration of assets in marketing systems.

Each wave of incremental technical change has led to the net displacement of labour, but has been biased hugely against casual female labour. Whether or not this displacement destroys livelihoods or 'merely' reduces drudgery does not depend only on the degree of commercialisation of the product, it also depends on the extent to which the labour relations of post-harvest processing have become commercialised. The first mechanised technology (the Lewis Grant huller, adapted in the early twentieth century from a coffee grinder and now very widespread, cost effective and made illegal in India) is the most female-labour-displacing of all because it replaces hand- or foot-operated machines worked by women.[17] The latest components (husk-fired driers) substituting for the public good of sunshine pose very serious threats to large quantities of female livelihoods in marketing systems. While Douglass North has hypothesised that technology is generally adopted so as to maximise the use of lesser-skilled workers who do not have the bargaining power to disrupt production (1990: 65), here, technology is adopted which does away with precisely those people least capable of bargaining or of withholding labour – the cheapest factor of marketing – female labour. The newest technical components are only cost-effective at market prices under conditions of high capacity utilisation which are difficult to achieve. Yet, inexorably, they are being adopted in the very reverse of a green-revolutionary development.[18] Perhaps the employment of armies of low caste people who happen to be women is more of a status-reducing expression of the contaminating caste relations of a merchant than a status enhancing expression of patriarchy. Technical change can not only concentrate the economic asset structures of the marketing system but also reinforce their gender power relations.

Liberalisation and masculinisation

If liberalisation is successful, it results in the development of more integrated national markets, which in turn entail not just the commercialisation of production and the scaling-up of post-harvest technology but also an increase in specialisation and interregional wholesale trade, not the least in staples. The development of long-distance interregional trading in female marketing systems has been observed to be dominated by men. In parts of West Africa, masculinisation may substitute for female trading (e.g. in northern Nigeria) while elsewhere they may be complements (e.g. Guinee Forestière). Female marketing systems may be articulated with national territorial markets without a reduction in female livelihoods. Indeed, these may very well expand. The point is that the integrated system as a whole is dominated, economically if not in numbers, by men. This domination places a new constraint upon female commercial accumulation. It is not necessary for a change in the gender division of work to occur. It is enough that there is expansion in precisely that type of work historically dominated by, if not entirely restricted to, men.[19]

The adaptive and productive inefficiency of gender roles in commerce

The most common question asked of markets concerns their efficiency. By virtue of there being no de-institutionalised marketing systems anywhere, efficiency is extremely difficult to evaluate. For the purposes of this discussion we can distinguish productive efficiency in which outputs from given inputs are maximised, from adaptive efficiency (North, 1990: 80–2) which involves judgements about the flexibility of the norms and institutions shaping the way an economy develops. In raising the issue of efficiency it does not follow that the World Bank's emphasis, particularly over the 1980s, on efficiency to the detriment of exploitation can be taken without question (see Elson, 1995). The point to be made here is that the economic consequences of the gendering of the rice marketing system reduces both sorts of efficiency in the examples we have used.

In Guinee, the gender division of labour has been calculated to cause losses in productive efficiency. Women face reduced incentives in production because of male control of the product of their labour, in processing because of the gendered stratification of technology and in trading because of the higher costs which were discussed earlier, which reduce their returns by 20 per cent.[20] The inefficient impact of these gendered relations is to raise consumer prices, leading to malnutrition, to raise the competitive advantage of imported over local rice (and imported rice is completely controlled by men) and to lead to massive female underemployment in the scarce season, which does not bode well for the nutritional status of their dependants (Pujo, 1997: 239–74).

In liberalising India, while gender roles, ideologies and the division of tasks in metropolitan conurbations may show considerable new elasticity (particularly among the 'middle classes') they seem to solidify with the inexorability of superglue outside such social territories, and are 'adaptively inefficient'. In a South Indian market town of some 100,000 people whose economy has been studied every decade from 1973, the adaptive inefficiency of the gendering of markets works differently from the West African case. Considerable strides have been made in female education and there is a small core of women doctors and lawyers. But women cannot own or manage commercial firms. The reasons given by the few women who want to enter trade are instructive. The state, in the guise of tax officials, blocks licensing on suspicion of bad faith and of intention to avoid tax by the family concerned. The state, in the guise of banks, also refuses to regard women as eligible for credit on the grounds that their registered collateral is 'benami' (bogus). With respect to the acquisition of skills and contacts, women's learning has to be confined to the domestic arena (to watching trade in a special room which can be a site – a private haven – for male business activity) and such women have faced male sanction on travel for purposes of commerce.

While there are no gender barriers to entry into high skill wage work such as computer programming in metropolitan cities and while the next stage of technical change in agro-commerce – automation – urgently requires computerisation, women in the marketing town who have somehow obtained relevant qualifications from the district capital's educational institutions are still debarred (on declared grounds of gender) from computer operation on commercial premises in the market town. The agro-commercial elite reject the female gendering of high-tech work, located socially (and physically) above their male labour force. The diffusion of computerisation is currently hindered and confined to the kind of simple accounting operations, which can be learned by trial and error by under-educated male family labour.

The commercial elite boasts many examples of what Sunder Rajan (1993) has ironically termed the 'new Indian woman': much more highly educated than their agro-commercial magnate husbands, these women have been imported for purposes of marriage from the metropolis. Their rare and always frustrated wish to enter commerce is seen as a natural outcome of a merchant capitalism construed everywhere as benevolent to them and massively reinforced in the popular English language media. Such 'modern women', confined to teaching the children of their elite peers and to philanthropic social work, with their roots in a carefully sanitised version of 'female tradition', accentuate the gap between their own apparent modernity and the alienated mass of women socially imprisoned by gender ideologies and by gendered material poverty.

Meanwhile, in this male marketing system the petty retail trade in staples which 20 years ago was an arena for women in the precincts of the Municipal Market has been taken over by men. Remaining women retailers are the most economically disadvantaged – widows and abandoned women with children. The older generation of women traders ceased this activity once their children were no longer economically dependent upon them. While a few elite women see large scale commerce principally in terms of its profitability and contemplate entry, poor women experience marketplaces as public, physically dirty and ritually polluting places and contemplate exit. For this latter class the non-participation of women is what they mean by development and progress. For the rich and poor aspirant to commerce alike, information, contacts and credit are the *sine qua non* of the ability of contingent acts of individual agency to consolidate themselves into a successful patterned challenge to gender roles.

Political organisation

Our search for gender-empowering action in marketing systems revealed very little.[21] In Guinee, agency is expressed in achieving micro-monopolies under competitive conditions, i.e. establishing niches, a regular clientele and repeated transactions so as to reduce competition. Otherwise gendered resistance and struggle is rare and is not acted out in the theatre of the marketplace. The division of labour in production and marketing is everywhere very close to ideological norms about the gendering of tasks and appropriate behaviour. If anything the measured input of women into rice *cultivation* is underestimated in normative statements.[22] This discrepancy between ideology and practice leads to men having greater control over the product than would be the case if tasks were actually performed according to gender norms. For women to take direct control of the means of production or the product is unusual. The resistance put up by women tends to take clandestine and petty forms: for instance hiding savings outside the home (part of the significance for women of gender-specific, rotating credit associations). But men also practise passive resistance in the same way. They also conceal savings and investments.

In India the micro-politics of casual male and female labour in marketplaces is quite different. Male casual labourers pull carts, load and unload, weigh and bag and act as millhands. Such labour tends to be permanent (albeit paid on piece rates or daily *coolie*) and unionised. Often casual male labour is organised in rival unions by competing political parties, unions run by professional politicians. Though this form of organisation smacks of 'divide and rule', unionised male labour has achieved some social change, e.g. the right to annual wage negotiations and the standardisation of piece rates in given localities.

By contrast casual female labour (which sweeps and cleans, dries and bags grain, separates and bags byproducts) is hardly organised at all throughout the subcontinent and even in states which have been ruled by the Communist parties. In fact their organisation is actively discouraged by the same mill owners prepared to negotiate with male unions. Over many years of fieldwork, I have encountered the stories of only two women 'foremen' who have sought to mobilise female casual labour. Both were harassed and sacked once the owners understood their purpose. Large unorganised female labour forces are *also* deliberately laid off by fractions in turn in order to avoid the welfare obligations towards permanent wage labour of the Factories Acts. Even in processing and trading firms which by dint of their male labour force are large enough to come under state regulation, there are no crèches, no sleeping areas for women, few latrines. Health and safety regulations are flouted. There are no muster rolls. Provident Funds, gratuities and lay-off compensations are ignored. The Factories Act inspectorate is widely co-opted and tends to collude with grain mill owners.

The working women forming the foundation of 'male' marketing systems are caught in a pincer. On the one side, technical change, on the other, the crudest of patriarchal commercial oppression threaten their livelihoods and their capacity collectively to improve their working conditions. Both in 'female' and 'male' marketing systems, and for a wide variety of reasons, it is no exaggeration to conclude that millions of female livelihoods worldwide are in jeopardy.

Notes

1 These ideas have been developed in dialogues springing from a comparison of my work in South Asia with that of doctoral students Laurence Pujo, working in Guinea and Elsbeth Robson, working in Nigerian Hausaland, to both of whom I am very grateful. The response of QEH's Centre for Cross Cultural Research on Women's seminar, where an earlier version was presented, and of Cecile Jackson, have also been very helpful. The remaining weaknesses are my responsibility.

2 See Humphrey, 1987; Baud, 1983; Clark, 1993 and Pearson here.

3 See Harriss-White 1995,1996 for developments of this point.

4 Bohannan and Dalton, 1962; Lawson, 1971; Hill, 1977; Christiansen, forthcoming.

5 Koopmans, 1990; Bauer, 1992.

6 In societies where divorce is common, such independence is required of women.

7 The first view has been advanced and discussed by Cordonnier, 1987, the second and third by Hopkins, 1973.

8 c.f. Bain, 1959.

9 Male and female child labour is crucial for the perpetuation of secluded women's trade in Nigeria. Their education may be denied them for this reason, or they may trade with other pupils at school (Robson, forthcoming).

10 The female casual labour force can number up to 700 in cotton ginning and whole-saling firms (see Harriss-White, 1996: Ch. 7).

11 'Coolie' in Tamil means wages for casual labour.

12 Female education leads to the lowering of birth rates (though not to reduced gender discrimination in regions of South Asia where this is practised: Das Gupta, 1987; Jefferey and Jefferey, Ch. 11 of the present book). But it is primary rather than tertiary education which achieves this result.

13 See Christiansen, forthcoming, for a pioneering study of the volumetric conventions in price formation by women in marketplaces in Benin.

14 The exception is in Hausaland where women can own livestock, though its disposal requires the compliance of the husband of the owner (Robson, forthcoming).

15 The vast bulk of this female economic participation, however, was from artisan craft work and agricultural labour rather than from petty trade, least of all in grains. However, the results show how complex the issue of the gendered consequences of the gains from trade is likely to be. For the original research see Samuels, 1989 on three desert villages of Rajasthan; Gillespie, 1988 on four tribal villages in Andhra Pradesh; Gibbs, 1986 on one village and Harriss, 1991 on two other villages in northern Tamil Nadu.

16 This increasingly appears to be less the case in India: see Erb, 1996 and Vera Sanso, 1997 for evidence of secular decline in the relative status of poor elderly people in rural and slum-urban settings respectively.

17 The process of displacement is most backward (and therefore acute) in the north-east of the sub-continent: see Greeley, 1987.

18 A revolutionary component should increase output per unit of input and thus lower total costs per unit of output.

19 It is also the case that forces other than liberalisation and the formation of national markets may masculinise trade: the expansion of Islamic seclusion ideology and practice is one, the gender ideologies of the colonial and post-colonial state are another.

20 Not more because male traders have a wage labour cost component which female traders do not have (Pujo, 1997: 263).

21 None of the researchers upon whose work we have relied deliberately sought out institutions initiating change wherever they might have been located. NGOs such as SEWA in India, BRAC and the Grameen Bank in Bangladesh have a limited success with the collective organisation of women in rice processing (Rowbotham, 1997). In the regions on which we have focused here, there has been no such activity.

22 This is not unknown in India! See Mencher and Saradamoni, 1982.

References

Agarwal, B. (1995) *A Field of One's Own: Gender and Land Rights in South Asia.* Cambridge University Press, Cambridge.

Agnihotri, S. (1996) 'Juvenile Sex Ratios in India – A Disaggregated Analysis, *Economic and Political Weekly* December: 3369–82.

Bain, J. (1959) *Industrial Organisation.* John Wiley, New York.

Bardhan, K. (1993) 'Social Classes and Gender in India: The Structure of the Differences in the Condition of Women', in Clark (ed.) (1993 pp. 146–178).

Batliwala, S. (1993) *Empowerment of Women in South Asia: Concepts and Practices.* FAO, New Delhi.

Baud, I. (1983) *Women's Labour in the Indian Textile Industry: The Influence of Technology and Organisation on the Gender Division of Labor.* IRIS Report 23, Development Reseach Institute, Tilburg University, Netherlands.

Bauer, S. (1992) 'Action to Assist Rural Women: Marketing Approach for Income Generating Activities in Four African Countries', in Cammann (ed.) (1992), pp.10–20.

Bhaduri, A. (1986) 'Forced Commerce and Agrarian Growth', *World Development* 14, 2: 267–72.

Bohannan, P. and Dalton, G. (1962) *Markets in Africa.* Northwestern University, Illinois.

Boserup, E. (1970) *Women's Role in Economic Development.* Allen and Unwin, London.

Braudel, F. (1985) *Civilisation and Capitalism in the 15th to 18th Centuries: Vol. 2 The Wheel of Commerce.* Fontana, London.

Cammann, L. (ed.) (1992) *Traditional Marketing Systems.* German Foundation for International Development, Feldafing.

Christiansen, B. (forthcoming) 'Unstandardised Measures and the Analysis of Price Efficiency: An Application' in Benin, in B. Harriss-White (ed.) ch 3.1.

Clark, A. (ed.) (1993) *Gender and Political Economy: Explorations of South Asian Systems.* Oxford University Press, Delhi.

Cordonnier, R. (1987) *Femmes Africaines et commerce: les revendeuses de tissu de la Ville de Lome.* L'Harmattan, Série Villes et Entreprises, Paris.

Das Gupta, M. (1987) 'Selective Discrimination against Children in Punjab', *Population and Development Review* 13.

Davis, J. (1992) *Exchange.* Open University Press, Buckingham.

Elson, D. (1995) *Male Bias in the Development Process.* Manchester University Press, Manchester, 2nd edn.

Erb, S. (1996) *Outcast from Social Welfare: Adult Disability in Rural India: Report to the Overseas Development Administration.* Queen Elizabeth House, Oxford University.

Folbre, N. (1986) 'Heart of Spades: Paradigms of Household Economics', *World Development* 14, 2, pp.245–256.

Folbre, N. (1994) *Who Pays for the Kids? Gender and the Structures of Constraint.* Routledge, London.

Fourie, F. C. von N. (1991) 'A Structural Analysis of Markets', in G. Hodgson and E. Screpanti (eds) (1991).

Gibbs, C. (1986) 'Characteristics of Household Expenditure in a Tamil Village, South India. BA dissertation, Newnham College, University of Cambridge.

Giddens, A. (1992) *Sociology: A Brief but Critical Introduction.* Macmillan, London.

Gillespie, S. (1988) 'Social and Economic Aspects of Malnutrition and Health among South Indian Tribal Groups.' Ph.D. thesis, London School of Hygiene and Tropical Medicine, University of London.

Gillespie, S. and McNeill, G. (1992) *Food, Health and Survival in India and Developing Countries.* Oxford University Press, New Delhi.

Greeley, M. (1987) *Post Harvest Losses, Technology and Employment: the Case of Rice in Bangladesh.* Westview Press, Boulder, Colorado.

Griffon, M. (ed.) (1990) *Economie des filières en régions chaudes: formation des prix et échanges agricoles.* CIRAD, Montpellier.

Guerrien, B. (1994) 'L'Introuvable Théorie du marché,' in Caille et al (eds).

Haddad, L., Hoddinott, J. and Adelman, I. (1997) *Intrahousehold Resource Allocation in Developing Countries: Models, Methods and Policy.* John Hopkins University Press, Baltimore, Maryland.

Harriss, B. (1991) *Child Nutrition and Poverty in Rural South India.* Concept, New Delhi.

Harriss, B. and Kelly, C. (1982) 'Food Processing: Policy for Rice and Oil Technology', *Bulletin of the Institute of Development Studies* 13, 3: 32–44.

Harriss, J., Hunter, J. and Lewis, C. (eds) (1995) *The New Institutional Economics and Third World Development.* Routledge, London.

Harriss-White, B. (1995) 'Maps and Landscapes of Grain Markets in South Asia', in J. Harriss *et al.* (1995) pp.87–108.

Harriss-White, B. (1996) *A Political Economy of Agricultural Markets in South India: Masters of the Countryside.* Sage, New Delhi.

Harriss-White, B. (forthcoming) *Agricultural Exchange and Markets from Theory to Practice: Field Methods and Field Experience in Developing Countries.* Macmillan, London.

Hill, P. (1977) *Population, Prosperity and Poverty: Rural Kano 1900 and 1970.* Cambridge University Press, Cambridge.

Hodgson, G. (1988) *Economics and Institutions.* Polity, London.

Hodgson, G. and Screpanti, E. (eds) (1991) *Rethinking Economics.* Elgar, London.

Hopkins, A. (1973) *An Economic History of West Africa.* Longmans, Harlow.

Humphrey, J. (1987) *Gender and Work in the Third World: Sexual Divisions in Brazilian Industry.* Tavistock, London.

Jorion, P. (1994) 'L'Économie Comme Science de l'Interaction Humaine vue sous l'angle des Prix: vers une Physique Social', in Caillie *et al.* (eds).

Kandiyoti, D. (1988) 'Bargaining with Patriarchy', *Gender and Society* 2, 3: 274–90.

Koopmans, J. (1990) 'Gender Issues in Food Production and Marketing: Core Issues in Africa's Food Crisis, in Griffon (ed.) (1990) pp.519–31.

Lawson, R. (1971) 'The Supply Response of Retail Trading Services to Urban Population Growth in Ghana', in Meillassoux (ed.) pp.377–99.

Meillassoux, C. (ed.) (1971) *L'Evolution du commerce en Afrique de l'ouest.* Oxford University Press, Oxford.

Mencher, J. and Saradamoni, K. (1982) 'Muddy Feet, Dirty Hands: Rice Production and Female Agricultural Labour, *Economic and Political Weekly Review of Agriculture* 17, 52: 149–67.

Moser, C. O. N. (1993) *Gender, Planning and Development: Theory, Practice and Training.* Routledge, London.

North, D. (1990) *Institutions, Institutional Change and Economic Performance.* Cambridge University Press, Cambridge.

Pahl, R. (1980) 'Patterns of Money Management within Marriage', *Journal of Social Policy* 9, 3: 313–35.

Palmer, I. (1991) *Gender and Population in the Adjustment of African Economies: Planning for Change*. International Labour Office, Geneva.

Pandya, A. and Dholakia, N. (1992) 'An Institutional Theory of Exchange in Marketing', *European Journal of Marketing* 26, 12: 19–41.

Penny, D. (1985) *Starvation: A Political Economy*. Australian National University, Canberra.

Polanyi, K. (1957/1985) *The Great Transformation: The Political and Economic Origins of Our Time*. Beacon Press, Boston, Mass.

Pujo, L. (1997) 'Towards a Methodology for the Analysis of the Embeddedness of Markets in Social Institutions: Application to Gender and the Market for Local Rice in Eastern Guinea'. D.Phil thesis, Oxford University.

Robson, E. (forthcoming) 'Gender, Households and Markets: Social Reproduction in a Hausa Village, Northern Nigeria'. D. Phil thesis, Oxford University.

Rodgers, G. (ed.) (1989) *Urban Poverty and the Labour Market: Access to Jobs and Incomes in Asian and Latin American Cities*. International Labour Office.

Rowbotham, S. (1997) 'Real Women of the Real World', *Guardian* 19 April: 21.

Samuels, F. (1989) 'Changes in Female Income and Status in Rural Rajasthan: a Survey of Three Villages'. MSc Dissertation, Queen Elizabeth House, Oxford University.

Sen, A. K. (1990) 'Gender and Co-operative Conflict', in Tinker (ed.) (1990) pp.123–49.

Shaffer, J. D. (1979) 'Observations on the Political Economics of Regulations', *American Journal of Agricultural Economics* 11, 2: 766–74.

Sunder Rajan, R. (1993) *Real and Imagined Women: Gender, Culture and Postcolonialism*. Routledge, London.

Tinker, I. (ed.) (1990) *Persistent Inequalities: Women and World Development*. Oxford University Press, Oxford.

Vera Sanso, P. (1997) 'Household Composition in Madras' Low-Income Settlements', *Review of Development and Change* 2, 1: 77–98.

Whitehead, A. (1981) '"I'm Hungry, Mum": The Politics of Domestic Budgeting', in Young *et al.* (1981) pp.54–68.

Young, K. Wolkowitz, C. and McCullagh, R. (eds) (1981) *Of Marriage and the Market: Women's Subordination in International Perspective*. CSE Books, London.

Part IV

POPULATION AND THE ENVIRONMENT

10

GENDER ANALYSIS OF FAMILY PLANNING

Beyond the 'feminist vs. population control' debate[1]

Ines Smyth

> The history of population control and the struggle for repro-
> ductive rights is far richer than a mere unfolding of economic
> forces or the playing out of political ideologies. This history
> becomes a complex and passionate enterprise when it focuses
> on the growth and development of the respective social move-
> ments – each of which takes shape through individuals and
> organisations who act powerfully in its behalf – attempting to
> define reality.
>
> (Thomas Shapiro, 1985: 12)

In recent years there has been an expansion, and deepening, of debates around
issues of population control versus reproductive rights. During the 1970s and
1980s discussions were marked by polarised arguments between those in favour of
population control policies and those who defended women's reproductive needs.
The framing of debates in terms of the catastrophic results of population growth
meant that these two positions were presented as being mutually exclusive. The
development of the argument that safeguarding women's reproductive rights and
improving women's status are prerequisites for reducing fertility has, however, created a potential area of common ground between the two sides. As the Cairo
Conference confirmed, those organisations that were once in favour of population
control are now talking the language of reproductive rights. This apparent convergence of voices serves to emphasise the need to clarify underlying theoretical
positions.

In order to address the above issue, this chapter considers the response of the
population establishment[2] to the criticisms voiced by feminists and health advocates. More specifically, the chapter tries to assess whether its adoption of feminist
ideas and language embodies their values or whether it hides fundamental differences. For this purpose, it is necessary first to describe the recent historical

events which provide the context for the apparent changes in the treatment of women by the population establishment. Similarly, it is essential to analyse feminist notions of reproduction, science and reproductive technologies, and how these inform critiques of family planning programmes. Such critiques are not uniform, in content or degree. Thus, to avoid oversimplification, this analysis must include the different feminist traditions from which they derive.

In confronting such issues, the intention of the chapter is to encourage policy makers in the field of population to consider seriously the principles contained in feminist critiques of family planning programmes. Failure to do so may lead to the kind of instrumentalism which, as will be discussed, characterises segments of the population establishment. Such instrumentalism alienates women and health advocates who are attempting to 'bridge the divide' (Kabeer, 1993) between those who are primarily interested in women's reproductive rights, and those whose main preoccupation is reducing fertility and population growth. Thus, it puts obstacles to the continuation of fruitful dialogues between the two.

The emerging debate

The improvement of the status of women, particularly in respect to education, health and economic autonomy, is a highly important end in itself. In addition, it affects and is in turn affected by demographic variables such as fertility and infant and child mortality

(UN, 1993: 11–12)

Every ten years since 1954 the UNFPA has organised an international conference on population and development issues. These international events are of great importance, because they reflect the dominant concerns in matters of population. They also influence the directions for thought and strategies for action for the following decade. Each of the conferences so far has epitomised the conventional wisdom on population for that specific decade. For example, the 1974 Bucharest Conference is recognised as the forum at which the definition of population growth as a problem was challenged from different perspectives (Marden *et al.*, 1982). Under attack were also the motives of the Western countries which set the conference agenda. In 1984 in Mexico City 'the pendulum swung back' (Hartmann 1987) in the sense that overpopulation was reconfirmed as the problem and family planning the solution.

Since then, the growing preoccupation with environmental depletion and deterioration, culminating with the Earth Summit held in Rio in June 1992, has ensured that (over)population has remained a compelling topic of public debate. The latest International Conference on Population and Development (ICPD) was held in Cairo, Egypt, in 1994. The topics and arguments which dominated the 1994 Conference and beyond reflect the different opinions and priorities of those institutions which are considered to be the population establishment.

The very heterogeneous nature of the population establishment and of the

218

opinions it holds should be kept in mind, despite the recent insistence of some of its representatives on 'global consensus' (Sadik, 1990). The current process of rewriting the history of the official population positions, and the formulation of the 1994 agenda in a way which emphasised harmony, glosses over the bitter disagreements voiced at Bucharest, and the problems caused later by US withdrawal of financial support to international organisations working on population.[3]

While the differences are very real, the preparations for the Cairo Conference displayed a new, shared interest in women. Women were never completely ignored in these events. The proceedings of the Belgrade Conference of 1965 include many mentions of women's fertility as an impediment to work (UN, 1966). At Bucharest in 1974, however, women were less visible in the agenda, though papers and discussions did contain references to the links between fertility and women's status. The conference aims also supported the elimination of all forms of discrimination against women (UN, 1974). At the Mexico Conference of 1984 the links between high fertility and the disadvantages women experience in employment, health and education were mentioned. In contrast to this, women were poorly represented, and only 18 per cent of all delegates were female (Wulf and Willson, 1984).[4]

The importance given to women's issues during the run-up to Cairo was shown by the themes of some of the additional meetings convened on special topics. For example, an expert group meeting on Population and Women was held in Gabarone in 1992, and a round table on Women's Perspectives on Family Planning, Reproductive Rights and Reproductive Health, was held in Ottawa in August 1993. The 'annotated outline' which represented the draft of the final document of the ICPD contained an early (II) chapter on 'gender equality and empowering of women'.[5]

The number and type of activities, the contents of discussions and documents, and the terminology employed are all indicative of a change in tone and scope. They also reveal a shift in approach from one which focused on the statistical correlation between women's fertility and their social position (as reflected by their education, health and employment status) to one which allegedly looks at population issues from a woman's perspective. Many countries' statements show a similar tendency. They give 'women's rights and gender equality' (Denmark) 'women's health' (USA) and 'women's rights to reproductive health and choice' (UK) considerable emphasis and high priority. Significantly, the same countries mention and endorse 'The Women's Declaration on Population Policies': a document prepared by a broad coalition of health and women's organisations across the world as a lobbying tool to influence the Cairo process.

Clearly these mentions are not comprehensive of all the activities and events of the Cairo Conference at the national and international level. They are, however, the most representative. The changes referred to can be read, with some caution, as hopeful signs that the population establishment was not simply 'adding women' to the array of topics of discussions and recommendations, but tried to adopt a more gender-sensitive perspective on all relevant issues.

Feminist critiques

Contraception alone does not provide the conditions requisite for freedom. If it assures women that the reproductive decisions they make can in fact be carried out, it does nothing to assure them that the decisions themselves are within their control

(Michaels, 1987: 211)

Clearly this shift of emphasis on the part of the population establishment has been gradual. Since the 1970s the material produced by the population establishment has given women increasing attention (see UNFPA 1977, 1989a, 1989b, 1992).

What is more important is that the changes have not been spontaneous. They are the result of the sustained efforts of considerable numbers of feminists and other concerned people and their organisations, those often referred to as the women's health movement (Dixon-Mueller 1983: 48). This is formed of 'those groups and individuals whose prime concern is to promote and protect women's reproductive rights and health' (Population Council, 1993). It is from this heterogeneous source that for several decades has come the 'most articulate and persistent voice' (Kabeer, 1993: 27) challenging the ideas and practices of the population establishment. Similarly, in the field of development more broadly, the last few decades have seen a transformation of the way gender inequalities are perceived, and sometimes acted on. This has been to a great extent the outcome of the challenges which feminists and women's advocates have posed to often reluctant governments and international institutions.[6]

What unifies the women's health movement is that its members share a feminist perspective. It should be noted here that the notion of a feminist perspective has meaning outside the specific arena of reproductive rights and population policies. It communicates something about the ultimate intentions of those who hold such a perspective and act from it. As stated by Spike Peterson (1992: 20): 'Feminists are by definition and determination critical of status quo social relations and committed to political transformation'. This political transformation goes beyond sex-based inequalities, as feminism 'is developing a profound philosophical world view that will point to change in all systems based upon racial, class and sexual oppression' (Bleier, 1991: 255).

In the West, early campaigns to gain, expand or protect abortion rights often united women from otherwise different feminist leanings. They were expressions of the importance that feminists have always attached to reproductive matters and fertility control. The arrival in the 1960s of more effective methods of contraception in the guise of the hormonal pill seduced Western women into thinking that these would be the definitive tools for control. It also led them to believe that this would be the avenue for personal liberation as well as sexual freedom. On the contrary, what soon appeared clear was that modern contraceptives, and the family planning programmes which manage and distribute them, can bring new threats to the physical and social integrity of women (Keysers and Smyth, 1989). This is particularly the case for the developing world and for the poor.

There is abundant documentation to show that such threats can be very real. Here it is sufficient to mention some examples. Large numbers of poor women have been sterilised in Puerto Rico, Brazil, Bangladesh and India. This has taken place in the absence of proper information, of adequate facilities, of consideration for the desires, circumstances and health status of the women in question (Mass, 1976; Hartmann and Standing, 1989; Kabeer, 1992). Since the 1960s, new contraceptives have been tested on women in developing countries, frequently with very limited, if any, information being imparted to them or to health workers (Atkinson; 1986; Sumati Nair, 1989). Abuses are not limited to countries of the South. In the 1980s Aboriginal women in Australia were being routinely injected with Depo Provera (McLaren, 1990). Other forms of abuse can be found in those programmes where, as in Indonesia (Smyth, 1991) or South Africa (Norsigian, 1987), women have little say about what contraceptive method they can use and no medical back-up for failure or negative effects of the method they do use. Similarly, there are countries where certain categories of women (unmarried, poor, rural) have no access to either family planning or health services. Finally, abuse can be seen in the widespread neglect of women's health which allows over 500,000 of them to die yearly of preventable causes related to pregnancy or childbirth, including unsafe abortions.

Abuses are not limited to women. Men have also been at the receiving end of coercive and violent practices in family planning, as in the case of Indian men during the Emergency. However, the fact remains that family planning programmes direct their interventions almost exclusively to women, from the contraceptive methods developed and deployed, to information, education and communication (IEC) activities.

As a reaction to these situations, feminists and health advocates have been extremely critical of the aims and practices of family planning programmes. While opposition to the abuses is shared by all, the contents of such critiques reflect differences within the feminist ranks. Beyond the commitment to the promotion and protection of women's reproductive rights and health, the feminist perspective is not uniform. As in the case of the population establishment, it encompasses many differences, making it more accurate to talk of 'feminist perspectives'.

Reproduction

The notion of reproduction is central to feminist thinking, but in a differentiated manner. The elements which differentiate various feminist positions fall broadly within the divisions identified as characterising separate strands of feminism. The classification between liberal, radical and Marxist/socialist feminist employed by Alison Jaggar (1983) is a useful one, though trying to slot all feminist ideas (on reproduction, family planning or any other subject) neatly into such a rigid framework denies their complex and changeable nature (Bryson, 1992: 4).

For liberal feminists, control over fertility is simply one of the legal rights women should have to enable them to participate in society as rational and autonomous individuals as fully as men. Thus their attention tends to be on the availability of family planning services. Their critique of family planning is inclined to be muted, and to confront only the most blatant abuses for which those services are responsible.

Reproduction has the most cardinal role in the analyses closer to radical feminism. This is because radical feminists see male domination as primary and ubiquitous, and based on the relations constituted around human reproductive biology (Jaggar, 1983). The preoccupation with women's bodies is a direct outcome of this: '[Radical feminism] has stressed women's control of our bodies as crucial to liberation, giving rise to analysis and action within the health movement, in the naming and analysis of violence against women, and in the analysis of sexuality and the imposition of heterosexuality as an institution' (Rowland and Klein, 1991: 305).

The approaches which have relied on a socialist tradition have located the roots of women's social position in the nexus between relations of production and those of reproduction in different historical settings (Kuhn and Wolpe, 1978; Bryson, 1992). It should be said, however, that this categorisation falls short of exposing the complexity of the relationship (labelled the 'unhappy marriage' by Lydia Sargent, 1981) between feminism and a Marxist tradition. Thus, in the words of Louise Johnson (1991) 'socialist feminists inhabit, critique and reconstruct'. The categorisation also erases the variety of feminisms which select from Marxism what is useful to feminist analysis through these critiques and reconstructions.

Science and reproductive technologies

An object of feminist enquiry which feeds directly into the critiques of family planning programmes relies on the development of feminist positions on science and technology. Feminist scholarship has joined other recent intellectual traditions in questioning the role of science and technology, their methods and their ethics.

The optimistic conviction that scientific discoveries and technological advancements would overcome the biological differences on which gender inequalities were seen to be based (Firestone, 1971) was of short duration. It was soon supplanted by a more sceptical attitude towards science and its neutrality. This sees science as constituting human beings, and particularly women, as objects (Hubbard, 1990). Here too we find differences among various feminist perspectives. From a radical feminist point of view, science is the domination of nature. Hence, it results in the domination of women, whose reproduction represents the forces of nature (Rowland, 1992).

Ecological feminism is deeply rooted in radical feminism. Among other things, it maintains that technology based on the artificial division between an active and passive principle has led to the colonisation of land and other natural resources, and to the devaluation of women (Shiva, 1992). These views of the links of women to nature (and of men to culture), are problematic because of their essentialism, and the attendant biological notions that are traditionally used to justify women's subordination. Similarly, such notions deny the historical nature of the factors which shape women's relations to nature (Leach, 1993). The debates in favour and against this dualistic notion, which equate women to nature and men to culture, are part of the vast body of intellectual work which ecofeminism is generating.

The view of science and technology just summarised results in a perception of reproductive technologies (of conception, contraception and childbirth) as inherently inimical to women, as they hand to men control over their distinctive source of power (Rowland, 1985; Corea, 1985). For these reasons, according to radical feminists, all reproductive technologies should be questioned and, for some, rejected outright (Mies, 1987, 1989).

Those critical of the ideas summarised above rightly note that many radical feminist positions on science neglect the fact that women have participated in the development of scientific ideas since antiquity (Rowbotham, 1993). It is true that their contribution to science and technology has been erased from historical accounts (Rose, 1987), and 'We women have been robbed of the history of female technical initiative, imagination and invention. We have lost our place in defining and shaping technology' (Hynes, 1989: 11). It is also true that women as practitioners of science still experience considerable difficulties in entering and working in their chosen fields. At the same time, it cannot be denied that though hidden from history, the participation of women in science must have influenced the directions in which scientific thought and practices have proceeded. The process of recovery which feminists have undertaken with respect to women's historical relations to science is in itself a contribution to science, in reproduction as well as in other sectors.

It is more useful to focus on the contexts in which science is employed, rather than to search for inherent properties which make any technology, including reproductive technologies, inevitably hostile to women (Feldman, 1987). This less absolutist position maintains that reproductive technologies can only be evaluated by taking into account the differences between various technologies and between women, and the broader social and economic circumstances which shape women's lives (Rose, 1987). Similarly, Patricia Spallone (1989) stresses context by stating that technologies can create a repressive ethic of reproduction, but that it is repressive social relations which allow certain technologies to be developed and used. As Bryson says in relation to new reproductive technologies: 'Once again the issue must be related to other areas of patriarchal control, and the struggle over reproductive rights must be fought in this context, rather than isolated as a simple cause of or the key to liberation' (1992: 207).

This type of analysis has led to the identification of the specific contextual elements which make reproductive technologies questionable. They include the fact that women themselves have had no say in what technologies are developed and deployed; that male scientists have preferred female contraceptive methods for fear of endangering male sexuality; that effectiveness dominates the choice of technology promoted by family planning programmes; that field tests take place without 'informed consent'; and that certain contraceptive methods are promoted in locations with inadequate medical infrastructures and expertise (Dixon-Mueller, 1983).

Family planning programmes

Feminist perspectives have not only challenged the nature of reproductive technologies, but also many family planning programmes which promote and employ them. These critiques go beyond the documentation and condemnation of violent practices and of the abuses of human rights mentioned earlier. One type of critique, from what could be described as a liberal feminist position, focuses on the quality and range of family planning services provided. This has been translated into a useful inventory of basic elements deemed necessary to reshape and improve family planning programmes: choice of methods, comprehensive information, technical competence of staff, good interpersonal relations – in other words a comprehensive package of back-up and other services (Bruce, 1989).

At a more profound level, criticism is based on the legitimate belief that family planning programmes worldwide are developed and implemented with the stated or implicit aim of reducing fertility rates and population growth, rather than with the intention of promoting women's health and reproductive freedom. This will be discussed in more detail later. There is another crucial aspect of this more fundamental criticism. This is that family planning programmes with a demographic goal may be implemented by governments upholding Malthusian notions of the relationship between population growth and socio-economic development. In many cases, however, such programmes are a reflection of international power imbalances, where national policies are a response to outside pressure. This pressure was reflected recently in the conditionality for loans imposed by international financial agencies, and in the practice by donor countries of targeting financial assistance to nations with the largest populations (Hartmann, 1992; Dixon-Mueller, 1983).

While all feminists are in broad agreement with the centrality of these two elements in the critique of family planning, there is considerable variation within feminist positions. Rather than dichotomise distinct radical or feminist critiques it is more accurate and useful to recognise a continuum of positions, within which specific critiques emphasise different combinations of the two elements.

Nevertheless, it is possible to distinguish a dominant feminist critique from the increasingly marginal radical feminist positions, parallel to the distinction made between feminist environmentalism and eco-feminism (Jackson, 1993a). The former locates these debates firmly in the context of development, seeing the contradictory pressures of, on the one hand, global and economic crises which make fertility limitation part of poor women's constrained livelihood strategies and, on the other, the population policies and family planning programmes of national and international institutions which see fertility limitation as the route rather than the result of economic development (Hewitt and Smyth, 1992).

Within this dominant feminist approach, family planning programmes are not necessarily nor always considered to be against women's interests; on the contrary, family planning is seen as an integral part of overall strategies to combat women's subordination (Dixon-Mueller, 1988). But this entails the demand for a profound transformation of the existing programmes. They must abandon the demographic rationale and substitute as their objective the safeguarding and enhancement of the health, general welfare and social position of women – especially poor women in the South. This is what is considered to be a woman-centred perspective on family planning. Moreover, the feminist critique has also been directed at the exclusion of men, and at an understanding of the dynamics of gender relations from family planning programmes and population control policies (Berer, 1993: 10). Men should be integrated as actors both in making fertility decisions and as family planning users, but in a context which prioritises women's needs rather than subordinates women's well-being to demographic imperatives.

From the perspective of radical feminism, the demographic rationale and the international political and economic order can be seen as manifestations of the workings of the capitalist patriarchy on a world scale (Mies, 1989) which has enmeshed women in a double set of oppressive controls from the rise of colonialism onwards. Whilst this position is rightly contextualised in an analysis which emphasises the centrality of biological and social reproduction in creating and maintaining women's oppression, the conclusions drawn by writers from this position are problematic. Not only does the radical feminist position entail the, previously discussed, blanket condemnation of science and technology as misogynist, it also leads to the unqualified rejection of all existing family planning programmes.

This extreme position can be said to be represented by the Feminist International Network of Resistance to Reproductive and Genetic Engineering (FINRAGE), though not homogeneously. A recent flyer prepared for the IPCD by FINRAGE (People's Perspectives on Population, 1993), together with several groups from developing countries, defined official family planning programmes as forms of population control (see the earlier definitions of these terms). Such programmes were described as 'racist, sexist, imperialist', aimed at eliminating the poor. Science and technology were deemed to be generated by 'capitalist-patriarchy to reinforce and reproduce capitalist patriarchal relations'.

This position, drawn from a radical feminist perspective, shares the essentialist position discussed earlier. Not only does it see reproductive technologies as subverting women's 'natural' situations, it ignores the multiplicity of women's experiences and their needs in terms of reproductive choice, which may include the desire and ability to limit their fertility (Feldman, 1987). It also sets up a dichotomy between the situation and requirements of women in the South and those in the North (Mies, 1989; Alexander, 1990). This opposition precludes the deconstruction of the multiplicity of identities and demands of women within both parts of the globe (see Keysers and Smyth, 1991 and Peter Waterman, 1993 for an extended discussion of these issues).

But, most importantly, such an uncompromising critique is unhelpful for those engaged in forging strategies which would make reproductive rights accessible for women in both the North and the South. The outright rejection of family planning services might be a genuine and principled rejection of both the objectives of family planning policies and abuses experienced in service delivery. However, as Dixon-Mueller (1983: 33–34) points out, these 'radical' critics are 'throwing the baby out with the bath water' in their total dismissal of all contraceptive technologies and family planning programmes.

Shared visions?

The previous sections have demonstrated the range of positions within feminist critiques of population policies and family planning programmes. To some extent, the population establishment also contains a broad array of positions; moreover, as outlined above, there has been a considerable shift on the part of many of the major providers to accommodate and incorporate concern for some of the issues raised by feminists. However, its notions are in many cases still based on profoundly different principles and visions from those upheld by the women's health advocates. Furthermore, segments of the population establishment have adopted certain feminist concerns and terminologies in a superficial and instrumental manner. This is alienating sections of the women's health movement, especially those who subscribe to or sympathise with a radical feminist view of reproductive technologies and family planning.

The rationale of family planning programmes

There is one main divergence of ideas between the population establishment and the women's health activists. This has already been mentioned in an earlier section, where it was said that the core of the feminist critique of family planning programmes is their demographic rationale. Philipps distinguishes three separate objectives which have overtly motivated family planning programmes in the South (Philipps, 1990). The first is the demographic objective: population growth is viewed as a fundamental cause of poverty, underdevelopment and environmental degradation, and fertility reduction through family planning programmes is seen as their solution. A second objective is to promote maternal and child health: family planning is intended to prevent maternal mortality in pregnancy and childbirth, to improve women's health and to reduce child mortality through birth spacing. A third objective is to advance human rights, where these are defined to include knowledge of and access to safe contraception (UN, 1990).

Most women and health advocates rightly maintain that the population control

226

motive is dominant in most official family planning programmes (Jaquette and Staud, 1985; Hartmann, 1987, 1992; Freedman and Isaacs, 1993). The enhancement and safeguard of women's reproductive and general health and their rights are sacrificed to this rationale. A commitment to their reproductive autonomy is actually deemed to be contrary to it and counterproductive to its aims (Keysers and Smyth, 1989). Such factors are taken into account only when considerations of costs or efficiency demand it.

The dominance of the demographic motive can explain the use of incentives and disincentives of various types, and of numerical targets (Smyth, 1991), both of which are often the immediate causes of coercive practices in family planning. This rationale also leads many population institutions to have an instrumental approach towards the broader socio-economic policies which should provide women with the means to achieve better health and reproductive autonomy. Both at the national and international level, policies advocated to foster women's education or their employment opportunities too often have an ulterior goal: that of controlling population growth through reducing fertility. For example, the Amsterdam declaration states that:

> The participants to the International Forum on Population in the Twenty-first Century recognise that women are at the centre of the development process and that improvements in their status and the extent to which they are free to make decisions affecting their lives and that of their families will be crucial in determining future population growth rates.
>
> (UNFPA, 1989a: 1)

This instrumentality is common to many development policies which are recommended for the benefit of women but have other aims: for example accelerating economic growth, or mobilising unpaid labour (Newland, 1991; Postel-Coster, 1993; Smyth, 1993). In the 1991 World Development Report, the World Bank (1991: 56) lists the benefits of educating women as: reducing the need for community health programmes; lowering infant mortality, thus compensating for the absence of medical facilities; increasing the use of contraception. Clearly economic and demographic objectives are paramount, rather than those pertaining to women's self-improvement and life chances.

A more sophisticated version of instrumentalism is reflected in the notion of synergism that underpins the policies of a number of development agencies, including the World Bank. This approach is based on an assumed model of the environment and human society as one system, with women as the crucial axis of articulation between 'nature' and society. From this it is concluded that one set of policies can be utilised to effectively address a diversity of issues, so that interventions aimed at improving women's position will also, supposedly, achieve environmental, economic or demographic objectives, and vice versa (Jackson, 1993a, 1993b).

States may legitimately develop policy objectives based on a given understanding of a country's demographic or economic conditions. However, one of the most serious dangers of instrumentalism is that changes in such perceptions may lead to complete reversals in policy aims and practices, thus rendering women's needs vulnerable to shifts in political-economic outlooks at the national and international levels. Evidence of the effects of such transformations can be drawn, most obviously, from the post-Communist countries of East Europe. Reproductive policies in the former GDR were largely dictated by the need to replace the labour force. Falling birth rates during the 1960s led to the introduction of various material incentives designed to induce women to increase their family size. The switch to policies of marketisation and labour force rationalisation following German Unification resulted in the reduction of paid leave to care for sick children from five weeks to five days per year, a policy change that was most likely to affect negatively those women who had been encouraged to have more children under the old regime (Einhorn, 1993: 83–86).

Thus, the means through which demographic objectives are achieved should never jeopardise women's reproductive rights. In particular, policies should never be based, either in design or implementation, on a disregard for women's health through practices which intimidate, misinform, coerce or subject women to moral or financial pressures. On the contrary, such policies should offer women safe, accessible and free services which correspond to the different needs that women of different classes, ethnic groups and ages have. Above all, such policies must not be a substitute for comprehensive interventions aimed at improving women's social condition through education, employment, financial support for child care, and broader public services. These provisions would strengthen women's position *per se* and, in addition, free them from identification with the single role of motherhood that often underpins high fertility.

Reproductive rights

One of the central concepts of feminist perspectives on reproduction and family planning is that of reproductive rights. As the summary on pp. 213–14 of this chapter has shown, the language of rights and choice has recently been adopted by the population establishment. Thus it is important to see whether the understanding of the terms coincides with the way in which it is intended by feminists.

Among feminists there has been an evolution in the meaning of reproductive rights, which still continues. Western feminists of the so-called 'second wave' originally used the slogan 'Women's Right to Choose' with reference to abortion. Though powerful in the various campaigns mounted to defend or expand abortion legislation, the notion has proved problematic for several reasons. Both 'right' and 'choice' were seen as ideas based on a Western, individualist understanding. As such they failed to take into consideration both the importance of the social structures which encompass all aspects of women's lives and which pre-determine and mediate reproduction and reproductive choices, and the regional and historical differences between these structures. Additionally, the call for women's rights in reproduction was seen as a claim made from within a given social order which did not necessarily entail a challenge to that order, despite the notion of rights being an important legal safeguard. Furthermore, it soon appeared as an idea which could be easily used to support the essentialist position of biological reproduction as women's fate (Petchesky, 1985), in other words, a return to the notion of 'biology as destiny' to which feminists are unanimously opposed.

In order to overcome some of these problems, the language of needs has been applied to reproduction (Kabeer, 1993). This, too, is fraught with problems, since it can lead to perceiving 'reproductive needs' as part of 'basic needs' to be satisfied with a simple, technical solution (family planning programmes) (Alexander, 1990). So far, these complications have not led to the abandonment of 'reproductive rights' as a central concern for feminists. Rather, they have inspired caution. They have given rise to initiatives which instead of pre-defining such terms, seek to ascertain what meanings different women give to 'reproductive rights' and what demands and priorities they attach to their attainment (IRRRAG, 1993; WGNRR, 1993). Such attempts allow the notion of reproductive rights to encompass a consideration of the differences between women in their reproductive behaviour, perceptions and needs; of the various ways population policies affect them; and of the differences between the social settings in which women are located.

The examination of the possible meanings of the central concept of 'reproductive rights' also signifies a shift from an individualistic perspective to one which retains the notion of *self-determination* in childbearing (if, when and with whom to have children) as the crucial element. Here, the emphasis is on a woman's own determination against that of others, rather than on the self as individual. It implies the acceptance of the fact that self-determination in reproductive matters cannot be understood or achieved in isolation from self-determination in all other spheres of life. This entails access to and command over material and non-material resources far beyond contraceptives and family planning programmes. In other words, individual reproductive behaviour is influenced by systems of gender relations and those are embedded in social, economic and political norms and structures (Dixon-Mueller, 1983: 112). Thus, as Berer states, 'From a women-centred point of view, increasing women's currently limited life choices as well as reproductive rights are the first principles upon which any policies and programmes on fertility should be based' (1983: 10).

The population establishment's interpretation of reproductive rights and choice is different. An essay which decries the decline in contraceptive research is illuminating (Wymelenberg, 1990). In the essay, the author states that the factor uniquely responsible for women's low status in society is their uncontrolled fertility. Clearly this understanding of the complex articulation between women's personal and social position and their fertility is completely counter to any of the feminist analyses summarised above. The author significantly equates the expansion of women's reproductive choice with the expansion in the number and types of modern contraceptives available (1990: 62). This also seems to be the interpretation adopted by the World Bank, which sees it as a type of consumer's choice. Thus, the Bank advocates the broadening of such choice by the elimination of what it considers unnecessary constraints on the types of contraceptives available, for example, the use among governments of essential drug lists which 'mistakenly' include some contraceptives, and 'excessive medical screening requirements' (World Bank, 1993b: 5).

This notion of reproductive rights and choice goes hand in hand with the demographic rationale of family planning programmes since, for the World Bank, providing choice of different contraceptive methods is a requirement to attract 'clients', in order to raise acceptance rates (World Bank, 1993a: 39–41).

The population establishment's perception of reproductive rights also differs from a feminist one at another level. For the latter, reproductive autonomy is 'a basic right for every woman' (Freedman and Isaacs, 1993: 23); thus every woman should have access to the means necessary for the exercise of such right, including contraception and safe abortion. For the population establishment, on the other hand, contraception through family planning programmes is promoted for poor women and poor countries – those, in other words, whom they perceive to be responsible for unacceptable rates of population growth (Mass, 1976; Michaelson, 1981; Hartmann, 1992). For example, the World Bank (1990: 82) states that:

> Family planning programmes, where they have been implemented, have brought birth rates down . . . Other factors in reducing birth rates, however, should not be overlooked. Rapidly developing economies can bring about some modest decline even with weak family planning programmes. But, in the poorest countries (such as India and Indonesia) strong family planning programmes are necessary to slow population growth.

Family planning is also targeted on racial grounds. For example, South African policies reflected the wish by the government to reduce the growth of the black population (Klugman, 1993).

Quality of care

Perhaps it is with the issue of quality of care that the population establishment has come closer to adopting a woman-centred perspective. It is undeniable that there has been a genuine and widespread concern for the quality of the services provided by family planning programmes. The Population Council, for example, has spearheaded a sustained effort to clarify the principles on which improvements to the services provided to family planning acceptors should be based (Bruce, 1989). However, there is considerable worry among health advocates worldwide that were these improvements in services to become the norm, this might well take place against the background of basic health services constantly eroded by financial and other reforms, which would also put them out of reach of the general population.

Furthermore, in this context too the demographic rationale is often present. It is in fact obvious that far too often the support for such improvements has little to do with safeguarding women's health and rights; rather it is a means to improve acceptance rates and thus achieve population reduction targets. In documents discussing organisational aspects of family planning programmes, the World Bank evaluates choice in contraceptive methods, community participation and users' perspectives in family planning, all elements which in different ways should contribute to the quality of services. But they are frankly acknowledged to be tactical means to increase contraceptive prevalence and continuation rates by improving the 'interface' between providers of services and users and through more advanced management styles (Green, 1992).

Should this difference in the motive behind the support for improvements in the quality of services worry the women's health movement? I am inclined to say that if the population establishment can translate quality of care statements into good, comprehensive and free reproductive health services for women which respond to their varied needs, and which are provided by adequately qualified personnel in a dignified and respectful manner, perhaps it is immaterial that this is done to achieve maximum effectiveness, rather than to adhere to genuinely held feminist principles.

This conclusion does not eliminate the need to remain alert to the many dangers inherent in the demographic rationale of family planning programmes. It also does not lessen the dissatisfaction with the empty adoption of the language of feminism and the instrumentality evident in the use of feminist notions by certain segments of the population establishment. The UNFPA has appropriated terms such as self-determination and choice in childbearing (UNFPA, 1992). Similarly those who advocate the marketing of new fertility-enhancing technologies have adopted a language of choice (Alexander, 1990). The World Bank too makes liberal use of expressions such as 'women's empowerment' (World Bank, 1992). According to Hartmann (1992) this 'doublespeak' clothes perceptions and interests which are very different from feminist visions.

Conclusions

The population establishment has embraced some crucial feminist ideas, but only partially and instrumentally. A consequence of this has been that many women and health advocates, and in particular those who support radical feminist views, remain deeply distrustful of the population establishment.

They see dangers in the process of institutionalisation of women's issues and in the dialogues between the women's health movement and population organisations. After many decades of neglect, planners and policy makers have responded to the growing interest in women. Institutionalisation takes place at different levels, from the establishment of women's bureaux in multilateral and bilateral aid agencies and governments, to the encouragement of research and women's projects, and to the organisation of 'gender awareness' training and international conferences. It has spread even to institutions – like the World Bank – which had previously been impervious to such considerations (see the *World Development Reports* for 1991 and 1992).

One perceived danger of the institutionalisation of women's issues has been their removal from the domain of struggle, to one where technical solutions can be negotiated leaving basic social relations unchanged. The other dangers are related to the entrance of women into population establishment institutions. Women's absence from the public arena is an old preoccupation among Western feminists (Wollstonecraft, 1965). Women's exclusion from public life and from positions of authority has been perceived as both symptom and cause of women's subordination in developing countries as well as in Western nations. For some, this exclusion is analytically linked to the separation of the private from the public sphere, and the relegation of women to the former (Grant, 1992). In this view, formal power resides in the latter and is governed by the male values of dominance and control. Feminists have sought to institute styles of organisation based on the reverse principles of non-hierarchy and participation (Savage, 1992: 21). A crucial aspect of women's organisations is their independent status, and groups active in reproductive rights have espoused these politics of autonomy (Correa, 1993).

Because of this commitment to non-hierarchy and to autonomy, the entrance of women into positions of power within population institutions is reawakening fears that women in powerful positions will become concerned with careerism, be co-opted into conforming with the culture and the objectives of their employers and reject the women's movement for its naivety (Watson, 1992).

There is also distrust of dialogues. Institutions like the Population Council and other national and international agencies frequently create opportunities for encounters and exchanges of ideas. In particular, in preparation for the 1994 Conference, many governments opened up to consultations with non-governmental organisations, professional associations and women's groups. One of the possible dangers identified is that, given the superior power (in resources and influence) of population institutions over the women's health movement, priorities and terms of the debates will be set by the former, forcing the latter to take a reactive stance. The same power imbalance can lead women's health advocates to be side-tracked away from urgent and controversial concerns. Finally, there is concern for the possibility that the population establishment can use dialogues as a way to 'engineer consent' around specific activities, thus silencing oppositional voices (Richter, 1993).

In summary, the population establishment may have moved a little closer to understanding and accepting some of the principles embodied in a woman-centred perspective in family planning. The change is, however, a partial and superficial one. For the radical feminists, who already hold profound reservations about family planning programmes, this is direct confirmation of their unacceptability.

For all feminists this generates fears that dialogues and co-operation are fraught with dangers of co-option, of marginalisation and of trivialisation of women's issues. The dangers are very real, and the warnings should be heeded. However, it is also important to stress that working for women's reproductive rights and health does not necessarily cease to be a struggle when placed in the context of dialogues or in institutionalised environments, though these may necessitate the development of new analytical and strategic tools. It is also important to remember that when they have occurred, different forms of collaboration between women's health advocates and the population establishment have led to misunderstandings and unhappy compromises. At the same time, they have also been the medium through which women's health advocates have influenced policies in directions much more responsive to women's needs, and through which they have gained a foothold in political arenas otherwise inaccessible to them (Coote and Campbell, 1982; Barroso and Bruschini, 1991). To use the words of Hartmann (1993: 3) awareness of dangers

> does not mean that one does not push for policy reform or engage in dia-
> logue with those within the system, but one has to do it, in my mind, with
> a clear understanding of the limitations and from a critical perspective,
> which includes careful use of language.

For the reasons given at the very beginning of this chapter, the Cairo Conference of 1994 offered an important opportunity for the population establishment to review its thinking because of greater awareness and responsiveness to women's perspectives in family planning. Feminists have developed principles which are essential to this rethinking. However, it is not sufficient for the population establishment to display a notional adherence to such ideas, to advocate them only in the pursuit of ulterior aims, or simply to use their language without their substance. This manner of operating is already causing considerable worries among some women's health advocates, and may compromise the possibility for long-term, fruitful exchanges between those and the population establishment.

Notes

1 This chapter first appeared in *Feminist Economics* 2(2), Summer 1996. I wish to acknowledge the useful suggestions and encouragement of Maria Black, Claudia Garcia Moreno and Loes Keysers.
2 These include national governments and international organisations such as the UNFPA (The United Nations Fund for Population Activities), the Population Council, the IPPF (International Planned Parenthood Federation), the World Bank and USAID (Marden *et al.*, 1982).

3 Support was withdrawn from programmes supporting abortion in any way. See Hartmann (1987) for the role this played in casting the population establishment in the role of 'defenders of reproductive rights' (1987: 125).

4 Figures for other conferences were not available. However, reports from participants clearly indicate that there were a large number of female representatives at Cairo.

5 It is worth noting that the sections dealing with women's reproductive and sexual health were at the centre of the most heated debates at the conference.

6 This, however, does not mean that the loosely integrated coalitions which formed, and still form, the women in development movement have ever been either all powerful or unified. See Kathleen Newland (1991) for an analysis of the movement's main weaknesses and divisions.

References

Alexander, Jacqui. 1990. 'Mobilising against the State and International Aid Agencies: "Third World" Women Define Reproductive Freedom', in Marlene Gerber Fried (ed.) *From Abortion to Reproductive Freedom: Transforming a Movement.* Boston: South End Press.

Atkinson, Linda. 1986. 'Two Decades of Contraceptive Research: Prospects for the Century'. Paper presented at the Population Council Meeting, New York (8–9 October).

Barroso, Carmen and Bruschini, Christina. 1991. 'Building Politics from Personal Lives: Discussions on Sexuality among Poor Women in Brazil', in Chandra, T. Mohanty, Ann Russo and Lourdes Torres (eds) *Third World Women and the Politics of Feminism.* Bloomington: Indiana University Press.

Berer, Marge. 1993. 'Population and Family Planning Policies: Women-centred Perspectives', *Reproductive Health Matters* 1: 4–13.

Bleier, Ruth. 1991. 'Science and Gender', in Sneja Gunew (ed.) *A Reader in Feminist Knowledge.* London: Routledge.

Bruce, Judith. 1989. *Fundamental Elements of the Quality of Care: A Simple Framework,* The Population Council Programme Division, Working Paper 1, New York.

Bryson, Valerie. 1992. *Feminist Political Theory: An Introduction.* London: Macmillan.

Coote, Anne and Campbell, Beatrice. 1982. *Sweet Freedom: The Struggles for Women's Liberation.* London: Picador.

Corea, Gena. 1985. *The Mother Machine: Reproductive Technologies from Artificial Insemination to Artificial Wombs.* New York: Harper and Row.

Correa, Sonia. 1993. DAWN Research Effort 1992/94: Population and Reproductive Rights Component. Platform Document, mimeo.

Dixon-Mueller, Ruth. 1988. 'Redefining Family Planning: Feminist Perspectives on Service Delivery'. Paper presented at the Annual Meeting of the Population Association of America, New Orleans, April.

Dixon-Mueller, Ruth. 1983. *Population Policy and Women's Rights: Transforming Reproductive Choice.* Westport: Praeger.

Einhorn, Barbara. 1993. *Cinderella Goes to Market. Citizenship, Gender and Women's Movements in East Central Europe.* London: Verso.

Feldman, Rayah. 1987. 'The Politics of the New Reproductive Technologies', *Critical Social Policy* 9(7): 21–39.

Firestone, Shulamith. 1971. *Dialectic of Sex: The Case for Feminist Revolution.* London: Jonathan Cape.

Freedman, Lynn P. and Isaacs, Stephen L. 1993. 'Human Rights and Reproductive Choice', *Studies in Family Planning* 234(1): 18–30.

Grant, Rebecca. 1992. 'The Sources of Gender Bias in International Relations Theory', in Rebecca Grant and Kathleen Newland (eds) *Gender and International Relations*. Milton Keynes: Open University Press.

Green, Cynthia P. 1992. *Strategic Management of Family Planning Programme*. World Bank WPS976, Washington.

Hartmann, Betsy. 1987. *Reproductive Rights and Wrongs: The Global Politics of Population Control and Contraceptive Choice*. New York: Harper and Row.

Hartmann, Betsy. 1992. 'Population Control in the New World Order', *Development in Practice* 2(3): 210–15.

Hartmann, Betsy. 1993. 'The Present Politics of Population and Reproductive Rights', *Women's Global Network for Reproductive Rights Newsletter* 43: 1–3.

Hartmann, Betsy and Standing, Hilary. 1989. *The Poverty of Population Control*. London: Bangladesh International Action Group.

Hewitt, Tom and Smyth, Ines. 1992. 'Is the World Overpopulated?' in Tim Allen and Alan Thomas (eds) *Poverty and Development in the 1990s*. Oxford: Oxford University Press.

Hubbard, Ruth. 1990. *The Politics of Women's Biology*. New Brunswick: Rutgers University Press.

Hynes, H. Patricia (ed.) 1989. *Reconstruction Babylon: Essays on Women and Technology*. London: Earthsan.

IRRRAG (International Reproductive Rights Research Action Group). 1993. *Report on the First Year*, February.

Jackson, Cecile. 1993a. 'Doing What Comes Naturally? Women and Environment in Development', *World Development* 21(12): 1947–63.

Jackson, Cecile. 1993b. 'Questioning Synergism: Win-win with Women in Population and Environment Policies', *Journal of International Development* 5(6): 651–68.

Jaggar, Alison M. 1983. *Feminist Politics and Human Nature*. Brighton: Harvester Press.

Jaquette, Jane and Staud, Kathleen. 1985. 'Women as "At Risk" Reproducers: Biology, Science and Population in US Foreign Policy', in Virginia Shapiro (ed.) *Women, Biology and Public Policy*. Beverly Hills: Sage Publications.

Johnson, Louise C. 1991. 'Socialist Feminist Interventions', Introduction in Senja Gunew (ed.) *A Reader in Feminist Knowledge*. London: Routledge.

Kabeer, Naila. 1992. *From Fertility Reduction to Reproductive Choice: Gender Perspectives in Family Planning Discussion*. Paper 299, Institute of Development Studies, Brighton.

Kabeer, Naila. 1993. 'Bridging the Gap, *People and the Planet* 2(1): 27–8.

Keysers, Loes and Smyth, Ines. 1989. *Family Planning: More than Fertility Control? Women in International Development*. Michigan State University Working Paper No. 198.

Keysers, Loes and Smyth, Ines. 1991. 'Reflections of Global Solidarity for Women's Health and Reproductive Rights', *VENA Journal* 3(1): 26–31.

Klugman, Barbara. 1993. 'Balancing Means and Ends: Population Policy in South Africa, *Reproductive Health Matters* 1: 44–57.

Kuhn, Annette and Wolpe, AnnMarie 1978. 'Feminism and Materialism', in Annette Kuhn and AnnMarie Wolpe (eds) *Feminism and Materialism*. London: Routledge and Kegan Paul.

Leach, Melissa. 1993. *Rainforest Relations: Gender and Resources Use among the Mende of Gola, Sierra Leone*. International African Institute, London.

Marden, Parker, G. Hodgson, Dennis G. and McCoy, Terry L. 1982. *Population in the Global Arena: Actors, Values, Policies and Futures.* New York: Holt, Rinehart and Winston.

Mass, Bonnie. 1976. *Population Target. The Political Economy of Population Control in Latin America.* Toronto: Women's Press.

McLaren, Angus. 1990. *A History of Contraception.* Oxford: Basil Blackwell.

Michaels, M. W. 1987. 'Contraception, Freedom and Destiny: A Womb of One's Own', in Stuart F. Spicker, William B. Bondeson and H. Tristam Engelhardt (eds) *The Contraceptive Ethos: Reproductive Rights and Responsibilities.* Dordrecht: Publishing Company.

Michaelson, Karen L. (ed.) 1981. *And the Poor Get Children: Radical Perspectives on Population Dynamics.* New York: Monthly Review Press.

Mies, Maria. 1987. 'Why Do We Need All of This? A Call Against Genetic Engineering and Reproductive Technology', in Patricia Spallone and Deborah B. Steinberg, *Made to Order: The Myth of Reproductive and Genetic Progress.* Oxford: Pergamon Press.

Mies, Maria. 1989. 'What Unites, What Divides Women from the South and from the North in the Field of Reproductive Technologies'. Paper presented at the FINRAGE-UBINIG conference Comilla, Bangladesh, 18–25 March.

Nair, Sumati. 1989. *Imperialism and the Control of Women's Fertility.* Amsterdam: Campaign Against Long Acting Contraceptives.

Newland, Kathleen. 1991. 'From Transnational Relationships to International Relations: Women in Development and the International Decade for Women', in Rebecca Grant and Kathleen Newland, *Gender in International Relations.* Milton Keynes: Open University Press.

Norsigian, Judy. 1987. 'Reproductive Choice in Jeopardy'. International Policy Perspectives, Presentations at the Biennial Conference of the Association for Women in Development, Washington, April.

Palomino, Nancy. 1993. 'Unity in Diversity', *Women's Global Network for Reproductive Rights Newsletter* 43: 7–8.

Petchesky, Rosalind P. 1985. *Abortion and Women's Choice.* London: Verso.

Philipps, David R. 1990. *Health and Health Care in the Third World.* New York: John Wiley & Son.

Population Council. 1993. Day of Dialogue on Population and Feminist Perspectives, Aide-Memoire. London, 20 November.

Postel-Coster, Els. 1993. 'The Instrumentality of Indonesia's Policy towards Women', in Jan-Paul Dirkse, Franz Husken and Mario Rutten (eds), *Indonesian Experience under the New Order.* Leiden: KITLV Press.

Richter, Judith. 1993. 'Report on the Workshop Population Policy and Reproductive Choice in South Asia'. Oxford, 2–4 September 1992.

Rose, Hilary. 1987. 'Victorian Values in the Test-Tube: the Politics of Reproductive Science and Technology', in Michelle Stanworth (ed.) *Reproductive Technologies: Gender, Motherhood and Medicine.* Cambridge: Polity Press.

Rowbotham, Sheila. 1993. 'Feminist Approaches towards Technology '. Paper presented at the Workshop on New Technologies and Women's Employment, UN University, Maastricht, The Netherlands.

Rowland, Robyn. 1985 . 'Reproductive Technologies: the Final Solution to the Woman Question', in Rita Arditti, Renate Duelli Klein and Shelley Minden (eds) *Test Tube Women.* London: Pandora.

Rowland, Robyn. 1992. *Living Laboratories: Women and Reproductive Technologies.* London: Lime Tree.

Rowland, Robyn and Klein, Renate. 1992. 'Radical Feminism', Introduction in Sneja Guew (ed.) *A Reader in Feminist Knowledge*. London: Routledge.

Sadik, Nafik. 1990. 'The Role of the United Nations – From Conflict to Consensus' in G. Roberts (ed.) *Population Policy: Contemporary Issues*. New York: Praeger.

Sargent, Lydia. (ed.) 1981. *The Unhappy Marriage of Marxism and Feminism: A Debate on Class and Patriarchy*. London: Pluto Press.

Savage, Mike. 1992. 'Women's Expertise, Men's Authority: Gendered Organisations and the Contemporary Middle Classes', in Mike Savage and Anne Witz (eds) *Gender and Bureaucracy*. Oxford: Blackwell.

Shapiro, Thomas. 1985. *Population Control Politics: Women, Sterilization and Reproductive Choice*. Philadelphia: Temple University Press.

Shiva, Vandana. 1992. 'The Seed and the Earth: Women, Ecology and Biotechnology', *The Ecologist*. 22(1): 4–7.

Smyth, Ines. 1991. 'The Indonesian Family Planning Programme: A Success Story for Women?' *Development and Change* 22: 782–805.

Smyth, Ines. 1993 'A Critical Look at the Indonesian Government Policies for Women', in Jan-Paul Dirkse, Franz Husken and Mario Rutten (eds) *Indonesian Experience under the New Order*. Leiden: KITLV Press.

Spallone, Patricia. 1989. *Beyond Conception*. London: Macmillan.

Spike Peterson, V. (ed.) 1992. *Gendered States: Feminist (Re)visions of International Relations Theory*. Boulder: Lynne Reinner Publishers.

UN 1966. *Proceedings of the World Population Conference Summary Reports. Vol. I.*

UN 1974. *The Population Debate: Dimensions and Debates*, Papers of the World Population Conference, Bucharest 1974, Vol. I.

UN 1990. *Population and Human Rights*, Proceedings of the Expert Group Meeting on Population and Human Rights, Geneva, 3–6 April.

UN 1993. International Conference on Population and Development – Annotated outline of the final document of the Conference – Note by the Secretary General; A/48/_/Add.1.

UNFPA 1977. *Women Population and Development Population Profiles*, No. 7, New York.

UNFPA 1989a. 'A Better Life for Future Generations: The Amsterdam Declaration', *Population* 15(12).

UNFPA 1989b. *Annual Report* 1988.

UNFPA 1992. Population Issues: Briefing Kit.

Waterman, Peter. 1993. 'Hidden from Herstory: Women, Feminism and New Global Solidarity', *Economic and Political Weekly* 30 October.

Watson, S. 1992. 'Femocratic Feminism', in Mike Savage and Anne Witz, *Gender and Bureaucracy*. Oxford: Blackwell.

WGNRR 1993. *Newsletter 43*, Report on the International Conference 'Reinforcing Reproductive Rights', Madras, 5–8 May.

Wollstonecraft, Mary. 1965. *A Vindication of the Rights of Women*. London: Everyman's Library.

World Bank 1990. *Development Report 1990: Poverty*. New York: Oxford University Press.

World Bank 1991. *Development Report 1991: The Challenge of Development*. New York: Oxford University Press.

World Bank 1992. *Development Report 1992: Development and the Environment*. New York: Oxford University Press.

World Bank 1993a. *World Development Report 1993: Investing in Health*. New York: Oxford University Press.

World Bank 1993b. *Effective Family Planning Programme.* Washington, DC: World Bank.

Wulf, Deirdre and Willson, Peters. 1984. 'Global Politics in Mexico City', *Family Planning Perspectives* 16(5): 228–32.

Wymlenberg, S. 1990. *Science and Babies: Private Discussions and Public Dilemmas.* Washington, DC: National Academic Press.

11

SILVER BULLET OR PASSING FANCY?

Girls' schooling and population policy

Patricia Jeffery and Roger Jeffery

Ever since the end of the eighteenth century, population issues have cast a shadow across debates about how more equitable and sustainable social change might be encouraged. When Malthus disputed with Condorcet, Godwin and others about the relationships between population growth, the growth in agricultural output, and the mechanisms through which these might be related, he was contributing to lively debates in political economy, debates that were crucial in the foundation of modern economics (Sen, 1996). Since the Second World War, as economic development programmes have become central features of national and international projects, population issues have rarely been far below the surface. But only since the early 1970s have these issues been explicitly addressed in terms of their gender and class implications. The major decennial international population conferences – in Bucharest in 1974, in Mexico City in 1984 and, most recently, in Cairo in 1994 – provide invaluable windows into current arguments about how population issues should be understood. Each conference exposed different fault lines. Each is remembered for different messages – about the priority that should be attached to population growth compared to (say) the international and national redistribution of resources or to women's empowerment programmes – though these messages may bear little relationship to everyday policy. Thus, 1974 is linked to the statement by Karan Singh, the Indian Minister for Health and Family Planning, that 'Development is the best contraceptive.' Yet within two years he was party to one of the most coercive attempts to use population control to assist in Indian development by forcibly sterilising more than 10 million Indians during the political Emergency.

It is too soon to tell what the long-term impact of the Cairo conference will be. In the Western media, its defining image was the attempt by the Vatican (in collaboration with conservative Islamic governments) to prevent agreement on a Program of Action by demanding that abortion and contraception issues should be left to religious and patriarchal leaders to decide. Such moves were ultimately defeated, and media interest then almost completely ceased, perhaps because the final Program of Action seemed otherwise to represent a basic consensus. Some academic discussion has welcomed the Cairo documents, stressing the strong statements about the significance of the 'empowerment and autonomy of women' as goals in themselves as well as essential for the achievement of other goals, such as sustainable development (Petchesky, 1995; see also Germain and Kyte, 1995). Furthermore, reproductive rights are described as an aspect of human rights, and the documents recognise diverse family forms as well as women's rights to control over their own fertility. Indeed, much in the Program of Action resulted from the determined activities of women's groups from around the world, lobbying and drafting to ensure their views were not merely represented but accepted over alternative formulations emanating from conservative governments (McIntosh and Finkle, 1995).

Two major criticisms have nonetheless been made of the Cairo Program of Action. The first is that it represents merely an opportunistic shift in rhetoric that dominant actors in the population field (especially the World Bank) are happy to accept because it gives a (false) sense of change which allows them to continue with 'business as usual' (Hartmann, 1994, 1995). The second is that, even if the change in terminology might reflect real changes in orientation, the Cairo documents fail to critique the market-driven solutions imposed under structural adjustment programmes. In this policy context, any changes in orientation are unlikely to be implemented successfully (Petchesky, 1995: 157).

In part at least, the discussions of population policy and the significance of the Cairo conference recapitulate some of the arguments about the sources of women's subordination that have been central to feminist debates since the late 1960s. Women's empowerment has been an important linking theme, but opinion has been divided about the appropriate strategies to achieve it. Some strands of feminist thinking regard women's reproductive capabilities as their defining, natural and essential characteristics, since they (apparently) differentiate women most clearly from men. From these perspectives, the control of women's sexuality and fertility is a major source (if not the root cause) of women's oppression, and empowering women so that they can control their own sexuality and fertility is the key priority. For many others (ourselves included), such essentialising frameworks are deeply flawed, because women themselves are far from homogeneous. Gender differentiation and the domestic and wider politics of reproduction are socially organised. Women's experiences of their sexuality and fertility, leave aside their work and access to resources and so forth, are contextually specific. Thus there are extremely varied patterns of intersection between gender and other structured inequalities such as class and ethnicity, both within and between nations. Women's circumstances, their interests and perceptions may differ markedly.

One implication is that the preference of international agencies for the global implementation of formulaic 'silver bullet' remedies is based on seriously misguided assumptions: they are not addressing issues that are the same the world over, but socially organised ones in which questions of context and power are crucial. Another is that, although women's groups have tried to ensure a wide representation of women's views in development activities, the voices and priorities of successful women have generally been more audible during policy framing than those of grassroots (and often poorer) activists. Many commentators have seen the Cairo conference as a radical departure from earlier population conferences. For some, this creates optimism that women's oppression (especially in relation to controls over their reproductive capacities) has been taken seriously; for others, women's empowerment brings the horror of disruption to traditional family life. Yet, arguably, the Cairo agenda is a cautious one and belief in its efficacy is misplaced. The world order is not seriously endangered by talk of empowering women if schooling girls and getting them into jobs are the key policy initiatives chosen. Nowhere could such an individualistic framework for social change tackle structural inequalities at either national or international levels. And, as Betsy Hartmann points out, 'while educating girls is a laudable goal in and of itself, it is also politically safer than advocating other forms of empowerment, such as letting women organise independent trade unions in free trade zones or on plantations' (1995: 134).

In this chapter, then, we consider some key assumptions of the Cairo conference, and the debates and research carried out in preparation for it. In particular, we will address a number of dilemmas for those involved in gender and development research in relation to population issues.

Women and population programmes

Much of the policy-oriented writing about gender and development has tended to essentialise women. In the early modernisation literature, for example, women were largely ignored as irrelevant to the development process, or regarded as repositories of 'traditional' thinking who were responsible for retarding development. More recently, when the environment and sustainable development came to centre stage, other images of women have been expressed, sometimes as idealised 'noble female savages' for their supposedly conservationist environmental practices, but also, contrariwise, as key villains of the piece, because of their high fertility.[1] In environmental programmes, one concern has been to make programme managers involve women rather than ignore them. But, especially since the mid-1970s, women have been the main target in population programmes, to the virtual exclusion of men. In many parts of the world, including South Asia (from where we will be drawing most of our examples), not only have population programmes been aimed primarily at women, but population concerns have also tended to subvert other policies which are apparently designed to improve women's positions.

Population programmes have been the focus of numerous critiques, many centring around the politics of reproductive health.[2] Particularly in South Asia, but not only there, population programmes tend to focus on fertility limitation to the exclusion of other issues. Very often, population programmes have been separated from the general health services. Since 1980, for example, the Population Division in Pakistan has been part of the Ministry of Planning and Development. It was separated from the Ministry of Health in order to integrate population planning with other planning, and this led to the creation of a network of Family Welfare Centres whose primary concern has been with first aid and non-surgical contraceptive methods. In India, family planning has always been funded as a central government programme, which has given the Government of India (and donor agencies) the opportunity to channel funds to female health workers in Primary Health Centres. In this way, maternal and child health services have been provided as a subsidiary part of the family planning programme. Women's reproductive health provisions (maternity services, treatments for reproductive tract infections, immunisations, etc.) have been used as 'sweeteners' to persuade women to be sterilised. In Bangladesh, the separate family planning services have offered substantial financial and other incentives to women to be sterilised (Hartmann and Standing, 1985). In all three countries, government health services for women have been weakened and deformed by the pressure to concentrate on fertility limitation. The delivery of contraception has been the key intervention aimed at women, often through inundation tactics. This stereotypes women as mothers and marginalises other aspects of women's reproductive health (PID, infertility, and other gynaecological complaints) and women's health status in general.

Moreover, the anti-natalist state population control programmes in India and Bangladesh have often used coercive means to limit the fertility of their citizens. As a result, many critics have stressed the broader human rights issues of informed consent.[3] Planners and programme managers have regarded a need for population control as sufficient reason to sideline questions about the safety and control of technologies, and to ignore adverse findings. In India, only determined opposition from women's groups forced the government to delay the introduction of hormonal contraceptive technologies such as Depo-Provera and Norplant while safety issues were addressed. In Bangladesh, Norplant has been introduced into the government programme, despite objections from women's groups that women are prevented from choosing safer methods and are often unable to demand the removal of the implants when they experience side-effects. Anita Hardon (1992: 763) argues that Norplant's acceptability was tested in Bangladesh through methods which look much more like a marketing campaign than responsible science. Other South Asian countries, however, have taken very different decisions on the acceptability of Depo-Provera and Norplant. Indeed, the controversies about them have had minimal impact in Pakistan, where feminist activists have seen women's limited access to contraceptive technologies of any kind as a much more serious issue. In Sri Lanka, medical trials seem to have been carried out in more ethically acceptable ways, and the quality of government maternal health service provision is much higher. But throughout the region, medical contraceptive technologies have been 'provider-dependent', which tends to leave power in the hands of medical practitioners, and to allow considerable opportunities for abuse. Most obvious are the financial incentives for contraceptive acceptors, usually restricted to those who accept one of the permanent sterilisation methods, and the loss of pay, humiliation or 'punishment transfers' meted out to workers who fail to meet their sterilisation targets. Briefly, South Asian women are often unable to make informed choices about contraception or to reverse procedures if they change their minds (Hartmann and Standing, 1985; Hartmann, 1995).

Coercive top-down population programmes target women but exclude them from any input into the planning, implementation or assessment of the quality of what is provided. But domestic relationships also severely restrict women's ability to determine their own fertility. Very often, indeed, pro-natalist domestic authorities are more effective at controlling women's bodies than is the state. For example, in Pakistan and northern India, rural women and many urban women tend to remain subordinate within patriarchal household structures and levels of contraceptive use are low, even in India where contraceptive techniques have been made widely available by the state (albeit on terms which are certainly not ideal). Feminists, then, must find ways of critiquing not only state population programmes but also such family systems, while avoiding ethnocentrism.

Moreover, in some parts of north India (Uttar Pradesh and Bihar, for example) the quality and availability of female health workers may be so poor that many women are dependent on private practitioners, rarely trained in Western medicine but nonetheless offering Western medicines. Alternatively, women may have access only to local medical systems, whether popular and folk (including traditional birth attendants) or practitioners of the 'high culture' medical systems of Ayurveda or Unan-i Tibb.[4] Consequently, feminists also have to position themselves in relation to local knowledge systems, some elements of which may certainly have positive value for women, but in which demeaning images of female physiology and reproduction, for instance, may also be closely tied to the legitimation of gender inequalities. Thus, although states often act to undermine women's reproductive rights, there may also be situations in which they may seem (and, in limited circumstances, may even be open to feminists to use as) a means through which women can enhance their reproductive rights.

Relationships between population and other women's programmes

Population control agendas have often been closely linked to longer-term programmes ostensibly aimed at other objectives. Here again, within these programmes, universalising global policies are played out in local contexts, very often showing little concern for local specificities. In South Asia, for example, population programmes have ambiguous relationships to maternal and child health programmes, which appear to be concerned with the laudable goals of reducing maternal and child morbidity and mortality. Particular examples – intuitively attractive to feminists, and apparently taking account of some of the criticisms outlined above – include programmes to train local birth assistants and programmes to expand women's economic opportunities.

In the 1980s, the World Health Organisation was the key advocate of programmes to enhance women's and children's health by training traditional birth attendants (TBAs). Apparently, such programmes took note of feminist critiques that health services were distant from the population they were trying to serve: involving TBAs in health service delivery seemed to redress the balance somewhat towards an acceptance of local women's knowledge of ante-natal screening, birthing procedures and post-natal care. Unfortunately, such programmes rarely entailed true collaboration between lay and professional workers, but became standardised teaching packages which ignored local skills and incorporated and neutralised immanent critiques of Western medicine (Jordan, 1989). In South Asia, moreover, TBA training programmes have been repeatedly reinvented since they were first introduced by British doctors in the 1860s. There is little sign that they have done more than provide a poorly paid low-level health worker to carry out the tasks which state-employed nurse-midwives regard as menial and degrading (Jeffery and Jeffery, 1993a).

Income generation programmes have also been seen as a tool for women to enhance their domestic power. These programmes may be fuelled by the assumption that kinship structures prevent women from exercising choice over their fertility and that independent income can enhance their capacity to do so. Following arguments based on theories of household economics, it has often been argued that an employed woman and other members of her household are likely to see a trade-off: if such a woman has another child she will lose income when she is pregnant, breast-feeding and rearing small children. But the calculations are probably more complex than this. Women may choose not to reduce their work obligations (or they may be unable to choose to do so), and they may even not need to do so, for alternative childcare-providers are often available. Women may also be able to combine childcare with many forms of rural and informal sector work, or high-input childcare leading to schooling may not be viewed as a high priority (Weller, 1984: 161). In the 1980s, attention turned to the effects of women's paid work, and for a while it was thought to be enough that women were workers for them to be 'empowered'. But it soon became clear that women's economically productive work (however that might be defined) was not sufficient to make a difference to their influence inside the household: only when that work provided an income which was under women's control could paid work be relied upon to empower women. Furthermore, as Linda Mayoux (1995) has pointed out, many women's co-operatives set up in India as part of programmes for women's empowerment have had major problems ensuring their economic viability and preventing the agendas of men taking priority over those of women. Introducing co-operative production by itself does not necessarily lead to any greater changes in women's position than employment in private industry (for a similar argument about credit schemes, see Chapter 1 by Baden and Goetz, this volume).

Since the mid-1970s, expanded schooling for girls has also been promoted. Supporters of population control programmes have attempted to harness the efforts of feminists who have argued for better schooling for girls, on the grounds that schooling enhances women's autonomy and that women with the capacity to make choices will choose low rather than high fertility.[5] Girls' schooling is often regarded as a basic requirement for other 'empowerment' policies to succeed or, at the very least, as a significant contributor to them.[6] Advocating girls' schooling is also usually non-controversial, since it is hard for any group in most societies to argue against more schooling, particularly if the state (or the religious leadership) remains in control of the curriculum. Female education has indeed become a rallying cry for international agencies, most notably the World Bank. Other donors, including non-governmental ones, are generally also in favour of this line of argument. A clear statement of the argument in favour of using female education as a solution to a range of problematic issues in current development is provided by Laurence Summers (Vice-President Development Economics and Chief Economist in the World Bank at the time):

> An educated mother faces a higher opportunity cost of time spent caring for the children. She has greater value outside the house and thus has an entirely different set of choices than she would have without education. She is married at a later age and is better able to influence family decisions. She has fewer, healthier children and can insist on the development of all of them, ensuring that her daughters are given a fair chance. And the education of her daughters makes it much more likely that the next generation of girls, as well as boys, will be educated and healthy as well. The vicious cycle is thus transformed into a virtuous circle.
>
> (Summers, 1993: vii)

Because of the high profile girls' schooling has achieved, particularly since the Cairo conference, the rest of this chapter concentrates on issues raised by the problematic relationships between education, women's autonomy, and fertility decline, and some of the hidden and debatable assumptions of those who promote female education as a 'silver bullet' to resolve many environmental and developmental issues at a stroke.

Female schooling and fertility

In most places, the statistical correlations between women's schooling achievement and their fertility are strong. The amount of schooling a woman has had is, of course, likely to be closely correlated with her husband's schooling, his socioeconomic status, and residence in towns rather than in rural areas. After controlling for these variables, the apparent impact of a girl's own schooling on her later fertility is halved, in statistical terms. Even so, maternal schooling is the strongest predictor of fertility in many countries experiencing declines in fertility (Cleland and Jejeebhoy, 1996).[7] These statistical relationships are not straightforward, though. There are, for instance, so-called 'threshold effects': going to school for just a few years – the precise number varies from place to place, but is usually less than six or seven years – provides a much less robust statistical relationship with fertility. Patterns also vary within South Asia:

[T]he nature of the relationship between women's schooling and their fertility . . . [is] . . . also affected by cultural conditions, notable among which is the position that women occupy in the traditional kinship structure. Thresholds are particularly evident at low levels of development and in highly gender stratified settings, such as Bihar and Uttar Pradesh, rather than in more egalitarian settings such as Kerala and Tamil Nadu . . . in more egalitarian or developed settings in the region . . . even modest amounts of schooling are sufficient to trigger changes in women's autonomy, in ways that then influence their reproductive behaviour. In the more gender stratified settings . . . improvements in autonomy do not occur until relatively high levels of education have been attained.

(Cleland and Jejeebhoy, 1996: 104, 105–6)

Furthermore, it appears that the overall level of schooling achievement in a locality makes a considerable difference to whether there are any clear contrasts between schooled and unschooled women. Where general levels of schooling are high, schooled and unschooled women appear much the same; where general levels are low, then differences tend to be greater. In some cases, the relevant population for comparison may be social groups such as castes (*jāti*) within which marriages are arranged. This emerges clearly from our study of Jats and Sheikhs in Bijnor. Whether girls' schooling was widespread (as among the Jats) or very uncommon (as among the Sheikhs), there were few noticeable differences in fertility between schooled and unschooled Jats or between schooled and unschooled Sheikhs. There were, however, considerable differences between the Jats as a whole and the Sheikhs as a whole (Jeffery and Jeffery, 1996). But these differences seem to have little to do with women's autonomy, at least as measured by the best available indicators. Similarly, on the basis of a detailed study of women in four districts in Gujarat and three districts in Kerala, Leela Visaria concluded:

The association between fertility – average number of children ever born – and any of the autonomy indices is not clearly established within the districts. At every level, however, women of Ernakulam and Palghat districts in Kerala have fewer children than the women in either Malapuram or in the districts of Gujarat. Evidently, 'district' and/or other factors appear to be important in understanding fertility differentials.

(Visaria, 1996: 263)

Moreover, once schooling is controlled for, wife's employment often has little relationship with reproductive behaviour, although the data here are very confusing.[8] Indeed, two studies, both published in 1995 and both using district-level data from the 1981 Census of India, come to different conclusions about the relative significance of female labour force participation rates in predicting total fertility rates. In Malhotra, Vanneman and Kishor (1995), the best models for predicting fertility suggest that female literacy has a small and non-significant positive relationship, whereas the female share of the labour force is statistically significant (and negative) in five of the six models. In Murthi, Guio and Drèze (1995) female literacy and female labour force participation are both statistically significant and correlate strongly with lower levels of fertility. Part of the difference may be explained by the fact that Malhotra, Vanneman and Kishor use different statistical techniques to estimate the relationships for the north, south and east of the country from Murthi, Guio and Drèze. If regional patterns are different, in the ways acknowledged by Malhotra, Vanneman and Kishor, this would reinforce Leela Visaria's point quoted on p. 242.

Despite such qualifications, however, these very widespread statistical correlations between high levels of female schooling and low fertility are often read off as causal links, in which schooling is seen as a progressive and positive mechanism for broadening people's minds, raising women's autonomy at the same time as it reduces their fertility. But the purported causal link between female schooling, female autonomy and low fertility is problematic. In many parts of South Asia, indeed, evidence of fertility decline should not be interpreted as a result of higher female autonomy, itself a consequence of girls' schooling, but as the outcome of the logics of male-dominated family systems in which low fertility has come to be seen as economically rational (Jeffery and Jeffery, 1996; Jeffery and Jeffery, 1997). As Ester Boserup puts it, 'when rural development raises men's interest in family limitation, the inferior status of women may actually serve to reduce fertility, because it is usually the husband who decides on family size' (1990: 59). In other words, it is a mistake to see schooling for girls as a straightforward panacea for their lack of autonomy, any more than for the 'population problem'.

Evidence for this latter point can also be derived from some recent instances of regions seeing dramatic declines in fertility without major investment in girls' schooling, for example, two rather different regions in South Asia (the state of Tamil Nadu in India, and Bangladesh) (Cleland and Mauldin, 1991; Ravindran, 1993; Savitri, 1994).[9] Following the same line of argument, we can also point to examples of the Philippines and the countries of west Asia (notably Jordan), where female schooling is widespread yet there has been no rapid decline in the high levels of fertility. There are also areas within India – such as the northern states of Haryana and Punjab – where girls' schooling is widespread and fertility is low, but commonly used indicators suggest that women's autonomy is also low (Dyson and Moore, 1983).

Where girls' schooling is widespread, fertility is likely to be low. But spreading girls' schooling does not inevitably result either in rises in women's autonomy or declines in fertility, even though they may co-vary in some places. Women's autonomy may have nothing at all to do with these relationships; or it may operate in the opposite direction, as in places where women are already relatively autonomous, and girls may be better able to attend school for longer than elsewhere. In other words, interpreting the correlations between girls' schooling and fertility decline is far from straightforward. Indeed, other possible explanations of the observed relationship are sufficiently telling that they must be taken seriously.

Girls' schooling and women's autonomy

The problematic relationships between schooling and fertility are not the only reasons for questioning the orthodoxy that emphasises the empowerment of women via education.[10] Precisely how education supposedly enhances women's autonomy is rarely specified. Authors routinely say 'education' when they mean 'schooling', and the demographic literature on this topic exposes a depressing naivety about the efficacy of schooling. A number of consequences flow from this.

To begin with, calling schooling 'education' bathes the whole topic in a warm positive glow, and draws attention away from the circumstances in which children are actually socialised and learn about the world around them. Since schooling is usually only a small part of this learning process, talking casually about differences between educated and uneducated women ignores the ways in which unschooled women are nonetheless highly educated in the specifics of their social worlds. Further, in the demographic literature (and in much of the policy debate) education is, in practice, usually measured simply by years of schooling, rather than by taking cognisance of the quality and content of schooling, or considering adult and non-formal education. Schooling is also usually regarded unequivocally as a 'good thing', but feminists must surely ask whether and how gendered school curricula critique gender inequalities. Indeed, schooling often endorses images of the good wife and mother (as well as class and other inequalities), and may provide an education for consent rather than for independent thinking. In general, understandings that are commonplace within a critical sociology of education seem not to have impinged on demographic discussions.[11]

Nevertheless, schooling is widely regarded as a panacea by those desperate to find a way to reduce population growth. Three different kinds of mechanism are discussed in the literature. First, if girls spend longer at school, they are likely to marry later, which by itself can help to reduce their fertility. Second, schooling is said to introduce a number of changes which have generally gone under the heading of modernisation. Schooling is regarded as synonymous with access to new ideas, especially (but not only) through the written word; with more willingness to change patterns of social life; and in particular, with a greater faith in and understanding of the benefits (usually unquestioned) of modern institutions like Western medicine, banks, and so on – all trappings of bureaucratic, scientistic progress.

Here, though, we want to focus on the third mechanism by which schooling of girls is believed to affect fertility, through the impact of schooling on women's autonomy. In path-breaking analyses, Susan Cochrane (1979, 1983) and Karen Mason (1985) both concluded that improving women's status led to lower levels of fertility.[12] Confusingly, by 'women's status', they meant both 'women's positions in society', and also a sense of the prestige of women *vis-à-vis* men. As Jack Caldwell (1986) has pointed out, a woman who can take more decisions about moving around (empowerment) might find that she has lower status (in the sense of prestige). The use of 'status' and 'role' has also been heavily criticised for appearing to focus on the division of labour, and for failing to deal adequately with issues of power and conflict (for instance over labour-power within the domestic arena). To highlight the location of women within gender relationships, many authors now prefer talk of 'women's autonomy'. Women's roles in the world of work, aspects of their control over resources, including the disposition of their own income and time, and their access to public space have been the subject of particular attention. Without the ownership or control of her income and significant economic resources, a woman's work, by itself, need not improve her position or her freedom to take decisions.[13] Such insights have clarified some ways in which women may find that their attempts at empowerment are restricted. In South Asia, for example, families may strive to raise their general prestige by restricting women's access to the public sphere, and by enforcing norms of avoidance of social contact with unrelated members of the opposite sex. Yet, despite the increasing sophistication of some of these discussions, as Francine and Etienne van de Walle (1993) note, much of the demographic literature retains its faith that it is sufficient to know how women participate in the labour force and how many years of schooling they have received in order to understand women's status.

In South Asia most women are not employees outside a household enterprise and girls' schooling has received an almost fetishistic celebration as the policy initiative most likely to lead to fertility decline. Improvements in the status of women, high female literacy and education, low infant and child mortality, are sometimes given more priority in policy statements than the family planning programmes. Two prominent demographers in the World Bank, a major funder of South Asian fertility control programmes, argued as follows:

> [t]he reason for expecting a negative influence of primary education on fertility is that primary education, by providing basic functional literacy and numeracy, enhances women's status within and outside their immediate family and increases their exposure to information and ideas disseminated through printed material . . . [and] improvements in female education can be expected to influence fertility behaviour even without simultaneous changes in other factors such as increased opportunities for them to participate in the paid labour force.
>
> (Nag and Jain, 1993: 2)

Yet neither of them, nor other authors writing in this vein, seem to have explored the *meanings* of girls' schooling for the girls themselves or for their parents. Evidence from much of South Asia suggests that many parents keep their daughters in school in order to enhance their position in the marriage market, not as a route to their economic independence.[14] Carol Vlassoff, writing about a village in Maharashtra that she studied in 1974–75 and again in 1987, found little relationship between schooling experience and female autonomy, and suggests that:

> Part of the explanation for this lack of relevance [of schooling] to female autonomy seems to lie in the fact that female schooling had become a

prerequisite for marriage. An educated girl, for whom an adequate dowry had been paid, was deemed more likely to lead a secure and happy life in her husband's family. This feeling, while evident in 1975, was much more pronounced in 1987. Hence, the role of schooling was viewed more in terms of its 'buying power' than of its potential contribution to the development of female autonomy. In other words, schooling had become a matter of prestige, rather than of autonomy.

(Vlassoff, 1996: 232)

Likewise, our research in rural Uttar Pradesh has made us doubt that girls' schooling is necessarily empowering. School curricula there do little to challenge local notions of family honour and respectability, in which the demeanour of girls and women is so crucial. Rote learning and an unquestioning respect for teachers and other authority figures are required. Teaching rarely moves beyond the textbook. Girls are expected to use respectable forms of speech expunged of earthy turns of phrase and to adopt forms of body language that reflect well on their own reputations.[15]

Crucially, girls' schooling is generally regarded as a preparation for marriage in an increasingly competitive marriage market. Parents and young married women alike deny that paid employment outside the home is desirable, although they might also say that it could enable a woman to 'stand on her own legs' in a calamity (such as widowhood or marital breakdown). Parents want to arrange their daughters' marriages into 'good homes', and sending their daughters to school is an important part of the strategy to achieve this end. The importance of marriage rather than employment is also reflected in girls' subject choices. Most of the women who had attended school beyond primary level had taken liberal arts subjects (Hindi, Sanskrit, Art, Home Economics) and there was a great emphasis on homemaking skills such as sewing, embroidery and cooking. Rarely can academically inclined girls insist on continuing at school, unless their parents also wish it. Conversely, several women had continued studying long after they had lost interest because their parents insisted they did so in order to attract a suitable marriage offer.

Parents ambitious for their daughters face a dilemma, however. School credentials are vital counters in the marriage market, but they might be obtained only by sacrificing family honour. Adolescent girls are a particular source of vulnerability and anxiety. Indeed, few villages have secondary schools, and girls are often removed from school at the end of class 5 or 8 rather than be sent to another village or nearby town to continue their schooling, precisely because of the danger of unmonitored contact with boys. Those girls who are allowed to attend schools outside their village must be constantly circumspect about their behaviour. Some wealthy rural families establish satellite households in nearby towns so that the children can be chaperoned by one of the household's older women, or children may be boarded out with relatives living in town. Given such considerations, girls in urban families clearly have a much greater chance than village girls of continuing their schooling. Many rural families who opt not to send their daughters to high schools as 'regular' students register them as 'private' students who complete their studies at home, using correspondence course materials supplemented with private tuition, and only attending a college to take the examination. Since there is little need for the 'private' student to meet strangers, this solution protects family honour. It also combines a home-based study regime with learning domestic tasks from female family members, an ideal preparation for a married life in which the in-laws require a daughter-in-law skilled in domestic matters and sufficiently knowledgeable to guide her children with their school work. Studying at home, of course, gives a girl little experience in dealing with the world beyond her home, arguably important in developing self-confidence and the ability (or desire) to act autonomously. Such differences in the context of 'education' do not show up in statistics of 'years of schooling'.

In any case, in rural areas, girls and young married women are locked into much the same domestic structures, irrespective of their level of schooling. Young women's marriages are generally arranged by their parents, often without the girls' knowledge or consultation, and the bride must migrate to her husband's village on marriage. Indeed, in some respects, young rural women who have been highly educated are more likely to be in domestic situations which are less conducive to autonomy than women with little schooling. Lengthy schooling is a strategy that is effectively open only to relatively affluent parents: schooling entails direct costs, but, additionally, highly educated young men not only want comparably educated brides but can command much higher dowries from their in-laws than the less educated. Dowry harassment is widespread in ambitious and relatively affluent circles, and it seriously disempowers young married women. Moreover, considerations of honour are likely to mean a more strict regime of seclusion than is possible among the less wealthy.[16] Young women with *more* schooling are also more likely to be sharing a household with older in-laws, who expect to have a say over matters which affect a young woman's life. Indeed, living in a joint household with the mother-in-law is locally construed as a major restriction on autonomy for married women in their childbearing years (for whom fertility decisions are matters of the moment). In these ways, then, *more* schooling often seems (if anything) to translate into *less* autonomy within the domestic unit (Jeffery *et al.*, 1989; Jeffery and Jeffery, 1993b, 1994, 1996).[17]

In brief, then, girls' schooling in its own right has a questionable impact on women's autonomy. The curriculum content and the parental motivations that lie behind schooling girls tend to entail docility rather than open rebellion. Indeed, many young women explicitly denied wanting to have the freedoms (and responsibilities) that 'autonomy' would involve. But even if these women's experience of schooling had raised their consciousness of the world and their position in it, consciousness-raising must not be confused with empowerment. Women will not be empowered by their schooling if they remain embedded in structures that limit their room for manoeuvre. Clearly, schooling may indeed empower women in some contexts. But the educational provision and the forms of domestic organisation that are typical of rural north India provide an important angle from which to critique the homogenising and universalising assumptions of 'silver bullet' programmes to empower women through schooling girls.

Our argument that girls' schooling does not *inevitably* contribute to women's empowerment (and in that way, to lower fertility) presents feminists with a dilemma, however. On the one hand, we are extremely wary of seeming to side with those who oppose special efforts to provide better schooling for girls because they fear the social effects of women's empowerment. In that respect our position is similar to that of donor agencies who believe their main opponents to be in the ranks of conservative religious leaders, as was evident in Cairo. Further, even as we critique the schooling that girls currently receive, there are increasing dangers of retrenchment in social sector expenditure in many developing countries, especially where Structural Adjustment Programmes demand the rolling back of the state and reduced expenditure on those items (health, education) thought to hamper the restructuring of the economy.

On the other hand, we cannot align ourselves unambiguously with the Cairo consensus. In the Programme of Action, the notion of 'empowerment' is much deployed to legitimise inputs into the educational sector, while the notion of 'unmet needs' for contraception is used to argue the case for empowering women so that they can successfully demand the contraception they are said to want. There are, however, serious dangers in being seduced by such tantalising shifts in vocabulary in the major donor agencies, although we should not leap to conclude that these rhetorics are merely smokescreens. Nevertheless, unless we are convinced otherwise, the most prudent stance is to suspect a hijacking of feminist vocabulary that masks a fundamentally unchanged population control agenda and that engages with girls' education only as a means to that end. In other words, we are probably not seeing a serious commitment to girls' education as a value in its own right. As Betsy Hartmann (1995: 134) asks, would the same support be there if women used their autonomy to have larger families? With hindsight, moreover, we can see how other passing fashions (for example, for TBA training and income generation schemes) have been sidelined when they seemed not to 'work' to reduce fertility. Continuing vigilance is required to prevent the examples of fertility declines in Tamil Nadu and Bangladesh, achieved without substantial investments in girls' schooling, being used to justify expenditure cuts in female education. In addition, the Cairo consensus is basically silent about the implications of Structural Adjustment Programmes. If girls' schooling seems not to be necessary to achieve fertility declines, pressures to reduce spending in the educational sectors are likely to be particularly concentrated on girls' schooling, since boys' schooling apparently has more potential for translation into 'economically productive' labour.

When arguments are so polarised, it becomes difficult to position ourselves. Yet it is important to stress that in critiquing the schooling that is currently available for girls and in arguing that the purported links between girls' schooling and women's autonomy are not as clear-cut as current policy fashions would suggest, we are most definitely not arguing that girls' schooling be given a lower priority. On the contrary, girls' access to mind-broadening schooling can and must be defended in terms of women's rights to literacy and numeracy, even if schooling does not necessarily enhance their autonomy.

Conclusion

Rather than drawing formal conclusions, we want to end with some questions about how feminists can respond to debates in development discourses about fertility and education and their connections. These raise serious policy issues about women's education and training and about women's reproductive rights – as well as about how these are all linked to broader social and economic changes.

Difficulties in arriving at our position in relation to complex issues are compounded by problems about how to convey the complexities and ambiguities in the situation. Can we develop critiques of population control programmes (such as we outlined at the beginning of this chapter) without being read as wishing to deny women their reproductive rights (in which access to safe contraception when women themselves want it is a core feature)? How do we express our views on education for girls, perhaps critiquing the content and form of schooling as currently provided and its connections to (coercive) population programmes, yet also asserting the positive potential of some types of schooling? How likely is the provision of woman-friendly health and family planning services or of school systems that educate in the widest sense of that word? What is the potential of the sectorally based state provisions (education, health and other social services) to achieve beneficial social changes – especially when their potential efficacy is liable to be undermined (from one side) by pervasive everyday sexist practices in the household and elsewhere and (from the other) by secular trends in national and global economies that may be inimical to women's reproductive and other rights? Just where should we focus our efforts to advance the cause of women's empowerment in its own right, and not as the handmaid of other policy initiatives?

Notes

1 For examples of how women are being expected to solve environmental problems and improve their own positions at the same time, see Jackson, 1993.

2 For recent representative examples, see Freedman and Isaacs, 1993; Hartmann, 1995; Sen and Snow, 1994; Sen, 1994.

3 For more details on how the overt coercion employed by Indian government employees in 1975–77 was merely an exaggeration of covert tendencies before and since, see Vicziany, 1983; Ravindran, 1993.

4 For more detail on the kinds of health services available to women in Bijnor, Uttar Pradesh, see Jeffery et al. 1989: Chapter 9.

5 Mass (1976: 229) cites a USAID document calling for research on 'female education, employment opportunities, and other activities which offer alternative choices to traditional domestic responsibilities since slower population growth seems to follow improvement in the status of women'. But as Hull (1977: 43) pointed out, policy-

makers rapidly embraced early findings to claim that 'female employment and education are the keys to fertility decline' without bothering to look further into the probable causes and mechanisms behind the findings.

6 Lockwood and Collier (1988: 53), argue, for example, that 'family planning and direct nutritional programmes will be more successful when they are integrated with policy on other factors with which fertility and nutrition are interrelated', of which maternal schooling is a major example, they cite.

7 Cleland and Jejeebhoy also note the exceptions to this generalisation: the Caribbean, where wife's schooling is a worse predictor of her fertility than is husband's schooling; and many Arab countries, where the differences are marginal.

8 This finding suggests that, in South Asia at least, raising schooling achievements for girls does not necessarily lead to higher opportunity costs of children to mothers. We cannot explain their lower fertility in this way, *contra* the position of Birdsall (1994: 265).

9 Indonesia is an additional example of a country where fertility decline has preceded widespread girls' schooling (see Cleland and Jejeebhoy, 1996: 80).

10 For more details on many of these issues, see Jeffery and Basu, 1996, especially the editors' introduction, and Basu, 1996.

11 Classics of the critical sociology of education in the West include Willis, 1977; Bowles and Gintis, 1976; Bourdieu and Passeron, 1977. Stanworth, 1983, and Chanana, 1988, provide good insights into the gender dimensions of schooling in the UK and in India respectively. For a rare example of a concerted attempt to use ethnographic methods to view schooling in developing countries from the perspective of the schoolgirl, in this case in Calcutta, see Ray, 1988. Lindenbaum, 1990, is an exceptional account of the meanings of schooling in Bangladesh.

12 See also, e.g. Cain, 1984; Safilios-Rothschild, 1982; and Sathar et al., 1988. More recent – and nuanced – accounts can be found in Mahmud and Johnson, 1994, and Mason, 1993. Martin, 1995, is a recent statistical analysis. For an influential account of how female schooling worked to reduce child mortality, see Levine, 1980.

13 See, for instance, Agarwal, 1994.

14 This is a key theme in Mukhopadhyay and Seymour, 1994.

15 Kumar, 1986, provides a general account of text-centred pedagogy in India. See also Ray, 1988.

16 We have no intention of romanticising the position of women in poorer families: the lack of household resources, a woman's need to work outside the home and the risk of sexual and other forms of harassment, make poor women vulnerable in many ways.

17 These findings are not restricted to our data. For example, Bradley, 1995, on the basis of Kenyan data, suggests that schooling can make women more vulnerable to violence within the household.

References

Agarwal, Bina, 1994. *A Field of One's Own*. Cambridge: Cambridge University Press.

Basu, Alaka, 1996. 'Female Schooling, Autonomy and Fertility Change: What Do These Words Mean In South Asia?' pp.48–71 in Roger Jeffery and Alaka Basu, eds, *Girls' Schooling, Women's Autonomy and Fertility Change in South Asia*. New Delhi and Newbury Park, CA: Sage Publications.

Birdsall, Nancy, 1994. 'Government, Population and Poverty: A Win-Win Tale', pp.253–74 in Robert Cassen and contributors, *Population and Development: Old Debates, New Conclusions*. New Brunswick and Oxford: Transaction Publishers.

Boserup, Ester, 1990. 'Population, the Status of Women, and Rural Development', pp.45–60 in Geoffrey McNicol and Mead Cain, eds, *Rural Development and Population: Institutions and Policy*. New York: Oxford University Press.

Bourdieu, Pierre and Jean Claude Passeron, 1977. *Reproduction in Education, Society and Culture*. (Translated from the French by Richard Nice.) London and Beverly Hills: Sage Publications.

Bowles, Samuel and Herbert Gintis, 1976. *Schooling in Capitalist America: Educational Reform and the Contradictions of Economic Life*. London: Routledge and Kegan Paul.

Bradley, Candice, 1995. 'Women's Empowerment and Fertility Decline in Western Kenya', pp.157–178 in Susan Greenhalgh, ed., *Situating Fertility: Anthropology and Demographic Inquiry*. Cambridge: Cambridge University Press.

Cain, Mead, 1984. *Women's Status and Fertility in Developing Countries: Son Preference and Economic Security*, World Bank Staff Working Papers no. 682, Population and Development Series no. 7, 1984.

Caldwell, John C., 1986. 'Routes to Low Mortality in Poor Countries', *Population and Development Review*, 12(2): 171–220.

Chanana, Karuna, ed., 1988. *Socialisation, Education and Women: Explorations in Gender Identity*. New Delhi: Orient Longman.

Cleland, John and Shireen Jejeebhoy, 1996. 'Maternal Schooling and Fertility: Evidence from Censuses and Surveys', pp.72–106 in Roger Jeffery and Alaka Basu, eds, *Girls' Schooling, Women's Autonomy and Fertility Change in South Asia*. New Delhi and Newbury Park, CA: Sage Publications.

Cleland, John and William P. Mauldin, 1991. 'The Promotion of Family Planning by Financial Payments: The Case of Bangladesh', *Studies in Family Planning*, 22(1): 1–18.

Cochrane, Susan H., 1979. *Fertility and Education: What Do We Really Know?* World Bank Staff Occasional Papers, no. 26. Baltimore, MD: Johns Hopkins University Press.

Cochrane, Susan H., 1983. 'Effects of Education and Urbanization on Fertility', pp.587–626 in R. A. Bulatao, R. D. Lee with P. E. Hollesback and John P. Bongaarts, eds, *Determinants of Fertility in Developing Countries*, Vol. 2. New York: Academic Press.

Dyson, Tim and Mick Moore, 1983. 'On Kinship Structure, Female Autonomy and Demographic Behaviour in India', *Population and Development Review*, 9(1): 35–60.

Freedman, Lynn P. and Stephen L. Isaacs, 1993. 'Human Rights and Reproductive Choice', *Studies in Family Planning*, 24: 18–30.

Germain, Adrienne and Rachel Kyte, 1995. *The Cairo Consensus: The Right Agenda for the Right Time*. New York: International Women's Health Coalition.

Hardon, Anita P., 1992. 'The Needs of Women versus the Interests of Family Planning Personnel, Policy-Makers and Researchers: Conflicting Views on the Safety and Acceptability of Contraceptives', *Social Science and Medicine*, 35: 753–66.

Hartmann, Betsy, 1994. 'The Cairo "Consensus": Women's Empowerment or Business as Usual?' *Women's Reproductive Rights Newsletter*, Fall, 1/4.

Hartmann, Betsy, 1995. *Reproductive Rights and Wrongs: The Global Politics of Population Control and Contraceptive Choice*. New York: Harper and Row (First edition 1987).

Hartmann, Betsy and Hilary Standing, 1985. *Food, Saris and Sterilisation: Population Control in Bangladesh*. London: Bangladesh International Action Group.

Hull, Valerie J., 1977. 'Fertility, Women's Work, and Economic Class: A Case Study from Southeast Asia', pp.35–80 in S. Kupinsky, ed., *The Fertility of Working Women*. New York: Praeger.

Jackson, Cecile, 1993. 'Questioning Synergism: Win-win with Women in Population and Environment Policies?' *Journal of International Development*, 5: 651–68.

Jeffery, Patricia and Roger Jeffery, 1994. '"Killing my Heart's Desire": Education and Female Autonomy in Rural North India', pp.125–71 in Nita Kumar, ed., *Women as Subjects: South Asian Histories*. Calcutta: Stree, and Charlottesville: Virginia University Press.

Jeffery, Patricia and Roger Jeffery, 1996. 'What's the Benefit of Being Educated?: Girls' Schooling, Women's Autonomy and Fertility Outcomes in Bijnor', pp.150–83 in Roger Jeffery and Alaka Basu, eds, *Girls' Schooling, Women's Autonomy and Fertility Change in South Asia*. New Delhi and Newbury Park, CA: Sage Publications.

Jeffery, Patricia, Roger Jeffery and Andrew Lyon, 1989. *Labour Pains and Labour Power: Women and Childbearing in India*. London: Zed Press, and New Delhi: Manohar.

Jeffery, Roger and Alaka Basu, eds, 1996. *Girls' Schooling, Women's Autonomy and Fertility Change in South Asia*. New Delhi and Newbury Park, CA: Sage Publications.

Jeffery, Roger and Patricia Jeffery, 1993a. 'Traditional Birth Attendants in Rural North India', pp.7–31 in Shirley Lindenbaum and Margaret Lock, eds, *Knowledge, Power and Practice in Medicine and Everyday Life*. Berkeley and London: University of California Press.

Jeffery, Roger and Patricia Jeffery, 1993b. 'A Woman Belongs to her Husband: Female Autonomy, Women's Work and Childbearing in Bijnor', pp.66–114 in Alice Clark, ed., *Gender and Political Economy: Explorations of South Asian Systems*. Oxford and New Delhi: Oxford University Press.

Jeffery, Roger and Patricia Jeffery, 1997. *Population, Gender and Politics: Demographic Change in Rural North India*. Cambridge: Cambridge University Press.

Jordan, Brigitte, 1989. 'Cosmopolitan Obstetrics: Some Insights from the Training of Traditional Midwives', *Social Science and Medicine*, 28(9): 925–44.

Kumar, Krishna, 1986. 'Textbooks and Educational Culture', *Economic and Political Weekly*, 31(30) 26 July: 1309–11.

Levine, Robert A., 1980. 'Influences of Women's Schooling on Maternal Behaviour in the Third World', *Comparative Education Review*, 24(2/2): 53–105.

Lindenbaum, Shirley, 1990. 'The Education of Women and the Mortality of Children in Bangladesh', pp.353–70 in Alan C. Swedlund and George J. Armelagos, eds, *Disease in Populations in Transition: Anthropological and Epidemiological Perspectives*. New York: Bergin and Garvey.

Lockwood, Matthew and Paul Collier, 1988. *Maternal Education and the Vicious Cycle of High Fertility and Malnutrition*. Policy, Planning and Research Working Papers (WPS 130) in Women in Development, Population and Human Resources Department, The World Bank, Washington DC.

McIntosh, C. Alison and Jason L. Finkle, 1995. 'The Cairo Conference on Population and Development: A New Paradigm?' *Population and Development Review*, 21: 223–60.

Mahmud, Simeen and Anne M. Johnson, 1994. 'Women's Status, Empowerment and Reproductive Outcomes', pp.151–9 in Gita Sen, Adrienne Germain and Lincoln Chen, eds, *Population Policies Reconsidered: Health, Empowerment and Rights*. Cambridge, MA: Harvard University Press.

Malhotra, Anju, Reeve Vanneman and Sunita Kishor, 1995. 'Fertility, Dimensions of Patriarchy, and Development in India', *Population and Development Review*, 21: 281–305.

Martin, T C., 1995. 'Women's Education and Fertility: Results from 26 Demographic and Health Surveys', *Studies in Family Planning*, 26: 187–202.

Mason, Karen Oppenheim, 1985. *The Status of Women. A Review of its Relationships to Fertility and Mortality*. New York: The Rockefeller Foundation.

Mason, Karen Oppenheim, 1993. 'The Impact of Women's Position on Demographic Change during the Course of Development', pp.19–42 in Nora Federici, Karen Oppenheim Mason and Solvi Sogner, eds, *Women's Position and Demographic Change.* Oxford: Clarendon Press.

Mass, Bonnie, 1976. *Population Target: The Political Economy of Population Control in Latin America.* Brampton, Ontario: Latin American Working Group.

Mayoux, Linda, 1995. 'Alternative Vision or Utopian Fantasy?: Co-operation, Empowerment and Women's Co-operative Development in India', *Journal of International Development,* 7(2): 211–28.

Mukhopadhyay, Carol C. and Susan Seymour, eds, 1994. *Women, Education and Family Structure in India.* Boulder, CO: Westview Press.

Murthi, Mamta, Anne-Catherine Guio and Jean Drèze, 1995. *Demographic Outcomes, Economic Development and Women's Agency,* London School of Economics, London: Discussion Paper 61, The Development Economics Research Programme.

Nag, Moni and Anrudh Jain, 1993. 'A Note on the Importance of Female Primary Education for Fertility Reduction in Developing Countries' (mimeo). New York: Population Council.

Petchesky, Rosalind P., 1995. 'From Population Control to Reproductive Rights: Feminist Fault Lines', *Reproductive Health Matters,* 6: 152–61.

Ravindran, T. K. Sundari, 1993. 'The Politics of Women, Population and Development in India', *Reproductive Health Matters,* 1: 26–38.

Ravindran, T. K. Sundari, 1994. 'Women's Health Policies: Organising for Change', *Reproductive Health Matters,* 6: 7–11.

Ray, Raka, 1988. 'The Contested Terrain of Reproduction: Class and Gender in Schooling in India', *British Journal of the Sociology of Education,* 9: 387–401.

Safilios-Rothschild, Constantina, 1982. 'Female Power, Autonomy and Demographic Change in the Third World,' pp.117–32 in Richard Anker, Myra Buvinic and Nadia H. Youssef, eds, *Women's Roles and Population Trends in the Third World.* London: Croom Helm.

Sathar, Zeba, Nigel Crook, Christine Callum and Shahnaz Kazi, 1988. 'Women's Status and Fertility Change in Pakistan', *Population and Development Review,* 14(3): 415–32.

Savitri, R., 1994. 'Fertility Rate Decline in Tamil Nadu: Some Issues', *Economic and Political Weekly* 29(29): 1850–52.

Sen, Amartya K., 1996. 'Fertility and Coercion', *University of Chicago Law Review,* 96(3): 1035–61.

Sen, Gita, 1994. 'Women, Poverty and Population: Issues for the Concerned Environmentalist', pp.215–25 in Wendy Harcourt, ed., *Feminist Perspectives on Sustainable Development.* London: Zed Books.

Sen, Gita and Rachel C. Snow, eds, 1994. *Power and Decision: The Social Control of Reproduction.* Boston: Harvard School of Public Health.

Stanworth, Michelle D., 1983. *Gender and Schooling: A Study of Sexual Divisions in the Classroom.* London: Hutchinson in association with the Explorations in Feminism Collective.

Summers, Lawrence H., 1993. 'Foreword', pp.vii-ix in Elizabeth M. King and M. Anne Hill, eds, *Women's Education in Developing Countries: Barriers, Benefits and Policies.* Baltimore and London: Johns Hopkins University Press.

van de Walle, Francine and van de Walle, Etienne, 1993. 'Women's Autonomy and Natural Fertility in the Sahel Region', pp.61–79 in Nora Federici, Karen Oppenheim

Mason and Solvi Sogner, eds, *Women's Position and Demographic Change*. Oxford: Clarendon Press.

Vicziany, Marika, 1983. 'Coercion in a Soft-state: the Family Planning Programme of India', *Pacific Affairs*, 55(3): 373–402, and 55(4): 557–92.

Visaria, Leela, 1996. 'Regional Variations in Female Autonomy and Fertility and Contraception in India', pp.235–68 in Roger Jeffery and Alaka Basu, eds, *Girls' Schooling, Women's Autonomy and Fertility Change in South Asia*. New Delhi and Newbury Park, CA: Sage Publications.

Vlassoff, Carol, 1996. 'Against the Odds: The Changing Impact of Education on Female Autonomy and Fertility in an Indian Village', pp.218–34 in Roger Jeffery and Alaka Basu, eds, *Girls' Schooling, Women's Autonomy and Fertility Change in South Asia*. New Delhi and Newbury Park, CA: Sage Publications.

Weller, Robert H., 1984. 'The Gainful Employment of Females and Fertility – with Special Reference to Rural Areas of Developing Countries', pp.151–71 in Wayne A. Schutjer and C. Shannon Stokes, eds, *Rural Development and Human Fertility*. New York: Macmillan.

Willis, Paul, 1977. *Learning to Labour*. Farnborough: Saxon House.

12

QUESTIONABLE LINKS

Approaches to gender in environmental research and policy

Cathy Green, Susan Joekes and Melissa Leach

Introduction[1]

Since 1980, linkages between gender, the environment and development have become a major focus of research attention. Over the same period, social issues have received increasing attention in environmental policy formulation and in project design, and in many instances policy-makers and project designers have specifically addressed gender issues as part of that effort. But the interventions have not been notably successful: indeed, they have often been counterproductive, neither improving women's command over natural resources nor assisting project effectiveness in environmental terms.

The purpose of this chapter is to examine the extent and ways that environmental policies and programmes have attempted to incorporate a concern for gender, drawing on certain strands of research while ignoring others. Focusing on four contrasting policy areas – forestry, water resources management, urban environmental management, and cross-sectoral legal and institutional reforms – we illustrate the lack of success to date. This outcome, we argue, can be attributed in large part to flaws in the conceptualisation of social relations of gender and their relation to environmental change underlying the measures used. Those measures stemmed from the recommendations advanced by two linked schools of thought: the 'women as environmental managers' or women, environment and development school (WED), and (certain strands of) ecofeminism. Both of these schools have elements in common with the women in development (WID) approach, so that the failings of attempts at gender-sensitivity in the environmental field parallel the failings of policies based on the WID approach in other development sectors.

In contrast, feminist research has now offered several alternative conceptualisations of gender–environment relations which can broadly be thought of as translations of gender and development (GAD) into the environment domain. In highlighting key issues and social and political dynamics ignored by the WED/ecofeminist approaches, these GAD-inspired perspectives both help explain policy failures to date and suggest some ways forward.

The treatment of gender issues in standard environmental policy and programme approaches

We begin by describing ways in which environmental policies and field interventions in several illustrative 'sectors' have hitherto taken account of the position of women. This entails a necessarily summary review of changes over time in the approach to social questions, and within that, of the attempts that have been made to incorporate gender issues. The discussion focuses on the policies and programmes of governments and major donor agencies, rather than on NGO and 'grassroots' activities.

It will become clear that in overlooking how social relations of gender are intertwined with and determine environmental resource use, policies have failed to match up to the difficulties of involving women in projects ostensibly designed for their benefit. Not surprisingly, projects have often fallen short in implementation and failed to benefit women as intended, and have often in consequence also failed to meet their objectives of improved natural resource management.

Forestry

Over the last decade standard forestry sector policies have begun to lay more emphasis on environmental and social issues. In a departure from earlier stress on industrial forestry, it is now more common for forest resources to be managed with a view to sustainable resource use, conservation and biodiversity protection, and for trees and forests to be recognised as a vital source of livelihood for local peoples (Gregersen *et al.*, 1989). Donor funding of forestry projects over the last 15 years has switched emphasis accordingly:

> Forests have to be seen in a new light – as a valuable economic resource having multiple uses and multiple users. Consequently, the practice of forest management has to undergo a change – from tree management to ecosystem management in which people play a significant part.
>
> (D'Silva and Appanah, 1993)

Recent forestry policy addresses at least three interrelated levels: conservation of large forest blocks and reserves, social or 'community' forestry, and farm forestry. In relation to large forest blocks or reserves, there has been a move towards 'conservation with development' which has gained the support of conservation agencies such as the World Conservation Union (IUCN) and the Worldwide Fund for Nature (WWF), multilateral donors such as the World Bank and bilateral donors such as the Department for International Development (DFID) (UK). It marks a shift away, at least in theory, from exclusionary reserve approaches which, in advancing the interests of local elites or in prioritising global concerns for biodiversity conservation, had, in effect, often forced forest and forest-fringe dwellers to 'steal' from a resource base which had formerly provided them with a vital source of livelihood. This evolution of policy clearly links into the sustainable development arguments of the 1980s, which brought social and economic concerns to bear on biological conservation objectives (Leach, 1994; cf. WRI/IUCN/UNEP, 1992). Thus, policy documents such as the Food and Agriculture Organisation's (FAO's) (1985) Tropical Forestry Action Plan now highlight the importance of involving, rather than excluding, local people in forest conservation.

'Conservation-with-development' programmes generally advocate protection of a core reserve area, with management plans for surrounding buffer zones focused on a varied mix of state/commercial and local livelihood interests.[2] Local-level support for reserve protection is sought by giving forest dwellers a stake in revenues generated within the reserve, perhaps through ecotourism, or by ensuring their access to locally valued forest products, for instance, in 'extractive reserves'. Local institutions may also be drawn into reserve protection, by regulating or directly policing access to particular areas or products. A first wave of integrated conservation-development projects (ICDPs) has been implemented world-wide (Wells et al., 1992).[3] However, the few evaluations of ICDPs that have been undertaken at this early stage tend to emphasise the low quality of participation engendered within the projects, whether for social, historical or administrative reasons (Wells et al., 1992; Pimbert and Pretty 1994). Gender issues are rarely mentioned in this literature; it is safe to assume that they lie outside the main concerns of the approach, which thus strongly risks compromising women's resource interests (cf. Leach, 1994).

It is in other areas of forestry policy that explicit attempts have been made to incorporate women: those concerned with village and community forests, whether 'natural' or planted woodlots, and those concerned with smallholdings, including those lying within reserve buffer zones.

Community and joint forest management, as have been promoted particularly in India and Nepal and in West Africa, are increasingly seen as a way to build up local peoples' incentives for sustainable forestry. Many such programmes continue to ignore women, focusing on an undifferentiated 'community'. In others, women and women's groups have become a special target group and institutional focus for activities in woodlot planting, rehabilitation or protection (cf. FAO, 1993). Certain Joint Forest Management schemes in India have prioritised women's participation, for instance (Sarin, 1995). Such social or community forestry projects have also highlighted the importance of secure tenure in creating incentives for planting or conservation, specifically the rights of women to land and trees, and donor policy documents now commonly echo this concern (see FAO/SIDA, 1987; World Bank, 1991a). Related to this is an attempt to increase women's incentives for participating in social forestry by improving their access to extension services, to technical forestry training (World Bank, 1991b; UNCED, 1992) and to markets for forest products. In this view, where incentives are adequate, conservation becomes a 'rational' choice for women.

These efforts represent a delayed recognition of the role of trees and forest products in the household economy, the role of women in their collection, and the specific knowledge they have developed in the process. It is certainly preferable to women's complete invisibility in forestry activities (Leach, 1992). However, the focus on women seems to have an 'efficiency' rationale in the WID mould – put simply, projects benefit from women's labour input, their experience as environmental managers and their knowledge about forest products (cf. FAO, 1993). Thus 'Forestry programs that do not consciously plan for women's needs can miss significant opportunities to increase returns on forestry interventions' (World Bank, 1991a: 53). The mobilisation of women's labour has, however, frequently been undertaken without due regard to the time, energy expenditure and other opportunity costs of their involvement in projects. Women's labour is viewed as malleable despite their generally inflexible work regimes. Socially obliged to contribute labour to community woodlots, for example, women have often had to switch labour away from their own crops (cf. Leach, 1991), perhaps denying themselves a source of independent income.

Moreover, women's input into social forestry projects at higher levels, in planning or project management, has usually been minimal. Men dominate decision-making bodies and control high status activities and women's interests have often been ignored as a result. In the Joint Forest Management schemes in India, for example, there are many instances where village authorities have closed forested areas off to allow the regeneration of trees, cutting women off from their major supply of firewood (Sarin, 1995; Shah and Shah, 1995).

The interest in women and women's groups as the locus of forestry interventions tends to present women as a homogeneous group separate from men, distracting attention from the micro-level conflicts, bargaining and trade-offs within the household generated by differences of gender, age and status. Men may, for instance, obstruct individual women's rights or interests in relation to forest and tree products (cf. Shah and Shah, 1995). Even where many women are *de facto* heads of households because of male outmigration, men may still retain tight control over environmental resources as migrants and women acquiesce for reasons of personal livelihood security (cf. Alaoui, 1995).

The complex gender dimensions of tenure have also been overlooked in social forestry projects. A tendency to focus on titular land ownership has, for instance, often obscured the fact that women hold secondary rights to trees and tree products as land users (Rocheleau, 1987a, 1987b; Fortmann and Bruce, 1992; Leach, 1994). Women's often less visible rights thus risk being subordinated or even eradicated (Leach, *et al.*, 1995; cf. Rocheleau, 1992a; Berry, 1987). For instance, community woodlots planted on areas of common property have often excluded women from gathering sites. Granting women rights to new trees has often proved a poor substitute where the new species mix (not of their choosing) has not provided the same range of products.

Influenced by donor concern, recent forestry policy in many countries has emphasised greater levels of privatisation, including smallholder tree growing, farm forestry and agroforestry. The smallholder approach is expected to generate greater incentives for sustainable resource use since, so it is argued, the products and labour inputs can be captured more directly by contributors.

In this context, women's incentives for participating in farm forestry activities have become an overt concern of some donors. For instance, the World Bank (1991a: 81) states that successful interventions depend on 'a full appreciation of local social and cultural values, customs and traditions. These include rights to tree and forest products; gender-based distinctions in the allocation of land, labor and capital; and the complex issues of land and tree tenure.'

In practice, however, many farm-level approaches continue to assume that there is a single homogeneous household with unitary interests to which the costs and benefits of forestry accrue. Agroforestry schemes have often failed where gender divisions of labour have required women to tend plants from which men alone reap the benefits (cf. Leach, 1991; Rocheleau, 1992b).

Water resources management

The large-scale technology-driven projects that have consumed the major part of donor funding for irrigation schemes have come under increasing scrutiny because of their poor performance on efficiency, productivity and equity grounds (Lenton, 1992). Small-scale participatory projects that draw on the experiences of indigenous community-managed irrigation systems are now considered to be a more sustainable option (Vincent, 1990; Yoder, 1994). Policy interventions in large-scale irrigation have almost invariably ignored women's productive activities as agriculturalists and as users of irrigation systems and have therefore often disregarded them as a target audience.

The International Drinking Water and Sanitation Decade (1981–1990) marked a change in emphasis from the large to the small-scale in approaches to water supply and sanitation (WSS). Over the decade there was a shift away from top-down, technically oriented provision towards decentralised community-based approaches reliant on local-level management, maintenance and, in some instances, financing of water services. The USAID Water and Sanitation for Health Project (WASH), for instance, which provides technical assistance to USAID missions on the design and implementation of WSS projects, has moved in this direction. The effectiveness and sustainability of services are now considered higher priorities than unqualified technology transfer and meeting of coverage targets (Baden, 1993).

The policy focus on decentralisation and user participation implies a need for increased sensitivity to local conditions and priorities. Systematic attempts to incorporate women into community-based WSS projects have been made, with women's groups as an institutional focus for mobilising them. Women's multiple roles as providers of domestic water, as managers of water at community level and as guardians of family health give donors a clear rationale for integrating women into water sector initiatives (cf. Rodda, 1993). The sector is viewed as having multiple beneficial spin-offs – according to the World Bank (1992) improvements in water supply and sanitation provision are 'win-win' policies – and is therefore an area in which women's roles cannot be ignored. The PROWWESS (Promotion of the Role of Women in Water and Environmental Sanitation Services) project was set up by UNDP to promote the involvement of women in the sector. Some of its literature has even gone so far as to claim that water and sanitation are a 'women's sector' (e.g. INSTRAW/PROWWESS, 1989). This view is also adopted by NGOs such as the African Water Network, which, in its promotion of sustainable water development in Africa, notes that it 'intends to achieve this by increasing the participation of women at every level of water development projects' (cited in Rodda, 1991: 104).

There is a clear efficiency rationale behind this focus on women. The World Bank's thinking on women and water is explicit in the claim that 'Women who are trained to manage and maintain community water systems often perform better than men because they are less likely to migrate, more accustomed to voluntary work, and better entrusted to administer funds honestly' (World Bank, 1992: 113).

Project-level experience with involving women in WSS projects is now considerable, and many donors and research institutes have developed guidelines and checklists for good practice on integrating women into projects (Baden, 1993). Even so, shortcomings of the approach are evident. WSS policies and projects have tended to assume that women's participation will, of itself, advance their interests. The term 'participatory' covers a wide range of applications, from projects premised on labour utilisation to those concerned with community financing of services to those that attempt complete community control over interventions. The nature of women's input within WSS projects has varied markedly as a result and is not always of benefit to them.

Donor assumptions of the complementarity of gender roles at the local level have denied intra-community divisions: the problems of working through community-level social institutions that reflect and reproduce gender hierarchies are often not recognised in the policy literature. 'Consultation with community organisations' generally signifies consultation with men, whether as community leaders or heads of households (Baden, 1993: 5). Gender hierarchies can often limit the quality of women's participation on water committees by muting their expression of interests in public or by limiting their ability to take on responsible official duties. Even where attempts have been made to draw women into village water supply management, their involvement is commonly restricted. Three women who sat on a village council in Hyderabad, India, only attended water supply management meetings when summoned by male elders (IRC, 1992 cited in Baden, 1993: 19). Women tend to be allocated tasks perceived as an extension of their 'traditional' responsibilities, even if donors propose alternative approaches. In a project in Mali, where women were given minimal influence over project planning and kept out of key decision-making responsibilities, men lacked incentive to manage the project properly because water was 'women's domain' and women lacked interest in following water use rules over which they had no influence

(Purves and Bamba, 1994). In consequence, water supply projects have often drawn on women's labour, without any provision to increase their technical or managerial skills. This low level of participation has often contributed to project failure; for instance, men trained in well or pump maintenance may be unaware of breakages because their daily routines do not take them near water supply equipment, so that women may have to use other, perhaps more reliable, but less healthy, sources of water. This compromises both health and water supply objectives. Low quality participation can also lead to gender-specific preferences relating to water quality, quantity, reliability or 'willingness to pay' for water services being overlooked within local-level policy-making processes.

Donor interest has turned recently to integrated water resources management (IWRM) in which conservation and the reallocation of existing supplies have replaced the previous emphasis on supply extension. Cost recovery is key to the approach and applies to both WSS and irrigation sectors. The pricing of water resources is assumed to give users an incentive to pursue efficient utilisation; users of water for low value purposes will be induced to limit demand, thereby freeing up supply for high value uses (e.g. domestic supplies in urban areas).

Rigorous assessment of the economic costs and benefits of water resource development could lead to better recognition of the economic value of women's work in water collection and management (Whittington et al., 1990; Kamminga, 1991). Nevertheless, the water pricing argument adopts the 'household' as the unit of analysis, leaving potential conflicts of interest and preference within the household unexamined. Opinions as to what constitutes a high value use for water, for instance, are likely to differ by gender. With pricing, poorer individuals (including women in households) may be unable to use water for small-scale income-generating activities or could face reduced returns on these activities. The use of water for non-marketable purposes or in the production of low value crops (i.e. crops for own consumption) may also be vulnerable to the imposition of water charges: pressures which would deprive some women of a vital source of independent income, while constraining the ability of others to fulfil their familial obligations.

In response to the current policy emphasis on pricing, a body of literature on willingness to pay for water services has emerged. This research suggests that while the income elasticity of demand for improved water supplies is low, the price elasticity is high, i.e. costly water connections and charges have a significant deterrent effect on take-up and use. A study by the World Bank Water Demand Research Team (1993) found instances where women were willing to pay for improved services. However, they were unable to commit financial resources due to constraints on their ability to influence household decision-making. It is not surprising, therefore, to find that rates of recovery have proved to be unexpectedly low in some cost-recovery schemes (Baden, 1993). The problem is most acute where affordability studies had focused solely on men's incomes, and responsibility for meeting the costs of water services had later been transferred to women. There is an obvious danger, however, that if water is priced differently to make it

265

affordable to women, all the cost will be shifted onto women and no pressures will be in place to modify men's expenditure priorities to cover optimal levels of household water consumption. Intra-household dynamics over income, expenditure and decision-making thus have important implications for both the success and the gender equity of water pricing policies; yet they have largely been ignored in the policy literature to date.

Urban environmental management

Until recently urban environmental problems had received far less donor attention than those of rural areas (Atkinson, 1994: 98). This is now changing, with donors having dramatically stepped up support for urban 'brown agendas' and a profusion of high-profile programmes having been established to look into ways of improving urban environmental planning and management.[4]

This policy concern recognises that urban environmental problems differ qualitatively from those of rural areas. Key differences are that the day to day activities of the urban poor generally have less impact on the environment than in rural areas;[5] and processes of urban environmental degradation affect health more immediately than income (Leach and Mearns, 1991: 26). Rapid urbanisation and population growth in many Third World cities have outpaced the provision of basic environmental services and infrastructure. Environmental regulations, where they exist, have proved inadequate for dealing with growing problems of urban pollution. As a result, urban populations suffer exposure to a range of environmental pollutants, such as industrial waste, toxic chemicals, air pollution and biological pollutants derived from inadequate water, sanitation and drainage services (Hardoy et al., 1992: 204).

Other environmental problems in urban centres include overcrowded housing, dwellings built on environmentally hazardous (dumps, floodplains, steep slopes) or ecologically fragile sites, noise pollution and road congestion (Bartone et al., 1994). Low income groups tend to bear the major brunt of urban environmental problems (Leach and Mearns, 1991). They are more likely to be located in polluted and hazardous areas, to reside in overcrowded dwellings and to have less secure housing tenure, and thus to lack incentives for investment in buildings and in the land and services surrounding them (Bartone et al., 1994). Low income women are particularly vulnerable because of their close interaction with contaminated water sources and their responsibility for household sanitation and waste disposal.

Urban environmental management issues are complex in that they 'often involve more than one environmental medium, economic sector and administrative jurisdiction; institutions, policies and problems are not synchronised; and municipal capacity can seriously affect environmental quality' (Leitmann, 1994: 126). Nevertheless, most policy literature on the urban environment is sectorally focused and concerned mainly with site-by-site solutions to specific technical problems. The sectoral bias in analysis and planning has proved ill-suited for dealing with complex and multifaceted environmental problems. In particular, social concerns have proved to be a fundamental determinant of the acceptability of environmental services.

Although the research literature on gender/environment issues in the urban context is patchy – gender analysis of 'brown agenda' issues lags far behind that of 'green' natural resource management concerns – sectoral analyses of water, housing and land demonstrate a very high level of involvement of women in activities consistent with their household obligations. While the literature dwells on the effects of urban environmental degradation on women's roles as resource users (Bell, 1991; cf. Dankelman and Davidson, 1988; Sontheimer, 1991), it also indicates that gendered patterns of resource preferences, access and control, community participation and labour mobilisation are as relevant to urban environmental policy as to other natural resource management (NRM) sectors.

Yet in policies and programmes, gender-specific preferences relating to the location of standpipes, the cost, quality and reliability of water, the location or timing of waste disposal services, etc. have rarely been taken into consideration (Hardoy *et al.*, 1992: 215). Recent attempts by the Government of Bangladesh to expand public latrine provision in slum and peri-urban areas have been criticised for failing to take into account women's concerns for security and modesty. Public latrines were sited in a way which did not allow women to stay in seclusion, as required under prevailing cultural norms (Baden *et al.*, 1994).

Recent policy emphasis on 'sustainable cities' stresses the linkages between environment, health, poverty and economic productivity, and suggests a shift towards a more integrated approach to the urban environment. Urban environmental problems are increasingly seen as issues of service provision rather than of intrinsic natural resource scarcities,[6] and conceptualised as problems of governance. As such, they require legal, administrative and institutional solutions (Hardoy *et al.*, 1992: 205).

Donor investments are now being directed at institutional capacity-building of municipal and other local authorities to improve service coverage, delivery and management within city-specific environmental planning and management action plans (Bartone *et al.*, 1994). Other areas of assistance include support to NGOs and other community organisations to mobilise public support for and participation in environmental improvement programmes, and an emphasis on cost-recovery from improved facilities, with service users expected to pay for their resource use via charges, fees or taxes. This approach is authenticated by extensive research into willingness to pay for refuse, water and sewerage services which suggests that such services are highly valued by both low- and high-income groups (Coolidge *et al.*, 1993).

The new policy emphasis on building partnerships between government authorities and urban residents shows a sensitivity to the need for local identification of problems and solutions. Yet there is little attempt to disaggregate by gender.

The majority of environmental improvement initiatives at community level have been stimulated from the bottom up by community groups who have put pressure on local authorities to act on problems (Hardoy and Satterthwaite, 1989). In

Bangkok, for example, many low-income communities have taken over environmental management by organising periodic neighbourhood clean-up campaigns and regular waste collection services (Atkinson, 1994: 174). Local schemes for environmental improvement often draw heavily on the labour input of 'volunteer' women because these activities are seen to extend logically from their existing responsibilities.

A study of a low-income community in Guayaquil, Ecuador, showed that NGOs, rather than municipal authorities, were the main providers of environmental, education and health services to the area following public expenditure cutbacks in 1983. To ensure service delivery local women had to devote unpaid labour to the projects, in some cases forcing elder daughters to pick up the responsibility for the reproductive tasks their mothers no longer had time to undertake, with negative effects on their school attendance (Moser, 1992). The new policy focus on community environmental management needs to be aware of the risk that using women's labour has such negative effects.

Housing tenure is central to the urban environmental management issue. Residents of squatter and slum settlements face a continual threat of eviction which lessens incentives for investment in infrastructure and services. Lack of housing or land rights restricts access to credit which could be used for housing and other environmental improvements. Donors are beginning to tackle this issue. Granting of secure land tenure to slum occupants in Solo, Indonesia, for example, resulted in significant investments in housing, environmental services such as water supply, waste disposal and sanitation (Bartone *et al.*, 1994: 61). Equality of tenure rights is especially important where households are under female headship. Secure housing tenure may also be particularly important for women who work at home in income-generating activities.

Legal and institutional reforms

Various legal and institutional reforms with intended environmental – as well as other – outcomes have recently been promoted by donor agencies. Broad themes in such reforms – which cross-cut and affect simultaneously different environmental 'sectors' such as those considered above – include land tenure reform, administrative decentralisation and local institutional capacity building. The prominence of these themes partly reflects a concern to improve the economic incentives for environmental use and management, but it can also be seen as an attempt to address implementation failures in the past and as a response to a broader 'good governance' agenda now being pursued by donors.

Government and donor attention to the reform of tenure arrangements is partly driven by a general agreement that insecure rights to land and resources are antithetical to sustainable resource management. But policy-makers disagree over how to tackle the issue. Some donors and governments favour privatisation, in the belief that indigenous systems – where non-exclusive and often non-codified rights prevail – are thought to invoke less conservation-minded behaviour because of their apparent insecurity. Others are beginning to argue that customary tenure arrangements can be effective and efficient and that these rights should also be clarified, as in current policies for rangeland management.

To date, most attempts to privatise land have focused almost exclusively on men as 'heads of households' – women have seldom gained legal title. Customary tenure arrangements have, however, often continued to function in instances where individual titling has occurred, resulting in confusing and often ambiguous dual systems. However, there is evidence that this lack of clarity has sometimes been useful to women, providing them with a means to extend such contingent rights as they can lay claim to (e.g. Mackenzie, 1995).

With their exclusive focus on land ownership, land titling policies have tended to overlook the multiple, in-nested subsiduary use rights held within and dependent on broader, prior rights to land and trees which other users may hold over the same plot. In many cases, such contingent rights are particularly important to women, yet risk being undermined or obliterated. Neither do land titling policies recognise the extended livelihood aspects of tenure. Not all resource management activities are undertaken for immediate individual short-term gain. For example, where rights are contingent on others' rights, as tends to be the case for women, resource management practices may be part of a social strategy aimed at cultivating relationships which can be turned to in times of future need (Rocheleau et al., 1995).

Some donors and governments are now beginning to recognise the importance of working within customary tenurial arrangements. In Papua New Guinea, for instance, the government has recognised that customary communal land tenure actually provides more effective land rights than would a privatised system. Families hold indefinite rights to farm a plot of land, but clans control sales of land. Communal tenure confers entitlements over a specific piece of land to a range of individuals, who all have a stake in ensuring its sustainable use (Markandya, 1994: 265).

Administrative decentralisation for environmental management – often as part of broader reforms in governance – is expected to improve cost recovery and to create cost savings in service administration. But the emphasis on cost recovery may have unfortunate consequences in this context. There may be costs for women where jobs previously undertaken by men for wages are transferred to women at the local level and undertaken on a 'voluntary' basis. That women do undertake these jobs is a reflection of 'the male dominance of public office, the presence of women's groups facilitating the mobilisation of women, and the realisation by women that if they fail to do such work, it remains undone' (Jackson, 1993b: 1951).

Policies for administrative decentralisation also include a concern for upgrading the skills of local staff. Sometimes, as in the water sector, for example, it is stated that female staff should participate equally with men in training (as in World Bank, 1993a). While this offers an excellent opportunity for sensitising staff at all levels to gender issues in resource management, and for developing more gender-attuned extension services and participatory approaches, much of the policy literature instead emphasises the need for highly technical training, forgoing an opportunity to support the development of expertise for shifting towards more 'people-centred' and gender-sensitive development.

Policies to build up the capacity of local institutions link with a growing consensus, post-UNCED, that the implementation of sustainable development should be based on local-level solutions derived from community initiatives (Holmberg, 1992; Holmberg *et al.*, 1993). These are based on the view that strengthened or rejuvenated local institutions can be a useful vehicle for using and building up local capacity to deal with natural resource management problems, mediating and resolving conflicts between different interest groups, for building consensus over natural resource management, and mobilising community backing for tenurial arrangements.

However, as illustrated in the case of water resource management, it cannot be assumed that gender-equitable arrangements will be promoted by local institutions. Local institutions and organisations are part of – or at least emerge from – social and gender relations, reproducing their biases. Locally evolved rules about resource use tend to reflect the interests of dominant parties and, as recent experience with Joint Forest Management schemes in India has shown (Sarin, 1995), women's less visible rights of access to natural resources are often obliterated by decisions made within these hierarchical bodies. Ironically, then, devolution of control over land and property to the local level can have the effect of excluding women from their rights of access to natural resources for the first time.

'Gestion des terroirs' ('land management') approaches to local natural resource management, popular among NGOs and government agencies operating in Sahelian West Africa, have been similarly insensitive to socio-economic differentiation (Painter, 1991), whether by gender, class or seniority. While aiming to strengthen local institutional capacity for responding to specific local environmental conditions, they have ignored important differences in resource use, control, knowledge and preferences. Local institutions have tended to become dominated by local elites who have taken on new community roles in such projects as a means of promoting their own interests.

The focus on the institutional dimensions of NRM is a useful step towards incorporating social concerns. However, it does not of itself guarantee that gender issues will be recognised and adequately addressed within environmental policy. A sole focus on traditional NRM organisations at the expense of the more complex and often less visible social institutional arrangements which operate in parallel, which shape gender/environment interactions, and which may be important in promoting women's interests, may undermine policy objectives (cf. Leach *et al.*, 1997).

Evaluation of past experiences and their intellectual origins

Even the brief reviews above are sufficient to suggest that across environmental 'sectors' there are some striking similarities in the ways that gender issues have been addressed. Detailed project results have not been given here and are not always available, but there is enough evidence to suggest that past efforts have rarely been beneficial to women, and have often actually been damaging.

While there clearly have been efforts to fine-tune policy in women's favour, this concern is partial, so that parallel strands of policy within single sectors continue to say very different things about gender issues. Thus, in the forestry sector, conservation-with-development policies for forest reserves have focused on an undisaggregated 'community', while women have been drawn into social forestry schemes on a massive scale. In water sector policies, while women and women's groups have become a central focus of water supply and sanitation issues, the irrigation sector has continued to target interventions mainly at male farmers in their role as 'household heads' and as productive users of water.

More fundamentally, where environmental policies and programmes have tried to take account of gender issues they have consistently been based on a particular vision of social life, positing parallel – and virtually unconnected – male and female worlds of work, economic activity and interactions with the environment. This orientation, closely allied with the WID model of gender and development, is betrayed especially by the following common programme characteristics: their exclusive focus on women's current, mainly sustenance, roles; their focus on the identification of women's roles without any consideration of dynamic interactions with men's roles; their view of women as efficient resource managers and as an untapped pool of labour; their assumption that participation in a project will of itself benefit women; and their presentation of all women as the same, assuming a homogeneity of interest by virtue of their sex. These tendencies can be seen, in turn, as stemming logically from the intellectual approaches which have informed these policies, implicitly or explicitly: the Women, Environment and Development school, and certain strands of ecofeminism.

Women, environment and development

Within the large specialist literature on links between gender and environmental issues which has developed over the last 15 years, the 'women, environment and development' (WED) approach was the first to highlight women as having a special relationship with the environment, and it has remained the most directly influential in policy circles. Women were described as the main 'users' and 'managers' of natural resources at the local level (cf. Dankelman and Davidson, 1988; Rodda, 1991 for an exposition of the approach).

Like the WID approach, the starting point for WED is the gender division of labour. WED points out that women's work involves them closely with the environment and its resources. Typically it is women within a community who are hewers of fuelwood and haulers of water, and who play a major, though often unacknowledged, part as cultivators. Women's responsibilities make them closely dependent on, and give them distinct interests in, natural resources, especially those which provide food and fuel. Women are also acknowledged to have deep and extensive knowledge of natural resources, deriving mainly from their intimate

271

daily experience of them. By extension, it is argued that women's interests lie in sustainable environmental management and resource conservation; women's interests are thus identical to, or at least complementary with, those of environmental programmes and projects.

As with WID itself, in WED there is an almost complete focus on women, and a virtual exclusion of men and of men's resource-related activities from the picture (cf. Munyakho, 1985; Martin-Brown *et al.*, 1992). Furthermore, no attention is given to differences among women, which might be associated with other social stratifiers such as age and class; women tend to be treated unproblematically as a single, cohesive social group.

The emphases of WED discussions have shifted over time. In the early 1980s WED approaches commonly portrayed women as the primary victims of environmental degradation, bearing the brunt of pollution and deforestation and the major responsibility for coping with shocks such as drought. This was epitomised by powerful images of women struggling to find food and fuel in degraded land- and tree-scapes. Natural resource degradation was seen as undermining women's ability to perform their sustenance roles, and as imposing increasing costs on their time and energy. In the late 1980s women came to be seen less as 'victims' and more as efficient environmental managers and conservers of natural resources, on the basis of evidence that women were heavily engaged world-wide, according to the terms of local agro-ecological practices, in environmental protection and rehabilitation: building conservation terraces, planting trees, and dealing with seeds and wild plants to safeguard biodiversity, for instance.

Notwithstanding – perhaps even because of – its conceptual simplifications, WED produces clear guiding principles for policy: women are to be incorporated fully into programme activities. This is to ensure both that women benefit directly from environmental projects, and that projects are not undermined by the exclusion of women, who are the primary environmental resource management agents. Women's groups are thus often proposed as the appropriate vehicle for 'community' environmental action.

WED prescriptions have been taken on board in the environmental policies of many NGOs and donor agencies. The World Bank's 'synergistic' approach to environment and gender, arguing for a general identity of interest between women and environmental resources and thus for treating women as the best (most expert) agents for ensuring resource conservation, is the most comprehensive statement of the rationale for the approach (cf. Jackson, 1993a). WED assumptions have also been assimilated into the literature on the community-based approach to sustainable development known as primary environmental care (PEC),[7] which is widely advocated by NGOs and donors (DGCS 1990; Oxfam *et al.*, 1992). Women are conceptualised as the pivot around which the central planks of PEC – caring for the environment, meeting basic needs and community empowerment – rotate, because of their knowledge of and experience with environmental management (Davidson *et al.*, 1992: 151).

The practical application of the WED approach typically requires of policymakers and project designers, first, knowledge of the environmentally related tasks carried out by women under the gender division of labour, so as to 'bring women in' to project activities, mobilising the extra resources of women's labour, skill and knowledge; second, the delivery of project and programme resources to the 'right people', i.e. those (men or women as appropriate) currently engaged in a particular activity and benefiting from it; and third, the inclusion of women in the implementation of environmental projects in NRM sectors in which women are heavily involved, commonly through women's groups. The WED approach should be credited with pioneering a coherent, if flawed, model of social differentiation, and with inspiring interest for the first time in the position of women, and the implications for policy and projects, among environmental policy-makers. Nevertheless, the narrowness of the WED prescriptions has as we have seen often had disappointing and, in some cases, even damaging results. Despite efforts to include women, many projects have not, in the event, benefited women, or have not ensured the conditions for women's participation.

Ecofeminism

Ecofeminism is a group of approaches based on the notion that women are especially 'close to nature' in a spiritual or conceptual sense.[8] Philosophically, ecofeminism is associated with 'ecocentric' strands of radical environmentalism, such as deep ecology. Although largely of Northern origin, ecofeminism has an increasingly vocal international presence – for example through the work of the Indian writer Vandana Shiva (1988).

Ecofeminism shares in the post-modern feminist critique of scientific knowledge in general and of the applied sciences in 'mainstream' development in particular (cf. Merchant, 1989). The versions most influential in international circles extend to a general critique of conventional approaches to and definitions of development. The dominant model of development is perceived as a male construct (Mies and Shiva, 1993). Economic development is argued to have been harmful both to women and to the environment by trampling alternative, local knowledge, especially women's knowledge, associated with organic conceptions of people and nature as interconnected; by disregarding the spiritual and sacred in people's attitude to their environment and women's special role therein; and by overriding holistic and harmonious environmental practices. Economic development of this kind is similar to and goes along with the social subordination of women. Both processes suppress the 'feminine principle' (cf. Shiva, 1988). Nevertheless, ecofeminists consider that the feminine principle is not quite extinct in the environmental context, but still manifest in a residual, near instinctual wisdom which some women have been able to retain in the face of developmental pressures. In the ecofeminist view, therefore, hope for environmentally sustainable and gender-egalitarian development lies in the recovery of the feminine principle. 'Third World women' are portrayed as the last bastion of feminine environmental wisdom and they provide the key to its retrieval.

273

Ecofeminist arguments are, like those of the WED approach, heightened by the lack of reference to men. In Shiva's (1988) work, for instance, any reference to men tends to be subsumed within references to 'peasants' or 'tribes'. Another similarity with the WED approach lies in ecofeminists' emphasis on the importance to social survival of women's environment-related 'sustenance' or 'survival' activities, related to everyday provisioning of water and fuelwood, gathering and producing food. These subsistence activities, and the non-monetised, 'reproductive' sphere in general, are ascribed high spiritual value. Women, as environmental nurturers and caregivers, are seen to have interests and values that are intimately linked with and serve to promote environmental conservation.[9]

Ecofeminism has appealed to a large, popular international audience, and represents the views of many environmentalist movements, in both North and South, in respect of gender issues. Echoes of ecofeminist discourse are contained in many donor and NGO documents as preambular justification for special women's projects. It also colours the Miami declaration adopted by a large international conference of women activists prior to the Earth Summit at Rio.

In terms of policy recommendations,[10] the practical thrust of the ecofeminist approach is similar to that of WED. First, it suggests that policy-makers should identify women as allies – indeed as the prime or even only movers – in resource conservation projects. The strong inference is that separate, women-only projects are the only legitimate and effective form of intervention. However, no concrete recommendations are put forward for the design and implementation of such projects: the only prescription is that activities should be directed at women. Second, as in the WED approach, the prescription is a general one: 'women' are portrayed as a homogeneous group, with no suggestion made that particular women might have to be targeted over and above others in local environmental interventions. Third, 'women's groups' are seen again as appropriate vehicles for environmental conservation activities.

Such is their generality that these prescriptions are of limited value to policy-makers and project designers. Where they have been adopted in spirit, the actual measures that have been derived to implement the approach are identical to those recommended by the WED approach: targeting of projects to women, either in their entirety or by way of a special component and their 'incorporation' in project activities. The limited and sometimes counterproductive outcomes discussed above have been the consequence.

Typical outcomes at field level

WED and ecofeminist-inspired development interventions have led to several types of failure, which the discussions of forestry, water resources and urban environmental management illustrated in different ways. First, project 'success' has often been secured at women's expense, by appropriating women's labour, unremunerated, in activities which prove not to meet their own needs or whose benefits they do not control. New 'environment' chores have been added to women's already long list of caring roles. Women have sometimes been treated, in effect, as a source of cheap labour for environmental projects. The tasks they are given to do are often low status without any technical or managerial content; it is assumed that women as resource users have the incentive to do the work, whereas the situation is often that work schedules are badly designed and women lack the authority within the project context to modify procedures for the better.

Second, community management approaches, and the use of women's groups in that context, can act against women's interests. Women typically have a small political presence in community councils. This can actually serve to worsen instead of improve women's position, when new project resources are allocated by such councils to men, and when councils formalise access to and use rights in resources and downplay or squeeze out women's traditional rights in the process. Third, project efforts to include women do not always materialise, resulting in generalised failure. Women often resist activities which are not in their interests; for instance, they can refuse to tend trees which they perceive as men's or to take on new project-related tasks where this would force them to neglect others. Fourth, a focus on women's groups, overlooking differences among women, has often marginalised the interests and concerns of some (e.g. poor) women, often not well represented in such organisations.

Finally, the poor performance of WED and ecofeminist-inspired project interventions may be especially unfortunate in another way. WED and ecofeminism may have stoked up expectations that women, as environmental managers, have the ability to 'fix' environmental problems. The failure of environment sector projects that have attempted to address gender issues to deliver such a result may lead to disillusionment among policy-makers in their attempts to take account of gender concerns. It is important that failure of project attempts so far is understood to be due to limitations in the prescriptions that have been on offer from advocates of the WED and ecofeminist schools, and to unrealistic expectations. More analytically sophisticated and realistic policy prescriptions are required.

Towards gender analysis in environmental research and policy

A set of alternative approaches to the conceptualisation of gender–environment relations does exist in the literature, contributing to what may be broadly thought of as the application of a GAD approach to environmental questions. These alternative approaches, which include feminist environmentalism, feminist political ecology and gender, environment and development (cf. Braidotti *et al.*, 1994), have distinct emphases. For instance, feminist environmentalism tends to stress the material aspects of the gender–environment link (e.g. Agarwal, 1991), while feminist political ecology draws more attention to the nature of gendered knowledge, the link between cultural and resource use practices, and the importance of the macro context (Rocheleau, 1991; Fortmann and Nabane, 1993; Cornwall *et al.*, 1994; Leach, 1994; Thomas-Slayter and Rocheleau, 1994; Rocheleau *et al.*, 1996).

Nevertheless they share a number of core ideas, centring around a conceptuali-sation of gender in terms of dynamic social and political relations.

As we go on to show, such approaches direct attention to issues and relation-ships ignored within the limited model of gender and environment interactions developed under the WED and ecofeminist approaches. In so doing, they indicate ways in which attention to gender issues in environmental policy-making and pro-gramme and project interventions could be improved. Many of these ideas are, of course, commonplace to debate in the field of gender and development research more generally, although they have proved rather more difficult to translate into development practice. That they are still relatively novel within environmental policy debates underscores the extent to which environment has lagged behind other development arenas in its sensitivity to gender issues, for reasons which are beyond the scope of this chapter.

A GAD analysis challenges the assumption, in both WED and ecofeminism, that women, a priori, have a 'special' relationship with the environment. Instead, women's (and men's) relations with the environment are seen to emerge from the social context of gender relations, and are as such dynamic. If certain women are 'closely involved' with natural resources, this may reflect gender-divided roles and lack of any other economic opportunity, rather than any inherent caring rela-tionship: for instance, women may gather tree food products from communally managed land partly because they lack access to income from trees on private holdings (cf. Rocheleau, 1988; Agarwal, 1991). Moreover, women may, because they are locked into environmental resource dependence and deprived of access to other more lucrative activities, have little fundamental incentive for environ-mental sustainability or improvement. Their preference may be to move into other areas of production, as they see men do. This amounts to a fundamental challenge to the WED assertion that women's and environmental interests are synonymous.

Gender, environment and development approaches also avoid the WED/ecofeminism implication that women and men are homogeneous groups, emphasising the possible differences among sub-groups of men and sub-groups of women (of different ages, status, etc.). Such differences clearly do exist and can be strongly relevant to resource management practices and incentives. For example, older women may not be concerned with fuelwood supplies if they are able to devolve responsibility for collecting it onto younger women (Jackson, 1995) and some women with fewer household duties may be able to pursue economic oppor-tunities not immediately dependent on local resources (Hassan et al., 1995). In the project context, a 'land user approach' – rather than a gender division of labour or gender roles approach – can be used to identify particular resource users and analyse their specific incentives and constraints, and the nature of their environ-mental knowledge, in order for their interests and capabilities in environmental management to be understood (cf. Rocheleau 1987a, 1987b).

GAD perspectives also shift the focus from gender roles to relations. They emphasise that it is not only activities, but also relations of tenure and property, control over resources, products, and decision-making which shape people's environmental interests and opportunities. Power relations and bargaining processes within social institutions, such as marriage, affect resource use decisions. Women's environmentally related rights and responsibilities are almost always contingent on kin and household arrangements. In consequence, women's resource position varies amongst individuals according to their social position. Moreover, gender boundaries are clearly not fixed with respect to resource activities and control, but dynamic and interactive, related to and interwoven with each other, and liable to change. As economic and social circumstances alter, whether due to changes in global or regional market conditions or to shifts in the policy context, so rights and responsibilities may be redefined.

Property relations have been a particular emphasis of feminist environmentalist/political ecology, with recent work emphasising a more nuanced understanding of both the layers of contingent rights, and the informal practices, which underlie formal arrangements (e.g. Mackenzie, 1991; Agarwal, 1995). This work should warn policy-makers to be aware that environmental interventions of all types – not only those concerned explicitly with tenurial reform – may affect property regimes. The property rights of different women need to be understood at the outset of, and actively monitored throughout, the life of a project, if policies and programmes are not to discriminate against women either in terms of formalisation of new property rights or by (however unwittingly) obliterating pre-existing 'informal' rights. Women's less visible property rights in environmental resources are upheld by an array of social institutions and through various political mechanisms. An emphasis on strengthening and supporting women's organisations may often be correct, but work from a feminist environmentalist perspective suggests that policy-makers might also examine, support and build on the often less visible institutional arrangements and networks which provide channels for particular women to press their concerns and guard their entitlements in situations of ecological stress or environmental change. In particular contexts, support for different local organisational bases or coalitions may be more appropriate than purely gender-based associations.

Following on from this concern with access to and control over resources, gender analysis approaches point out the fallacy in assuming that women's participation in project activities is coterminous with benefit. Clearly, intra-household and intra-community decision-making processes can deny women control over resources which their own labour may have produced, including in a project context. And given the dynamics of intra-household income distribution, it cannot be assumed that women will benefit proportionally, in a 'trickle down' effect, from diverting their labour into project activities even if household incomes as a whole are expected to increase as a result. In the worst-case scenario, diversion of women's labour effort without remuneration may reduce their access to own-account income, as well as exacerbating the gender asymmetry in total hours of work.

Attention to gender inequities in the intra-household distribution of income and in the identification and expression of priorities in household consumption also suggests the need to review resource pricing and cost recovery policies and methods of price estimation. Policies need to take account of the likelihood first, that women have lesser command over cash than men and second, that where men take charge of household expenditure on purchased inputs and services they may not give proper weight to women's interests or priorities.

Finally, in drawing attention to the macro-context of gendered environmental relations, feminist environmentalist/political ecology perspectives point to the fact that women's relation to the environment emerges from a livelihood context in which resource-based activities are only one element. In some circumstances, sustainable environmental management may be best achieved by ensuring the availability of alternative income and employment, *in situ* or elsewhere, to reduce people's dependence on environmental resources. Likewise, progressive change for women may, in some circumstances, imply enhanced involvement in labour markets or trade. The need to widen people's, particularly women's, range of livelihood choices may sometimes imply a need for interventions encompassing activities not focused on the environment *per se*. This is consonant with the assumptions of standard economic policy, but contrary to the tenets of many environmental approaches and certainly contrary to the ecofeminist/WED conviction that women's fortunes and those of the environment are inextricably, synergistically entwined.

Notes

1 This chapter is based on a study supported by the Environmental and Natural Resources Policy and Training (EPAT) Project funded by the US Agency for International Development (USAID), which has been published in full elsewhere (Joekes, Green and Leach, 1995). Dr Nancy K. Diamond, Gender and Environment Officer (Office of Women in Development, USAID) prepared the scope of work for the original study and provided technical and editorial oversight. Responsibility for the views, interpretations, opinions and any errors in the study and in this revised version nevertheless rests with the authors alone.

2 In recognition of the multiple interests at play within forest zones, 'stakeholder' approaches which attempt to understand the conflicts and trade-offs between and within different groups have been developed (e.g. Grimble *et al.*, 1994).

3 E.g. the Korup National Park ICDP, Cameroon (Republic of Cameroon, 1990), supported by the DFID (UK), and, in Nigeria, the Oban ICDP, Cross River State (WWF, 1990).

4 For example, the UNDP/UNCHS/World Bank Urban Management Programme; UNCHS Sustainable Cities Programme; WHO Healthy Cities Programme; UNDP/World Bank Metropolitan Environmental Improvement Programme which is focused on Kathmandu, Metro Manila, Colombo, Beijing, Bombay and Jakarta (Bartone *et al.*, 1994: 5).

5 Two exceptions are when urban industry involves the poor as workers in environmentally damaging behaviour or where urban populations degrade rural resources such as forests beyond the urban boundary.

6 For example, illegal squatter settlements are often located in environmentally precarious locations, not because of land scarcities elsewhere, but because residents lack access to other more appropriate sites.

7 PEC has been defined as 'a process by which local groups or communities organise themselves with varying degrees of outside support so as to apply their skills and knowledge to the care of natural resources and environment while satisfying livelihood needs' (Pretty and Guijt, 1992:22).

8 Ecofeminism is a multifaceted school of thought and the brevity of our account fails to do justice to the many particular positions within it. Nevertheless, we hope to capture its philosophical essence here sufficiently to clarify the general type of policy prescriptions to which it has given rise.

9 Movements such as the Chipko (tree-hugging) movement in India, or 'Greenbelt' tree-planting in Kenya, have been portrayed as feminine environmental movements in support of this perspective. This position has, it should be noted, been strongly criticised on cross-cultural and historical grounds (Jackson, 1993b; Leach, 1994; Leach and Green, 1995).

10 Some ecofeminist thought is antithetical to any kind of development programmes, in a logical extension of the view that they are inherently and incorrigibly damaging to the environment and masculinist in orientation. An alternative model for development is sometimes advanced, which values subsistence, harmony with nature, disengagement from international capitalism and world trade, regional or national self-sufficiency in food, etc., and community and family institutions (Mies and Shiva, 1993).

References

Agarwal, B. (1991) *Engendering the Environment Debate: Lessons from the Indian Subcontinent,* East Lansing, Michigan: Centre for the Advanced Study of International Development, Michigan State University.

Agarwal, B. (1995) *A Field of One's Own: Gender and Land Rights in South Asia,* Cambridge: Cambridge University Press.

Alaoui, C. (1995) 'Women, Environment and Population: a Moroccan Case Study', *IDS Bulletin* 26 (1).

Atkinson, A. (1994) 'Introduction: The Contribution of Cities to Sustainability', *Third World Planning Review* 16 (2).

Baden, S. (1993) 'Practical Strategies for Involving Women as Well as Men in Water and Sanitation Activities', Briefing prepared for SIDA, Brighton: IDS, BRIDGE.

Baden, S., Green C., Goetz, A. M. and Guhathakurta, M. (1994) 'Background Paper on Gender Issues in Bangladesh', Prepared for the British High Commission, Dhaka, Brighton: IDS, BRIDGE.

Bartone, C., Bernstein, J., Leitmann, J. and Eigen, J. (1994) *Toward Environmental Strategies for Cities: Policy Considerations for Urban Environmental Management in Developing Countries,* Urban Management Program Policy Paper 18, Washington, DC: World Bank.

Bell, J. K. (1991) 'Women, Environment and Urbanization: A Guide to the Literature', *Environment and Urbanization* 3 (2): 92–103.

Berry, S. (1987) *Property Rights and Rural Resource Management: The Case of Tree Crops in West Africa,* Working Papers No. 122, Boston University, African Studies Centre.

Braidotti, R., Charkiewicz, E., Hausler, S. and Wieringa, S. (1994) *Women, The Environment and Sustainable Development: Towards A Theoretical Synthesis,* London: Zed Press.

Carney, J. (1994) 'Gender and the Sustainability of Irrigated Farming in The Gambia' in I. Yngström, P. Jeffery, K. King, C. Toulmin (eds), *Gender and Environment in Africa,* Edinburgh: University of Edinburgh, Centre for African Studies.

Coolidge, J. G., Porter, R. C. and Zhang, Z. J. (1993) *Urban Environmental Services in*

Developing Countries, EPAT/MUCIA Working Paper No. 9, Madison: University of Wisconsin-Madison.

Cornwall, A., Guijt, I. and Welbourn, A. (1994) 'Acknowledging Process: Challenges for Agricultural Research and Extension Methodology', in I. Scoones and J. Thompson (eds) *Beyond Farmer First: Rural People's Knowledge, Agricultural Research and Extension Practice*, London: Intermediate Technology Publications.

Dankelman, I. and Davidson, J. (1988) *Women and Environment in the Third World: Alliance for the Future*, London: Earthscan.

Davidson, J., (1990) 'Gender and Environment: Ideas for Action and Research'. Paper presented at the conference on Environment, Development and Economic Research, ODI, London, 27–28 March.

Davidson, J., Myers, D. and Chakraborty, M. (1992) *No Time To Waste: Poverty and the Global Environment*, Oxford: OXFAM.

DGCS (1990) *Supporting Primary Environmental Care: Report of the PEC Workshop Siena, Jan 29–Feb 2, 1990 to the OECD/DAC Working Party on Development Assistance and the Environment*, Rome: DGCS.

D'Silva, E. and Appanah, S. (1993) *Forestry Management for Sustainable Development*, EDI Policy Seminar Report No. 32, Washington, DC: World Bank.

FAO (1985) *The Tropical Forestry Action Plan*, FAO, World Bank and UNDP, Rome: FAO.

FAO (1993) *The Challenge of Sustainable Forest Management: What Future for the World's Forests?* Rome: FAO.

FAO/SIDA (1987) *Restoring the Balance: Women and Forest Resources*, Rome: FAO.

Fortmann, L. and Bruce, J. (1992) 'You've Got to Know Who Controls the Land and Trees People Use: Gender, Tenure and the Environment', in *Gender, Environment and Development: Some Interlinkages*, Stockholm: SIDA.

Fortmann, L. and Nabane, N. (1993) *The Fruits of their Labours*, Working Paper, Harare: Centre for Applied Social Sciences, University of Zimbabwe.

Gregersen, H., Draper, S. and Elz, D. (1989) *People and Trees: The Role of Social Forestry in Sustainable Development*, EDI Seminar Series, Washington: World Bank.

Grimble, R. J., Aglionby, J. and Quan, J. (1994) *Tree Resources and Environmental Policy: A Stakeholder Approach*, NRI Socio-economic Series 7, Chatham: Natural Resources Institute.

Hardoy, J. E. and Satterthwaite, D. (1989) *Squatter Citizen: Life in the Urban Third World*, London: Earthscan.

Hardoy, J. E., Mitlin, D. and Satterthwaite, D. (1992) *Environmental Problems in Third World Cities*, London: Earthscan.

Hassan, R. M. Al-, Warner, M.W. and Kydd, J. G. (1995) 'Gender Versus Other Socially Defined Differences: Lessons for Policy Intervention', Development Research Insights for Policymakers, No. 16, London and Brighton, ODI and IDS.

Holmberg, J. (ed.) (1992) *Policies for a Small Planet*, London: Earthscan.

Holmberg, J. *et al.*, (1993) *Facing the Future: Beyond the Earth Summit*, London: IIED.

INSTRAW/PROWWESS (1989) *Women, Water Supply and Sanitation: Making the Link Stronger*, Dominican Republic: INSTRAW.

Jackson, C. (1993a) 'Questioning Synergism: Win-win with Women in Population and Environment Policies?', *Journal of International Development* 5 (6).

Jackson, C. (1993b) 'Doing What Comes Naturally? Women and Environment in Development', *World Development* 21 (12).

Jackson, C. (1995) 'From Conjugal Contracts to Environmental Relations: Some Thoughts on Labour and Technology', *IDS Bulletin* 26 (1).

Joekes, S., Green, C. and Leach, M. (1995) *Integrating Gender into Environmental Research and Policy*, IDS Working Paper 27. Brighton: Institute of Development Studies.

Kamminga, E. (1991) *Economic Benefits from Improved Rural Water Supply: a Review with a Focus on Women*, International Water and Sanitation Centre, IRC Occasional Paper No. 17, December, The Hague: IRC.

Leach, M. (1991) 'Engendered Environments: Understanding Natural Resource Management in the West African Forest Zone', *IDS Bulletin* 22 (4).

Leach, M. (1992) 'Gender and the Environment: Traps and Opportunities', *Development in Practice* 2 (1): 12–22.

Leach, M. (1994) *Rainforest Relations: Gender and Resource Use among the Mende of Gola, Sierra Leone*, Edinburgh: Edinburgh University Press and Washington: Smithsonian Institution Press.

Leach, M. and Green, C. 1995 *Gender and Environmental History: From Representations of Women and Nature to Gender Analysis of Ecology and Politics*, IDS Working Paper 16. Brighton: Institute of Development Studies.

Leach, M. and Mearns, R. (1991) *Poverty and Environment in Developing Countries: An Overview Study*, Swindon: ESRC.

Leach, M. Joekes, S. and Green, C. (1995) 'Editorial: Gender Relations and Environmental Change', *IDS Bulletin* 26 (1).

Leach, M., Mearns, R. and Scoones, I. (eds) (1997) 'Community-based Sustainable Development: Consensus or Conflict?', *IDS Bulletin* 28(4).

Leitmann, J. (1994) 'The World Bank and the Brown Agenda: Evolution of a Revolution', *Third World Planning Review*, 16 (2).

Lenton, R. (1992) 'Irrigation Management Strategies for the 21st Century', *Canadian Journal of Development Studies*, special issue.

Mackenzie, F. (1991) 'Political Economy of the Environment: Gender and Resistance under Colonialism: Murang'a District, Kenya, 1910–1950', *Canadian Journal of African Studies* 25 (2): 226–56.

Mackenzie, F. (1995) '"A Farm is Like a Child Who Cannot be Left Unguarded": Gender, Land and Labour in Central Province, Kenya', *IDS Bulletin* 26 (1).

Markandya, A. (ed.) (1994) *Policies for Sustainable Development*, FAO Economic and Social Development Paper 121, Rome: FAO.

Martin-Brown, J., Ofosu-Amaah, W. and Philleo, W. (eds) (1992) *Proceedings of the Global Assembly of Women and the Environment 'Partners in Life'*, Miami, 1991.

Merchant, C. (1989) *The Death of Nature: Women, Ecology and the Scientific Revolution*, San Francisco: Harper and Row.

Mies, M. and Shiva, V. (1993) *Ecofeminism*, London: Zed Books.

Moser, C. O. N. (1992) 'Adjustment from Below: Low-Income Women, Time and the Triple Role in Guayaquil, Ecuador', in H. Afshar and C. Dennis, (eds) *Women and Adjustment Policies in the Third World*, Basingstoke, UK: Macmillan.

Munyakho, D. K. (ed.) (1985), 'Women and the Environmental Crisis: A Report of the Proceedings of the Workshops on Women, Environment and Development, July 10–20th, Nairobi, Kenya', mimeo.

OXFAM *et al.* (1992) *Primary Environmental Care: A Practical Approach to Dealing with Poverty and the Environment*, leaflet sponsored by OXFAM, ActionAid, IIED, Groundwork Foundation, Oxford: OXFAM.

Painter, T. M. (1991) *Approaches to Improving Natural Resource Use for Agriculture in Sahelian West Africa: A Sociological Analysis of the Aménagement/Gestion des Terroirs Villageois*

Approach, Agriculture and Natural Resources Technical Report Series 3, New York: CARE.

Pimbert, M. and Pretty, J. N. (1994) *Participation, People and the Management of National Parks and Protected Areas: Past Failures and Future Promise*, Geneva: UNRISD.

Pretty, J. N. and Guijt, I. (1992) 'Primary Environmental Care: An Alternative Paradigm for Development Assistance', *Environment and Urbanization* 4 (1).

Purves, M. and Bamba, I. (1994) 'The Macina Wells Project: Final Evaluation Report', London: CARE, mimeo.

Republic of Cameroon (1990) *The Korup Project: Plan for Developing the Korup National Park and its Support Zone*, London World Wide Fund for Nature, Commission of the European Communities and Natural Resources Institute.

Rocheleau, D. 1987a, 'Gender, Resource Management and the Rural Landscape: Implications for Agroforestry and Farming Systems Research', in S. Poats, M. Schmink and A. Spring (eds) *Gender Issues in Farming Systems Research and Extension*, Boulder: Westview Press, pp.149–69.

Rocheleau, D. (1987b) 'The User Perspective and the Agroforestry Research and Action Agenda', in H. Gholz (ed.) *Agroforestry: Realities, Possibilities and Potentials*, Dordrecht: Martinus Nijhiff, pp.59–87.

Rocheleau, D. (1988) 'Women, Trees and Tenure', in L. Fortmann, and J. Bruce (eds) *Whose Trees? Proprietary Dimensions of Forestry*, Boulder: Westview Press.

Rocheleau, D. (1991) 'Gender, Ecology and the Science of Survival: Stories and Lessons from Kenya', *Agricultural and Human Values* 8 (1): 156–65.

Rocheleau, D. (1992a), 'Whose Common Future? A Land User Approach to Gendered Rights and Responsibilities in Rural Landscapes', in *Gender, Environment and Development: Some Interlinkages*, Stockholm: SIDA.

Rocheleau, D. (1992b) *Gender, Ecology and Agroforestry: Science and Survival in Kathama*, ECOGEN Case Study Series, Worcester, Mass.: Clark University.

Rocheleau, D. (1995) 'Gender and Biodiversity: A Feminist Political Ecology Perspective', *IDS Bulletin* 26(1): 9–16.

Rocheleau, D., Thomas-Slayter, B. and Wangari, E. (eds) (1996) *Feminist Political Ecology: Global Issues and Local Experiences*, London: Routledge.

Rodda, A. (1991) *Women and the Environment*, London: Zed Books.

Rodda, A. (1993) *Women in the Humid Tropics*, IHP Humid Tropics Program Series No. 6, Paris: UNESCO.

Sarin, M. (1995) 'Regenerating India's Forests: Reconciling Gender Equity with Joint Forest Management', *IDS Bulletin* 26 (1).

Shah, M. K. and Shah, P. (1995) 'Gender, Environment and Livelihood Security: An Alternative Viewpoint From India', *IDS Bulletin* 26 (1).

Shiva, V. (1988) *Staying Alive: Women, Ecology and Development*, London: Zed Books.

Sontheimer, S. (ed.) (1991) *Women and the Environment, A Reader: Crisis and Development in the Third World*, London: Earthscan.

Thomas-Slayter, B. and Rocheleau, D. (1994) *Essential Connections: Linking Gender to Effective Natural Resource Management and Sustainable Development*, Working Paper No. 242, Michigan State University: Office of Women in International Development.

UNCED (1992) 'Agenda 21, Chapter 11, Combating Deforestation', Greennet, mimeo.

Vincent, L. (1990) 'Sustainable Small-scale Irrigation Development: Issues for Farmers, Governments and Donors', *Water Resources Development* 6 (4).

Wells, M., Brandon, K. with Hannah, L. (1992) *People and Parks: Linking Protected*

Area Management with Local Communities, Washington: World Bank/WWF/USAID.

Whittington, D., Mu, X. and Roche, R. (1990) 'Calculating the Value of Time Spent Collecting Water: some Estimates for Ukunda, Kenya', *World Development* 18(2): 269–80.

World Bank (1991a) *The Forest Sector: A World Bank Policy Paper*, Washington, DC: World Bank.

World Bank (1991b) *Forestry: The World Bank's Experience*, Washington DC: World Bank.

World Bank (1992) *World Development Report*, New York: Oxford University Press.

World Bank (1993a) *Water Resources Management: a World Bank Policy Paper*, Washington, DC: World Bank.

World Bank Water Demand Research Team (1993) 'The Demand for Water in Rural Areas: Determinants and Policy Implications', *World Bank Research Observer* 8(1).

WRI/IUCN/UNEP (1992) *Global Biodiversity Strategy*, Washington DC: WRI.

WWF (1990) *Cross River National Park Oban Division: Plan for Developing the Park and its Support Zone*, World Wide Fund for Nature with ODNRI for the Federal Republic of Nigeria and the Cross River State Government.

Yoder, R. (1994) *Locally Managed Irrigation Systems: Essential Tasks and Implications for Assistance, Management Transfer and Turnover Programs*, Colombo, Sri Lanka: International Irrigation Management Institute.

INDEX